A Yankee in Meiji Japan

A Yankee in Meiji Japan

The Crusading Journalist Edward H. House

James L. Huffman

ROWMAN & LITTLEFIELD PUBLISHERS, INC.
Lanham • Boulder • New York • Oxford

ROWMAN & LITTLEFIELD PUBLISHERS, INC.

Published in the United States of America
by Rowman & Littlefield Publishers, Inc.
A Member of the Rowman & Littlefield Publishing Group
4501 Forbes Boulevard, Suite 200, Lanham, Maryland 20706
www.rowmanlittlefield.com

P.O. Box 317, Oxford OX2 9RU, United Kingdom

British Library Cataloguing in Publication Information Available

Library of Congress Cataloging-in-Publication Data

Huffman, James L., 1941–
A yankee in Meiji Japan : the crusading journalist Edward H. House / James L. Huffman.
p. cm.
Includes bibliographical references and index.
ISBN 0-7425-2620-8 (cloth : alk. paper)—ISBN 0-7425-2621-6 (pbk. : alk. paper)
1. House, Edward H. (Edward Howard), 1836–1901. 2. Americans—Japan—Biography. 3. Journalists—Japan—Biography. 4. Journalists—United States—Biography. 5. Japan—History—Meiji period, 1868–1912. I. Title.
DS832.7 .A6H85 2003
952.03'2'092—dc21

2002155382

Printed in the United States of America

∞™ The paper used in this publication meets the minimum requirements of American National Standard for Information Sciences—Permanence of Paper for Printed Library Materials, ANSI/NISO Z39.48-1992.

To
James and Nao, Kristen and Dave,
who lived so much of this writing with me

and to
Librarians and Archivists Everywhere,
those amazing people without whom I'd still be flailing aimlessly

Contents

Abbreviations

The following abbreviations are used in the notes:

BHT:	Benjamin Hold Ticknor Papers, Library of Congress
D-USMJ:	Department of State. Despatches for United States Ministers to Japan, 1869–1901, National Archives, Washington, D.C.
ECS:	Edmund Clarence Stedman Papers, Columbia University or Library of Congress, as indicated
EHC:	Samuel Langhorne Clemens Collection (the Edward House Collection), University of Virginia
HVP:	Henry Villard Papers, Houghton Library, Harvard University
JAG:	James A. Garfield Papers, Library of Congress
JH:	John Hay Papers, Brown University
JMPH:	Jōyaku misai Perokoku hansen Mariya Rūtsugo shinkoku kaimin rantai Yokohama e nyūkoku tsuki shochi ikken, Gaimushō (Foreign Ministry) Gaikō Shiryōkan, Tokyo
JRY:	John Russell Young Papers, Library of Congress
JWM:	*Japan Weekly Mail*
MTP:	Mark Twain Papers, Bancroft Library, University of California at Berkeley
OM:	Ōkuma monjo, Waseda University
USG:	Ulysses S. Grant Papers, Library of Congress
TBA:	Thomas Bailey Aldrich Papers, Library of Congress or Harvard University, as indicated
WEG:	William Elliot Griffis Papers, Rutgers University
WR:	Whitelaw Reid Papers, Library of Congress

Acknowledgments

Nothing in this study has been harder to write than the acknowledgments, partly because I fear that I will omit people to whom I owe a great deal, partly because it is impossible to express how deeply I am indebted to many who, for want of space, will receive only a mention in the lines below. A friend of mine commented after one of the many trips required by this project: "This is an expensive study!" She was right, though in ways she did not imagine. The study did indeed consume a great deal of other people's money, but it also drew on their time, their expertise, and their good will. I wish I knew how to give them a more adequate expression of thanks.

A few must have special mention because they helped in such special ways: David Barry, a Wittenberg University German professor, who read nearly all of the manuscript and helped me often to grapple with the work's ideas and hurdles; Uchikawa Yoshimi, the dean of Japan's press historians, whose insights undergird my understanding of Japan's press; Peter O'Connor, who knows Japan's English-language press like perhaps no other living scholar; Sally Hastings of Purdue University, whose critiques and suggestions have inspired many of my better ideas; Fred Notehelfer, whose thoughts have saved me from some bitter errors and made this a better book; and Chen-hui Yeh of Sun Yatsen University in Kaohsiung, who gave up two days to guide a man he never had met through the places Edward H. House visited in Taiwan.

I also am indebted to a remarkable group of Wittenberg students who have helped me with research, organization, and translation across the years: Jeff Shy, Cathy Parks (who, among other things, indexed the *Tokio*

Times headlines), Yuko Morizono (and her grandmother!), who helped with some very difficult Meiji prose, Petal Morais, Melanie Ziarko, Kaoru Abbey, and (especially) Dukho Koh. Several classes of Wittenberg students also have made me a better scholar by indulging in my constant "House stories" and suggesting new interpretations.

My Wittenberg colleagues deserve deep thanks too for their lively and encouraging reactions, as well as numerous suggestions about sources and approaches. Among those who simply must be mentioned are the members of the Works in Progress group (led by Tammy Proctor), my own history department, the East Asian studies faculty, Don Reed, Tom Taylor, Charles Chatfield, Al Hayden—and three brilliant administrative assistants who have given unsparingly of both their time and their expertise: Rosie Burley, Margaret DeButy, and Cathie Dollinger. I also am indebted to Wittenberg's Faculty Research Fund Board for grants that have enabled me to do research in Great Britain, Taiwan, Japan, and various American locations. Elsewhere, financial assistance also came from the Japan Center for Michigan Universities in Hikone and from the Northeast Asia Council of the Association for Asian Studies, currently headed by Linda Lewis

Nothing has been more satisfying, or humbling, during this project than getting to know a bit of the worlds of the archivist and the librarian. So many of them have given me their ears, their knowledge, and their time; they often have left me overwhelmed. At the International House in Tokyo, Higuchi Keiko and Koide Izumi deserve special thanks, as does Bradley Gernand at the U.S. Library of Congress. At Wittenberg, I owe particular thanks to Gina Entorf, along with Suzanne Smailes, Lori Judy, Ken Irwin, Alisa Mizikar, Holly Wolfe, Kathy Schulz, and Rita Osborne. Elsewhere, I must call attention to Ruth J. Simmons, who helped me with the William Elliot Griffis papers at Rutgers University, and to Henry F. Scannell, who gave large amounts of time to House's Boston roots. Beyond those, so many librarians and archivists helped me find the materials, many of them obscure, that provide the foundation of this work: Tomizuka Kazuhiko of Japan's Foreign Ministry archives, Shiraishi Hiroyuki of the Tokyo city archives, Nakano Minoru, chief archivist at the University of Tokyo, Marianne Curling, curator of the Mark Twain House in Hartford, Jeffrey M. Flannery at the Library of Congress, Janice Chadbourne and William Faucon of Boston Public Library, Sharon Defibaugh at the University of Virginia, Kathy M. Flynn of Phillips Library at the Peabody Essex Museum, Aaron Lisec at Southern Illinois University, Nicola Kennan of Oxford University's Bodleian Library, Colin Stevenson at the London Library, and several staff members at the Mark Twain Project at the University of California at Berkeley: Brenda Bailey, David Glenn Briggs, Rob Browning, Anh Bui, Victor Fischer, Robert Hirsh, and Lin Salano.

Then there are many in the broader scholarly community who have left me in their debt: Haruhara Akihiko, Roger Buckley, Charles Wordell, Kudō Tetsurō, Takashima Mariko, Mayuki Sano, William Steele, Patricia Sippel, and Ogawa Kazuo in Japan; Lung-chih Chang, Ts'ui-jung Liu (director of the Institute for Taiwan History at Academia Sinica), Caroline Tsai, and Tanya Hsu in Taiwan; and Timothy Cheek, Ya-chen Chen, Dennis Frost, John Dower, Aaron Martin Cohen, Jack Hammersmith, Bara Blender, Roger Hackett, Kenneth Pyle, Louis Perez, and Kimberly Ball in the United States. Two special groups also made this work better by critiquing parts of it in stimulating ways: the Midwest Japan Seminar, one of the most effective academic groups I have known, and the Lutheran Academy of Scholars led by Ronald Thiemann. I owe special thanks too to Susan McEachern, the energetic, astute editor of this work, for both her enthusiastic support and the things she did to make it a better manuscript.

Finally, the most important thanks of all must be reserved for those whose ties are personal as much as academic. I have been deeply enriched by House's granddaughter by marriage, Kuroda Hatsuko, one of the most lively (at ninety-six!) and gracious persons I ever have met, as well as by her own daughter-in-law, Kuroda Mitsuko, and by Saitō Motohisa, who helped me to locate the Kurodas. And my own family—James, Kristen, Dave, Nao, even Grace and Simon—know (but I need to tell them anyway) that they deserve more gratitude than can be expressed. They have lived House with me, suggested some of the most crucial leads, helped me interpret him, and searched the Internet for leads when I was scratching my head. And they have made an old parent feel young. I am in their debt most of all.

Credits

Thanks are due to the following libraries and archive collections for the use of letters and manuscripts.

The British Library: William Gladstone Papers.
Brown University Library: John Hay Papers.
Columbia University, Rare Book and Manuscript Library: Edmund Clarence Stedman Papers.
Folger Shakespeare Library (MS Y.C. 4286 [1], Edward H. House to Treasurer of Daly's Theatre).
Harvard University, Houghton Library: Henry Villard (bMS Am 1322 (234-236), Thomas Bailey Aldrich (bMS Am 1429 (2132-2145), and John Hay (bMS Am 2121 (1253) Papers.
Library of Congress: Reid Family, Edmund Clarence Stedman, Thomas Bailey Aldrich, Hamilton Fish, John Russell Young, Benjamin Holt Ticknor, Hamilton Fish, and Ulysses S. Grant Papers.
Ministry of Foreign Affairs, Japan, Diplomatic Record Office (Gaikō Shiryōkan): Dainihon Gaikō monjo, Vol. 5, edited by Research Department, Ministry of Foreign Affairs of Japan; Gaimushō Kiroku (3.6.3.12, Vol. 3), Diplomatic Record Office, Ministry of Foreign Affairs of Japan.
National Archives of Japan (Dokuritsu Gyōsei Hōjin Kokuritsu Kōbunshokan): W.G. Howell to Ōkuma Shigenobu, November 19, 1873.
Peabody Essex Museum, Phillips Library, Salem, Massachusetts: The Edward Sylvester Morse Collection (Correspondence Series E2, Box 7, Folder 9).

Princeton University Library, Morris L. Parrish Collection: Charles E. Reade Collection.

Rutgers, The State University of New Jersey, Archibald S. Alexander Library, Special Collections and University Archives: William Elliot Griffis Collection.

University of California, The Bancroft Library, Mark Twain Project.

University of Virginia, Clifton Waller Barrett Library, Albert and Shirley Small Special Collections Library: James Russell Lowell Collection (6219, Lowell letter), Mark Twain Collection (6314, letters from Samuel, Clara, and Susie Clemens), Edward H. House Collection (10762, letters from Edward H. House).

Waseda University Libarary: Ōkuma Shigenobu Monjo.

Introduction

America's first regular newspaper correspondent in Meiji Japan, Edward H. House (1836–1901), was a dynamic shaper of attitudes and policies on two sides of the Pacific Ocean. He also was a conundrum. A patriot's patriot who believed that the United States represented the peak of world civilization, he nonetheless preferred living in Japan and ordered that his remains be buried in Tokyo. Few people rivaled him for independence and integrity; he fought so hard for unpopular causes that some British journalists declared him "possessed of the devil." Yet he had no qualms about taking money from the Japanese government or serving as a secret agent when he thought an issue sufficiently pressing. For nearly twenty years, he was paralyzed from the waist down and riddled with pain, but his productivity never flagged. As a crusader—the role he cherished most—he damned imperialism yet remained an imperialist in more ways than he himself knew. And although he fought for women's rights, he tried to keep his own daughter from marrying when he thought she had lapsed into "that absorbing infatuation which is so pitiful and pathetic in women."[1] Like many of us, House acted so often in paradoxical ways that the search for his core is daunting.

But the search is worth the struggle. His importance is unassailable: he played a key role in creating the national reputations of men like John Brown and Mark Twain during his early years as a New York reporter; he persuaded the U.S. Congress to return a huge indemnity to Japan and was called by a Japanese foreign minister the "grand old man" of Japan's struggle to gain equal treaties with the imperialist powers;[2] and he edited Tokyo's first English-language newspaper, gave the world most of its knowledge of Japan's earliest imperialist military excursion, and became a pioneer, in his last years, in the introduction of Western music to Japan. His life also was more than usually interesting. The devil-may-care approach of his youth made him one of New York's more appealing personalities; so did the fact that he climbed mountains in four continents. He remained single but became the adoptive father of a Japanese judge's daughter who was on the brink of suicide, he spent a decade in a prime minister's wheelchair (when he was not in bed), and the tumult of his relationship with Mark Twain merits a study of its own. Due to the scarce, scattered nature of sources and the caprices of historical narrative, however, House has been overlooked by students in both the United States and Japan. With the exception of one scholarly article on his legal fights with Mark Twain, no one has written more than a few pages in English on House's life. Even in Japan, where he spent most of his last thirty years, a handful of articles comprise the whole of what has been written on him. His life cries for rediscovery.

Making the case for an examination of his life even more compelling is the passel of insights his experiences provide about international relations in the late nineteenth century. His communications with novelists, politicians, actors, railroad tycoons, financiers, dramatists, and newspaper editors shed intriguing light on the way people interacted in the small, interconnected world of late-1800s American opinion making. In Japan, he illustrates the complex role played by foreigners, many of them government employees, in helping Japan maneuver its way into a threatening, expansive world from which it had been secluded until the 1850s. He also shows the vicious battle that pro- and anti-Japanese Westerners fought to get control of public images, to determine whether the citizens of that archipelago would be seen as civilized compatriots or as sneaky exotics. Even more important, his life and writings provide provocative ideas about the impact of imperialism on a people who until the 1850s had been progressive but isolated. And he raises crucial questions about the role of image-making in international politics, about the Japanese leaders' keen understanding that any effort to change Western policies necessitated confronting both the Western leaders' perceptions of Japan and, in the words of historian Peter O'Connor, "the European master narratives of imperialism, modernity and colonialism."[3] Although House ought to demand our attention for the inherent interest of his many experiences, it is his involvement in so many of the era's key issues that makes this study imperative.

House is, however, only one of this work's foci. The other is Japan itself. Japan's Meiji era (1868–1912) stands out among historical periods for the aggressive way in which leaders and people alike confronted the most daunting of international challenges. The statesman Ōkuma Shigenobu, who became House's mentor in Japan, opened a two-volume analysis of the era in 1910 by proclaiming that although much of Asia remained in a "somnolent, if not a decadent, condition," Japan in just fifty years had "raised itself from its lethargy to such an extent that is has been able to cross swords with a leading military power of the West." In less than three generations, Japan had propelled itself from seclusion to world power status, from pacifism to military might, from the anti-commerce orthodoxy of Confucianism to economic strength that challenged the Western dominance, from a decentralized, feudal system to a constitutional monarchy with a popularly elected national legislature. In the oft-quoted observation of a British expatriate: "To have lived through the transition stage of modern Japan makes a man feel preternaturally old; for here he is in modern times . . . and yet he can himself distinctly remember the Middle Ages. . . . Old things pass away between a night and a morning."[4]

Like House himself, however, the Meiji era is little known in the Western world today. Scholarly studies on the era continue to appear, and there are a number of excellent histories of Japan's modern era as a whole. But general or more popular works focus mostly on the World War II years or on Japan's phenomenal development in the fifty years after the war. Indeed, the last general histories to concentrate on the Meiji era were George Sansom's *Western World and Japan* and E. H. Norman's *Origins of the Modern Japanese State,* both of them written before 1950. House would have found that distressing—but familiar. He gave half a life to trying, with mixed success, to correct what he saw as inadequate narratives: to explain what had been ignored and to change mistaken memories. Having lived through the Meiji years, he also would have understood just how remarkably his own times prefigured Japan's post–World War II successes—and how impossible it is to understand the dynamism of modern Japan without knowing what happened in the late nineteenth century. And being the kind of man he was, he surely would have written articles (and more articles, and then more articles still), along with hundreds of letters, and even a book or two, to make people aware.

It is in his spirit that this work attempts, more explicitly than usual, to interweave House's life with his times, to explain the era as intentionally as it explains the man. Since most English-speaking readers will have only a limited knowledge of Japan's late-nineteenth-century narrative, the book emphasizes context as well as life, presenting a brief, chapter-long description of Japan's historical development during each period that precedes a segment of House's life. The goal is not only to make House's life clearer by explaining its context but also to help the reader see Meiji Japan's historical experience on its own terms. It was that latter aim, after all, that motivated House himself for three decades. As he wrote in 1881: "To lead my own countrymen to a just appreciation of this pleasant land,

and of those who inhabit it, has been my self-assigned task for many years." When an American friend wrote in 1879 that "you have made a good deal of a Japanese patriot of me," House was delighted.[5] That his life should be used now, more than a century later, to introduce Westerners again to the land he admired seems appropriate.

It should be noted, lest the reader be confused, that the pages that follow employ the Japanese orthographical style. Surnames precede given names, except when quoting from a source that inverts the standard Japanese order. And macrons (lines over letters) are used to indicate long vowels in all Japanese words except those that have become common enough in English to appear in standard U.S. or British reference works (e.g., Tokyo and shogun).

NOTES

1. Though the first major U.S. correspondent in the Meiji era, House was not the first important American correspondent in Japan *per se*. That title probably should go to Francis Hall, a businessman in Yokohama who served as a regular correspondent for the *New York Tribune* from 1859 to 1866, submitting more than seventy articles to the paper. See F. G. Notehelfer, *Japan Through American Eyes: The Journal of Francis Hall, Yokohama and Kanagawa, 1859–1866*. For "possessed of the devil," see John Russell Young in *Tokio Times*, December 27, 1879; for "absorbing infatuation," House letter to Henry Villard, May 20, 1897, HVP, Harvard University.

2. Evaluation of Mutsu Munemitsu, in Ebihara Hachirō, *Nihon Ōji shimbun zasshi shi*, 128.

3. Peter O'Connor, "Informal Diplomacy and the Modern Idea of Japan," *Japan Forum* 13, no. 1 (2001): 1.

4. Ōkuma's comments are in his *Fifty Years of New Japan*, vol. I, 1; and "to have lived," in Basil Hall Chamberlain, *Things Japanese*, 1.

5. "Lead my own countrymen," in E. H. House, *Japanese Episodes*, 4; and "patriot," in Joseph Twichell to House, June 9, 1879, EHC, University of Virginia.

1

Incident in Yokohama Harbor

> He was one of those people who likes to try anything unusual, anything difficult, anything complicated—anything others are afraid to do.
>
> —Tokutomi Sohō about E. H. House[1]

A grumbling crew of twenty Peruvians sailed into Yokohama harbor on Wednesday, the tenth day of July 1872. The heat and humidity alone had to be aggravating, but on this day the summer weather was the least of their concerns. A more pressing worry was the storm that had embroiled them in the Pacific three weeks before, ripping away several of their little barque *Maria Luz*'s masts and forcing them into an alien port for repairs. The potential for trouble was large, given the unevenness of Japanese relations with the Western trading nations and the fact that Japan and Peru had no diplomatic relations. The work could take weeks, assuming the Japanese were cooperative, and cooperation was no sure thing. In any case, a great deal of extra time would be required before their cargo, purchased in Macao, would arrive at the Peruvian coast, and that period would be costly. Only on arrival would they receive the 3,220 pounds for which the 231 Chinese men aboard had been contracted.

The ship's captain, Ricardo Herrera, also was worried about the mental state of those Chinese. If his crew members were anxious, the passengers were seething, many of them downright rebellious. Some of these men were workers, some drifters, thirteen of them teenagers—and all of them victims of kidnapping or false promises about the jobs that they would be given in Peruvian mines and plantations. They had been aboard long enough by now to reflect on the contracts they had signed, long enough to understand loneliness and seasickness; long enough to project, from the shipboard crowding and tortures, what kind of treatment they might expect in Peru. Six of their fellows already had died during the 2,000-mile voyage from Macao, another lay near death, and nearly 10,000 miles of uncertain seas still lay ahead.

It was more than fear and separation that moved several of these laborers to action, however. As later investigations by Japanese authorities would show, their shipboard conditions bordered on the subhuman. The men were packed into a lower deck of about 2,000 square feet, giving them less than three square feet per man, with a heavy ceiling just six-and-a-half feet above the floor. Assertive types were thrown into the brig at an officer's whim; the more willful had their queues (pigtails)—the very symbols of their Chineseness—slashed off. And their food was barely enough to keep them alive. While the crew's quarters up on the deck boasted individual dinner plates and soup bowls for each man, thirty-three wine glasses, a cruet stand, and a gravy dish, along with seven tubs of duck eggs, seven boxes of tobacco and cigars, a sofa, and six chairs, the "Chinese galley" had a single tin plate for every 2.3 men—and one tin cup for each. The contract each man had signed, said a Japanese observer, made him "no longer a person but a chattel."[2]

There was nothing unique about these *Maria Luz* conditions. What the Chinese referred to as "buying men" had begun in the 1840s, and conditions on many vessels were even worse than those described here. It was not unusual for contractees to be packed so tightly, and the heat and stench to be so great, that more than half the workers died en route to the Americas. Just four years earlier, forty-nine Chinese laborers aboard the *Cayalti* had revolted off the coast of Peru, killed most of the crew, and forced the captain, at axe-point, to take them back to China—and hardly anyone in the West had paid attention. But several things assured that the *Maria Luz* would be more widely known. First, one of the passengers jumped into the black harbor waters a few evenings after the ship anchored at Yokohama and swam to the British vessel *Iron Duke*. Taken aboard "in a state of extreme exhaustion," he described his fellows' plight and begged protection. The British turned him over to Japanese officials, who returned him to the *Maria Luz* after receiving assurances from Herrera that the passengers were well treated and the escapee would not be punished.

The second factor was the presence in Tokyo of Britain's chargé d'affaires R. G. Watson. Hearing about the escape and the laborer's terrified screams after he had been returned to the *Maria Luz,* he decided to investigate. When he visited the Peruvian barque himself, however, he was refused access to the passengers. So when another worker jumped overboard and swam for help, Watson pressed the Japanese officials to launch their own investigation and to detain the ship until the survey had been completed. He told them of his own rude treatment by Herrera and reminded them that Peru's trade in Chinese workers had been "characterized by . . . barbarity," adding that Herrera's punishment of the escapees after promising leniency was "an insult to your Excellency's Government."[3]

A third reason the case became so important lay in the fact that Soejima Taneomi was foreign minister. A scholar from Saga prefecture on Japan's southern island of Kyūshū, Soejima saw here a chance for Japan to win a reputation for humane trade policies and to assert its sovereignty in dealing with the Western imperialist powers. Several men in the ruling councils opposed Japanese intervention in the case, afraid that the imperialist nations might take offense and resist even more actively Japan's efforts to get fair and equal treaties. For two decades, the Japanese had struggled under treaties that denied them sovereignty over their own tariff rates and deprived them of jurisdiction over foreigners living in Japan. Recently, the United States had shown some flexibility in treaty talks, however, and cautious officials feared any provocation that might irritate the powers and delay progress toward treaty equality. But Soejima prevailed, and Japan agreed to take up the case, thereby turning a rather ordinary episode into a cause célèbre.

This aggressive response surprised and alarmed most of the European diplomats in Japan. In the thirty years that Japan had been interacting with other nations, its diplomatic responses had been uniformly timid. Few saw any reason to expect a different approach now. Indeed, since Japan had no diplomatic relations with Peru and thus no channel for official communications, action would be doubly difficult in this case. Making matters worse, and suggesting to some that Soejima's opponents may have been right, the German, Italian, and Portuguese consuls general in Yokohama warned Japan that it had no legal right to make judgments about the barque's situation—while the Americans and Dutch equivocated, and the British alone supported an active response. But having won his case with his own fellow officials, Soejima persisted.

After removing all the Chinese passengers from the boat, Ōe Taku, whom Soejima had made governor of Kanagawa, launched an investigation. He took testimony from Herrera and some fifty of the workers, many of whom complained that they had been kidnapped in Macao, deprived of adequate food, beaten with rattan canes, and refused entry onto the ship's deck. One of his investigators reported that the Chinese aboard the vessel "began to gather around me with great cries, and in the most earnest manner begging for assistance. . . . I could hardly escape from their importunity." On August 26, Ōe found the captain guilty of forcibly detaining his passengers and abusing them within the Kanagawa jurisdiction. The prescribed penalty for this kind of offense was 100 lashes or

100 days of confinement, but the governor chose leniency and pardoned the captain, granting him permission to sail away. Instead, Herrera turned obstinate. He sued the Chinese workers, demanding that Ōe make them return to his ship.

The governor's written opinion was much longer this time, but it took the same tack. He cited twenty times when Japan had abrogated contracts under which "children have . . . been taken from their homes to be clandestinely conveyed from Japan to serve for a term of years" abroad. He discussed the "repugnant" nature of slavery and declared it Japan's policy "*that no labourers . . . shall be taken beyond its jurisdiction against their free and voluntary consent*." And he discussed the conditions of the passengers on the ship at length. Some said they had been abused vilely, others that treatment had been satisfactory, but the repeated attempts of the laborers to escape, the use of force to keep Watson from investigating, and the eruption of a rebellion on board suggested that most of the passengers had indeed been abused; so did the violation of international standards on the space that was to be provided per passenger. "The judgment of the court," Ōe wrote, "is for the defendant." On October 24, *The New York Times* reported: "The Japanese Government has liberated the coolies. . . . They will be sent to China."

With that, the defeated Herrera abandoned his ship and left for home. But the case did not end. The Peruvian government expressed outrage, and news reports from Lima said that a warship or two would be sent to East Asia. In the end, only one diplomat was dispatched: Aurelio Garcia y Garcia, who arrived in Yokohama the following February 27, demanding an apology and an indemnity. The Japanese refused to give either, and after four months of wrangling, the two countries asked the Russian czar to mediate. He took two years to examine the evidence, including more than eighty documents prepared by the Peruvians. His decision, on May 29, 1875, completely vindicated the Japanese. The *Maria Luz* itself had been sold by then for $7,250.[4]

The *Maria Luz* case marked an important moment in Japan's progress toward international respect and influence. Though Japanese officials still cowered frequently before the imperialist powers, they had proved that Japan would act strongly when relative strength allowed it to do so and that it would assert judicial independence when the treaties made it possible. Its leaders and diplomats also showed that they had the knowledge and inclination to follow accepted Western procedures in dealing with tangled legal cases. And they gained wide respect for their principled resistance to what was then called the "coolie trade." When Peru announced its decision in 1873 to ban the importation of Chinese laborers altogether and then began curbing the merchants who had handled the bulk of the human trade in Macao, foreign governments took note of Japan's growing capacity for exerting influence beyond its own shores.

It was not just the world of *big* issues that was shaped by this episode, however. At the individual human level, the *Maria Luz* affair dramatically changed the career of a thirty-seven-year-old Boston journalist who was just then feeling his way into Japan's political and social scene. Edward H. House had been more striking than handsome when he came to Japan in 1870, marked by a thin, sensitive face, a pointed noise, and penetrating eyes that more than once had broken down the tough façade of an interviewee. Called "Ned" by his reporter friends, he had brought to Tokyo the reputation of a celebrity journalist largely as a result of his reporting on the American antislavery movement and the Civil War for Horace Greeley's *New York Tribune.* His vivid stories about John Brown, the abolitionist crusader hanged in December 1859 for his uprising at Harpers Ferry, Virginia, had helped to turn Brown into a martyr in the prewar north. Months later, just weeks after the war began, House had been hurrying with Colonel Elmer E. Ellsworth down the steps of the Marshall House Tavern in Alexandria, when a proslavery Virginian leaped from the shadows and shot the colonel to death. "I think my arm was resting on poor Ellsworth's shoulder," he told the readers of the *Tribune* on May 26, 1860. "At any rate, he seemed to fall almost from my own grasp. . . . He dropped forward with that heavy, horrible, headlong weight which always comes of sudden death inflicted in this manner." House's account had dominated the press that day.

Ned's notoriety in New York itself also had had a personal side to it. In an era of swashbuckling, individualistic journalism, he was a leader of the brats, known as much for his drinking and devilry as for his vivid reporting. He belonged to a group of writers, actors, and artists who frequented the Pfaff beer cellar on Broadway for heavy drinking and spirited debate about politics, the arts, and just about everything else. His fellows there included the editor/novelist Thomas Bailey Aldrich, the poet Walt Whitman, the humorist Artemus Ward, and Samuel Clemens, whose pen name of Mark Twain was not yet widely known. Years later, Twain would write House a fond letter about "that day when bohemianism was respectable—eh, more than respectable, heroic."[5] Among the Pfaff group, House was considered one of the wildest, a man willing to risk life to have fun as much as to get a story. His reckless courage in disguising himself to secure a spot on the scaffold when John Brown was hanged became legendary in the House circle. So did one of his first escapades with Mark Twain. Early in 1867, it seems, Twain and House, both visibly drunk, visited the offices of one Charles C. Duncan to reserve a place for Twain on the *Quaker City* voyage to Europe and the Holy Land. Knowing that the tour was sponsored by the prominent clergyman Henry Ward Beecher,

House introduced Twain as a Baptist minister who would help out with shipboard sermons. The inebriated display irritated Duncan, though not enough to keep him from accepting Twain's $125 cash deposit.

Another thing that had set House off from his fellows in New York was an almost mystical fascination with those faraway islands known in America as Japan. The reasons for this fascination will be addressed later; for now, it is sufficient to note that when the *Tribune* gave him a chance to report there in 1870, only two years after a new government called Meiji had begun to transform Japan into a "modern" state, he did not hesitate. Nor did he hesitate, on arrival, to devour, like one famished, every dish the Japanese feast had to offer. Within weeks, he had climbed Mt. Fuji, even though the climbing season already had passed. He found a way to live in Tokyo, a city forbidden by treaty to all but a few selected foreigners. He made his way into the mountainous countryside, also generally off-limits. He dined with statesmen, visited the theater, studied Japanese, taught English to Japan's coming leaders, and spent more than a few evenings, in his own words, "cultivating a mild immorality."[6]

He also wrote—mainly about culture. Like most newcomers to an alien place, he was struck primarily by what was "different" about the country. Although he sent many essays and cables on political news back to the *Tribune* and to *The New York Times*, most of his longer pieces dealt with colorful features of Japanese life. He described the Fuji ascent with the detail of someone enraptured. His *Atlantic Monthly* account of theater life in September 1872 showed the eye of a man who himself had covered the arts and written plays. A story about dinner at an official's home was filled with ingenious gardens, fragrant teas, parents' indulgence of children, delicate lanterns, incorrigible chopsticks ("united at one end, like matches"), thirteen courses (each accompanied by "liquors of a bubbling and effervescent character")—and exquisite courtesy.[7] Japan was in the midst of cataclysmic political changes at this time, with the government threatened daily by imperialist designs abroad and opposition movements at home. House knew of these; his letters and newspaper pieces make that fact quite clear. But his longer writings slighted politics. From the work he sent home, it was clear that the arts and culture were his first love.

That changed forever when the desperate Chinese worker jumped off the side of the *Maria Luz*, however. No documents tell us why House took up the human-trade issue with such relish, but a couple of explanations appear plausible. First, his earliest Tokyo confidant was Charles O. Shepard, the U.S. consul in Tokyo at the time of his arrival. He shared a home with Shepard during his first months, and when the 1872 crisis occurred, Shepard was managing the American mission for Minister Charles E. DeLong, who was in the United States on leave. Like House, Shepard despised the buying and selling of Chinese workers, and when Peruvian officials asked his assistance in handling the dispute, he refused, even though the United States was Peru's diplomatic representative in Japan. His reason was expressed in an August 3 letter supporting the British chargé Watson. The evil of the trade transcended America's agreement to "extend friendly offices" to Peru, he said: "As she is in the inhuman, illegal 'Coolie trade,' I declined to lend in any way my aid or sanction."[8] Since House and Shepard were in daily contact, it is not surprising that an episode that enraged the diplomat would have engaged the journalist too.

The second reason lay in House's personality. From his earliest days, he had identified with underdogs and seethed over injustice. He saw slavery and the Civil War as a moral issue, he hated elitism, and he despised pretension. His short stories—and he wrote many in the 1850s and 1860s—typically featured a servant, a woman, or an urchin outstripping an upper-class snob. When he got to Japan, he displayed an immediate contempt for boorish merchants and chauvinistic diplomats who patronized or took advantage of the ambitious Japanese. In the *Maria Luz* episode, the issues that moved him came together: greedy foreigners, abused workers, and the underdog Japanese taking on an unequal, unfair trading system. When DeLong, his own nation's minister, reversed Shepard's approach after returning on August 10, supporting the Peruvians legally even while expressing contempt for the trade itself, House discovered issues enough to change his journalistic persona for all time. He would continue to write occasionally about cultural affairs, but politics would be central from then on.

House involved himself directly with the official maneuvering over the Peruvian ship that summer. He clearly worked with Shepard on the case, at times in a semiofficial capacity. He also helped the Japanese government prepare the argument against Herrera and the human trade. The primary document summarizing the episode was the *Case of the Peruvian Barque Maria Luz,* and although its title page lists no writer, sources uniformly attribute the writing to House. In strong prose with a typical House tone, the document outlines the whole complex case in two pages, then concludes, "The Government, therefore, leaves it to the candid judgment of the world. . . . Should the Captain or the contractor have any claim to make . . . both will have ample opportunity to make it before the authorities of China." Of even greater long-term importance than House's role as document drafter was this episode's role in initiating his friendship with Ōkuma Shigenobu, one of the most powerful voices in the small leadership clique and a man whose life would intertwine closely with the American journalist's for another three decades.[9]

House also covered the episode for the *Tribune,* beginning with a September 28 piece that promised a neutral recital of the events, "avoiding the expression of a single opinion," then damned the Peruvians with a string of highly opinionated anecdotes and observations. He quoted some passengers who "had been lured on board by false representations" and others who "had been kidnapped outright." He said one Chinese worker declared that when he hesitated to sign a contract "his finger had been pushed into an inkstand, and then jammed down upon the paper." He described his own visit to the *Maria Luz* with a team of three investigators: Captain Herrera's verbal abuse of the Japanese officials; the "few small holes" in the barque's keep for ventilation; the "reeking and sweltering . . . atmosphere which would extinguish the life of an American or European in half a day"; the "piteous cries" with which the Chinese workers "implored our intercession"; and Herrera's twice-repeated statement that it would be necessary "to kill" some of the passengers "after leaving Yokohama, in order to awe the others into submission." The article also pointed out that DeLong, on his return to Tokyo in August, had overruled Shepard and offered to help Herrera make his case with the Japanese authorities, but that the Japanese had decided to free the "captives without unnecessary delay"—a fact that was "positive" but had not yet been made public.[10]

Another House piece, written on October 23, accused the American government of complicity in the despised "coolie trade." The article lauded early efforts by Robert Van Valkenburgh, DeLong's predecessor as American minister to Japan, to prevent Americans from participating in the trade, and then quoted letters showing that in 1871 Thomas Settle, the U.S. minister to Peru, actually had "approved and assisted" in arrangements for the shipping of Chinese workers by Herrera and his patron, Fauro Armero. House gave examples of the viciousness of Peru's human merchandise operations, citing the case of the *Dolores Ugarto,* "on board of which 600 men were deliberately burned to death at the outset of a voyage from China to Peru." And he accused Minister DeLong of a "grave offense against humanity" for serving as a conduit for Peru's efforts to get the Chinese workers back. At the same time, House praised the British chargé Watson's efforts on behalf of the *Maria Luz* victims, reprinting Watson's long letter demanding an investigation of the *Maria Luz*: his description of his own rude treatment when he visited the Peruvian ship to check on the escapee's claims, his analysis of the overall "barbarity" of the trade, his call for the Japanese to keep the ship under surveillance, and his offer to help in the Japanese investigation of the whole affair. House ended with a ringing defense of Japan's actions, asserting, "If any public notice should be given of bad faith or false action on the part of the Japanese Government . . . I am ready to prove that their whole conduct has been perfectly consistent and upright." He also ran a brief piece in the *Tribune* on January 2, 1873, reporting on the return of the workers to China and noting China's expressions of appreciation for the way the Japanese had treated the envoy whom China had sent to bring the men home.

House's charge against the United States probably was unduly harsh; although individual Americans had engaged in the nefarious trade, and although diplomats such as DeLong and Settle winked at, or even played a direct role in, the human trade, U.S. policy against it was clear. Congress had taken strong action to outlaw the buying and selling of Chinese workers in 1862, and Secretary of State Hamilton Fish had chastised DeLong for even appearing to support Peru's position. But the core of House's charge was on target, and his allegations were carefully supported. The allegations were influential, too, because he was advocating a position that touched sympathetic chords among a people back home who had just fought to abolish slavery. He also had the ear, quite personally, of a number of America's public opinion leaders: journalists such as Whitelaw Reid and Horace Greeley of the *Tribune*, politician-writers of the ilk of John Hay and John Russell Young, and publicists like Mark Twain, all of whom worked to magnify House's condemnation of what Peru was doing.

In the *Maria Luz* case, then, House had found a compelling cause; in taking it up, he had stumbled upon an even bigger and more enduring issue: Japan's treatment at the hands of the imperialist powers. From this day forward, when he wrote about Japan, he would most often focus on Japan's international position. For three and a half decades he had been honing both the journalist's reportorial skills and the activist's value system, the combination that made him a powerful spokesman for the Japanese when they released the Chinese workers. For the next three decades, those same skills and values would turn him into one of Japan's most visible, most effective champions in the English-speaking world. The pages that follow will trace House's career—both the formative forces and the decades as "Japan's friend." For now it is sufficient to note than when an *Ōsaka Asahi Shimbun* editorialist wrote late in 1901 that House had "enthusiastically defended Japan's role for more than thirty years," he was describing a passion ignited by a single Chinese laborer who risked death in July of 1872 by leaping off the side of a little Peruvian slave ship.[11]

NOTES

1. Tokutomi Sohō, "Hausu sensei no omoide," 109.

2. "In the Kanagawa Kencho," *Case of the Peruvian Barque Maria Luz,* 12. Inventory details come from JMPH, V, Gaimushō Gaikōshiryōkan. The overall account of the *Maria Luz* episode is drawn from this document, as well as C. Harvey Gardiner, *The Japanese and Peru 1873–1973,* 7–16; Suzanne Jones Crawford, "The *Maria Luz* Affair," *The Historian,* 583–96; Jack Hammersmith, *Spoilsmen in a "Flowery*

Fairyland," 97–99; Payson J. Treat, *Diplomatic Relations between the United States and Japan 1853–1895,* vol. 2, 455–63, 487–93; and Wayne C. McWilliams, "Soejima Taneomi: Statesman of Early Meiji Japan, 1868–1874," 166–85.

3. R. G. Watson to Soejima Taneomi, August 3, 1872, *Dainihon gaikō monjo* 5, 415–17.

4. Ōe's quotations are from *Case of the Peruvian Barque Maria Luz,* 10–14 (italics in the original). Also see E. H. House, "The Coolie Trade," *New York Tribune,* November 28, 1872. The account of the investigator and the sale of the vessel are described in "Correspondence on the Subject of the Peruvian Barque 'Maria Luz,'" 15–16, and "Appendix to Correspondence on the Subject of the Peruvian Bark 'Maria Luz,'" JMPH, vol. 6 (not paginated), Gaimushō.

5. Samuel Clemens to E. H. House, January 14, 1884, MTP, University of California, Berkeley.

6. E. H. House to Whitelaw Reid, November 22, 1870, WR, Library of Congress, Washington, D.C.

7. E. H. House, "A Japanese Statesman at Home," *Harper's New Monthly Magazine* (March 1872); reprinted in E. H. House, *Japanese Episodes,* 185, 189.

8. Charles O. Shepard, August 3, 1872, JMPH, 420.

9. Shōwa Joshi Daigaku, ed. "E. H. Hausu," *Kindai bungaku kenkyū sōsho,* vol. 5, 385; also Takeuchi Hiroshi, ed. *Rainichi senyō jinmei jiten,* 291, and Ōtani Tadashi, "Edowādo Hausu senkō," *Senō Hōgaku Ronshū,* 243. For House's involvement with Shepard in the diplomatic maneuverings, see Treat, vol. 1, 455.

10. *New York Tribune,* November 28, 1872. It took long essays three to six weeks to arrive by ship and overland transportation in New York.

11. *Ōsaka Asahi Shimbun,* December 23, 1901.

2

The Prodigy: 1836–1870

Hard and anxious toil had a deal more to do with my standing in journalism . . . than any natural qualification.

—E. H. House to Henry Villard, August 31, 1898

Time to say the grace of your well-misspent youth.

—Gregory Fraser, "Rejoice"[1]

Nothing exceptional happened in Boston during the first days of September 1836. The city council voted to replace the wooden fence around the Commons with an iron one; Whigs in the state legislature supported Daniel Webster for the presidency; and the local papers ran ads on anything that might make life easier or more interesting: whale oil (4,000 gallons of it), sperm candles (1,000 of them), shellac and indigo from Calcutta, Russian feathers, Brazilian sugar, a biography of the missionary William Carey, bookkeeping classes at the Boston Academy, brandy, and guns. The local press also told readers about Henry Clay's "marvelous escape from death" when a bull gored and killed the horse he was riding, and about the Boston arrival of people from Smyrna, Calcutta, and London. What it did not report was that on Monday, September 5, Edward Howard was born into the artisan/musician home of Ellen Maria and Timothy House in Newtonville, just outside the city.

Information on the baby's parents is sketchy, but we do know that Ellen was just six months past her twentieth birthday and that Timothy was twenty-two. We also know that the mother was "beautiful" and an accomplished pianist, and that she would become the dominant influence in their son's life—but that is about all. Regarding Timothy, we know that he came from a Martha's Vineyard family and was on his way to becoming a prominent bank note engraver, eager to pass his skills on to Edward. Of British descent, Timothy supplemented his income by preparing portraits for illustrated books. And about the child, we know that he showed early signs of going in a different direction from his father. When he was just four, according to family stories, he called his mother's attention to a mistake that she had made in her playing, and not many years later he began composing music himself.[2]

It was natural then that in 1849, when he was thirteen, they enrolled him in Chauncy-Hall School, one of Boston's best boys' schools and the academy his father had attended briefly two decades before. Ned did not stay at Chauncy-Hall long enough to graduate, but its impact on him was significant. Founded by the businessman G. F. Thayer, it prided itself on innovation, openness, discipline, and patriotism—characteristics on which House would pride himself as an adult. The school was prosperous and lively. Lithographs from House's time show a stately, three-story gray building next to Boston's First Congregational Church with horses and carriages on the earthen street outside. The catalogue lists some 175 students in the preparatory and upper divisions, many of them, like House, from the communities surrounding Boston. And Chauncy-Hall attracted students from a wide range of classes and faiths. As one of the teachers recalled, it refused to favor "any special class in society or sect in religion. No questions were asked involving these subjects; no nationality was excluded."

Convinced that the environment affected learning, Thayer introduced a host of physical innovations at Chauncy-Hall: a school playground, classroom ventilation, an assembly hall with a stage at the front, blackboards, microscopes, a principal's office, adjustable chairs for students, and central heating. Five years after House's entry, he also pioneered in coeducation, admitting girls, and in another innovation: he insisted that reading lessons utilize "real literature" rather than the dull lessons then current in most schools. And to prevent student rivalries, he declared that all children who attended for a full year without "deviation" marks in conduct would receive equal commendations at the closing ceremonies. At the same time, the school brimmed with discipline. The 1849 *Catalogue* demanded that parents notify the school "in case of the pupil's failing, *on whatever plea,* to take his books home with him for study." It forbade days off for family affairs. It promised weekly performance reports in each subject—to be returned to school with the parents' signatures. And it urged "all parents, who love their children, and value their own happiness, to nip this spirit of self-conceit and wilfulness in the bud, unless they wish to gather, in after years, the fruit of disobedience, ingratitude, and misery." Central to the Chauncy-Hall system then was insistence on *"steady exaction on the part of the teacher, and hard work on the part of the pupil,"* on *"the maintenance of unlimited authority"* by teachers and *"implicit obedience"* by students.[3]

This approach worked well for most students. By the 1840s, Chauncy-Hall was sending six students a year to Harvard, a full 10 percent of a typical Harvard class. One of its better-known early graduates was the 1836 entrant Francis Parkman, historian of America's French and Indian Wars. For Ned House, however, although the Chauncy-Hall approach to coeducation and equality was formative, its authoritarian character was beyond the pale. There was no problem with his personal discipline, nor with his ability. But already, as an adolescent, he was cheeky and self-confident, not one to brook even a teacher's arbitrary authority. In what became a family legend, a Chauncy-Hall teacher praised one of his essays too much; it seemed too good, the teacher said, to have been written by a twelve-year-old. Might Ned have gotten help? The lad was indignant. He told his parents, wrote a letter about it to a Boston paper, and announced that he would leave the school. The fact that his father had stayed at Chauncy-Hall for only a year and wanted his son to become an engraver may have lessened the embarrassment of the withdrawal.[4]

House never enrolled in a formal educational institution again; instead, he studied at home. He balanced work at his father's firm with study. And by any reckoning, he was a driven adolescent. He gave the greatest portion of his time to music, playing the piano and studying orchestral music with a zest that attracted attention. Years later, he would recall his infatuation as a youth with the German Richard Wagner's opera *Tannhäuser.* "I set at work to copy every note in the crowded pages of the overture," he said, "as the only possible method of learning how its extraordinary and unprecedented effects were produced." He may have had Chauncy-Hall School tribulations in mind when he added that the copying gave him a "more thorough comprehension of orchestral capacities than a long course of previous study had given me." People began to talk about the appearance of a prodigy when one of House's pieces, "Composition for Orchestra," was performed by a Boston orchestra while he was still in his mid-teens.[5]

It was thus his mother's music, not his father's engraving, that led to Ned's next step, the acceptance of a job that would set his course for life. Actually, 1854, his eighteenth year, was seminal. On July 22, his mother died of tuberculosis, drawing note in the local press only as the thirty-seven-year-old wife of Timothy who lived in nearby Newton. There was no mention of her musical accomplishments nor of any of her family members. The second formative event of that year made him a journalist. According to family lore, he dashed off a review of a local musical performance one day, sent it to one of the Boston newspapers, most likely the *Courier*, whose arts coverage was weak, and received an offer to join the staff.[6]

When House went to work, the thirty-year-old *Courier* was the "favorite Boston journal" among "influential persons." Though officially nonpartisan, it took a conservative line and espoused protectionist trade policies: what then was generally called "the American system." Its writers had included the venerable Charles Francis Adams, poet James Russell Lowell, and William J. Snelling, whose accounts of life in the Minnesotan wilderness had a national following. By Ned's third year, 1857, the paper's circulation was 1,600, respectable for the time but not sufficient to garner the profits the owners desired. When they put the *Courier* on the market that year, a group of six journalists, including the twenty-one-year-old House, purchased it for $9,000. It did not take long, however, for the group to realize "that they had made a bad bargain." Possibly for that reason, but more likely because the head of the group, John Clark, took the paper in a pro-Southern direction, House severed his ties with the *Courier* the next year.[7]

The years at the *Courier* shaped House's approach to both life and journalism. For one thing, they gave him the confidence to take a paper's reportage in new directions—in this case, into the arts. One had to search hard, usually in vain, for stories on music and drama before he went to work there. By his third year, however, arts coverage had become a *Courier* forte, particularly in the "Musical and Dramatic" column that graced page one on many days. Unfortunately, the absence of bylines in 1850s journalism keeps us from saying with certainty which pieces House wrote. But his love of the arts, coupled with the dramatic drop in arts coverage once he left Boston in 1858, suggests that most reports and reviews were his. The reviews in particular oozed the expertise and sarcastic wit that would become his hallmark. Although the majority of reviews were favorable or informative, a number were witty and derisive. Late in February 1857, for example, he took on the aspiring actress, Mrs. Dennis McMahon, whose role as Pauline in the *Lady of Lyons* was a "complete and hopeless failure." Noting her "extravagant ambition," House quipped: "It is possible that, with much study and care, she might in time become a fourth or fifth-rate actress." On January 2, 1858, he described a benefit by a Mr. Davidage who "sang in a truly comical manner a not very comical song." On the whole, however, House admired Boston's art world and worked hard at nurturing the city's artists. Even when he left for New York, he continued to support Boston artists and musicians, providing counsel to the editors of a new journal, the *Boston Musical Times,* when it commenced publication in 1860.[8]

Another effect of these years was the honing of the reportorial approaches that would turn him into a national figure. Since most of House's personal papers and journals were destroyed when his grandson's home was burned in the World War II fire bombings of Tokyo, data regarding his early reportorial techniques are thin, but he said enough in later articles and letters to give us a fair sense of how these years educated him as a reporter.[9] A piece that he published decades later in *Harper's Weekly Magazine,* for example, shows a young man who was learning to work long hours and to be unfazed by the prestige of his sources. The piece recalls a Sunday evening when House, just over twenty, went searching determinedly for *Atlantic Monthly* editor James Russell Lowell's home in Cambridge, Massachusetts. Coming unexpectedly upon the middle-aged editor out walking with his daughter, House introduced himself as an *Atlantic* contributor and was invited home for a conversation that lasted until near midnight. First, Lowell told the neophyte that one reason he had published a recent book review by House was that he thought rejection would be too hard on his tender ego: "I judge that cutting up unnecessarily is not the best treatment for one of your kind, at your time of life." He suggested, however, that House stick to fiction and the short stories that had begun to give him a reputation. Next, Lowell advised him that "independence in thought and in expression" was the "most essential" characteristic of good prose, and that only second-rate authors mimicked the styles of the great writers. When Lowell commented that "every man who wrote with an earnest purpose was entitled to a hearing," House showed the chutzpah that later would irk many rivals, asking if the editor would publish an unpopular writer in *The Atlantic.* "Are you thinking of anybody in particular?" Lowell asked. To which House replied, "I was thinking of Whitman." It was a brash suggestion, given Lowell's well-known antipathy for the poet. But Lowell said yes, he would, and not long thereafter he did so. "In this way," recalled House, "almost through an accidental turn of conversation, the publication of Walt Whitman's early contribution to the *Atlantic Monthly* was brought about."

Lowell, whom House praised for a special "kindliness . . . toward young writers," perceived quite clearly several of the characteristics that the *Courier* years had given to the young House: his talent with words, his sensitivity to criticism, and his penchant for copying brilliant masters (as he had done with *Tannhäuser*). It is not so certain that he knew about two other characteristics: attention to the details of reporting and a willingness to work hard. Within twenty-four hours of the interview, House recalled, he had written down the entire Lowell conversation and sent it off in a letter to another journalist. "Nothing that could be recalled was omitted, and the familiar practice of the newspaper reporter was serviceable in the endeavor to reproduce the exact words that were used."[10] Evidence of this fastidiousness shows up in occasional references later to his "copying book" in which he would keep duplicates of each letter he wrote, as well as in his advice, years later, to Henry Villard, when the railroad magnate's son was considering a reporter's career. Aspiring journalists must remember, House wrote, that journalism "needs hard work, and above all honest work." He said it was his "unvarying rule" at the *Courier* "never to let the meanest or most trivial paragraph go to the printer until I had hammered it into its best."

> Dear me, I would twist and turn a wretched little item about a fire, or a street accident, until my head spun, rather than leave a slovenly stain on it; and I often turned back to my office from my house-door, after a hard night's work, only to rearrange a phrase that I found awkward at the last moment, or perhaps to change an infelicitous adjective. To this day, I recall a night of almost sleepless torment, owing to the sudden reflection after I had gone to bed, that I had used the word "troglodyte" in a sense not strictly applicable. If it had been a simpler word, I should not have been so disturbed; but I was oppressed with the fear that I would be suspected of aiming at grandiloquence.[11]

Referring to himself as a "fanatic in fastidiousness," he said the early care made him a rapid writer in later years.

House left Boston for New York in 1858. It was a big leap for a twenty-two-year-old, self-educated man with more ambition and talent than connections. Boston was a sophisticated place, the intellectual and literary center of the country, with the likes of Longfellow, Whittier, Thoreau, Emerson, and Hawthorne in or near there at the time, but it boasted only 170,000 inhabitants and its journalism was local. New York's newspapers, by contrast, had developed a national scope. When their editors and writers spoke, politicians from Washington to Chicago listened. And these were heady days for local reporting, too, as the city teemed with the human hurly-burly that gives journalism its romance. The city's population had nearly doubled, to nearly a million, in less than a decade thanks to waves of immigrants from Ireland and northern Europe, which meant that New York had become America's financial center, its liveliest port, and the heart of its growing railroad and commercial systems. Class and religious conflicts also abounded: old Protestants against new Roman Catholics, Irish against African Americans, new male workers against the farm girls who had been laboring for years in the textile mills. And the city was overrun by slums—human hives, as some called them, with huge families living in dank, windowless cellars, surrounded by garbage and stench on the street and children begging on the corner. House's new paper, the *Tribune,* had a few years earlier estimated that the least a family could scrape by on was $10.37 a week; yet most factories capped workers' weekly wages at five dollars. As late as 1863, young umbrella seamstresses were paid three dollars a week, *minus* the cost of the needles and thread they used.[12]

All of this produced the crime, the human conflict, and the need for cheap and easy-to-read information that had made New York the hub of the populist press during the quarter-century before House arrived. Benjamin Day had inaugurated "penny press" journalism in 1833, when he launched the *New York Sun* at one cent an issue (a sixth of the price of established papers), attracting readers with tales of tragedy, scandal, sex, and murder. His competitors sneered at his standards, but by the 1850s the emulators—James Gordon Bennett's *Herald,* Horace Greeley's *Tribune,* and Henry Raymond's *Times*—had become the establishment. They were more serious than the *Sun,* but they too survived now on illustrations, bold headlines, self-promotion, and endless stories of sex and scandal. The result was circulations approaching 40,000 for the *Tribune* when House arrived, and 75,000 for the *Herald,* twenty to forty times those of Boston's *Courier.*

The *Tribune* was, by most tellings, the best paper in the city. Founded by the egocentric Horace Greeley, it favored a contradictory set of political positions: protective tariffs to help big business, a national bank, improved railway and highway systems—balanced by calls for better working conditions, labor unions, workers' education, and free entry by women into professional life. Greeley opposed the theater as immoral, eschewed tobacco and alcohol, railed against marital infidelity, yet was notorious for his profanity. He printed Karl Marx's essays from London and emphasized the news of Europe. As one of his editors put it: "Greeley had something to say and must say it." He also made a great profit, watching the paper's worth go from $5,000 at its birth to more than $300,000 when House entered seventeen years later. And he did all this while building up "an outstanding editorial staff, perhaps the best in America at the time." As E. L. Godkin, Greeley's rival at *The Nation,* put it: "To get admission to the columns of The Tribune almost gave the young writer a patent of literary nobility."[13]

The move from the *Courier* to the *Tribune* was quite a step for the young House. But he was ready and jumped easily into coverage of the country's biggest stories: abolitionism, foreign visitors, and diplomacy. His leap was eased by the intellectual-artistic environment in which he had moved in Boston; self-taught though he was, he was no outsider to elite circles. Certainly, his aggressive personality helped him too. The most important factor, however, was his instant welcome by a group of literary figures who nurtured both his literary talents and his epicurean tastes. His fellow reporters at the *Tribune* were a free-wheeling, fun-loving lot, described by reporter John Russell Young as "resolute, brilliant, capable, irresponsible, intolerant—not above setting things on fire for the fun of seeing them burn." And his social life revolved around the Pfaff beer cellar at 653 Broadway, a famous haunt for writers, artists, and actors who wanted cheap food, good alcohol, and endless conversation. Located beneath street-side shops near Winter Garden Theatre, it had a long bar, often sticky with suds, and a clutter of small tables and chairs owned by Charlie Pfaff and presided over by King of Bohemia Henry Clapp, a one-time temperance speaker known for calling Horace Greeley "a self-made man that worships his creator." People varied in their assessments of the saloon's food (William Dean Howells loved the German pancakes) but praised its beers and liquors.

Pfaff patrons included a who's who of the day's literary establishment, some of them gay and some of them straight, along with many of the city's better-known eccentrics. There was the Queen of Bohemia Ada Clare, an actress and writer of uncertain marital status who had "friendships and amours" with the likes of Charles Dickens, Walt Whitman, and Dante Gabriel Rossetti. There were actors and journalists. There were aristocrats, one of whom had "the dignity, suavity, and learning to qualify him for being a bishop, but . . . much preferred writing plays, engineering shows and being an old Bohemian." There were writers Thomas Bailey Aldrich ("an official attendant" who "was usually glad to escape to the quiet of his little hall-room") and George Arnold; journalists William Winter, Edmund Clarence Stedman, and Frank Wood; dramatist Dion Boucicault; humorist Artemus Ward; and the poet Whitman, who came in sombrero and flannel shirt and sat silently, "roughly unpleasant, and plainly on exhibition." Above all, there was drinking, smoking, and conversation. Ward's manager, E. P. Hingston, said: "They knew everything down at Pfaff's. That which they did not know they assumed they did. . . . Many of them being young men, and all of them critics, the gentlemen who assembled at Pfaff's were encyclopaedic in their information, and never suspected the correctness of their opinions." When the gang at Pfaff's determined that Ward would be a hit in New York, Hingston relaxed: "As I have stated before—they were always right down at Pfaff's."

Whitman got the tone of it all in an unfinished poem about "the vault at Pfaffs":

> Laugh on Laughers!
> Drink on Drinkers!
> Bandy the jest! Toss the theme from one to another!
> Beam up—Brighten up, bright eyes of beautiful young men!
> Eat what you, having ordered, are pleased to see placed before you—
>   After the work of day, now, with appetite, eat,
> Drink wine—drink beer—raise your voice.

The Pfaff cellar also had what Stedman called a "pathetic side." Many of the regulars worked hard, made little, partied continuously—and died young. "No other such list of names that I remember could show such a death roll," Stedman said—nine dead within a dozen years of the Civil War. "That was New York's Bohemian Olympiad."

And Ned House fit right in, except for the early death. A practical joker who threw a raw egg at an actor during one play and pinned a small flag on an actress's stocking before she went on stage, he loved beer, writing, and conversation. He one day would regret the wilder side of his young life, confessing that this "wasn't the best road to take in entering life," and admitting that "the days (and nights) were sometimes too turbulent for anybody's welfare" and that "I wasted too much time." Indeed, he would write to Aldrich from Tokyo years later, wishing "I had some of it back again." But at the time, he participated without reserve. As his journalist friend—and later editor—Whitelaw Reid recalled, one never could predict what "escapades" or "mischief" Ned would indulge in "when he was crazed with drink." If the older House regretted the sprees, the younger man loved them. He was new to the city, new to elite journalism, new to the ideas and excesses of the New York arts world, "the keenest of the group," as journalist-diplomat John Russell Young recalled him.[14]

House threw himself into reporting as avidly as he did into merrymaking. Judged "among the most brilliant" of the *Tribune* writers, he attracted attention in the spring of 1860 with his richly detailed stories on Japan's first diplomatic mission to the United States. The series will be discussed below, but it should be noted here that this early encounter with men from a land that hardly had touched his consciousness back in Boston would prove seminal in two ways: it would clinch his reputation as a writer of descriptive prose, and it would initiate a personal link with Japan that would, in time, become almost mystical. Another of his early coups was a set of reports in October on the U.S. visit of the nineteen-year-old heir to the British crown, Albert Edward, Prince of Wales. It was the first trip to the United States by a member of the British royal family and House covered it with panache. He wrote that the visit seemed more like "a family reunion" than a solemn occasion of state, something altogether different from the "stateliness and frigid etiquette" of the Japanese in May. The atmosphere in the White House during the prince's reception was "loose, careless, essentially democratic. . . . There were men who appeared slightly unclean and possibly were so, and a few who spit on the carpets." On successive days, House described the prince's voyage down the Potomac to a dilapidated Mount Vernon; his love of dancing; a New York reception where the crush of people "imparted an excitement to the very act of standing still, with an elbow in every rib and a heel on each toe"; and a Boston appearance where 1,200 schoolchildren "shouted and cheered, and shook their handkerchiefs until the audience . . . shouted and cheered too." Always, he celebrated the boisterous, friendly, and democratic nature of the American spirit.[15] And his editors and readers loved it.

The reportage that turned House into a full-fledged star was his work on abolitionism and the Civil War, which sandwiched his reports about the foreign visitors. On October 16, 1859, his first big break had come when the white-haired abolitionist John Brown led twenty-one followers, five of them black, in seizing the federal arsenal at Harpers Ferry, Virginia. His intent was to set afire a slave rebellion throughout the South, but the seizure also ignited House's *Tribune* career. Brown was, by all accounts, a fanatic. His group of seven had murdered five proslavery men in Kansas in 1856, then had taken part in months of violent conflict between pro- and antislavery forces there. But his extremism was balanced by his sincerity in a time when the national debate on slavery was at fever pitch. Thus, when half of his small Harpers Ferry band was killed and he was captured by U.S. Marines two days later, the northern press trumpeted his cause rather than his means. When he behaved with courageous dignity during his trial and imprisonment, the abolitionists made him a martyr. As the *Tribune*'s lead reporter wrote on the day that the trial opened, October 27: "It cannot be pleasant to the sensitive slaveholders of Virginia to know that there are men like Old Brown and his associates—who are not afraid to risk their lives, their liberties, and their cash, in such a cause. It is not what one solitary fanatic can effect which constitutes the danger—but it is the fact that there is one such." On December 3, the day after his execution, the paper editorialized: "John Brown dead is verily a power—like Samson in the falling temple of Dagen. . . . Let us be reverently grateful for the privilege of living in a world rendered noble by the daring of heroes, the suffering of martyrs."

Leading the *Tribune*'s coverage of John Brown's trial and execution was the twenty-three-year-old House, the first of three reporters sent by Greeley to Baltimore to cover the case. It is difficult on most days to tell which articles, or parts of articles, were his due to the absence of bylines and the way that papers then combined several reporters' stories into a single article. But House's accounts gained enough notoriety to make his authorship clear in many cases. A long piece on December 5, for example, recounted Brown's last moments in painstaking detail, including even his conversation with the executioner on the gallows:

> Near ten minutes elapse before Gen. Taliaferro's chivalrous hosts are in their proper position, during which time John Brown stands with the cap drawn over his head, and the hangman's knot under his ear. . . .
>
> At last Virginia troops are arranged *à la mode.*
>
> "Capt. Brown, you are not standing on the drop—will you come forward!" said the Sheriff.
>
> "I can't see, gentlemen," was the reply; "you must lead me."

The Sheriff led his prisoner forward to the center of the drop. . . .

A moment after, the Sheriff springs the latch—the drop falls—and the body of John Brown is suspended between heaven and earth. A few convulsive twitchings of the arms are observed. These came after a moment.

John Brown is dead.

The Last Moments of John Brown *by Thomas Hovenden. The well-known painting was based on inaccurate information inserted by a* New York Tribune *editor into House's article about the hanging. (Courtesy of The Metropolitan Museum of Art, Gift of Mr. and Mrs. Carl Stoeckel, 1897 [97.5]. Used by permission.)*

How, the reader asks, could a reporter have known what was being said if the press was kept 150 feet from the scaffold? The answer, explained Stedman, one of House's closest lifelong friends, was that House disguised himself as a member of the surgeon's staff "and was on the scaffold with Brown, virtually taking his life in his hand, had his identity been discovered."

The same article inspired Thomas Hovenden's 1884 painting, *The Last Moments of John Brown,* which hangs in New York's Metropolitan Museum of Art and led to a row over the authenticity of House's reporting. The *Tribune* story described the prisoner kissing a black child as he left the jail: "He stopped for a moment in his course, stooped over, and, with the tenderness of one whose love is as broad as the brotherhood of man, kissed it affectionately. That mother will be proud of that mark of distinction for her offspring, and some day when, over the ashes of John Brown the temple of Virginia liberty is reared, she may join in the joyful song of praise which on that soil will do justice to his memory." Though the jailer called the account a fabrication, denying that Brown had touched any civilian, historians have argued about what really happened. The truth, House himself would explain years later, lay with the jailer. Although House had "supplied the greater part of the material from which the *Tribune* article was composed," an editor in New York ("Edward Underhill, I think") had inserted the kissing story without House's knowledge. By the time House learned of the addition, the tale "had already secured a hold upon public confidence, and defied contradiction until years had gone by." The hero-worshiping *tone* of House's reportage was not inserted, however. His belief in Brown, combined with his gift for vivid prose, prompted *The Atlantic*'s Lowell to recommend that he "make a little book of your adventures in Virginia."[16]

Where House's idealism came from is hard to say. From his commoner roots? From his sense of unfair treatment at Chauncy-Hall School? From his conversations with iconoclasts at Pfaff's? From passions ignited by the national slavery debate? Whatever the source, it was clear by the end of his first two years in New York that journalism would, for him, mean more than reporting facts or pretending objectivity. The reporter's profession, as he understood it, demanded an ideological commitment as well as an ability to sway readers. And those beliefs, for House, included not only freedom for slaves but skepticism about all pretenses of wealth and class. Just months before the Brown raid, he published one of his first *Atlantic* short stories, "Mien-Yaun," the witty tale of a Chinese aristocrat who wanted to marry a beautiful young woman from the despised merchant class. When people heard of the nobleman's marriage plans, said the narrator, "All Pekin was in an uproar. That is to say, the three thousand eminent individuals who composed the aristocracy had nearly lost their wits. The million and a half common people were, of course, of no account." Years later, House would say of another writer, "His sympathy with suffering was as quick and tender as his hatred of injustice was fiery and uncontrollable."[17] He could have been talking about himself as the novice reporter who tried hard to get the details accurately but made no pretense at objectivity once he had set upon a cause.

Just sixteen months after Brown's execution, the country was at war. It says something about both House's abilities and the state of journalism that a twenty-four-year-old school dropout, only three years in New York, would be included on the lists of preeminent Civil War reporters during the early months of fighting. The country had no veterans in war reporting then. As one of House's closest friends put it, "We pioneers were *creating* the profession of the War Correspondent in America"; this "was prentice work." That House was among the best of those "prentices" became clear weeks after the fighting began, in an event that "greatly stimulated the war feeling in the North." On Friday, May 24, 1861, House accompanied twenty-four-year-old Colonel E. Elmer Ellsworth to Alexandria, Virginia, with a thousand Zouaves troops who intended to wrest the city from Southern hands. Arriving at 5:30 A.M. on May 25, Ellsworth, House, and two others headed for the telegraph station to destroy the wires and disrupt communication with the South. En route, Ellsworth decided to take down a Confederate flag flying from the Marshall House Tavern.[18] At this point, it seems best to give the story over to House, whose account filled four columns of the *Tribune*'s front page the next day:

> The Colonel met a man in his shirt and trousers, of whom he demanded what sort of flag it was that hung above the roof. The stranger, who seemed greatly alarmed, declared he knew nothing of it, and that he was only a boarder there. Without questioning him further the Colonel sprang upstairs, and we all followed to the topmost story, whence, by means of a ladder, he clambered to the roof, cut down the flag . . . and brought it from its staff. . . . We at once turned to descend, Private Brownell leading the way, and Colonel Ellsworth immediately following him with a flag. As Brownell reached the first landing-place . . . a man jumped from a dark passage, and hardly noticing the private, leveled a double-barreled gun square at the Colonel's breast. Brownell made a quick pass to turn the weapon aside; but the fellow's hand was firm and he discharged one barrel straight to its aim, the slugs or buckshot with which it was loaded entering the Colonel's heart, and killing him at the instant. I think my arm was resting on poor Ellsworth's shoulder at the moment. At any rate, he seemed to fall almost from my own grasp. He was on the second or third step from the landing, and he dropped forward with that heavy, horrible, headlong weight which always comes of sudden death inflicted in this manner.

House then went on to describe how Brownell shot the assailant (who turned out to be the hotel's proprietor) and how the little group wrapped Ellsworth's feet in the flag, "stained with his blood." He concluded with a eulogy to the Colonel: "It may be said that his deed was rash, but I should not like to hear this reproach too largely urged against him. He was young, and ardent, and full of ambition, and perhaps knew not that sense of caution which a colder nature would possess. But it would be well for many of us if we were as . . . rich in manly virtues."

Years later, House related to his friend John Hay an additional episode to which he had referred only obliquely in the *Tribune* story. Knowing that Ellsworth wanted to disrupt cable service between Alexandria and the Confederate forces, House dashed off to the telegraph station following Ellsworth's murder, accompanied by two timid soldiers. "As there were several persons inside the building, and as I had no weapon," he recalled, "I thought it wisest to simulate, on the staircase, the approach of a considerable number of visitors, and the result was that the operating rooms were hurriedly vacated before I threw open the door." He strode into the empty room, "broke the instruments, snapped the wires, and did all I could to make the machinery temporarily useless," before returning to the Marshall House, and thence to Washington, to write his story.

Historians Louis L. Snyder and Richard B. Morris list House with a handful of others, including William Howard Russell of the London *Times* and the photographer Matthew B. Brady, in the "galaxy of brilliant journalists" who covered the first battle of Bull Run on July 21. Even before the actual battle, House had stirred things up by scooping the Washington press on July 7 with a report that "tomorrow is the day agreed on by the President and his advisers, including General Scott, for a grand combined movement on Manassas Junction by flank and center columns." The item was accurate, but supply problems forced a last-minute postponement—and General Winfield Scott was so furious about the leak that he clamped a heavy censorship on the press until the buzz of complaints forced him to remove it five days later.

House's behavior and reportage at Bull Run illustrated both the joy of engagement and the attention to detail that had become his hallmarks. In one often-repeated episode, he was walking in the setting sun one afternoon with two reporter friends, Stedman of the *New York World* and Villard of the *Herald,* when the latter, famished, decided to climb a cherry tree and get something to eat. By Villard's own account, Confederate troops began shooting at the Union soldiers while he was in the tree. There was a "mighty whizzing and clattering all around. . . . We were . . . right in the line of fire of a whole rebel brigade." Before he could know what was happening, Villard had been knocked out of the tree, shaken but uninjured. House recalled a "descent from mid-air into the heart of the First Massachusetts—to the amazement, I presume, of that gallant regiment, and to the envy of your colleagues, whom you had distanced by securing a point so far in advance." And Stedman recollected that "we all exchanged drinks, the sun being where it was, and no water in sight." Villard said "the music of 'bullet, ball, and grapeshot' never had much terror for me thereafter."

When the Union retreat turned Bull Run into an ugly rout, House, Russell, and Villard watched from a small hill. Most of the journalists returned at once to Washington to file their reports, but House, who blamed the defeat on confused communications from General Irwin McDowell's staff, stayed behind, along with Joseph Glen of the *Cincinnati Gazette.* He told his fellows that it "would be unseemly for a *Tribune* reporter to join the retreat" and that Greeley would be angry if he left. His skeptical colleagues suspected that inebriation was the real reason for his lingering, but whatever the cause, when he and Glen awakened the next morning, they found the house in which they had bivouacked occupied by Confederate soldiers. Posing as southern gentlemen, the two offered to make breakfast for the cavalrymen, then walked into the kitchen, out the back door into a morning drizzle, and off toward Washington, observing dead horses, demolished buggies, spilt food, and looters as they went. Several miles on, they came across a Union army wagon, hitched a ride to the capital, and wrote their stories.[19]

House seems to have spent a good deal of time in enemy territory during the war's early period. Thomas Bailey Aldrich, also a reporter then for the *Tribune,* talks of riding with Ned through the inhospitable woods of Virginia in October. And House would write Aldrich more than a decade later about "the night we passed together at Stahel's quarters—that dark night, dreary and unwholesome everywhere else around, but vivid with excitement and activity in the light of the Dutchmen's watchfires." An evening like that, he said, was "worth a little sacrifice." But after the war's early months, House's reportorial assignments shifted. By the second year of the conflict, he was off on other beats, sometimes in New York, at other times in London, Paris, or Washington. He also began devoting time to other kinds of writing: covering the theater for the *Tribune,* contributing to literary magazines, collaborating with the Irish actor-writer Dion Boucicault, even writing his own plays. Whether the *Tribune* editors reassigned him or he tired of day-to-day war coverage is unclear, though correspondence with his fellow journalist Stedman suggested that his restless nature drove him back to New York when battlefield action lagged in the east, while his own later expressions of regret about his habits in these years hint that the drinking and devil-may-care approach may have undermined his effectiveness in covering routine battles, even as they made him potent on the more dramatic stories.[20]

This branching out, however, was very much in keeping with House's personality. He had always been restless, leaving Chauncy-Hall School prematurely, leaping from engraving to music, then to the *Courier,* and on to the *Tribune.* The one constant had been writing. Even though his move to New York in 1858 had been as a reporter, he regarded himself even then more as a writer than as a reporter *per se.* As a result, he began at once that practice, which would intensify across the 1860s, of supplementing his newspaper work with literary work, publishing stories and essays for *Harper's New Monthly Magazine* and *The Atlantic Monthly.* Most of his fictional pieces were love stories in which hard work or integrity bested manners and pretense. "How the Snow Melted on Mt. Washington," for example, mocked the affectations of a rich woman who was furious that her young niece "passed a night upon a mountain with a stranger," even though the stranger had been there to save the niece's life during a sudden ice storm. In "Love by Mishap," the gallant Fred Timmerton thought one Julia Daisley beautiful but frigid during an outing in Central Park. As she gently nursed him back to health after a near-fatal riding accident, however, he decided that his quick evaluation had been wrong, and the two fell in love. "There is nothing in the world like the beautiful devotion of a woman to the sick," House wrote, in the respectful but stereotyped tone of his age. "From woman life comes; she feels that it is hers to guard it."[21]

Perhaps the least predictable of House's growing interests was eastern Asia. The western Pacific was as far removed, both geographically and psychically, as one can imagine from the hurly-burly of New York journalism. Still, for reasons that no one, including House himself, has been able to explain (beyond the confession that "Japan was always a point of tenderness with me"), he began demonstrating an infatuation with Asia soon after his arrival in New York. The first evidence was the above-mentioned *Atlantic Monthly* story, "Mien-Yaun," which showed a deeper understanding of China than one could have expected in a light literary fantasy of the late 1850s, an understanding that could have come only from serious reading or discussion about the Middle Kingdom.[22] The second piece of evidence came in his response to Japan's 1860 diplomatic embassy to Washington. When he learned that the mission had been dispatched, he immediately began work on a twelve-page essay introducing Japan to the readers of *The Atlantic Monthly.* Drawing heavily on *Japan as It Was and Is,* published five years earlier by his friend Richard Hildreth, House presented a sympathetic, surprisingly accurate account of Japan's historical development, focusing on the nation's tumultuous first engagement with Europeans in the sixteenth and seventeenth centuries. He quoted the missionary Francis Xavier's observation that the Japanese "are truly the delight of my heart," derided Catholic squabbling that got the Europeans thrown out of Japan early in the 1600s, absolved the Japanese of blame for the centuries of seclusion ("if Christianity has suffered, the errors of those who misrepresented it were the cause"), praised Matthew Perry's "firmness, prudence, and energy" in opening Japan to the West, and argued that Americans had treated Japan more kindly than Europeans had. He also said that since Perry's arrival, the Japanese had "showed themselves especially alive to the civilizing influences of foreign cookery, and manifested a particular . . . appreciation of such refinements as whiskey and Champagne, to whose beneficent influences they gave themselves up with ardor."

The tone of the piece—praised decades later by Lafcadio Hearn (who happened on it at a secondhand store) as "a very good article . . . for that time, considering that the writer found it necessary to correct the then popular error that the Chinese and the Japanese were the same kind of people"—provided a foretaste of the way House would approach Japan for the next forty years. His facts were generally accurate, and his tone differed from that employed by most Western writers on Asia. Although he assumed that American civilization was superior, he avoided condescension and eschewed that era's typical depiction of the Japanese "as a dishonest, childlike and backward people in need of moral and technological instruction."[23] Even the two centuries of seclusion, for which other writers damned Japan, were blamed on the European military and religious threat. House took the Japanese seriously, in other words, and gave them as much benefit of the doubt as other writers gave to European nations.

This attitude stood him in good stead when the *Tribune* assigned him to cover the arrival of the diplomatic mission in Washington on May 14. The embassy represented a unique moment in American history, the first time the United States had been visited by Asian diplomats. Seventy-seven men strong, the mission's ostensible goal was to exchange ratifications of the 1858 commercial treaty between Japan and the United States, but the real purpose was to show respect to the nation that had prompted Japan's reentry into the broader world. Few of the embassy's members held important posts back home; half a dozen were teenagers, and most were younger than forty. Lacking many diplomatic responsibilities, the ambassadors were free to do all manner of sightseeing and to engage in social activities. And their American hosts were free to gawk: at their impassive faces, their curious gifts of silk and folding screens, the samurai robes, the swords (two per man), the straw sandals, and the leaders' stern dignity. The visitor who drew the most attention was Tateishi Onojirō Noriyuki, a teenaged interpreter-trainee nicknamed "Tommy" by the press, who wrote love letters to American suitors and awed reporters with his good looks and irrepressible personality. Whitman penned a poem to herald the visit, President James Buchanan gave them a banquet, New York City gave them a parade with 7,000 military escorts, and 10,000 New Yorkers attended a ball in their honor.

Three members of the 1860 mission to the United States, which introduced the world of Japan to House, posed for a photo with the famed photographer Matthew Brady. The man on the right is thought to be Kawasaki Dōmin, the embassy physician. (Matthew Brady Collection, U.S. National Archives)

And House chronicled their story, working day and night for weeks to the point of feeling "used up." On the embassy's arrival in Washington, he told of looking "from my window down into the open area, where numerous Japanese are wandering among the crowds . . . distributing curiosities about with a lavish hand." He pronounced himself moved by this "meeting of two extremes of civilization." About Tommy, he wrote: "He perpetually laughs or sings. He says droll things at the most unexpected times. . . . He is rather short and plump, with a full, round face, and always overflows with mirth." And about the leaders of the mission: "Of the courtly and gentle manners of the Japanese Embassadors it is impossible to speak in too high terms. . . . It was not over pleasant to contrast their demeanor with that of a very considerable number of the Americans with whom they came in contact." When the entourage visited President Buchanan, he continued the theme: "The dresses of the Japanese were much more gorgeous than any they had previously appeared in. The first Embassador wore robes of blue and purple crape, with richly embroidered trousers of silk."

House also was interested in what the members of the embassy had to say, treating their ideas with the respect he accorded their demeanor and dress. Foreshadowing the agnosticism for which he later would become known, he noted the leaders' observation that while religious beliefs were necessary for the lower classes, "the higher and educated classes in Japan—even those in whom there is any degree of cultivation—do not believe that stars or spirits have any such influence." He also quoted their explanation to a group of visiting American doctors that the scientific approach had become standard among Japanese physicians and that syphilis was very common in Japan. When one of the leaders, Morita Okatarō Kiyoyuki, invited him to his room, House reveled in "an atmosphere of Oriental fragrance" and indulged in a round of pipe smoking. He loved the "soft and smooth" tone of the visitors' language. And Tommy kept reappearing in his stories. In Washington, the young heartthrob confided to House his "earnest desire to discover a suitable wife in this country," but the reporter's story pointed out that when older women thrust themselves at Tommy, he was "generally taken with a fit of business." Two weeks later the inevitable report came from New York: Tommy had "come to grief"; he had become "the victim of a hopeless passion." What came of that passion, House never related.

It was obvious to *Tribune* readers that House too had been overcome with a passion. Some of the enthusiasm might have been rhetorical; overwriting to attract readers was standard in journalism then. But House's sense of amazement clearly was more than verbiage. Other reporters' reactions to the embassy covered the spectrum of surprise, curiosity, criticism, respect, and condescension. But for House, there was constant approval, even the suggestion of an almost-spiritual affinity for a way of life he had not observed before. He always had been drawn to things that were new, he loved beauty and dignity, and he respected decorum. And these men had all of those qualities, with a pleasure-loving streak thrown in. More than he could have realized at the time, this early contact with the Japanese would change his life course.[24]

After the midpoint of the Civil War, House began showing signs that New York journalism, like that of Boston before, would not be able to satisfy his restless spirit forever. The *Tribune* editors offered him a new assignment as the paper's drama critic. It should have been a happy offer, given House's previous work in Boston and his love of the arts. But drama was hardly a plum at a paper whose editor equated the theater with sin. So although he took the assignment, he did not thrive in it. Instead, he turned increasingly to avenues outside the paper for fulfillment, developing friendships with actors and writers, trying his hand at theater management and playwriting, taking his skills to London and Paris. The *Tribune* remained his base, but his heart began to roam.

One of his new enthusiasms was a friendship that began to develop in 1867 with Mark Twain. House and Twain were introduced on a January morning by the publisher-writer Charles Henry Webb, who had set up an office on Nassau Street after achieving success as a publisher in California. Still largely unknown in the East but determined to make a name there, Twain was in Webb's office that day talking about publishing and speaking ventures when House happened to stop by. Within weeks the humorist had become a part of House's (and Webb's) bohemian circle, drinking at Pfaff's and engaging in pranks like the drunken minister impersonation, referred to earlier. "Clemens was a good deal in House's company" that year, according to Twain biographer Albert Paine. The two had similar natures: huge ambition and just as much self-confidence, a gift for language, and a propensity for hell-raising. Twain later would describe the youthful House as "young, brisk, handsome, and polished and engaging in his manners," adding that his "capacity as a journalist was high and confessed." They seemed made for each other.

It was more than fun and conversation, however, that kept them together after the first weeks. They found each other useful. House discovered good copy in Twain, and Twain realized that House's friendship would yield publicity. He was working feverishly to get his eastern career on the road (and to put food on the table), seeking out publishers, dreaming up lectures and tours, and badgering agents for writing and speaking contracts. And House was the drama man at one of the city's leading papers. Indeed, the episode that cemented the friendship was House's enthusiastic review of Twain's inaugural New York lecture, on May 6, 1867, at the Cooper Institute, which had the largest lecture hall in the city. Although the house was packed and enthusiastic, the *Sun, Times,* and *Herald* critics were unimpressed. House, by contrast, filled half of a *Tribune* column with praise, writing: "The mantle of the lamented Artemus Ward seems to have fallen on the shoulders of Mark Twain, and worthily does he wear it." With the exception of Ward, "no other lecturer . . . has so thoroughly succeeded in exciting the mirthful curiosities, and compelling the laughter of the hearers." Twain pronounced himself "very grateful to him for making so much of me." And well he should have, because that review was seen by many as pivotal in launching his eastern success.

The Twain friendship would become the richest of House's American life, lubricated by hundreds of letters, countless gifts, weeks at a time in each other's company, and endless conversation about politics, religion, Japan, baronial England, the Twain daughters' fantasies, and Twain's wife Olivia's unuttered profanities. It also would become the source of some of House's greatest pains and most serious financial stresses, when a dispute over *The Prince and the Pauper* would lead to lawsuits and estrangement. But the pain would come decades later. In these post–Civil War days, when Mark was seeking new audiences and Ned was thirsting for fresh releases for his creative energies, they experienced a special spark in each other's company. They were like minds, finding each other useful, stimulating, and fun.[25]

Other friendships that emerged from House's increasing concentration on the arts world after the war included Bret Harte, the editor of *Overland Monthly* and author of *Luck of Roaring Camp*; the Irish actor-playwright Dion Boucicault; and Artemus Ward, whose book of humor reportedly lay beside the Bible on Lincoln's White House desk. Nothing tells us whether Ward, whose real name was Charles Farrar Browne, had known House when he was in Boston in the 1850s as a struggling teenager. They became friends in New York, however, after arriving there within a year of each other. When Ward sailed for England on June 2, 1866, to commence his successful, but ultimately fatal, London appearance, House was with him. The reporter only stayed a few months. By the fall, he was off on a continental vacation, and by November he was back at the *Tribune's* New York office, where Ward would write him, describing his glowing British reception ("absolutely tremendous . . . like fireworks") and asking that a few of the London reviews "be smuggled into the *Tribune.*" House was still in New York the following January 23, when Ward gave his last London lecture and went off to Jersey Island to recuperate from pulmonary tuberculosis, as he was on March 6, when the thirty-three-year-old humorist died.[26]

But House was in London again soon thereafter. Indeed, he spent a good deal of time in Europe during the post–Civil War years, especially after William Winter replaced him as *Tribune* drama critic in August of

1867. The record for these years is spotty, but we know that he already had begun crossing the Atlantic frequently even before the Civil War began, sometimes as a journalist, sometimes as a vacationer. By 1867 he had, according to his own account, used all the trans-Atlantic steamship companies at one time or another—and had concluded that the least expensive steamers provided the best service. He made it as far as Egypt once, as well as to Switzerland and Germany. The first Atlantic crossing for which we have records brought him to a vacation in Paris early in 1861, when his audacious style led to an encounter with the German composer Richard Wagner who was in the city for the French premiere of *Tannhäuser*. When House overheard rumors that the city's art patrons were going to hoot the opera out of existence before they even had heard it, he decided he should warn Wagner. First, he wrote the composer a note. Then, receiving no reply, he went to his apartment, gaining admittance from a "slow-witted concierge," and secured tickets to the dress rehearsals from the master himself. He repeated what he had heard to Wagner, who was more impressed by House's chutzpah than by the rumors.

We also know that House was in London at the end of 1863, staying with the popular British novelist Charles Reade when William Thackeray was found dead in bed on December 23. And we know that just days before that he filled a third of a page in the London *Times* with a raw, vivid story on the famous prizefight between American John Heenan and Briton Tom King. The story actually should have been written by the *Times*'s own reporter, whom House had accompanied to the match, but when the strain of the day and drinks at House's apartment left him drowsy, he sought help from his *Tribune* friend. First, House described the universal predictions that Heenan would win. Then, paragraph after paragraph, he detailed the ebbs and flows in the match—and in the crowd's moods. Heenan knocked King to the ground four times in the early rounds, and the crowd screamed "in hungry accents for closer fighting and more blood." Then the fight turned, and King struck "the American full in the mouth a dreadful blow" that caused heavy bleeding. Back and forth it went, until "the two gigantic naked forms, urged forward by their seconds," came stumbling out for the twenty-fourth round, "almost insensible." When King won, House reported, the crowd turned against Heenan. "Among pugilists," he concluded, "there is no mercy for the defeated. Fair or foul, there is yet only one morality with them—success."[27]

In the years after the Civil War, London became House's second home, filled with the same kind of attractions as those that had brought him to New York a decade earlier. The British capital was home to more than four million people of all classes and occupations, site of the contradictory, exhilarating forces that brimmed from the novels of his friends Reade and Dickens. At the city's center were the houses of Parliament, bastions of democracy at home and imperial rule abroad, sitting two and a half miles upriver from the symbol of intolerance and political machination, the Tower of London. Intersecting the filthy Tudor-era alleyways were the broad avenues of Fleet Street and Holborn, where carriages transported business barons and press lords. The squeals of dying pigs and sheep at the Smithfield slaughterhouse mingled with the peals of the St. Paul's Cathedral chimes a few blocks south. And across the street from St. Bartholomew's hospital lay St. Sepulchre cemetery, where "resurrection men" often earned a few illegal pence by digging up corpses for sale as cadavers. It was a smelly city on market mornings, Dickens said, with the "ground . . . covered nearly ankle-deep with filth and mire, and a thick steam perpetually rising from the reeking bodies of the cattle, and mingling with the fog."[28] And it was a wondrously exciting city. When one added the ale-induced conviviality of London's pubs and the energy of its literary and theater worlds, it is not hard to see why it attracted the young House.

House described his relish for urbane variety in an 1867 *Galaxy* piece about his other favorite European spot, Paris's "Passage de l'Opéra," where he met Wagner and came to know the actress Pauline Déjazet. Over "a small bottle of red or white *vin ordinaire*," he wrote, "you may see a dignified chevalier of the Legion of Honor struggling to extract intelligence from the *Moniteur* at one little table, while at the next a merry *grisette* giggles over her *Journal pour Rire;* a rosy-faced *gamin* cuts jokes with his fresh fruit, in a corner, while a grim-visaged *huissier,* just opposite, attempts to sour all the wine in his neighborhood by the morose glances which he sends forth." London, he found, had just as much appeal and even more variety, along with an easier language (though he was comfortable with French), greater opportunities for making money, and a world of good friends—including Robert Browning, Dickens (at whose home he played card games), Reade, and Boucicault. So it was very much to his satisfaction when, late in 1867, the *Tribune* agreed to install him as correspondent there. He grumbled, as he would in Tokyo three years later, when the paper paid him by the article rather than giving him a salary.[29] But London seemed a happier workplace than New York.

House's most important nonjournalistic role in London was in the theater. For a time, he assisted in the management of St. James's Theatre, a thirty-year-old, thousand-seat house not far from Buckingham Palace, where Dickens's *Oliver Twist* had been performed to hoots for a single disastrous night in 1838, and where late in 1866 Henry Irving made his London debut in a Dion Boucicault play, *The Two Lives of Mary Leigh.* Irving's performance went unheralded at the time, but what House referred to as his "toil and travail" eventually would make him the country's leading Shakespearean actor. Like all of the "old theatres" of the day, the St. James's had a seedy quality: "inconvenient entrances, narrow winding passages" and the odors of "escaped gas, orange peels, tom-cats, and mephitic vapours." But it still was one of the city's more fashionable houses, favored by royalty and in the midst of something of a renaissance in the late 1860s. *Times* reviewers gushed often over the "brilliant audiences," the revivals of old classics, and the rhetorical skills of that "word-spinning genius W. S. Gilbert."[30]

One of the St. James's most popular performers in this period, and the apparent reason for House's connection with it, was Boucicault, who had spent most of the 1850s and early 1860s in New York. The Boucicault relationship gave rise to one of the more tantalizing features of House's career, the writing of plays. References appear repeatedly in biographical sketches to the plays that he wrote or helped to write, some of them obscure, others well known. And each of them involves either a mystery or a controversy. One, *Larcher's Victories,* is credited to House without question—but beyond that fact, we have little information on it. Set in New York in "about 1860," it narrates the humorous encounter of several socialites, one of them obsessed with wearing color combinations that fit the mood of the occasion, another determined to secure a young woman's hand through blackmail, a third in danger of losing both her fortune and her reputation. In the end, the color-obsessed Larcher uncovers the blackmailer's true self and saves everybody else through a combination of cunning and good will. That much we know. But when the play was finished, where it was published, and whether it actually was produced remain unclear. Another, House's dramatization of Twain's *The Prince and the Pauper,* became the source of the House-Clemens estrangement in the late 1880s and will be discussed at length below. And two of the mysteries center on Boucicault's Irish plays.

In one case—the assertion by a Japanese writer that House "coauthored *Colleen Bawn* with his friend, the famous dramatist and actor Dion Boucicault"—the safest conclusion seems to be that the writer was mistaken, as no substantiating evidence appears in the Boucicault or House papers, or in any primary sources. More complicated is the question of how much House collaborated with the Irish actor in what many have called Boucicault's most original work, *Arrah-na-Pogue,* an 1864 romantic tale that drew inspiration from Ireland's eighteenth-century independence struggles. Although no one doubts that Boucicault wrote the original script, it is clear that House had a hand in several changes that were made before its March 22, 1865, London opening, including the excision of a duel and the addition of a scene in which the hero, Shaun, escapes from jail by scaling a wall that sinks dramatically beneath the stage floor to intensify the viewers' illusion of height.

When Boucicault sued *London Herald* editor Joseph Berger in May 1865 for serializing *Arrah* without permission, House was the co-plaintiff, listed as the "joint author" and one of the "sole proprietors of the said . . . piece," who had made "certain additions and alterations to the play." And when the play was registered in the United States, he was named co-proprietor again and given its U.S. production rights. House also was named as coauthor in the American edition of the play's most popular song, "The Wearing of the Green," an old Irish folk song that became the unofficial anthem of the Irish freedom movement after its revision and reintroduction in *Arrah.* And Twain years later would recall that House "told me more than once that he wrote the bulk of" the play and that "his share of the proceeds was $25,000." Twain, who was fighting House over *The Prince and the Pauper* at the time of his recollection, added dismissively that "a theatre manager assures me that Mr. House merely wrote a few lines . . . to protect Mr. Boucicault's rights here against pirates."

The truth obviously lies somewhere between House's alleged claims and Twain's latter-day conclusions. That House made revisions is undisputed. What remain unclear are the specific things that House did on the play. The suit indicates that his revisions were substantial, and some have suggested that he helped Boucicault come up with the play's original theme. Moreover, the London judge accepted the plaintiffs' claim that both House and Boucicault were being damaged palpably by the *Herald's* "paraphrase in the shape of a stupid and sleepy novel." On May 11, he enjoined the paper from publishing any more "scenes or passages" of the play and left open the possibility of other relief for the playwrights "as the nature of the case may require." In the eyes of the law, *Arrah* was the property of both men. The fact that this legal verdict was rendered in London undercuts Twain's suggestion that House and Boucicault made the claim of joint ownership merely to protect Boucicault's rights in the United States.[31]

One other certainty is that House was with Boucicault in 1863 when he met the fifty-year-old Charles Reade, the popular Victorian author (said by the *Times* to be "as clever as he is crotchety") who became his closest British friend. House was in London, apparently on a reporting assignment, when Boucicault took him to Reade's home at Number Six Bolton Row for an interview. The novelist's "portly frame completely filled an exceptionally spacious armchair," which had been placed beside a large table on which he was writing *Hard Cash.* Reade's physical size symbolized his spirit, House said; he "left upon me an impression of breadth and amplitude which . . . remained undisturbed throughout the course of a long and unbroken friendship." The fact that Reade considered Americans his "true public" impressed the patriotic House, too.

Across the next decade House stayed at Reade's home often when he was in London, sometimes for months on end. In 1867, after Reade had finished *Griffith Gaunt,* the two men took a trip together through Wales, where House listened bemused as the novelist described Welsh women as "hideous," Welsh taverns as "mean," and the Welsh "hatred of the Saxon" as disturbing. On the other hand, House said, Reade "was passionately fond of simple music, and listened with delight for hours . . . to the old Welsh lays." In 1869, at a party, he saw Reade talk kindly to a young man who had abused him not long before in print. And on several occasions he had "lively" discussions with Reade and his companion Laura Seymour over how the "lower orders" should be treated. A few days after House had taken the side of a household servant caught reading—an activity well above her status!—Reade gave him a long manuscript on "domestic servants . . . defending their rights and privileges, and charitably extenuating their follies and weaknesses." "There," said Reade, "perhaps that will suit your republican highness."

One basis for the friendship was the fact that House was an American. As nephew Compton Reade put it, the novelist "never lost an opportunity of cultivating American ladies and gentlemen, and of displaying his preference for all things American." And American readers returned the affection. At his death, *Harper's Weekly* commented that if he had visited America "his reception would have cast into the shade that of any other foreign author, not excepting Charles Dickens." Even more important to the friendship were House's theater ties; though Reade made his money and reputation by writing novels, he would have preferred success in acting. "Theater was his passion," House wrote. "He would willingly have surrendered all his fame as a novelist in exchange for a single unqualified triumph upon the stage." His friend John Coleman recalled a dinner with Reade and House, where the novelist read from a play he had written based on Tennyson's "Dora"; "He was never happy out of the theatre," Coleman commented. Unfortunately, thought House, Reade's pretensions in that sphere amounted to "sheer nonsense."[32]

In many ways, House greeted the end of the 1860s as frustrated about his own career as Reade was about the stage. He still was writing for the *Tribune,* but his work lacked the compelling qualities that had fired him in the early 1860s. His engagement in the London theater was titillating but not a grand success. His friends were numerous and prominent, but even that fact induced discontent, since many of them had become more prominent than he was. And he was rootless. The death of his fifty-year-old father from dysentery in 1864 had left him without a place to call home; his only relatives were aunts and uncles to whom he was not very close. He owned no residence, he was single, and it was not clear whether he belonged more in London or New York. That he was successful no one would deny. But it was not the level of success that the prodigy had envisioned when his teenage symphonies were performed in Boston, or when, as a twenty-five-year-old, he set America talking about John Brown.

At the same time, House was free—free to dream of worlds he had not visited, free to *go* to those worlds if opportunity presented itself. He also had developed a set of skills that could be applied in untried directions: an agile mind, a facile and eloquent pen, an ability to make friendships quickly among those who held power, and perhaps most important, connections in America that would give his writings a hearing. What was more, while he had matured beyond the wildness of his early New York years, he had not lost his thirst for things unusual. It was thus not surprising that he began thinking again about that part of the world that had captured his spirit a year before the outbreak of the Civil War, when those curiously clad Eastern diplomats visited America. Early in 1870, he made a trip to Washington, with glowing letters from Greeley and the *Tribune's* managing editor Whitelaw Reid, seeking a diplomatic post in Japan where, he commented, "It is well established that no foreigner can now penetrate the country without some accredited position from a treaty power." Greeley wrote Secretary of State Hamilton Fish that House had done "excellent work on the Tribune" and was "a gentleman and a scholar" who would be a "most competent and faithful officer in Japan." The letters and inquiries failed to pry open a post, however, so House decided to "go to Japan as an outsider," armed with *Tribune* promises of ample pay for the articles he sent back as their official correspondent. "It was the happiest thought in the world for me, that of starting out" in a new Asian career, House would write later. The long trans-Pacific voyage would do more than take him to a mysterious land; it would give him a fresh start in a place even richer in opportunities than London had been a decade earlier. It would change his life as dramatically as if he had been born anew. And it would bring to Japan's shores one of the most vocal, consistent—and influential—American friends that the Asian archipelago ever would know.[33]

NOTES

1. "Anxious toil," from HVP, Harvard University; and "say the grace," from Gregory Fraser, "Rejoice," *The Southern Review* 36, no. 3 (summer 2000): 499.

2. Material on life in Boston in September 1836 comes from the *Boston Courier,* September 6–7, 1836. Sources divide over whether House was born on September 5 or October 5; evidence that it was September 5 is in his letter to Samuel Clemens, September 8, 1887, MTP, University of California. The story about correcting his mother is in "Hausu o omou," *Yomiuri Shimbun,* December 28, 1901.

3. Quotation about class and religion from Thomas Cushing, *Historical Sketch of Chauncy-Hall School,* 41; *Catalogue* quotations come from 14–16 (italics in the original). For additional information on the school, see Edward H. Cole, *A School—and a Man.*

4. This story was recounted by a Japanese friend in "Hausu o omou," *Yomiuri Shimbun,* December 28, 1901; also see Tokutomi Sohō, "Hausu sensei no omoide," 108.

5. E. H. House, "Wagner and Tannhäuser in Paris, 1861," 411. His compositions are discussed in Shōwa Joshi Daigaku, ed., "E. H. Hausu," 380.

6. For his mother's death, see *Boston Daily Evening Transcript,* July 22, 1854, 2; *Boston Herald,* July 25, 1854, 2; and Record of Death, Archives Division, Commonwealth of Massachusetts (D003232). For the stories of his first job, see Shōwa Joshi Daigaku, ed., "E. H. Hausu," 381.

7. Material here taken from "Biography of the *Boston Courier," Historical Magazine,* 45–46.

8. Material on Mrs. McMahon is in the *Boston Courier,* February 24, 1857, 2. For his advice, see letters from House to "My Dear Parker," February 8 and 11, 1860, in my personal collection.

9. House died in Tokyo in 1901 in the home of his adopted daughter, Kuroda Koto. His grandson, Kuroda Masao, said in a conversation on June 17, 1971, that the family's extensive House papers were burned in the 1945 fire bombings by American planes.

10. E. H. House, "A First Interview with Lowell," 850. I am indebted to my colleague Robert Davis for insight into Lowell's general attitudes toward Whitman, including the fact that he had *Leaves of Grass* removed from the Harvard library.

11. For "copying book," see House to John Russell Young, JRY, Library of Congress; and for advice, E. H. House to Henry Villard, August 31, 1898, HVP, Harvard University.

12. Description of New York based particularly on John A. Garraty, *The American Nation,* vol. I, 293–300; also on Howard Zinn, *A People's History of the United States,* 223–30.

13. For circulation figures, see Sidney Kobre, *Development of American Journalism,* 254; Edwin Emery, *The Press and America,* 3rd ed., 172; and James L. Crouthamel, *Bennett's New York Herald and the Rise of the Popular Press,* 117. Greeley's outspokenness is in John Russell Young, *Men and Memories,* vol. I, 112; for the evaluation of his staff, see Kobre, 255, and Royal Cortissoz, *The New York Tribune,* 16.

14. For the evaluation of *Tribune* reporters, see Young, 114; for material on Henry Clapp, see John J. Pullen, *Comic Relief: The Life and Laughter of Artemus Ward,* 35; for the Howells comment, see W. D. Howells, *Literary Friends and Acquaintances,* 72; for comments on Ada Clare, see Pullen, 37; for description of Aldrich, Ferris Greenslet, *The Life of Thomas Bailey Aldrich,* 41; for characterization of Whitman, E. P. Hingston, *The Genial Showman,* 102; for comments on Ward and conversation at Pfaff's, Hingston, 96, 97, 100; for Whitman's unfinished poem, Pullen, 36; for Stedman's lament, Laura Stedman and George Gould, *Life and Letters of Edmund Clarence Stedman,* vol. I, 208; for House's recollections, E. H. House to Thomas Bailey Aldrich, February 25, 1876, TBA, Harvard University; for Reid's comment, Whitelaw Reid to John Hay, July 2, 1886, JH, Brown University; and for Young's comment, Ōtani Tadashi, "Edowādo Hawādo Hausu senkō," 241. A vivid account of the role of Pfaff's in New York's bohemian world is found in Albert Parry, *Garrets and Pretenders,* 14–61.

15. "Most brilliant," in John Russell Young, *Around the World With General Grant,* vol. II, 590. Coverage of the visit of the Prince of Wales is in the *New York Tribune,* 1860: October 6 ("family reunion"), October 9 (Mount Vernon and dancing), October 13 (New York reception), and October 20 (Boston reception).

16. For Stedman comments, see *Boston Transcript,* January 20, 1902; and for kissing incident, "Hovenden's 'Last Moments of John Brown,'" *The Index,* September 17, 1885, Stedman to House, May 25, 1886, ECS, Library of Congress, and House letter to *Japan Weekly Mail,* November 3, 1894. Lowell's suggestion is in his letter to House, December 31, 1859, EHC, University of Virginia.

17. E. H. House, "Mien-Yaun," *The Atlantic Monthly* (June 1859): 677; for evaluation of the other writer, E. H. House, "Anecdotes of Charles Reade," *The Atlantic Monthly* (September 1872): 539.

18. The pioneer quality of the reporting is in Laura Stedman, vol. 1, 203; for "greatly stimulated," *Battles and Leaders of the Civil War,* vol. 1, 179.

19. "Brilliant journalists," Louis L. Snyder and Richard B. Morris, *A Treasury of Great Reporting,* 133. For discussion of the July scoop and reporters riding with McDowell, Emmet Crozier, *Yankee Reporters 1860–1865,* 86–88, 93; for the cherry tree episode, Henry Villard, *Memoirs of Henry Villard,* vol. I, 185–86, E. H. House to Henry Villard, August 31, 1898, HVP, Harvard University, and Laura Stedman, vol. 1, 252; and for account of House remaining at Bull Run, Crozier, 120, 125.

20. For the recollection of demolishing the telegraph office, see House to John Hay, January 15, 1890, JH, Brown University; Aldrich recollections recounted in Ferris Greenslet, *The Life of Thomas Bailey Aldrich,* 56–57; also see House to Stedman, n.d., ECS, Columbia University (a marginal note indicates that it was written in August 1861). The night with Stahel refers to an evening after Aldrich had become a war correspondent, with General Julius Stahel, a Hungarian who commanded a reserve unit at the first battle of Bull Run and then went on to top positions in the Union army; see House to Aldrich, February 25, 1876, TBA, Harvard University.

21. "How the Snow Melted on Mt. Washington," *Harper's New Monthly Magazine* (January 1860): 234; and "Love by Mishap," *Harper's New Monthly Magazine* (December 1862): 47.

22. Another House story set in China was "The Silent Lover," *Galaxy* (1867): 426–31. One analyst argues that Ta-uen, the hero of that story, symbolizes the never-married House's struggle with his own sexual identity, concluding that House "probably realized that he was a homosexual." Though occasional remarks in letters suggest that House was sexually active, I have found no evidence to either support or contradict this speculation. See Michelle Renee Gunnell, "The Silent Lover: A Reading," www.grad.cgu.edu/Egunnellm/webpage/10house.htm.

23. The article ran in June 1860. Hearn paid half a yen for that *Atlantic Monthly* copy, which contained an article by Oliver Wendell Holmes and a poem by Walt Whitman; reference found in Lafcadio Hearn, "Hearn's Notes on Japan," Notebook 4, Case 346, Lafcadio Hearn Collection, University of Virginia; and Japan as childlike, in Charles Wordell, *Japan's Image in America,* 32.

24. House refers to himself as being "used up" in letter to E. C. Stedman, May 28, 1883, ECS, Library of Congress; for the way the mission impressed him overall, see Shōwa Joshi Daigaku, 382. House's reports appeared in the *New*

York Tribune of 1860: May 17 ("from my window"), May 22 ("the dresses" and "the higher"), May 26 ("an atmosphere"), and June 12 (Tommy's passion).

25. The early meeting between House and Twain is described in Justin Kaplan, *Mr. Clemens and Mark Twain*, 25. For the frequent contact of the two, see Albert B. Paine, *Mark Twain: A Biography*, vol. 1, 311; and for discussions of the Cooper Institute lecture, see Andrew Hoffman, *Inventing Mark Twain*, 118, 121–22; Kenneth Eble, *Old Clemens and W. D. H.*, 9; and Paul Fatout, *Mark Twain on the Lecture Circuit*, 79–81. Twain's comments about House and the review are in Samuel Clemens, "Concerning the Scoundrel E. H. House," unpublished, 5–6.

26. The mutual voyage to England is noted in Edward P. Hingston, *The Genial Showman*, 348; the European vacation is referred to in David Gray to John Hay, October 10, 1866, JH, Brown University; and the November 17, 1866 letter from Ward to "Dear Ned" about his London reception is quoted in John J. Pullen, *The Life and Laughter of Artemus Ward*, 149.

27. For his comment on steamship companies, see E. H. House, "Hints for Visitors to Paris," *Galaxy* (March 1, 1867): 509. The Wagner story is recounted in E. H. House, "Wagner and Tannhäuser in Paris, 1861," *The New England Magazine* (June 1891): quote from 418. Another Paris encounter, possibly from the same trip, is described in his "Dejazet," *Galaxy* (June 1867): 179–90. For House's report on the King-Heenan fight, see "The Great Prize Fight," *The Times*, December 11, 1863, 7, reprinted in *The New York Times*, December 26, 1863; the circumstances under which he came to write the story are described in House, "Anecdotes of Charles Reade," *The Atlantic Monthly* (October 1887): 535.

28. From *Oliver Twist*, in Stephen Inwood, *A History of London*, 429.

29. See House, "Hints for Visitors," 515. For card games at Dickens's, see Samuel Clemens to House, October 1, 1883, MTP, University of California.

30. The connection with the St. James's Theatre is described by his friend, attorney George Scidmore, a vice president of the Meiji Musical Society, which House had helped to found, in the *Japan Weekly Mail*, December 28, 1901. House reveals an insider's knowledge of the St. James's and describes Irving in his *New York Herald* article, "Booth in London," November 7, 1880, 7. I have been unable to find sources in the theater's archives confirming the connection; extant records contain very little on anyone except the actors. In "Edwin Booth in London," *The Century Illustrated Magazine*, (November 1897–April 1898): 277, House refers to "having once had to do with theatrical management in London." The description of theaters then is from John Hollingshead, *Gaiety Chronicles*, 6; material on the St. James's from Barry Duncan, *The St. James's Theatre*, especially 1, 44, 126, and from The Theatre Museum, London, archives.

31. The use of "Wearing of the Green" was so inflammatory as an Irish freedom hymn that it was banned for years in England; see Townsend Walsh, *The Career of Dion Boucicault*, 104–105, 193–96. *Colleen Bawn* claims are made in "Mr. E. H. House," *Japan Weekly Mail*, December 21, 1901, as well as in Shōwa Joshi Daigaku, "E. H. Hausu," 403, and in W. B. Mason, "The Foreign Colony in Early Meiji Days—III," *The New East* (March 1918): 243. Material on the *Arrah-na-Pogue* suit comes primarily from Chancery Proceedings (C16, Pleadings, No. 251, B146; and C33, No. 1108, p. 863), Public Record Office, London, and the *Times*, May 12, 1865;

the suit is discussed in Richard Fawkes, *Dion Boucicault,* 157–58. For the Twain comments, see Clemens, "Scoundrel," 19–20.

32. Material on the Reade relationship comes primarily from 1887 articles by House in *The Atlantic Monthly,* "Personal Characteristics of Charles Reade" (staying with him, 155; passion for theater, 147); and "Anecdotes of Charles Reade" (first impressions, 525–26; Wales trip, 528–29; Reade party, 537–38; discussion of servants, 536; inability in the theater, 531). For Reade's love of Americans, see Charles and Compton Reade, *Charles Reade: A Memoir,* 335. House also wrote at length about Reade's relationship with Seymour, arguing that although the affection between the two was deep, there was no sexual relationship; he was critical of Reade for not marrying her so as to save her from scandal ("Personal Characteristics," 151–55). The *Times* comment on his cleverness ran on May 31, 1870, the *Harper's Weekly* piece on April 19, 1884. The dinner is described in John Coleman, *Charles Reade As I Knew Him,* 234.

33. His father's death is recorded in Copy of Record of Death, Archives Division, Commonwealth of Massachusetts (D003233). House's efforts to secure a government posting are discussed in a series of letters to Reid, all of them dated only by days, not by the year, WR, Library of Congress; the subject matter and the people named in the letters make it clear that they were written early in 1870; Greeley's evaluation is in Greeley to Hamilton Fish, January 23, 1870, Hamilton Fish Collection, Library of Congress. For "happiest thought," see House to Aldrich, February 25, 1876, TBA, Harvard University.

3

Japan to 1870: Dizzying Change

Don't despise the lodger;
Tomorrow he may be the Minister's secretary.

—Japanese song, 1870s[1]

Japan was in tumult when Ned House arrived late in August of 1870. A mere seventeen years had passed since Matthew Perry's American squadron had forced the island nation out of two centuries of relative isolation and into the ferment of the imperialist age, touching off tidal waves of domestic discussion and dissent. And just two and a half years had gone by since the Tokugawa family government had been toppled, ending 268 years of semifeudal, generally stable government by the shogun. Since then, hardly a month had passed without some momentous change. The emperor had been brought from Kyoto, where his family had resided for a millennium, and resettled in the shogun's old Edo castle. Edo's name had been changed to Tokyo or "eastern capital." The people of Japan had been promised public discussion of government policies and the abolition of status groups, along with a worldwide search for knowledge. The streets teemed with rumors of rebellion as word spread that the new administration was talking about abolishing the centuries-old feudal domains and placing all regions under the new, national government. During the two months before House's arrival alone, society had been hit with news of the suicide in the south of the governor of Kagoshima, who thought the changes were propelling Japan toward destruction; the resignation of Morioka's governor in the north, so that his domain could be made into a modern prefecture; the commencement of work on an Osaka-Kobe railroad in the west; riots by 400 workers at Takashima coal mine near Nagasaki; and a government decree prohibiting Chinese from buying Japanese children for sale abroad. Within another three weeks, commoners would be allowed, for the first time in history, to take surnames. The times, House would find when he stepped ashore, were alive with danger and potential.

No one who really knew this archipelago would have suggested that premodern Japan had been backward or undeveloped, except perhaps—and even then, only perhaps—in some fields of science and technology. The Tokugawa order, which had been constructed in the early 1600s, was among the most sophisticated—and interesting—political systems in the world. Based on divisions that already had existed when the Tokugawa family took military control at the beginning of the seventeenth century, the structure has been labeled "centralized feudalism," a system carefully balanced between the Tokugawa administration, called the *bakufu* or "tent government" in Edo, and more than 200 domain or *han* governments in the regions. The *han* lords, called daimyo, were allowed the freedom in their fiefs to raise taxes, maintain armies, and enforce laws as long as they remained loyal to the Edo regime, kept the peace, and paid assessments when asked. One of the more unusual supports for this system, labeled "alternate attendance," required the daimyo to serve in the shogun's Edo administration for alternating periods of six months or a year, depending on how far away from the capital their fief was, and to keep their wives and children in Edo permanently. As a result, the shogun always retained the daimyo's family as hostages, and the lord himself was forced to bear the financial burden of maintaining castles and administrative staffs in two locations. Nor was the lord ever away from Edo long enough to plan and carry out a regional insurrection.

The Tokugawa order had supported a dynamic cultural and intellectual life for more than two and a half centuries when House arrived, partly because of its heavy emphasis on education and partly because of the alternate attendance system. The network of roads and towns necessary to support the frequent travel by hundreds of lords and thousands of retainers served to integrate the country both physically and culturally. The cities experienced almost staggering growth. Edo, for example, which had been a small castle town at the end of the 1500s, had a population of 1.1 million by the mid-1700s, making it the biggest city in the world. Every domain had a large castle town, and a number of regions sprouted *zaigōmachi*, or commercial towns, with no particular connection to the surrounding fief. Pleasure quarters in the urban centers coupled with the wealth of a rising merchant class to produce a plethora of new literary, visual, and performance arts: the amorous and materialistic novels of Ihara Saikaku and the bawdy travel tales of Jippensha Ikku; Andō Hiroshige's woodblock prints of daily life and Kitagawa Utamaro's depictions of stars in the pleasure quarters;

broadsides recounting the latest double suicide or temple scandal; the all-male kabuki theater with its vernacular dialogue and spectacular scenery; and the geisha's world of song, dance, and drink. Confucian scholars bemoaned the moral decline, but the samurai cultural dictators partook anyway, even if they had to go to the entertainment centers in disguise.

Equally impressive was the accumulation of wealth that made such dynamism possible. Although most samurai were poor, forced to get by on fixed government stipends, the merchant class flourished in the Tokugawa years, displaying a propensity for entrepreneurship, creating sales networks and large capital reservoirs both within and across regions, developing multiproduct, family-based companies with names such as Mitsui and Sumitomo, and establishing financial and credit systems that loaned money at high interest rates. The urban merchants and artisans, who numbered 600,000 in Edo alone by the mid-1700s, also spawned a large labor force made up of both women and men.

Education flourished, too, with more than 10,000 home or temple schools, many of them run and taught by women, providing instruction in writing, math, and reading for hundreds of thousands of children—and supporting the production of at least 7,000 textbooks or copybooks in the late Tokugawa years. The result was that by the early 1800s Japan had one of the world's highest literacy rates, with roughly 40 percent of boys and 10 percent of girls able to read after some fashion. It also had a lively intellectual world. At the center were neo-Confucianists who defended the existing regime as a reflection of the natural order. Taking a more critical stance were large numbers of national learning scholars who questioned the Tokugawa order for having shunted the emperor to the edges of power. There also were what the historian Maruyama Masao has called the "premodern nationalists," who demanded a stronger place for Japan in the broader world, along with devotees of Western learning. And by the nineteenth century there were large groups of merchant intellectuals and peasant scholars, as well as samurai activists and radicals who questioned the regime's authoritative nature and devised schemes to get around the authorities. It would be hard to imagine a world where intellectual life was more invigorating.

These groups communicated widely with each other, too, through books that sold tens of thousands of copies; through courier networks, street-side sermons, and flimsy manuscript books (*shahon*); and through weekly discussion groups and lecture meetings. Among the most worrisome intellectuals to the Tokugawa rulers were the scholars of Western learning, followers of the eighteenth-century physicians Sugita Genpaku and Yamawaki Tōyō, who insisted that empirical observation precede theory and demanded that Western ideas about science and society be taken seriously. These men operated under constraints, since it was illegal to possess most kinds of Western writing. But the fact that there were hundreds, probably thousands, of such students by the middle of the 1800s says much about Japan's intellectual level when Perry arrived. As Gilbert Rozman puts it: "In virtually every instance in which a quantitative indicator has been introduced, Japan's rate has turned out to be extraordinary for a premodern society. Repeatedly, the country chosen as most similar to Japan has been England, which . . . normally appears as an exceptional case at the forefront of social development." If that was true of most sectors of society, it was particularly so of intellectual life.

The exceptions to this generalization, and the source of the Western image of Japan as uncivilized, were twofold. First, Japan was relatively isolated from the world. Early in the 1600s, the Tokugawa government, fearful of the destabilizing potential of Christianity, guns, and trade, had forbidden foreign travel by Japanese and banned all but a few Dutch and Chinese ships from coming to Japan. Even those few vessels allowed in were restricted to Nagasaki, a thousand miles to the southwest of the capital. Although the ban was never as complete as "closed country" tales suggest, its effects were massive. It meant that Europeans and Americans had little reliable information about Japan before Perry's arrival and that Japan's knowledge of the West was restricted and uneven. The seclusion policy also was partly responsible for the second exception to Japan's high level of development: its scientific and technological mediocrity. Although Japan's rulers kept themselves quite well informed about European politics, the country's scientific world fell out of step with Western developments. One can argue that Japan's scientific knowledge was impressive in a number of fields (anesthesia, for example, was first used for breast surgery in Japan in 1805, four decades before the use of ether in the West); certainly, scientific standards were appropriate to what the country needed at the time. But there is no denying that much scholarly progress was held in check by the conservative Tokugawa bureaucracy and the way that the samurai class, whose leaders favored the status quo over innovation, dominated intellectual life. Thus, Japan had no railroads or clipper ships, no telegraph, and few modern weapons when the West arrived. Itō Hirobumi, a young Turk in the clique that overthrew the Tokugawa, commented years later that "what was lacking in our countrymen of the feudal era was not mental or moral fiber, but the scientific, technical, and materialistic side of modern civilization."[2] And that absence was serious in a time when imperialist nations were wont to use force against other lands.

The result was an unprecedented sense of crisis when Perry arrived at the Edo Bay village of Uraga with four black ships and sixty-six guns in the summer of 1853, demanding that Japan establish relations with the United States—and sending villagers to the hills and Shintō priests to their prayers. If the villagers were panicked, the rulers were nearly paralyzed. They already had been criticized, over the past few decades, for allowing Russian, British, and American sailors to challenge the seclusion policy on occasion. The lack of a coastal defense policy had, in fact, prompted several of the stronger domains to begin rethinking their allegiance to the Tokugawa. Now, when Perry handed over his demands to shogunal officials, saying that he would return the next spring for an answer, many bureaucrats felt a sense of terror. Their first reaction was to request advice from the daimyo, but that helped little, yielding only dissension and a spreading sense that the government no longer had the power to act decisively. When Perry came back in February with nine ships (almost a fourth of the U.S. navy), the *bakufu* decided there was no choice but to capitulate. The officials signed a treaty opening two ports, Shimoda and Hakodate, and providing for the start of diplomatic relations. Four years later they agreed to a commercial treaty, opening Japan's door so wide that it never could be shut again.

The most immediate result of the Treaty of Kanagawa, as the agreement with Perry was called, was an eruption of domestic controversy. For two centuries, seclusion had been a bedrock of national policy. Now, its sudden abrogation did more than shock people; it triggered a serious opposition movement. One rebel group consisted largely of young samurai zealots, many of them several steps removed from the power centers. Called *shishi* (men of spirit), most of them had weak ties to their domain government but intense loyalty to at least one "loyalist" scholar, and all of them sought direct action to "honor the emperor and expel the barbarians" (*sonnō jōi*)—in other words, to get rid of the Tokugawa. The activist scholar Yoshida Shōin from the western domain of Chōshū called the *shishi* "humble heroes," whereas some scholars have dubbed them history's first urban guerillas. The young Tokugawa translator Fukuchi Gen'ichirō learned just how zealous these men were when one of them invited him out for drinks. Midway through the conversation, the friend took the severed head of a Western sympathizer from his bag, laid it in front of Fukuchi, and said he ought to curb his tendency to praise Westerners. On March 24, 1860, a band of eighteen *shishi* assassinated the regent Ii Naosuske because he had signed the commercial treaty with the United States two years earlier—in defiance, they said, of the emperor's will. Such tactics did not directly threaten the ruling regime, but they did undermine confidence in its ability to maintain order, and they encouraged several highly placed officials to join the opposition.

The growing opposition within the establishment took many forms. Its intellectual core lay in the Mito School, whose scholars argued that the emperor (not the shogun) was the core of the nation and that Western values would undermine Japan's fundamental character. Operating more practically were several court nobles who worked hard now to get the shogun to submit to imperial directives. Leaders in the southwest domains of Satsuma, Chōshū, and Tosa also began inserting themselves more aggressively into the Tokugawa's decision-making process, taking matters into their own hands when they thought officials were treating the foreign threat too lightly. In 1862, for example, several Satsuma samurai killed a British merchant, Charles Richardson, for refusing to show proper respect to the domain's daimyo. And in June 1863, Chōshū troops fired on Western ships in Shimonoseki harbor for refusing to obey a *bakufu* order that foreigners leave the country. The Satsuma and Chōshū actions prompted harsh foreign responses, but the most frightening thing for the government was that activist domain officials no longer felt the need to wait for Tokugawa orders before acting.

In the summer of 1864, radical troops from Chōshū went so far as to launch an attack on the city of Kyoto, attempting unsuccessfully to bring the emperor's court under their direct control. And in 1865, an anti-Tokugawa faction staged a coup in Chōshū and took charge of the domain government. The pace of developments quickened after that, and although the story is too complex to tell here, the result was a coup d'état on January 3, 1868—the Meiji Restoration—in which troops from Satsuma seized the Kyoto palace and had the fifteen-year-old emperor Meiji assume direct imperial rule. Shogun Tokugawa Yoshinobu staged a brief military resistance, then announced in February that he would turn his lands over to the emperor so as to spare the nation a bloody civil war. Some of his distraught followers continued to resist for another year and a half, and by the end of 1869, more than 8,000 had died in battle. But the center of power moved to the new rebel-led government as soon as the shogun resigned, and Japan entered the Meiji era.

Tokyo was thus the scene of colliding forces during the two and a half years before House's arrival. A new government may have come to power, but old structures remained and impediments to change were omnipresent. The threat of conquest by the imperialist powers kept the new leaders awake at night and energized their strategy sessions during the daytime. Most of the regional domains stood ready to assert their own independence or to turn back to the Tokugawa if the chance arose. Finances presented a grave problem, too, since the old system had produced massive financial obligations but no national tax system or unified currency. Nor was there an effective national army. Or navy. Or banking system. Or plan for running the country. Or network for communication. Even trade was rendered largely useless as a revenue source by the unequal treaties that prevented Japan from charging more than 5 percent duty, on average, on imports. It would be hard to imagine a more daunting list of problems for any group of officials trying to put together a stable administration.

Yet, when House arrived, the Meiji government was well on its way to establishing firm control. It could be argued that two things undergirded its success. First, the leaders were young and unfettered by traditional organizational structures. Second, they were pragmatists, wedded to no ideology except national strength. Power was commandeered in the Restoration by a group of samurai, mostly of middle rank, from the southwestern domains (particularly Chōshū and Satsuma), ranging in age from their mid-twenties to their early forties. All of them had had administrative experience in their own fiefs, all had had strong loyalist leanings, several had had some experience with the West, but none had been at the top rungs of power. Above all, they all were brilliant, hard-headed realists who devised practical slogans such as *fukoku kyōhei* (rich country, strong military) and *bunmei kaika* (enlightened civilization). One of the most telling examples of the pragmatism lay in their approach to Europe and the United States. As rebels, they had vowed, some in oaths signed with blood, to get rid of the foreigners; now, as rulers, they turned to the same imperialist powers for models and assistance. Having learned that getting rid of the foreigners was not an option, they set out to learn from the imperialists and to emulate them. Unable to throw the West out, they would make Japan the great power of the East. Thus, on April 6, 1868, just three months after taking over, the new government issued the Charter Oath, promising, among other things, to seek knowledge around the world, to exchange the "evil practices" of the past for international norms, to unify the classes, and to convene an assembly. Coming from elitists who only recently had sought to eradicate foreign pollution, the oath was stunning evidence that nothing mattered so much now as making Japan strong.

It should not be assumed, however, that these new leaders were unified in their opinions about how Japan should be governed. The challenges of the age were clearer than the solutions, and officials fought with the vigor one would expect of people in unknown wilds without a compass, often heading in one direction, then another. On the very day that the five-article Charter Oath was issued, the new rulers appeased traditionalists by handing down "five prohibitions." There would be no direct petitions to the emperor, no factions or cliques, no congregating of Christians, no free movement by commoners to new domiciles, and no untoward political activities. When a Grand Council of State was established, its members were to be elected from among the ranks of top officials, but when conservatives worried about "democratic" precedents, the council quickly scrapped the elections.[3] And the vigorous councilor Kido Takayoshi's proposal that the old domains be replaced with prefectures spurred such animosity that one vice-minister was assassinated and a group of 2,000 irregular troops from Chōshū rose in revolt. Indeed, those within the ruling councils fought constantly over everything from budget allocation to how

Japan should interact with its Asian neighbors. Their policies might look decisive from the vantage point of later generations, but at the time the only thing that unified the leadership was an agreement that Japan must be strong to survive.

For those outside of power, the impact of the early-Meiji policies varied greatly—from the cities, where people had to deal with change on a daily basis, to the small towns and villages, where a full 90 percent of the population lived much as they had for generations. The American educator William Elliot Griffis, writing from Fukui in 1871, commented that life seemed as it would have if "the world were to roll back and the ages with it." He wrote: "There are no railroads, nor snorting locomotives, nor telegraph wires, nor printing press, nor pavements, nor parks, nor milkman, nor newsboy." In actual fact, Fukui was changing quite a lot when Griffis arrived there; it had hired an American chemistry teacher, after all. But on the surface the change appeared minimal. Similarly, the villagers west of Tokyo, whose lives schoolteacher Nagatsuka Takashi described in his late-Meiji novel *Soil*, might well have been living in medieval times. They suffered unprotected from both heat and cold; they toiled in the fields from dawn to dusk; they lived in ignorance of the outside world. And if the weather turned mean or fires came, they worried ceaselessly about whether their food would last until another harvest.[4]

Their urban fellow citizens, on the other hand, particularly the elites with whom House would interact, already were becoming immersed in the sea of modernity. One of the most dramatic transformations in Tokyo was quite negative: the population had dropped by more than half in the Restoration years, from more than a million at mid-century to 480,000 at the beginning of the 1870s, due largely to the return of provincial aristocrats and their staffs to the regional castle towns. But most of the other changes were more positive, or at least more interesting. Westerners in suits and top hats were seen regularly now on the streets of the city, as were Japanese dandies who took to the latest fashions. The first railroad was under construction. Meat was finding its place onto local menus. The new Tsukiji Cattle and Horse Company was promoting the drinking of milk. And the Western system of keeping time had replaced the old method that divided the periods of daylight and dark into six units each. On January 1, 1871, a mere four months after settling into his new home, House attended a hospital opening in Waseda, a broad area six miles from the palace. After the formal speeches, several actors presented a comic play in which the Spirits of Science and Truth tricked the Geniuses of Neurosis, Paralysis, and Pyrosis into drinking poison—and thus assured the triumph of human development. House concluded his report on the event by praising "that cultivated development, the progress of which, in this land, it is our constant pleasure to applaud."[5]

There was one group that did not win House's smile, however. That was the foreign community, whose presence had helped to make the atmosphere of the Tokyo region in the 1870s so dramatically different from what it had been two decades earlier. The *gaijin* or foreigner center was Yokohama, the port city just to the southwest of Tokyo, which had been little more than a cluster of seaside huts scattered among vegetable fields until the *bakufu* selected it as the region's first commercial port a dozen years earlier. Across that span, it had turned into an energetic little town, home to hundreds of Europeans, Americans, Japanese, and Chinese, all of them engaged one way or another in the life of the tradesman. At one end of the settlement was a "swampy area . . . filled with the concentrated essence of life and drainage," and beyond that was an area known as Bloodtown, home to a collection of taverns, brothels, and gambling houses, as well as more than its share of "hair-raising knife fights between seamen." Here, said one writer, were the "little nooks into which you entered by a sliding panel," the places where the "moosmes" sat "in rows on the verandah," waiting for the gentleman who would choose them for an hour or two.

Yokohama had its complement of upstanding expatriates, including the missionary educator Samuel Brown and the physician-linguist James Hepburn. It had diplomats, too, some of them quite cultured. And it had a few journalists, though one of those, the minister-editor M. Buckworth Bailey, was known as much for his feuds with church organists as for his writing. The town was most renowned, however, for its Wild West quality, with shootings and assassinations far too frequent. It was hard to find anyone who did not at times second the diplomat who called Yokohama the home of "the scum of Europe." Only a handful of women lived there until the 1870s, so social life centered on horse riding, races, and drinking. A typical businessman's daily schedule included a visit to the bar of the "gentleman's club" late in the morning, another visit at lunch, and still another late in the afternoon. As one observer described it, "The merchants generally arrived at their offices, if at all, around 10 A.M. and quit at four, but out of those six hours, at least two would have been spent at the club or in one of the hotels." After 4:30 P.M., wrote another, "the offices would be deserted." The community also boasted many "beachcombers" from the West who made their way by theft and short stints of work when the money ran out.

House disliked this community from the day he arrived, and he would spend much of the next decade fighting with it. The thing that drew his ire was not the carousing; he had been no slouch at that himself. He was angered by the attitudes of expatriates toward the Japanese. One historian of the treaty ports notes that most of the Yokohama community "thought of themselves as being the representatives of a superior society"—little matter that they themselves had been opium smugglers or jobless before coming here. Others have noted the Westerners' general lack of interest in Japanese development, as well as their unwillingness to learn the Japanese language. They were in Japan for trade and profit, nothing else. All of that disgusted House, the Bostonian reared on ideas of fairness and love of the underdog. His article on the hospital opening noted that only two foreigners had showed up to observe what, for Japan, was a momentous event. Not surprising, he sniffed; had the event included "fuliginous sham-fights" or "other lurid accompaniments," they would have come. He described the typical foreigner on a Japanese roadway as someone "who deems it expedient and tasteful to proclaim his pluck by whirling a vicious whip-lash about him as he rides, enjoying the panic of startled women and children, and fancying himself at once a hero and a pioneer of civilization."[6]

For a reporter like House, Japan could have been a hell or a paradise in August 1870. The potential snares were many: an unknown and difficult language, weak communications lines with home newspapers, an absence of the human connections that had made him influential in New York and London, and an atmosphere that could be physically threatening and psychologically paralyzing. But by the same token, Tokyo was brimming that summer with news, vitality, and potential. Change was the coin of the day. There were few newspaper correspondents of any kind, giving an enterprising reporter the field to himself. Strange and exotic customs beckoned. And for House the concoction was more beguiling than alcohol or the theater ever had been. Very soon, as we shall see, his propensity for searching out the curious and the important would make him influential in ways beyond anything he had imagined possible when he left New York. Japan was a treasure house for House in 1870, a place ready-made for the very abilities he had honed most ferociously during the previous fifteen years.

NOTES

1. Stewart Lone, *Army, Empire and Politics in Meiji Japan,* 8 (capitalization modified).

2. For comparison to Britain, see Gilbert Rozman, in Marius Jansen, ed., *The Cambridge History of Japan,* vol. V, The Nineteenth Century, 566. Itō's comments are found in Ōkuma Shigenobu, *Fifty Years of New Japan,* vol. I, 124.

3. These prohibitions and the early election system are discussed in Okada et al., eds., *Nihon no rekishi: Meiji ishin,* 156–57.

4. Relief programs are discussed in Nihon Fūzoku Gakkai, *Shiryō ga kataru Meiji no Tokyo hyaku wa,* 38; Griffis's comments are found in Robert Rosenstone, *Mirror*

in the Shrine, 91; and Nagatsuka's novel, *Tsuchi,* was serialized in the newspaper *Tokyo Asahi* in 1910 and came out as a book in 1912.

5. The change in time systems is discussed in Nihon Fūzoku Gakkai, *Hyaku wa,* 40. House's article is "A Japanese Doctor and His Works," *The Atlantic Monthly* (December 1871): 689.

6. The swampy area and fights are described in Harold Williams, *Foreigners in Mikadoland,* 90–91, 99–100; "moosme" was the corrupted pronunciation of the Japanese word *musume,* or young woman. The comment on European scum is in Hugh Cortazzi, *Victorians in Japan,* 60; Williams describes the typical day in *Tales of the Foreign Settlements in Japan,* 51; and the deserted offices are described in Olavi Fält, *The Clash of Interests,* 31–32. The foreigners' self-conceit is discussed in *Japan's Treaty Ports and Foreign Settlements,* 6. For House's early comments, see "Japanese Doctor," 678, 681.

4

The Newcomer: 1870–1873

> Less than a month in this fantastic and delightful country . . . I see no reason to repent my visit.
>
> —House to Whitelaw Reid, September 21, 1870[1]

Travelers tell us that Yokohama harbor was steaming and busy on summer days in 1870, filled with small sampans, huge steamships, row boats, middling schooners, fishing barks, and ferries bringing half the town out to meet incoming passengers—with Mt. Fuji's misty visage looming some fifty miles away. Thus it would have been on August 26, when Edward House arrived aboard the Hong Kong–bound steamer *Great Republic,* hoping to stay in Japan for a year or two. But the atmosphere had a different scent that day. Although the bustle was typical, the Japanese and foreign communities were full of anti-American sentiments; many were saying they would rather not have the Americans around. The problem sprang from that fact that an American passenger steamer, the *City of Yedo,* had blown up at the beginning of August on its daily Tokyo-Yokohama run, killing seventy-one Japanese and five Europeans, and wounding the other sixty-two passengers. The cause lay in human error, the "ignorance and gross carelessness" of an engineer who had let the water level in the ship's boiler get too low, and as a result the Yokohama community was surly. It was not a propitious time for an American journalist to arrive.

If the young *Tribune* reporter was worried, though, he never expressed it. After leaving New York at the beginning of June, he had taken "a slow journey westward" across the United States, then sailed from San Francisco in early August. Following a brief stay in Yokohama, he found lodging with Consul C. O. Shepard at the American legation in Tokyo, a city dismissed by U.S. minister Charles E. DeLong (whose forte was not spelling) as "a wilderness of uninhabitable dwellings," with "streets filled with shiftless reckless people, beggars and lasy soldiery." Europeans and Americans usually preferred to live in Yokohama with its larger houses and Western social life; indeed, when land went up for sale in Tokyo's own foreign quarters in Tsukiji, just as House had been leaving New York, an hour passed before anyone made a bid on the first lot. But House chose Tokyo. He was a reporter, he knew that several of the diplomats had settled there, and he was more interested in meeting influential Japanese than in getting to know his fellow Westerners.[2]

Edward H. House as a youthful reporter. (Courtesy Meiji Shimbun Zasshi Bunkō, University of Tokyo. Used by permission.)

Most Westerners regarded Tokyo as DeLong did, as a place to be avoided. The buildings in Tsukiji were described by one engineer as "a set of mean little conventicles," and transportation was difficult, since even rickshaws were rare at the beginning of the 1870s. Fires posed a daily threat. The population decline of the late-Tokugawa years had given the city a feeling of decay. Foreigners were the objects of gawking. The missionaries, in particular, grumbled about the prevalence of prostitution and nakedness. Many of the Europeans and Americans also regarded their Tokyo hosts as arrogant, echoing the *Japan Weekly Mail* writer who huffed on February 11, 1871, that Japanese "vanity" was "a disease of sufficient malignity" to blind most of them to "the enormous gulf which separates Japan from the civilized world." And nearly all of the foreigners felt nervous when they rode, or walked, the city streets, afraid of drunken brawlers and thieves who occasionally preyed on Americans and Europeans. The clergyman William Elliot Griffis, who arrived four months after House to teach at the new government college, Kaisei Gakkō, said that when he and the school's assistant head, Guido Verbeck, went riding, "we were accompanied by armed guards." Verbeck, he said, "always looked carefully to his revolver to see it was in good order" because of "the murderous ronins [sic], to say nothing of drunken loafers, ruffians, and wild characters of every sort" on the streets. Griffis carried a Smith and Wesson.

House, on the other hand, laughed at such timidity and chauvinism, declaring Tokyo a safe, exciting place for anyone who loved new experiences, respected the Japanese, and valued progress. "To me, existence here is a perpetual delight," he wrote just weeks after his arrival. "The climate is lovely; the people (natives, I mean) are kind; hospitable, and courteous to a degree which more than justifies all that has been said in their praise; the language is easy to attain, for all practical purposes; the scenery inexhaustibly attractive, and the cost of living is light." He talked about the "gentleness and lightness of the Japanese people" and argued that the truly dangerous ones were the foreigners who carried weapons. "I never felt myself safer in any part of the world than here," he added. "I go every where, alone, and at any hour of day or night. I never had a rude word, and probably never shall, and as for weapons, I look upon them as absurdities."[3]

One reason for his bright evaluations obviously lay in his personality: the bond he had felt with the Japanese ever since reporting on their early mission to America, as well as his propensity for embracing new things. Another source was his determination to see as much of Japan as possible—on its own terms. From the very first, he traveled about with the energy of an explorer. Within days of getting to Yokohama harbor, for example, he joined a small group planning to hike up Mt. Fuji the first week of September, even though the climbing season already had ended. He chuckled about the necessity of rising at 2:30 A.M. "in a dazy stupor which stifles all exhilaration and excitement" and praised the singing insects ("they are not content with humming, but have learned to sing, in this land"), the porters who carried the entourage effortlessly across a single-rope suspension bridge (with "white water raging among the rocks below"), the "spectacles of cloud-pageantry" from the mountainside, and the silence of the peak itself, broken only by "the shrill scream of a hawk that flew over us." He also relished an eerily rapid descent down a lava slide, the breakfast of eggs and beer served on the way home, and the Yokohama harbor at twilight, which stretched out "like a sheet of gold" when the trip was over. House visited a number of the region's other scenic spots as well, going "many and many a mile beyond the treaty limits," and took almost daily walking and riding excursions around Tokyo. Griffis's diary records visits he made with House to Shiba Shrine, the Tokugawa tombs, the temples of Asakusa where "religion and innocent pleasure join hands," sundry tea-stands, and wrestlers' training stables. Five months after settling in, the restless wanderer of Europe would write: "There is hardly an inch of the city that I don't know by heart."[4]

House put equal energy into the reporting tasks that had brought him to Japan. He was tireless in cultivating sources among Japanese and Westerners alike. A November 1870 letter reported him "living comfortably" in a Tokyo villa, "studying the language, cultivating a mild immorality, and establishing friendly relations with Japanese officials, who are continually visiting me, or inviting me to their houses." By November, he told Reid that the "chief Foreign Minister and members of the Privy Council" were coming to his home "almost every other day" for dinner, making it clear that he had initiated a friendship with Ōkuma Shigenobu, the rising official from southern Saga Prefecture who would become the key to his Japanese successes. His reputation as a well-connected writer for a leading American paper obviously did him no harm with Japanese officials eager to gain influence abroad, nor did his enthusiasm for things Japanese. Among the foreigners living in Japan, on the other hand, he made contacts only when they were potential news sources. The American minister DeLong, a man who could not "write a phrase, or speak a sentence with decent approach to correctness," consulted with him regularly, asking for advice on the wording of reports and giving him inside information. House also got to know the British Minister Harry Parkes, finding him brighter and more influential, if less sensitive to Japanese perspectives. And when the American E. Peshine Smith arrived the next spring as an advisor to the Foreign Ministry, House was willing to overlook his widely discussed drunken visits to the Yoshiwara prostitute quarters once he found out what a rich source of information he could be.

The result was what one might have expected of a reporter with House's drive and skills. His biweekly letters to the *Tribune* were filled with the best intelligence then available: regular discussions of the instability of the young Meiji government and of rumored rebellions in the provinces, explanations of the emperor's figurehead role, indictments of DeLong's ineptitude, paeans to Japanese progress, a report on former Secretary of State William Seward's 1870 Tokyo visit, inside information on a Bostonian engaged in efforts to start a "coolie" business in Japan, and the sad physical condition of the American legation. He also included private background notes, not for publication, including the stories of Smith's behavior at a "public whore-house" and DeLong's trip to Kyūshū to meet with "a number of the disaffected leaders" plotting against the regime.[5] The *Tribune*, under Reid, was busy creating America's most ambitious foreign correspondence service, and although Europe received the greatest attention House's reports made the paper a leader in Asian coverage, too.

Not everything pleased House in the early months, however. For one thing, there were the chauvinistic expatriates whose condescension and coarseness disgusted him so much. For another, he was oppressed by the sense of personal isolation from the only foreigners he really liked or admired, those back in the United States and England. His first letter home pointed out that it took three weeks to make contact, even by cable, since the nearest telegraph office was twenty sailing days away in Ceylon. Again and again he wrote about how hard it was to get news from the States, or about misunderstandings that occurred because he could not talk directly to his editors, or about the months it took to find out how the *Tribune* had handled his news reports. By December of 1871, cable service was available from Nagasaki, but it still took the better part of a week to get most information to Nagasaki from Tokyo, and the cable from there cost $26 for twenty words! House doubted that he ever would use it. In one communication that month, he listed the number of letters he had received from American friends over the past sixteen months: a total of seven, including two from his editor friend David Gray in Buffalo and two from Mark Twain. "I know how easily and naturally a person drops out of everybody's recollection, even when he wanders only to a short distance—much more, of course, when he goes to the ends of the earth." It was a complaint that he would repeat many times across the years. House's other frustration lay in the financial arrangements he had with the *Tribune*. He was more than happy with the amount Reid paid for each article, but the paper refused to give him a regular salary, leaving his remuneration at the mercy of editorial decisions about whether or not to run his contributions. Though the *Tribune* published almost everything he wrote, House complained constantly until changes were made during a brief trip back to New York in 1873.[6]

The frustrations, however, were a minor theme in House's early Tokyo months, muted by a symphony of challenging and satisfying experiences. Near the end of the year, he was offered lucrative new work teaching

English literature at the Kaisei Gakkō. It would require only his morning hours, leaving afternoons free for reporting, and would pay $3,000 a year, an amount that House estimated to be worth at least $10,000 in New York and enough to live quite splendidly in Tokyo where, according to Verbeck, a bachelor "of careful habits" could get by on $800 a year. For a journalist who had earned $1,560 a year for full-time reporting at the *Tribune* during the Civil War, $3,000 was a fortune. And housing was provided free inside the school grounds. So by January, he had settled into a routine that balanced two lives, teaching and reporting. He would get up at six, teach from seven until noon, have lunch, then "roll about like a daimio, visiting Japanese officials or giving counsel at a newspaper office." In the evening, he reported to Reid, "I go virtuously to bed at 9 or at least half past 9. Truly bucolic." It was a far cry from the Parisian brawler's life. By every account, he loved it.

House's good fortune resulted from a remarkable new government policy: the hiring of great numbers of foreigners to help Japan down the road to modernity. The employees—called *yatoi*—came from all walks of life and in great numbers. In the year that House went to work, they included more than 200 Britons, a hundred Frenchmen, fifty Americans, and a smattering from Germany, the Netherlands, China, Italy, Norway, Portugal, Belgium, Switzerland, Malaya, and the Philippines. Across the era, there were nearly 8,000 such workers, regarded by many Japanese as "live machines" capable of spewing out the skills and knowledge needed in Japan's drive to become a powerful nation. The Japanese never had any thought of making these *yatoi* permanent fixtures, but in the 1870s they were used at a rate of 400 to 500 a year to build railroads, write sanitation plans, run lighthouses, mint currency, teach English and chemistry, run customs offices, drill armies, survey land, develop harbors, take photographs, staff woolen mills, advise police departments, construct mines, design buildings, and advise officials in everything from educational systems to constitutional law and treaty revision. They were remunerated well, too. The top 7 percent were paid more than cabinet ministers and generals, and House's salary was double that of the best-paid Japanese newspaper editor at the time.[7]

Teaching English may have been a rather ordinary way for a newcomer to Japan to supplement his income, but the kind of English teaching that House did was not typical. The Kaisei Gakkō had been created by the government as a vanguard institution to train the country's brightest young men for official service. As a result, it presented both challenges and opportunities unlike those of any other school in the country. Located in a walled, "wildly overgrown" compound that had been donated to the state by the rich daimyo family named Maeda, the institution attracted an unusually talented, ambitious group of students. On arriving there in

1871, House said he found nearly all of his protégés "as hungry for new food as robins." The challenge would not be to make them work but to satisfy their uniformly curious minds.

His fellow foreign teachers were less uniform. A dozen strong, some of the teaching contingent were bohemian and undisciplined, known for smoking and swearing while teaching, skipping class when they had hangovers, and visiting prostitutes or gambling houses in the off-hours. "While the great harvest was ripening, the laborers able to handle skillfully the sickle were few," lamented Griffis. On the other hand, the men selected to teach Class One, all of them Americans, were brilliant and disciplined. They numbered four: Verbeck, the school's assistant director and one of the era's most important government advisers; Griffis, author of the classic *Mikado's Empire;* William Veeder, later a physics professor at the University of Tokyo; and House. And they were a close lot, living together within the college walls and socializing continually. Griffis's journal shows him calling on the convivial young Bostonian, or going about the city with him, almost daily at the beginning of 1871 and again in 1872, after returning from a year's teaching stint in Fukui. After one lively evening, he called House the "soul of the party." And when Griffis's sister Margaret came to teach at Japan's first government girls' school two years later, she noted that House was a "charming conversationalist" and a "loveable person."[8]

The Class One schedule was not for slouches. House taught five hours each morning, with a single thirty-minute break. Most classes lasted sixty minutes, with no time scheduled between sessions. At first, only three free days were observed per month (the first, the eleventh, and the twenty-first), though the officials eventually made Sunday a holiday at the insistence of Christian teachers. Any student who arrived more than fifteen minutes late to a class was told to stay away for an entire half-day. And House was as stern a taskmaster as any in the school. Though hired as a professor of English literature, he essentially was a language instructor, teaching twenty-nine weekly sessions of grammar, composition, reading, penmanship, and history. Driven in teaching as he was in reporting, he thought his students should show the same diligence that he had evidenced in copying Wagner's *Tannhäuser* to learn musical composition. One of his best students described his style as "conscientious and painstaking"; he said he never had seen another "teacher possessing such personal magnetism or such a power of imparting instruction."

House's great joy at the school lay in his students. They studied hard and learned quickly, and many of them rewarded him by going on to national leadership. One of House's boys, Takahashi Korekiyo, became prime minister in 1921 and, after that, one of prewar Japan's most effective finance ministers, before being assassinated by an ultranationalist in

1936; another, Komura Jutarō, graduated from Harvard Law School and impressed the world with his tough diplomacy as foreign minister following the Russo-Japanese War; Sakurai Jōji became known in Japan as the father of organic chemistry; Hozumi Nobushige became the country's first doctor of laws, a drafter of the 1898 Civil Code, and president of the Privy Council; and Sugiura Shigetake, one of the era's most influential thinkers, tutored Crown Prince Hirohito and published the opinion journal *Nihonjin.* The teacher's favorites, however, were a pair of fourteen-year-olds: Kojima Noriyuki, whose heart was set on architecture, and Mitsukuri Kakichi, who had begun studying Western subjects when he was eleven and still at home. Both lads dreamed of studying in America, and when business took House home briefly in 1873, the boys went with him. They went by steamer to San Francisco and Panama, by rail across the isthmus, then up the Atlantic coast to New York. After a meeting with the Twains, House arranged for Hartford friends to lodge them and enrolled them in the local high school, from which they eventually graduated prior to going on to Yale University and Rensselaer Polytechnic Institute, respectively—and to later becoming prominent University of Tokyo professors. House's correspondence during the years of their American sojourn oozes with pride over their successes.

For all their pleasure, the teaching-reporting years also left House with physical problems, possibly the result of the grinding daily schedule, more likely the effect of genetic characteristics or the profligate habits of earlier years. Not long after returning to Tokyo from Fukui in February 1872, Griffis found his friend in bed, nursing a painful case of gout in his foot joints. That was on Saturday, the twenty-fourth; by the next Wednesday, the pain kept House from the classroom, so Griffis substituted for three days running. It may be of some significance that the vocabulary lists that House prepared for his students included "gout" as an example of illnesses. His eyes also began giving him trouble. In letters home in the summer of 1872, he began complaining about how hard it was to see some days. "My eyes, which were always weak, often trouble me seriously," he wrote in a dictated letter on July 18. "I can hardly write legibly, at times, without pain." The problems did not worry him or slow him down much. They were just nuisances—but more portentous nuisances than he could have known at the time.[9]

If teaching in the mornings gave House enough money to ignore Verbeck's warning about "careful habits," the afternoon reporting and writing still defined his persona. He may not have been salaried, but he was described in the *Tribune*'s columns as its "regular correspondent in Japan," and he took the job seriously. Each day, he would call on his sources, particularly in the foreign ministry and at the legations. Even (especially!) socializing had information gathering as its main goal. Then every two or three weeks, he would send a lengthy "letter" off to Reid, along with a personal note providing background information and off-the-record rumors and reports likely to titillate the managing editor. The newspaper "letters" typically interspersed lengthy excerpts from official correspondence with House's summaries and comments.

The first of House's reports arrived in San Francisco on October 16, 1870, aboard the steamer *Great Republic* (along with Mrs. J. S. Bourdon's 6,559 containers of tea and 353 packages of silk), and appeared on page one of the *Tribune* the next day, bearing bulletin accounts of Japan's increasing involvement in the new, imperialist world. Subsequent letters appeared monthly, each of them about three weeks after House had dispatched it from Tokyo. His first lengthy news story, a three-column essay that took up a significant portion of the *Tribune's* first page on December 29, showed both his patriotism and his sensitivity to what would interest American readers. Under the headline, "The Mikado Unvailed," House waxed enthusiastic about the emperor's October 8 reception for former Secretary of State Seward. The emperor had given audiences to foreign ministers before, but never to a private citizen. What was more, those earlier visitors "had only been allowed to look upon a part of his person at a time—the lower extremities or the face being always concealed." But this time the Mikado was wholly visible, "entirely unvailed by screen or curtain." House saw the episode as a signal that Japan wanted to modernize its foreign relations, to "relax the severity of old usages." The fact that the favor had been granted first to an *American* was significant—and thrilling. Another missive, on February 22, 1871, illustrated the breadth of his reporting, with pieces on the opening of a modern hospital in Tokyo; the pending appointment of missionary doctor James Hepburn as interpreter at the American legation (a prospect that "overjoyed" House, though it never actually materialized); completion of telegraph lines to Singapore, with a Hong Kong extension promised soon; and a report that a Japanese expedition to Korea was set to sail in mid-April, accompanied by the British minister to China. House's accompanying note to Reid regretted that his job at the Kaisei Gakkō would keep him from accompanying the expedition, and suggested that he might be able to arrange to go anyway if the *Tribune* would pay him as much as the teaching job did.

The most consistent theme of House's journalistic letters in these first months was the instability of the Tokyo government. Soon after his arrival he predicted that Tokugawa Keiki, the deposed shogun, would reenter politics soon and create a "rupture" in the new governmental system. He continued that theme throughout the next two and a half years. In November, he visited the mountains of Hakone to interview leaders of a group of rebels. When their plot miscarried, he expected that it would "be renewed in a few months," since "there is immense dissatisfaction with the present government," even among those who had helped install it. His most detailed discussion of the situation was a three-column *Tribune* piece, on January 27, 1871, arguing that Japan was "in a state of agitation which may at any moment break out into active revolution." He described the military preparations of several domains whose support for the Meiji government was shaky and predicted that within six months there would be a "reopening of the great question" of who would rule Japan. By the following September, House found it "really astounding" that no uprising had resulted from the government's "repeated invasions of the cherished rights of the old daimios" and noted that Tokyo was "in a perfect tumult," albeit a "tumult of discussion." Later that fall he commented again on the "lively state of combustion here" and predicted that "this artificial tranquillity can't last perpetually."[10]

From the hindsight of later decades, the new Meiji government actually had consolidated its power quite effectively by now. From the perspective of contemporary onlookers, however, the picture was muddier. Internal strife over policies and offices was nasty and endless, and rumors were rife. An outsider from the West, a man whose journalistic teeth were cut on civil war, hardly could have been faulted for not sensing how weak the opposition really was. House's view of the regime began to brighten, however, as the months passed and his connections to well-placed officials deepened. A lengthy piece early in 1872 on the "most important Commission that has ever left Japan"—the high level Iwakura mission sent for "general scrutiny and study of the social, commercial and political institutions of the various nations with which Japan now has diplomatic relations"—noted the confidence the mission's leaders were displaying by handing Japan over to caretakers while they went off to the other side of the globe. By the conclusion of his first Tokyo stay, early in 1873, he had decided that a daimyo uprising no longer was likely, though he remained uncertain about several other groups, including the samurai of the southwest.[11]

House's Tokyo friends in this period remarked often on what a charming dinner partner he was: on his incisive wit, his keen insights, his gracious manner, his mastery of the day's events. His editors, by contrast, often found him curmudgeonly. It was never enough for him to be frenzied in seeking out news stories; he also was obsessive about how the editors treated his copy. When they changed his prose, he was not above calling the revisions "idiotic" (at least once, Reid penned a note in the margin, saying he thought House right; the editor had been a "cruel butcher"). He grumbled when, at first, he was not given the right accorded to the *Tribune's* most prestigious correspondents, to have his initials printed at the end of articles. He was indignant when people questioned the reliability of one report, snipping: "Whenever I speak *positively* on any point I do so only after close and very cautious investigation. Whenever a doubt as to fact or theory arises in my mind, I shall take care to state it." And the delays and uncertainties involved in communicating across half a globe provoked endless gripes. Especially galling was the irritation of sending important pieces, then not being able to ascertain for two full months whether they had been published or not. "I ought to have asked you, if my communications were not used, to have taken the trouble to save them," he wrote in the fall of 1871. "Then I should have asked my uncle to call for them and dispose of them" at another publication. "It never could have occurred to me," he added "that subjects which seem so vital as the Coolie Trade . . . would be out of place; and I'm sure that somebody would have considered them worth using." Still fuming, he added later in the letter: "If you had wished for nothing from me, you might have let me understand so. I've had too much newspaper work to care about doing any *en amateur* at this late day."[12]

Nor did he issue his threats about sending material elsewhere idly; for although the *Tribune* was his publishing home in these first Japan years, he published a good deal in other venues, too. Some of his articles appeared in the rival *New York Times*, and he wrote numerous longer essays, mostly on Japanese culture, for magazines. His first major Tokyo essay, "A Japanese Doctor and His Works," appeared in the December 1871 issue of *The Atlantic Monthly*, describing the opening ceremonies of a modern 100-bed hospital in Tokyo. House poked fun at himself for wearing shoes in the building while the Japanese wore slippers; he liked the director's ingenuity in brewing beer that could be used in treating patients and praised his "democratic" spirit for charging patients just fifty cents a day. He also described the vocalist's solo with the wit he once had used as a Boston arts critic: "The voice of the very gifted singer is heard warbling and vibrating in that strange involution of shake and trill which constitutes the highest form of Japanese vocalization. . . . We vow that we are enchanted—and are in the mood to enjoy anything—but we do not press her to a repetition." A *Harper's* piece in March 1872, "Japanese Statesman at Home," took the reader to a lavish December dinner at the home of the imperial councilor Hirosawa Saneomi, replete with sweet jellies, rare teas, soup spiced with seaweed, raw fish, prawns, sliced chicken, beer, champagne, and sweets. The reporter's favorite experience that evening may have been watching the indulgent way in which children were treated. "There seems to be no system of discipline or training, as we understand it," he wrote. "Throughout all classes, high and low alike, the treatment of the young is almost extravagantly affectionate and considerate." He said he never had seen violent punishment. Yet Japanese children were the best behaved in the world. "It has seemed to me that the early admission of children to intimate and confidential association with their parents . . . gives an ease and an early development which act with equal good for all." The next time he visited Hirosawa's home was much sadder, House wrote in a coda to the article. That was in March 1871, after the statesman had been assassinated (hewn to pieces, as House put it) by a dissident band of the very sort he had been worrying about in his letters to Reid.

He also wrote a fifteen-page *Atlantic* story about a day at a Japanese theater, revealing an eye for critical details that only a career in the theaters of London and New York could have made possible. But after writing that piece, which came out in September 1872, his Tokyo journalism turned a corner. Although Japanese culture never would cease to interest him, he largely stopped writing about it except in fictional works. Not long after the *Maria Luz* sensation, which consumed so much of his reportorial energy in the summer and fall of 1872, he penned a serious analysis for *Harper's* on "The Present and Future of Japan," analyzing where Japan stood early in 1873. Labeling Japan's progress "one of the social marvels of modern times," he described the bungling and uncertainty of the new government's efforts to restore order. When they removed the daimyo from power, he said, "the whole fabric of feudalism . . . was blown away with a single breath." And when they had given the "native press" freedom to discuss public life, they invited chaos. He criticized the foreign merchants and diplomats who had imposed unequal treaties that made it difficult for Japan to get on its feet economically. He also criticized Westerners generally for treating Japan's 30 million inhabitants "with an indifference which is bestowed upon no other people of ancient or modern times." But he criticized Japan's own leaders even more for trying too much too fast. "In spite of the sincerity of its wishes for reform, the government has thus far displayed more rashness than reason in the prosecution of its aims. . . . The race against time has been too rapid." The future was bright, though. Japan's officials were shrewd, quick to learn from mistakes. He predicted "a time of overstrained effort and forced vitality, then a period of prolonged depression and anxiety, and subsequently a laborious but certain rise to a respectable, perhaps a prominent, position among the civilized countries of the world."

This piece revealed all of the major themes that had become important to Japan's new friend during his first thirty months in Tokyo. There was, first of all, deep respect for the Japanese themselves. His respect had a patronizing quality, the tone of a friend who assumed, perhaps unconsciously, that Japan should emulate the systems of the Western powers. But he loved Japan's culture, admired the intelligence of its leaders, and stood in awe of their ability to stimulate change. A second theme was the conviction that Japan was a land of opportunity for America, but that the opportunities were being undercut by inept diplomats. He wished John Hay, his journalist friend from Civil War days, would seek a diplomatic post in Tokyo. He also urged Washington to recall DeLong, a man who was equally corrupt, insensitive, bungling, and illiterate.

House's third theme approached obsession. Balancing his admiration for the Japanese was an overweening contempt for most of the foreigners who had taken up residence in Yokohama and Tokyo. He talked in the *Harper's* piece on Japan's future about the "rapacity" of the mercantile community, "tolerated, if not fostered, by the diplomatic authorities whose duty it should be to protect" Japan against unfairness. Elsewhere, he talked repeatedly about expatriates' insolence and arrogance, their determination to rob the Japanese of rightful profits, their defiance of Japanese laws, and their propensity for sending home inaccurate reports that slandered Japan. By the summer of 1872, he had developed a special antipathy toward a new contingent of Westerners whom most others treated with deep respect: the missionaries. House actually had expressed sympathy toward Christianity when he arrived in Japan. But two years had convinced him that missionary work was "extremely mischievous," an impediment to "the free progress of ideas and actions." He told Reid that he hesitated to write about this conviction, because "there is so much superstitious feeling in the matter that perhaps even the quietest treatment of it would not be well received." But he thought the impact of missionaries was "pernicious" and he offered to write a long essay on the topic if the *Tribune* wanted him to. It apparently did not.

House was thirty-six when he decided to make a short trip back home at the beginning of 1873. He gave family affairs and the need to get treatment for his gout as the reason. But a number of other things called him, too. He had been away for more than two and a half years, longer than he first had planned, and felt that he needed time with Reid to work out his relationship with the paper. His young students, Mitsukuri and Kojima, needed someone to settle them in an American school. And, in a hint of the future, Foreign Ministry documents suggest that he had agreed—officially but secretly—to lend the government itself a hand. Records compiled decades later, when the emperor decorated him shortly before his death, say that the government asked him to make a trip to America "in 1872–73" to talk with officials about the anti-Japanese activities of DeLong and British Minister Harry Parkes. Since there are no records of specific instructions or of financial promises, the arrangement likely was informal, probably between House and Ōkuma Shigenobu, the powerful force in foreign and finance ministries to whom he had become close. What is clear is that House had become enough of a Japanese partisan that such an arrangement would have suited him. Japan was eager to join the community of nations; it was beleaguered; and its leaders were capable, sincere, and willing to sacrifice for their people. Any American who valued democracy and progress ought to be willing to give Japan a hand.[13]

When House sailed into San Francisco with his young protégés on March 21, he was a different man than the restless writer who had left America. His body was weaker, but his soul was focused. He had found a suitor more engaging than any of the women in his *Atlantic* or *Galaxy* love stories. So he headed off for New York, where he would fail to persuade Reid to run a favorable review of Mark Twain's *Gilded Age* but succeed in getting him to print an attack on DeLong designed "to fairly kill a minister." The charges included accusations that DeLong had offended Japan by refusing to reside in the U.S. legation in Tokyo, that he had pressured the Japanese government to hire Americans, that he was "a virtual protector and defender of the coolie traffic," and that he had "actually participated in a conspiracy for the overthrow of the Mikado's sovereignty." He also accused the minister of telling the State Department that he had been asked to accompany the Iwakura mission to the West, when in truth "the ambassadors were especially anxious to avoid his companionship." When Japanese officials credited House with causing DeLong's recall that spring, he knew that the reasons were more complex than that. But he despised DeLong's diplomacy too much to correct the error.

House headed next to Hartford for several days with the Twains, swapping tales, discussing how to get the *Tribune* to treat Mark's novels better, and getting Kojima and Mitsukuri ensconced in high school. Then it was off to Boston, followed by a trip back to New York, to get his business affairs in order and to try—once again, unsuccessfully—to secure a regular salary from the *Tribune*. After a round of social affairs, he was ready by July to board the *City of Montreal* for England, where he would spend time with his novelist friend Charles Reade and catch another glimpse of the traveling Twain before heading back to Tokyo,[14] where his career would take a dramatic new turn. The first Japan stay had given him a sense of mission, a desire to show the world how much progress the Japanese were making and how desperately they deserved fairer treatment by Westerners; the second would provide more concrete ways to tell that story. It also would take House to the peaks of influence and the depths of acrimony.

NOTES

1. WR, Library of Congress.

2. House's arrival is reported in the *JWM,* August 27, 1870; the *City of Yedo* explosion comes from *JWM,* August 6, 20, 1870; House's journey across the United States is described in House to Whitelaw Reid, June 4, 1870, WR, Library of Congress; DeLong's comment is taken from his despatches to Hamilton Fish (January 30, 1871), quoted in Jack L. Hammersmith, *Spoilsmen in a "Flowery Fairyland,"* 92.

3. The description of Tsukiji buildings is in E. G. Holtham, *Eight Years in Japan 1873–1881,* 218. Riding with guns is in William Elliot Griffis, *Verbeck of Japan,* 235. Two of the Kaisei Gakkō's foreign teachers were indeed attacked by drunken men early in the morning of January 14, 1871; the foreigners, however, appeared to

Griffis to be guilty of provocation and breaking regulations by going about in the early hours without guards "in the company of a native girl," 245; also see *Japan Weekly Mail,* January 14, 1871. House's evaluations of Japan's delight and safety are found in his letters to Reid, September 21, 1870, and January 23, 1871, WR, Library of Congress.

4. The Fuji descriptions come from House's "To Fuziyama and Back," *Japanese Episodes,* 72 (rising early), 88 (porters), 90 (singing insects), 107 (cloud-pageantry), 114 (summit), 119 (breakfast), and 154 (sunset). Griffis's recollections are in "William Elliot Griffis's Travel Journal 1870–71," Rutgers University, January 5 and 9, 1871 (quotation about Asakusa from Robert Rosenstone, *Mirror in the Shrine,* 16); and House's claims about going beyond the treaty limits and getting to know all the city are in his letters to Reid, September 21, 1870, and January 23, 1871, WR, Library of Congress. Griffis's January 5 entry seems to have mistaken Shiba Shrine (Shintō) for a temple, which would have been Buddhist.

5. The quotations are gleaned from House letters to Reid, WR, Library of Congress, November 22, 1870 (contacts with DeLong, Parkes, and Japanese officials, as well as DeLong's involvement with rebels); December 13, 1870 (foreign minister); and May 24, 1871 (Smith's brothel visits). DeLong's contacts with rebels also are discussed in the *New York Tribune,* May 3, 1873, 6.

6. House's discussion of the Nagasaki cable is in a letter to Reid, December 23, 1871, WR, Library of Congress; his discussion of friends in a letter to "My Dear Evans," December 20, 1871, WR, Library of Congress; and his complaint about remuneration in a letter to Reid, February 23, 1872, WR, Library of Congress.

7. Data on *yatoi* come from UNESCO, *Shiryō oyatoi gaikokujin,* 163, 493, and from Hazel Jones, *Live Machines,* particularly 11 (salaries), 125 ("live machine"), 148 (national figures), and 152 (salaries). The estimate of what it cost to live a year was made by Guido Verbeck, assistant director of the Kaisei Gakkō, in 1870, in Ardath W. Burks, "William Elliot Griffis, Class of 1869," *The Journal of the Rutgers University Library,* 95. House's Civil War salary is from Laura Stedman and George Gould, *Life and Letters of Edmund Clarence Stedman,* vol. I, 252. Evening habits are in House to Whitelaw Reid, February 18, 1872, WR, Library of Congress.

8. The estate is described by Griffis in Rosenstone, 130; students and teachers are discussed in Griffis, *Verbeck,* 240–41; House's personality is in Griffis's "Travel Journal 1870–71 and Japan Notes 1870–1874," March 20, 1872, WEG, Rutgers University. Margaret Griffis's comments, from February 18, 1873, and April 8, 1874, are recorded in Henshū Iinkai, ed., *Za yatoi,* 144.

9. Material on Kaisei Gakkō classes, students, regulations, and vocabulary lists comes from Shōwa Joshi Daigaku, ed., "E. H. Hausu," *Kindai bungaku kenkyū sōsho,* vol. 5, 395–400, and Shigehisa Tokutarō, *Oyatoi gaikokujin,* 161; Takahashi and Komura also are listed in Griffis's handwritten lists of the school's students ("Students' Names: Kai Sei Gakko") in WEG, Rutgers University. The recollection of House's teaching style is from *Japan Weekly Mail,* December 28, 1901. Discussions of Mitsukuri and Kojima are in Isono Naohide, *Mōsu sono hi sono hi,* 22. Settling the boys in is discussed in a spring 1873 letter from House to Mark Twain, Monday p.m., n.d., MTP, University of California. Griffis's observation of House's illness is in "Japan Notes 1870–1874," February 24–March 1, 1872, Rutgers University, while the description of the eye problems is in House to Reid, July 18, 1872, WR, Library

of Congress. Ebihara Hachirō calls House Japan's first "regular English professor" in *Nihon ōji shimbun zasshi shi,* 122.

10. The features of Japanese instability also are discussed in his letters to Reid (WR, Library of Congress): Tokugawa Keiki, September 21, 1870; Hakone plot, November 22, 1870; daimyo failure to rebel, September 6, 1871; and likelihood that tranquillity will not last, October 23, 1871 (year inferred from contents of this document).

11. The report on the Iwakura mission was sent from Tokyo on December 23, 1871, and ran in the *Tribune* February 3, 1872; his evaluation of the feudal lords was sent January 10, 1873, and appeared May 13, 1873. It is worth noting, in light of House's later concern with women's issues, that the December 23 piece called readers' attention to the fact that the several women on the Iwakura mission were of low status, not "princesses" or "goddesses," as he assumed (correctly) the American press would make them out to be.

12. Taken from letters from House to Reid (WR, Library of Congress): "idiotic editing," n.d.; use of initials, December 23, 1871 (Reid began including House's initials after long pieces in February 1872); reliability of his accounts, January 23, 1871; problems with telegraphic communication, June 20, 1871; and letters not being published, September 6, 1871.

13. See House to Reid, July 20, 1872; he also talked about the "cheek" of church officials in a September 6, 1871, letter, WR, Library of Congress. Also see "Gaikoku jokun zaken: Beikoku no bu," December 17, 1901, No. 282, Gaimushō Gaikōshiryōkan.

14. The DeLong article is discussed in House to Reid, May 1, 1873; WR, Library of Congress; an editorial listing the charges ran in the *Tribune* on May 3, 6. House's arrangements with the *Tribune* are taken up in his letter to Reid, July 29, 1873; WR, Library of Congress. The fact that Reid and House had quarreled over the paper's treatment of Twain is reflected in Reid's note to John Hay at the bottom of the second letter: "Do you think we can stand it to let House represent himself at all as connected with us again?" Hay responds: "I do not see why, under proper limitations, he is any less valuable than before."

5

Japan, 1870–1875: Consolidating Power

This calamity is upon us today. Indeed, this is the greatest political upheaval since the Restoration.

—Kido Takayoshi, on a split in the government, October 30, 1873[1]

The government was in an uproar when House arrived back in Tokyo on November 1, 1873, riven by infighting so intense that many thought it would fall. Even as House was sailing across the Mediterranean Sea and Indian Ocean that summer, members of the Iwakura mission were making their own trips back to Japan after a year and a half of studying the systems and methods of the West. Most of them had reached home before the peripatetic Bostonian did, and their arrival sparked a brouhaha that came to be known as the Crisis of 1873 or the Conquer-Korea Debate (*seikanron*), depending on whether one preferred to remember things by calendars or by maps. Although House played no role in the episode, its aftermath would send his career in unanticipated directions and ratchet up by several notches his identification with Japan's efforts to stand strong in the community of nations.

The heart of the dispute lay in a plan by the charismatic "elder" statesman Saigō Takamori to increase Japanese influence by force in Korea. The Meiji government had attempted to establish state-to-state relations with the Koreans several times, but the Koreans had resisted, preferring to maintain their ages-old dependence on China and fearful that Japan had more than friendly intercourse in mind. More than once, Seoul had dismissed Japanese envoys rudely. Irritated by the rebuffs and convinced that it was time for Japan to assert itself, Saigō persuaded the

Grand Council of State on August 17, 1873, to mandate a mission to Korea, which he would head, to demand an apology. Saigō was popular enough to win broad support for the plan, even among those who feared that it might lead to war, but several officials remained skeptical. Japan likely would win an armed conflict, but war would be expensive, particularly if China came to Korea's aid, and every yen was needed to meet the financial crises at home. Soejima Taneomi of *Maria Luz* fame, who favored the general approach but worried about its specifics, got the emperor to insist that Saigō wait until the leaders of the Iwakura mission had returned before heading off to the continent; when they arrived in September, fresh from observing the military might of Europe, they declared Saigō's plan foolhardy.

The result was a struggle worthy of the history books. Junior councilor Kido Takayoshi announced that such a mission would necessitate tax increases, which could, in turn, precipitate rebellion. Ōkubo Toshimichi, the regime's financial wizard and Saigō's boyhood neighbor, said that if a war kept Japan from paying its foreign debts, the European powers might intervene in Japan's internal affairs. Sanjō Sanetomi, head of the state council, suffered a nervous breakdown. And Iwakura, the new head, got the emperor to withdraw approval from the Korean mission, whereupon Saigō and his supporters stormed out of the government. Before the episode was over, half of the privy councilors and many members of the imperial guard had returned to their home provinces, some to agitate for a greater voice in the government for the old samurai class, some to take up lives as private citizens, and several to plot against the young regime. Historians would argue that the episode made the evolving clique of rulers tighter and more cohesive. At the end of October 1873, however, the disaster looked unalloyed. Several of the most capable officials had turned against the government; survival of the regime seemed in question.

The Korean crisis dramatized two of the major problems that faced Japan's leaders five years into the new era. First, it showed just how shaky their hold on power really was, making it clear that House had been more than a gloom-monger when he wrote about imminent rebellion. Second, it highlighted the fact that it was not enough for them to consolidate power at home; they also had to consider where Japan stood in the world. For two and a half centuries, the Tokugawa rulers had been able to shut themselves off from foreign lands, but the Meiji officials could not do that. The outer world pressed from a thousand directions now, economically, diplomatically, militarily, intellectually, even culturally. Should Japan resist the foreign forces? Should it bend to their demands? Should it become a Western-style dynamo? And what about imperialism? Should Japan merely build up enough strength to defend itself against the Westerners, or should it become an expansive power itself? By the time Saigō went back to his native Kyūshū, it was clear that each domestic cloud had a roiling international lining, that every domestic decision had to take into account Japan's relationship to the world at large.

The most threatening features of that autumn's cloud seemed to be domestic in nature, however, born of the endless obstacles to modernization. There were, for one thing, the problems of helping people maintain a decent living standard; providing ways for people to get around in Tokyo as it began growing again; finding jobs for hundreds of thousands of samurai who for centuries had not been allowed to do ordinary work; and helping people grapple with the disruptions that all the changes had introduced into their personal lives. House's friend William Elliot Griffis was only gone for a year from his teaching job in Tokyo, but when he returned early in 1872, he was stunned by the changes: telegraph poles and electric lines; striped barber poles heralding a brand new profession when samurai began cutting off their topknots; brick houses with glass windows; daimyo estates turned into cattle pastures; and a popular new shop called Maruzen, which sold Western books and magazines at Nihonbashi. "The City of Yedo is undergoing vast changes," House told the *Tribune* readers; "another twelve months will probably have divested it of nearly all of those quaint and captivating architectural features which made it the constant delight of curious observers."

Griffis saw this as progress, but others knew that it spelled disruption and lost jobs, which in turn threatened the new regime with grumbling and discontent. The rulers also had to deal with public safety issues, such as foreigners' endless complaints about ruffians and stealing; Japanese worries about rowdy foreigners; the frequent flooding of the Sumida River; and, above all, fires. Fires always had been a problem in the capital because of the combination of concentrated housing, charcoal-burning stoves, inflammable building materials, and earthquakes. During the first Meiji years, Tokyo seemed cursed. On February 26, 1872, a fire broke out in the old Aizu lord's mansion and spread throughout the Ginza and Kyobashi areas as well as the foreign residences at Tsukiji. Two months later, the "most disastrous fire within . . . memory" killed sixty people and left 50,000 homeless, wreaking havoc with the government's relief budget. And in May 1873, the imperial palace was immolated.

The rulers also had to contend with increasing political discontent, exacerbated by the Korean crisis. At the commoner level, there was constant complaining about the new policies, and even some activism. Tokyo construction workers and rickshaw pullers showed their irritation at Western-inspired antinudity laws by donning jackets made of mosquito nets. Some journalists criticized the lax way officials enforced new laws against prostitution, whereas others lambasted the very idea of banning prostitution. In Tokyo, Kanda shrine goers grumbled when their priests took away the shrine's tutelary deity, Kanda Myōjin, because, as a one-time rebel, he was no longer a good role model. In the countryside, the government was confronted by thousands on thousands of people who resented the increasing reach of national power into their mountain valleys. Many protested in 1873 when the new Western solar calendar (dubbed "Jesus Christ's New Year") confused their annual planting and festival cycles. Others were infuriated by a set of 1872–1873 laws that required farmers to send their children to school for three years of compulsory education, to give up their older sons to three years of active military service, to pay 3 percent annual taxes on land they owned, and to halt such "backward" customs as mixed bathing and public urination. Those laws helped to break down the ages-old gap between the samurai and the commoners, as did an 1871 provision that all households be registered uniformly, regardless of previous social rank. But at the same time, the regulations took labor and cash away from farm households, many of whom were barely eking out an existence anyway. And that caused wide resentment.[2]

Disgruntlement of this sort did not worry the rulers overly much, since local disputes were endemic to public life, more interesting to the newspapers that were beginning to show up than dangerous to the governing system. Even when the antipathy led to violent peasant rebellions in several hundred villages during the first Meiji years, the officials knew that government troops would have little trouble restoring order. What concerned them more was the rise, especially after the Korean crisis, of an organized, national opposition, led primarily by disaffected members of the old samurai elite. This development took two forms, one political and peaceful, the other more violent, and the rulers feared that it had the potential to turn street-side grumbling into something more widespread and ominous, something quite dangerous to the state.

The violent, samurai-led opposition started right after the 1868 Restoration, with sporadic acts by small groups of extremist samurai: the assassination in 1869 of War Minister Ōmura Masajirō when he suggested that commoners be allowed in the army, and the 1871 killing of House's friend, imperial councilor Hirosawa Saneomi. Once Saigō left the government, these rumblings threatened to become a movement, and their reverberations shook the power centers. When the former Justice Minister Etō Shimpei led several thousand ex-samurai against the local government in Saga Prefecture in central Kyūshū in 1874, official troops put the rising down quickly in "a series of trifling skirmishes"[3] and executed Etō almost as soon as they captured him. Although the forceful response put a temporary halt to open military challenges, officials remained aware that angry samurai throughout the southwest had blood on their agendas. They knew, for example, that the Hagi region from which several of the government's own leaders had come was full of fire-breathing hotheads, and that hundreds of Shintō loyalists in northern Kyūshū had formed a League of Divine Wind to fight change violently. They also knew that in Saigō's home region of southern Kyūshū small private schools (*shigakkō*) were being created to teach martial skills and Confucian values to young men—all in the name of resistance to the new system. The officials in Tokyo hoped that Saigō's loyalty to his land would hold his followers back from violence, but they knew too that his disaffection was deep and that the situation was volatile.

Almost as worrisome was the emergence of a nonviolent opposition, led by men from Tosa on the island of Shikoku. Following the young Restoration soldier Itagaki Taisuke, they created Japan's first political societies and attempted to counter what they saw as an increasingly autocratic government through speeches, memorials to the throne, and newspaper editorials. Early in 1874, Itagaki and several of his companions sent what House called an "intemperate" petition to the emperor "attacking the administration in violent terms and proposing radical and immediate reforms."[4] Actually, the proposals were "radical" only by the standards of the day—and of the regime. Urging the creation of a popular assembly that would give the "people" a voice in government, they triggered Japan's first thoroughgoing public debate. Daily newspapers, which had not even existed prior to 1871, hurled arguments about the proposed assembly back and forth with a virulence equaled only by their erudition. Pro-government dailies such as *Tokyo Nichi Nichi Shimbun* argued that the people were not ready for self-government: a national assembly was needed, but not until the populace was better educated. The Itagaki side, represented by the newspapers *Chōya* and *Yōbin Hōchi*, countered that an assembly must be created at once to check the leadership's increasing despotism. In truth, Itagaki's forces were not particularly democratic. They wanted to exclude most of the commoner class from the new assembly, and they demanded a continuation of public stipends to the ex-samurai elites. But they were excellent sloganeers, and their use of the *jiyū minken* or "freedom and people's rights" label introduced new ideas into the public sphere. They also made the Meiji officials feel vulnerable, prompting the creation of several structures intended to satisfy dissenters without giving them real influence.

One of the government's responses was to establish prefectural governors' assemblies in 1875, elite bodies with very few powers except the right to debate public issues. The more important response was to restructure—more than once—the Grand Council of State (Dajōkan) system under whose guidance all policy making was carried out. The Council, created right after the Restoration, was named Dajōkan after the government structure used in ancient times, to symbolize the fact that the emperor was supposed to be ruling directly now. In truth, he remained a figurehead. The structure also had other fictive features, including a legislative branch (variously called Giseikan, Sain, and Genrōin) whose members were selected by the top officials and given little actual authority. The core of the system, by the time it reached maturity in 1875, lay in a coterie of about ten councilors (*sangi*) who headed the ministries and talked together daily to decide policy. One result of the small size of this group was that decision making was quite efficient; another was that the ruling body took on more and more of the qualities of an oligarchy as time passed. And by the late 1870s, it was a narrowly based oligarchy, referred to often as the Satchō clique because most of its members came from the domains that had led the way in toppling the Tokugawa family, Satsuma and Chōshū.

The determination of the *sangi* to consolidate power so forcefully sprang partly from their own personal ambitions, but even more from their conviction that a strong state was needed "to give protection and tranquility to the people, and to maintain equality with foreign nations." The thing that made national strength seem particularly urgent was the looming threat of imperialist nations whose boats now anchored in Yokohama harbor. "There was a real danger," wrote the historian Tōyama Shigeki, "that Japan would become a colony," just as India, Burma, the Philippines, and the East Indies had. For that reason, although the domestic threats occupied the center of most days' councilor debates, the question of how to deal with the foreigners never was far from anyone's mind. If Japan failed to maintain tranquility at home, the foreigners might well send in troops; if it was unable to create effective domestic institutions, the United States and Europe would deny it a place in the international community. And for that reason, the move to modernity had to be made quickly, even if that meant curtailing discussion and letting a few men make the decisions. At least, that was the way most councilors saw it.[5]

As we already have noted, one consequence of these convictions was the decision to make a vigorous study of the ideas and institutions of the strong Western nations: to bring foreign specialists to Japan for everything from teaching English to building navy yards, to dispatch the Iwakura and other official missions, and to send hundreds of individuals to what the Japanese referred to as the "eastern" side of the globe to learn Western subjects of every kind. The things these Japanese encountered often left them amazed. Gaslights. Men opening doors for bare-shouldered women. Leather shoes. The unembarrassed eating of meat. "Penal restrictions on smoking and drinking." Museum items made of human hair. Elected legislatures. Children talking back to parents. Christians bowing before "pictures of crucified criminals, profuse with ruby-red blood." The list of things stupefying and puzzling had no end. But neither did the curiosity or brightness of the Japanese students. As a *New*

York Times essayist wrote from Washington on July 1, 1871, "Those who meet the Japanese speak of their wonderful intelligence."

One result of these encounters was the set of institutional changes that we have been discussing. Another was the eruption of a mania for things Western in Japan's major cities. By the early 1870s, it seemed that everything Japanese was in decline and everything American or European was in vogue—that, in the words of the journalist Tokutomi Sohō, "it was always 'America this and America that.'" In 1874, Tokyo boasted nearly a hundred foreign language schools. Translations of Shakespeare, the Bible, John Bunyan's *Pilgrim's Progress,* and Samuel Smiles's *Self Help* flooded city bookstores. Newspapers described the importance of eating meat ("always with onion") and advertised cigarettes, soaps, and patent medicines. And the use of English phrases—sometimes elegantly, sometimes awkwardly—became *de rigueur* in intelligent conversation. The literature specialist Basil Hall Chamberlain listed the following among business placards in Tokyo then: "Specialist for the Decease of Children," "Head Cutter" (outside a barber shop), and "Extract of Fowl" over a display of eggs. The backlash and downside of this Western craze will be discussed in a later chapter. The upside was that it made urban Japan wonderfully exciting in the 1870s; one could not spend the days there without feeling the energy. It also made Tokyo, in particular, a place of great intellectual vitality.[6]

One of the most important issues fueling the intellectual debates was the very question that triggered the Crisis of 1873: how a transformed Japan should relate to its Asian neighbors. That relationship had been easy to define across most of the previous millennium, when all Asian lands had fit into a comprehensive world order with power and wealth emanating outward from China. Though less willing to genuflect before the Chinese court than the other Asian kingdoms were, Japan's thinkers and rulers never questioned China's political, intellectual, or cultural superiority. Japan's first great advance in civilization, in the seventh and eighth centuries, had resulted to a large degree from the influence of scholars who spent years, even decades, studying at Tang dynasty temples and schools. Japan's writing script came from China; so did the models for its law codes and its major religious traditions. The founders of its major Buddhist sects—Tendai, Shingon, Zen, and Pure Land—had developed their theological understandings after lengthy sojourns in China. And during the recent Tokugawa era, the political order was built on an intentional adaptation of the ideas of China's neo-Confucian sages. Japan's intellectual core may have been at odds in certain ways with that of the continental giant. But until the middle of the 1800s most Japanese stood in awe of the ancient and sophisticated Chinese. "The China we envisioned as children," recalled the journalist Ubukata Toshirō decades later, "was noble, romantic, and heroic."

By the 1870s, however, Japan's leaders had begun having serious questions about China. Most still accepted the idea of Chinese cultural superiority, but respect for its political position had dimmed. Actually, doubts about Chinese dominance already had begun to appear late in the Tokugawa era, when scholars such as Ōtsuki Gentaku began searching out the writings of the West and deriding sinocentrism as "crude and . . . narrow." The questions had proliferated after mid-century, when China was humiliated by the challenges of Great Britain and France. And the Beijing government's difficulty in putting down domestic rebellions from the 1850s onward made the new Meiji officials turn away from China as a model for governance. As a result, when Japan signed a commercial treaty with China in 1871, she insisted successfully that it be on a strictly equal basis: no most-favored nation clause, no difference in tariffs, and mutual consular jurisdiction in both nations. When the Chinese failed to send diplomatic representatives to Tokyo for the first several years, the Japanese were not favorably impressed. The diplomats' absence, thought many Japanese, illustrated an inability to comprehend the rules of international intercourse.[7]

And this changing conception of China, along with the Meiji leaders' need to fortify their domestic base by showing themselves strong abroad, prompted a rethinking in the early 1870s of Japan's relationship with all of its East Asian neighbors. One reason for Saigō's eagerness to go to Korea lay in a desire to undermine the sway that China always had held over the peninsula; so in the aftermath of the 1873 debacle, officials decided to secure trade relationships not by invasion but by combining diplomacy and moderate displays of force. When a Japanese gunboat was fired on in Korean waters in 1875, the Japanese retaliated, then sent three gunboats early the next year, accompanied by armed transport ships, to demand that Korea negotiate a commercial treaty. The Kanghwa Treaty that resulted gave Japan the very diplomatic superiority in Korea that the imperialist powers had insisted on in their treaties with Japan. It also created two decades of bitter rivalry between China and Japan in Korea.

Farther to the north, the Japanese decided now to put space between themselves and Russia, as well as to demonstrate their strength, by insisting on recognition of Japan's control of several territories beyond Hokkaido. When they secured a treaty with Russia in 1875 recognizing Japanese sovereignty over the Kuril Islands, all the way north to Kamchatka, in exchange for recognition of Russian control of the island of Sakhalin, the public was generally pleased, seeing the negotiations as a sign that Japan had won respect among the international powers.

The other territory that concerned the government lay some 500 miles south of Kyūshū, in the Ryūkyū archipelago, a region that had maintained its own semiautonomous status for centuries as a tribute state of both

China and Japan's Satsuma domain. The Dajōkan coterie in Tokyo decided at the beginning of the 1870s to assert Japanese sovereignty there. In 1872, they announced that the Ryūkyūs were a Japanese domain and that their king (*sho tai*) would serve as lord of that domain. The Western powers accepted this assertion, while China protested and the islanders mistakenly assumed that it meant merely that their tribute status with Satsuma would continue. The lack of a Chinese diplomatic mission in Japan made communication about the disagreement difficult, so the Japanese next chose a novel tack to make their intentions clear. Learning that a group of Ryūkyū islanders had been massacred in southern Taiwan following a ship accident, the Japanese government decided to send a military expedition in 1874 to punish the Taiwanese for murdering *Japanese* subjects. The episode will be discussed at length in the next chapter, since it triggered a major change in the course of Edward House's career. For now, we need merely to note that the expedition illustrates many of the forces that were coming to define Japan's national life in the first half of the 1870s.

It demonstrates, first of all, Japan's determination to control the seas and islands around itself, even if that meant using moderate force, as long as the goals were limited and success was fairly certain. It also shows that relations with China were central to the leaders' thinking. Just as in Korea, the Ryūkyū-Taiwan dispute was intended primarily as a statement to the old continental patron that Japan no longer accepted China as the Middle Kingdom. Finally, the absorption of the Ryūkyūs demonstrated the close link between domestic policies and foreign affairs. The expedition to Taiwan was intended as much to win respect for the regime at home, and to pacify those who were angry over the refusal to send troops to Korea in 1873, as it was to achieve its diplomatic ends. The influential historian of Japan's international relations, Akira Iriye, has commented that Japan's longtime struggle in Korea "was but a context in which domestic rivalries were played out."[8] He could have said the same about the move in the 1870s to clarify the nation's sovereignty over other adjacent regions. Control of a changing and confused domestic political scene was, in many ways, up for grabs at the outset of the 1870s; by the middle of the decade, it was much more solid, even if samurai malcontents were not ready to admit as much. Although domestic policies were important, the regime's successes in moving onto the international scene probably were even more important in giving it legitimacy among the populace and thus assuring its growing stability. The future might cast clouds over the direction in which these international initiatives were beginning to move Japan, but at the time few (except the Ryūkyūans, Koreans, and Chinese!) saw them as anything more than a sign of just how civilized this new member of the international community was becoming.

NOTES

1. Kido Takayoshi, October 30, 1873, after Saigō Takamori left the government; see *The Diary of Kido Takayoshi,* vol. 2, 388.

2. Cattle farming and the new Maruzen store are described in Nihon Fūzoku Gakkai, *Shiryō ga kataru Meiji no Tōkyō hyaku wa,* 29, 32; Griffis's recollections are found in Robert Rosenstone, *Mirror in the Shrine,* 115, 186; House talks of the "vast changes" in the *New York Tribune,* January 2, 1873; and the great 1872 fire is discussed in a despatch from C. O. Shepard to Hamilton Fish, April 13, 1872, in JMPH, Gaimushō Gaikōshiryōkan, vol. 3, no. 9. The shrine discontents are discussed in Nihon Fūzoku Gakkai, *Meiji no Tokyo hyaku wa,* 45–46; and the peasants' term for the Western calendar is from Peter Duus, *Modern Japan,* 2nd ed., 104.

3. The phrase, by House, is from the *New York Herald,* April 4, 1874.

4. *New York Herald,* March 20, 1874.

5. "Protection and tranquility" are discussed in the rescript abolishing the feudal domains in 1871, in Walter W. McLaren, "Japanese Government Documents," 1914, 2. The danger of colonization is from Nagai Michio and Miguel Urrutia, eds., *Meiji Ishin,* 29.

6. Penal restrictions in Peter Duus, ed., *The Japanese Discovery of America,* 169; pictures of criminals in Duus, *The Japanese Discovery,* 176; and both are from Kume Kunitake's report on the Iwakura Mission. Tokutomi's recollection is quoted in Kenneth Pyle, *The New Generation in Meiji Japan,* 83. English expressions are found in Basil Hall Chamberlain, *Japanese Things,* 137.

7. Ubukata Toshirō, "Kenpō happu to Nisshin Sensō," 88, discusses the traditional view; Ōtsuki's contrasting opinion is quoted in Donald Keene, *The Japanese Discovery of Europe,* 26.

8. In Marius Jansen, ed., *The Cambridge History of Japan,* vol. 5, *The Nineteenth Century,* 745.

6

Writing for Japan: 1873–1876

> Bullets and bayonets were then, as they have generally been, the only trustworthy propagandists of Western Civilization.
>
> —Frank Brinkley, 1883 [1]

House never dreamed that the popular Saigō would be gone from the government by the time he returned to Yokohama late in 1873. Nor could he have had any idea what an impact Saigō's departure would have on his own career, how it would turn him from a writer who admired Japan to a publicist who loved it, served it, and fought many of its battles. Once the immediate outcry over the old leader's defection had quieted down, Home Minister Ōkubo Toshimichi and House's friend Ōkuma began laying plans for the Taiwan military expedition, discussed above, as a means of placating Saigō's supporters and establishing Japan's control of the Ryūkyūs. Before the planning was done, they would decide to let House accompany the troops as the first foreign correspondent ever to cover a Japanese military mission abroad. And by the time the expedition had ended, House would be drawn deeply enough into Japanese politics and diplomacy to render the line between reporting and advocacy almost invisible.

In early November, however, the Bostonian's plans were mundane. The only passenger to get off the San Francisco–bound *Great Republic* that Saturday, he met his old teaching colleague William Elliot Griffis and headed for Tokyo, where he settled down again at the Kaisei Gakkō, planning to resume the bucolic life of reporting and teaching. The foreign residents' directory for 1874 lists him as a teacher of English at the school, along with chemistry instructor Griffis, physics teacher V. Veeder, and superintendent Verbeck. As before, writing consumed him most. He published "Carnelian: A Romance of a Sleeping Car," a two-part love story in the *Overland Monthly,* replete with his usual gibes at snobbishness. He wrote his business agent in New York about having Japanese photographs printed on special paper to go with a manuscript on Japan that he was writing "with reasonable rapidity." And he filed newspaper stories at about the same intervals as before. There was a difference, however. Although he continued for a time to write for the *Tribune,* his principal venue changed. He had struck up an acquaintance in New York with James Gordon Bennett, Jr., the hard-living financial genius whose journalism House once had derided, and soon his letters were appearing more frequently in Bennett's *New York Herald.*

There also was a difference in the tone of House's stories. He had a good deal more confidence than he once had in the stability of the government, as his accounts of the ex-samurai uprising in Saga illustrated. A March 19 story called reports of the rebellion "wildly exaggerated" and sneered at British papers in Yokohama that seemed to desire a rebel victory. "Not a single one of the inflammatory reports with which the little settlement has overflowed . . . have been confirmed," he wrote. On April 4, when the government troops had triumphed, his *Herald* story commented that "the rebel collapse was coldly received by the foreigners generally in Yokohama." Three weeks later, another of his *Herald* pieces raised the Formosa issue, with a lengthy discussion of rumors that Japan was about to send an expedition to keep "marauding tribes" there "in proper subjection." House should have known about those rumors, since he already was on his way to Taiwan himself by the time this April 7 despatch had appeared in the *Herald*'s April 28 edition.[2] Not coincidentally, his old paper, the *Tribune,* largely missed the impending conflict—an indication that Reid's decision not to meet House's financial demands cost the *Tribune* readers severely.

Before heading off for that military adventure, however, House had a domestic encounter that would prove as important to his personal life as the relationship with Ōkuma would to his professional career. It occurred at Takebashi Girls School, Japan's first government-sponsored educational institution for girls. Established early in 1872 inside the Kaisei Gakkō grounds, it became the inspiration for several of House's projects and a good deal of his writing. The school opened with about forty students between the ages of eight and fifteen and provided a broad curriculum that would have been considered inappropriate for female students in earlier eras: zoology, botany, physics, and chemistry, as well as more traditional handicrafts and a great deal of Chinese and Japanese literature. Takebashi was not for everyone. The courses were demanding, much of the instruction was in English, and students came largely from the upper reaches of the old samurai class. Education historian Usui Chizuko says that Takebashi, popularly dubbed the "school of young princesses" (*ohimesan no gakkō*), was intended "as a substitute for the foreign study stints that elite males were receiving." It also was a harbinger of things to come; for although the Ministry of Education reported that only three middle schools in the entire country accepted girls in 1874, by 1876 there were 201 such schools with 1,030 female students, and by 1879 784 with more than 2,700 girls attending. Takebashi itself had 152 students in 1876.[3]

The school's significance for House was twofold. First, it provided one of the foci of his writing. Nothing except politics and diplomacy would stir his interest more keenly across the next fifteen years than the role of women in Japanese society, and his experience with the Takebashi girls provided the initial impetus for that interest. Second, the school introduced him to the person who would serve for nearly three decades as his deepest emotional support and most important intellectual partner: Aoki Koto. A native of the Nagoya area, she was a fourteen-year-old member of the first Takebashi class when House returned from America in 1873. In a student essay, she remembered her home region as a place where "people are honest and gentle and the women never go out without their girdle." Her mother had died when she was three, before Koto had learned to walk (!), and in 1868, after the Restoration, her father, Aoki Nobutora, brought her to Tokyo where he eventually would be named a judge. Koto was a model student, hard-working and bright. Nearly a century later, her son would recount family stories of people staring as she walked to Takebashi each morning, wearing a boy's formal robe or *hakama*, carrying English books, and practicing spelling drills as she passed the fish market. She was stylish when she sat for formal photos with her classmates: the nape of her neck bare, her left hand tucked modestly into her kimono sleeve, a formal hairpiece making her look chic. Her teacher, Margaret Griffis, called Koto "the most knowledgeable and thoughtful of my students" and gave her a Bible. And she was among the honor students chosen to meet the empress during an imperial visit in November 1873.

Griffis, who seldom mentioned individual students in her journal, also noted on March 5, 1874, that Koto would be getting married the next evening, wearing a Western-style wedding dress. Marriage was not unusual for Japanese girls of that age, but Aoki loved learning too much to settle into a domestic routine, while her husband, whom House later called "a worthless scamp," apparently valued neither learning nor an intelligent spouse. At any rate, the marriage was troubled, and after perhaps a year of

This formal photograph of Aoki Koto was taken while she was a student of Margaret Griffis at Takebashi Girls School. She was later adopted by House. (From the William Elliot Griffis Collection; used by permission of the Special Collections and University Archives, Rutger University Libraries.)

"unspeakable wretchedness," the couple was divorced. Few things were more disastrous in Japan than a publicly failed marriage; upper-class women were expected to be submissive and faithful and to endure anything. The situation was so agonizing that Koto had decided to take her own life—when her former teacher, House, intervened "to lessen the griefs of a suffering girl" and "to save her from subsequent humiliation." Single, yet more settled emotionally now, ready to appreciate "the value of a child," he offered to adopt his former student. When Koto and Nobutora agreed, a relationship commenced that was as deep, loving—and, on occasion, tumultuous—as any father and daughter ever knew.[4]

During the spring of 1874, however, while Koto was just beginning to find out what a "long disease" marriage could be, House's mind was on war. On February 6, the state council decided to send soldiers to Taiwan. In early April, Ōkuma was selected to head the Bureau of Savage Affairs and Saigō Tsugumichi, younger brother of the disgruntled Takamori, was appointed to head the expedition. The operation would not take place without opposition, however. The month of April produced struggles almost as bitter as the previous autumn's controversy over Korea. For one thing, China was utterly opposed to Japanese action, even though its officials had remarked to Japanese representatives in Beijing the previous June that, although China claimed all of Taiwan, the southern regions where the "raw aborigines" or *sheng fan* had killed the Ryūkyūans were "beyond the reach" of Chinese control. For another thing, the proposed cost of the mission—500,000 yen—caused an appalled Kido Takayoshi, Ōkuma's early patron, to quit the government in anger, much as Saigō had done the previous fall.

Equally worrisome to Ōkuma and Ōkubo was a crescendo of opposition from the foreigners. The foreign press in Yokohama railed against the idea of an expedition, just as it did against every Japanese assertion of independence. On April 28, for example, the *Japan Herald* predicted failure because Japanese soldiers were "low in the scale of intelligence, deficient in political knowledge, and wanting in courage and patriotism." Even more seriously, the foreign diplomats came out in active opposition to the proposed invasion—in part because they feared that Japan would attempt to colonize southern Taiwan, in part because they worried about war between China and Japan. Harry Parkes, Great Britain's minister to Japan, asked the Japanese not to use any British ships in the expedition unless China officially concurred with the mission. He and the British minister to Beijing, Thomas Wade, then warned Britons in East Asia not to cooperate with the Japanese and officially forbade the use of British vessels. Parkes's American counterpart, John Bingham, also fought the mission, urging the foreign ministry on April 18 not to use American ships or men unless China officially agreed to the Japanese expedition.[5]

Two things made Bingham's response particularly problematic for the Japanese. First, plans for the expedition were far enough along now to trigger a new domestic explosion if they were called off. Second, Japan already had secured the American vessel *New York* and hired three Americans as military aides: Lt. Commander Douglas Cassel of the Navy, Lt. James Wasson of the Army Engineers, and the aggressive General Charles LeGendre, who as U.S. consul in Amoy had handled the similar *Rover* episode in 1867–1868. Already under contract as the foreign ministry's Taiwanese expert at $12,000 a year, LeGendre was to go along as an advisor while the other two would serve as staff officers. For a time, it appeared that Bingham's protest might actually prevent the invasion, when the Council of State decided to send Ōkubo to Nagasaki to tell the troops not to sail. By the time Ōkubo got there on May 3, however, five shiploads of soldiers already had embarked for Taiwan, and Saigō, in a response that amounted to insubordination, said that his orders had come from the emperor, not the Dajōkan. He did agree to leave LeGendre behind and to withdraw his troops once the Taiwanese had been punished.

Just what lay behind this string of events may never be known: what caused Ōkubo to arrive late, whether there was a genuine intent to call the expedition off, and whether Cassel and Wasson would have complied with Bingham's demand if they had not already sailed. What we do know is that when the ships left Nagasaki on April 27, House was aboard, along with his two American fellows. We also know that the first of the 3,000 troops arrived in southern Formosa on May 6 and that the two American staff assistants stayed until mid-summer, when they received an ultimatum from the American consul at Amoy, J. J. Henderson, "to at once withdraw from the Japanese armed expedition . . . under penalty of arrest and trial." We know too that when Saigō came to Formosa on May 22, his boat was captained by a Scotsman, and when LeGendre attempted to join Saigō early in August, long after the end of hostilities, he was arrested in Amoy by U. S. Marines operating under Henderson's instructions. And we know most of this because the mission's English-language chronicler was House, who had been promised $600 for his reports by the "*Herald* people" and quite possibly $225 a month for salary and expenses by the Japanese government. He stayed with the force for two months, through a "pandemonimic of misery and hardship," then sailed back to Tokyo to report on the diplomatic aftermath of the fighting. When the episode had ended, he wrote a 231-page narrative, *The Japanese Expedition to Formosa,* which remains the most complete English-language account of the campaign.[6]

The book narrates the story chronologically, beginning in March 1867 with the killing of the American sailors aboard the shipwrecked *Rover,* and ending in April 1875 with China's attempts to begin asserting control over southern Taiwan. The heart of the account runs from May 3, when the initial boatload of 250 soldiers arrived at the Chinese coastal city of Amoy (packed into a vessel that "could not properly accommodate one hundred"[7]), through July 16 when House returned to Nagasaki. The tone is unabashedly, though not uncritically, pro-Japanese. House accepts Japan's disputed claims to sovereignty over the Ryūkyū Islands, he reminds readers that China had refused to take administrative control over the area in question, and he accepts at face value Japan's claim to having no long-term territorial designs on Taiwan. He also is hard on Bingham, noting that the American minister's opposition to the expedition came only "after the movement had actually begun" and after he already had approved a leave of absence for Cassel to join the Japanese troops (23). At the same time, House is meticulous in marshaling facts. And he balances detailed analysis with a journalist's knack for colorful details. The story he tells is thus riveting and significant, shedding important light on a seminal event in Sino-Japanese relations and in China's approach to national defense policy.

The central narrative begins with the creation of a base camp for the 3,000 soldiers, soon to arrive, on a table-flat hilltop near the village of Sheliao (House calls it Sialiao) on Taiwan's extreme southwestern coast. The camp sat within close view of a mountainous region where eighteen aboriginal groups, none of them more than 250 in number, long had resisted all efforts at control by outsiders. It was these mountaineers, particularly a group known as the Botan,[8] who were thought to have killed the Ryūkyū islanders. Sheliao itself provided a surprisingly hospitable site for settling in. Its houses, about a dozen altogether, were made of "cemented stone and fine red brick" and had "solid and serviceable" armchairs indoors "that would not discredit a New England farm house" (36). At the back of each home was a Buddhist shrine, and scattered about conspicuously were all manner of weapons: scabbards, matchlock guns, bows and iron-tipped arrows, spears, and lances. The women and the higher-ranking men wore trousers and vests, the rest loincloths. A number of the women also wore gold and silver bracelets, earrings, and artificial hair flowers. Beyond Sheliao lay even smaller hamlets dotted with thatched-roofed mud huts, and still further away, a dense mountain jungle where the "enemy" lived.

Nothing much of a military nature happened the first week; so House was free to learn about the local, coastal people, who proved cooperative once they were told that the Japanese would pay liberally for land and assistance and that as many as 25,000 more troops might be sent if there were trouble. He described the fear he and his colleagues felt the first day when they heard gunfire and saw a procession of perhaps thirty men and women carrying weapons in the village below the camp. More shots threatened panic until they learned that it was a wedding party celebrating. The day's only unpleasant episode occurred when villagers protested against Japanese who disrobed for their baths. Later the same afternoon, House decided to go swimming. After sporting "among the fishes" awhile, he fell asleep on the bank, half-naked, only to be awakened by some water buffalo that "had stopped on their way across the river to inspect the new animal that had come among them." They were followed by inquisitive dogs, and then by a woman who asked for a coin from the pocket of his coat, lying nearby. House gave it to her, then realized he had made a mistake when she returned with "a procession of women, various in age and quality, all clearly bent upon the accumulation of silver." He refused this time, and there ensued "a highly amicable consultation for an hour, without the interchange of a single idea" (41–44).

The next few days uncovered the capitalist instinct of the local peoples. Setting out to build a forty-acre camp on the flat-topped Turtle Hill, the Japanese announced that they would pay thirty cents a day for workers. Some 400 people came from across the region, one-third of them women. A tumult broke out when the Japanese refused to pay the full thirty cents to people who worked only half a day, and the next morning a village committee demanded a raise to fifty cents a day. When the Japanese held the line at thirty cents, the workers "raged furiously . . . and bore themselves as if fresh injuries had been heaped upon them." Work came to a halt until another ship arrived that afternoon with fresh Japanese troops and workers to replace the now jobless locals (56). The villagers quickly learned what kinds of goods the Japanese needed and began visiting the camp daily with eggs, pineapples, fish, chickens, candy, bananas, and, most popular of all, "a certain strong liquor, distilled from sweet potatos [sic] . . . with results not always creditable to the purchasers" (109).

The most difficult features of the first weeks were the unstable weather and the intense heat of the region. When it rained, it did so in torrents and for half a week at a time, until the camp would turn into "a lake of no trifling depth," despite its high location. Not a bit of food could be cooked, at one point, for forty-eight hours (69–70). And then the heat would come, an "intolerable and enfeebling" heat that bred illness. "The temperature is of a withering and prostrating intensity such as I have encountered in no other place excepting, possibly, the Red Sea," he wrote. To make it worse, the troops were billeted in "close and ill-ventilated" tents, made of a kind of canvas that "actually seemed to invite the sun's rays" (53–54). And "the hard, stony paths were so heated that the glow could literally be felt through the soles of thick shoes." To avoid heat prostration, House wore nothing but pajamas, a straw hat, and straw sandals (117).

House was particularly interested in the deportment of the Japanese soldiers, now that he had a chance to watch them up close. What struck him most was the contrast between their undisciplined jocularity off-duty and their bravery on. In the camp, fun and games were the rule, quarrels unheard of. The men, few of them more than twenty-five years old, drank great quantities of beer and spirits, ate extravagantly, bathed when they felt like it, discarded "refuse and offal" wantonly, and spent the evenings in wrestling and other sports. "A merrier little army never made day and night lively with jests and songs" (34, 96). Once they were called into action, however, "the instinct of implicit obedience" appeared. On trek, they followed orders; they showed self-control; and they were brave, sometimes beyond wisdom. The Japanese military man, House said, "is far from a finished soldier, according to our strict notions of routine and drill"; he also was capable of strategic blunders. But "in his self-denying patience and his ready, hearty, willing spirit, he is often a hero even more than in the reckless daring of his actions" (34, 127).

All was not jollity the early camp days, however. The soldiers represented the vanguard of Japan's first foreign military excursion in almost 300 years, and there were immediate contacts with the men from the mountains, some of them diplomatic, others violent. The Sheliao headman, Miya, helped the Japanese set up a May 15 meeting at the edge of the mountains between the expedition heads, Cassel, and four aboriginal leaders. The mountaineers' spokesperson, named Isa, chewed betel nuts and wore heavy steel plates in his ear lobes, but struck House with his "vigorous, resolute and intrepid" demeanor and his "tall and muscular" stature. His eyes, almost colorless, were "remarkable and quite exceptional." Communication was difficult, since every sentence had to be translated four ways: from the original language to Chinese, to English, to Japanese—and vice versa. As a result, little was accomplished in the initial meeting beyond establishing contact, but the tone was congenial, and the talks ended with a pig feast (62–67).

One of the more important bits of information that House gleaned in the first days was that there were fewer "savages" than their reputation abroad had suggested. The largest of the eighteen groups, the Botan, numbered only 250 men, while the smallest, the Koalut, who had murdered the *Rover* crew, had only fifty, and the total male population of the region was just 2,360. Even this figure House calculated to be an exaggeration, so the number available for fighting was no more than 400 (105–06).[9] The small numbers did not, however, make the Botan less frightening to the Japanese soldiers, particularly after several run-ins with armed villagers. Despite constant warnings not to stray from the camp, several soldiers decided on Sunday, the 17th, to explore a nearby village whose roofs were visible above the bushes. They wandered among the huts, attracting no apparent attention, then left. As they were returning to camp, however, shots rang out, and one was killed. The rest of the group fled, and when an official party came back, they found the fallen comrade's body naked and headless. Two days later, Admiral Akamatsu

Noriyoshi returned from a surveying cruise along the coast to report that his "boats had been fired upon by savage warriors who were believed to belong to the Koalut country" (69). And on the following Thursday, an official party of a dozen men engaged in the expedition's first exchange of fire. After searching the area of Sunday's shooting and finding nothing, they headed for another village two miles beyond. En route, they encountered a group of Botan men who opened fire. A battle ensued, leaving two Japanese injured and a villager dead. The Botan quickly vanished into the jungle, however, and the Japanese returned to camp angry and frustrated.

The next day, May 22, General Saigō arrived in Sheliao, with 1,500 more men, to launch the formal expedition. He was too late, however, to take part in the expedition's decisive battle. On that very morning, another unplanned encounter had resulted in a spectacular fight that ended the Botan resistance before a serious war even started. The incident, called the Battle of Stone Gate (*sekimon* in Japanese, *shimen* in Chinese), would take its place in the lore of Japan's dramatic military engagements. Though neither House nor the majority of the Japanese troops were on location when the encounter took place, Saigō took him along when he and his squadron visited the scene ten days later, and House's account of what happened is the dramatic highlight of *The Japanese Expedition.*

Two companies of men had set out from the base camp on Friday morning, May 22, to investigate the area where Thursday's altercation had occurred. Once they reached the spot, they decided to press forward over the mountain trail along which the tribesmen had vanished. Soon, they found themselves at a treacherous pass filled by a thirty-foot-wide stream, with "rocky acclivities" stretching up "at sharp angles, and often perpendicularly," 500 feet high on the north side and 450 on the south. The stream dashed "in foam over rough rocks through the greater length of the pass" and had only one fordable, waist-deep section (119). It was behind this pass that the Botan lived, secure in the impregnability of their "stone gate." And it was here, at the pass, that the Japanese met their first enemy force, seventy men strong. The Japanese had twice that many men themselves, but only forty in a position to fight.

When two dozen unsuspecting Japanese waded toward the pass, looking for a place to ford, the invisible Botan began firing from behind a line of boulders, killing two or three and wounding a dozen others. The Japanese scrambled for cover behind rocks in the river, then fired back. Others entered the pass, and the process was repeated. Sensing an impossible situation, the commanding officer ordered a retreat, but his men, "now thoroughly aroused," ignored him. "Thus irregularly," reported House, "and with no directions except those suggested by their own minds to the participators, the contest went on for nearly an hour, the Japanese steadily, though very slowly, getting nearer their opponents."[10] Finally, the commander ordered several men to scale the rocks on the north. It was a preposterous command; from the bottom, large areas of the cliffs "looked like sections of smooth and polished stone, affording no hold for feet or hand." But using "some insect-like property of adhesion," the troops gradually moved upward, at last springing "upon the topmost ledge with gestures of triumph and shouts" that "vigorously echoed" in the valley. Seeing them, the Botan "broke in a body and made for the riverbanks," leaving behind sixteen mortally wounded fellows, including the chief's son. Another fourteen, the chief among them, died later. Japanese fatalities numbered seven, the wounded thirty. "A complete understanding of the difficulties" of the battle could not be conveyed with words, said House. When he retraced the soldiers' route ten days later, he began to wade across the stream and quickly found himself "in water so deep and so rapid that no strength of mine could stem it." Looking up, he saw an officer heading toward him, "wearing nothing but a benevolent smile." The man picked him up, handed him to another soldier, who handed him to a third, "and so following" until he was on firm ground. "The incident was almost too slight to be worth narrating," House wrote, "but I cannot look upon anything as altogether trifling that helps to illustrate the thoughtful kindliness of these instinctively warm-hearted people" (124–25). The Botan, under attack by outsiders in their own land, might not have described the Japanese troops quite that way.[11]

After the Stone Gate encounter, the Japanese expedition met no other serious resistance. But Saigō's mission was not finished: the Botan had not been punished yet, nor had they been pacified. On May 25, the expedition leaders met again with the friendly Kaolut leader, Isa, who was rewarded with swords, silk, woolens, cottons, and "a few tubs of Japanese 'sake'" for promising to see that the Botan were "all extirpated, together with their unruly neighbors" (98). Then the next week, on June 1, Saigō started his troops out on the mopping-up mission, accompanied by House. Even before they reached Stone Gate, they came upon the mass grave of the murdered Ryūkyūans at the edge of a village occupied by Chinese descendants. Puzzled about finding the grave outside the Botan territory and miles away from the coast, they were told that the Botan had mistaken the shipwrecked islanders for native Chinese and brought them here for a ransom. When the villagers refused to pay, the Botan had killed the castaways. House expressed doubt about the story but thought it had a ring of truth.

Next, the troops marched into the Botan region, burning villages, killing stragglers who had not fled into the jungles, and setting up patrols to guard the region. The trek took the soldiers through unmapped territory,[12] across dozens of streams, up steep mountainsides, along slippery ledges, and over tangled mounds of fallen trees that had been piled up to block their progress. It also made them subject to occasional gunfire from invisible mountaineers. When night fell after the first day of the operation, neither a campsite nor food could be found, so the famished men simply dropped wherever they could find a spot. When an officer produced two cigars for diversion, Ned regretted that he was not a smoker. Later in the week, when a wounded man being carried by soldiers offered House his own shoes, the leg-weary reporter said he felt humbled. And when Saigō offered him a palanquin, he said no, commenting: "In truth I was hardly able to stand, but I could not acknowledge myself beaten." He did not decline that night, however, when offered "a bundle of biscuits and some claret" (136).

By June 4, the extirpation was complete and the troops returned to Sheliao. On June 9, Saigō had another meeting with the cooperative non-Botan chiefs, who agreed after considerable negotiation to allow Japan to establish another base on the eastern coast as a "point of departure against the hostile tribes" in the case of future difficulties (142). On June 11, the base was set up, followed by an impromptu banquet hosted by the chiefs, complete with vast quantities of a potent, heated liquor that tasted like "very inferior Irish whiskey." The normally "stern and unbending" Isa got drunk that night and was last seen "trying to walk through a fishing net that hung in his way" (149). The next day, June 12, a telegram to Tokyo "announced the completion of the subjugation of southern Formosa."[13] And four days after that, two men sailed for Beijing to inform Chinese officials about what had happened.

It was not yet time, however, for the expedition to return to Japan. From the beginning, Japan's major diplomatic dispute had been with China, partly over which nation was sovereign over the Ryūkyūs, partly over whether Japan had a right to invade southern Formosa. Until that issue was settled, the troops would remain. As a result, the next months saw the camp settle into a "prolonged stagnation." Some efforts were made to bring "civilization" to the coastal villages. Saigō tried to start an experimental farm with new varieties of plants; he also sent doctors into the local villages, in what House called "the most effectual appeal to barbarian confidence all over the world"; and he proposed setting up schools. Squadrons also were sent out regularly to inspect the pacified mountain. And the village chiefs put on more feasts. But mostly there was monotony. "We were reduced to the feeblest expedients for sustaining mutual interests," House reported. "Fancy making the experiment of chewing betel-nut for absolute want of anything else to do. I tried it, on one occasion, for half an hour or more, without a result worth mentioning . . . unless it may be in the flow of red saliva which it promotes" (154–57).

The one significant diversion for the top officers was the arrival of Chinese diplomats on June 21 to begin negotiating an end to the expedition. The talks were difficult, with the Chinese representative Pan Wi maintaining that since "the legitimate sway of China extended over all Formosa," Japan's actions had been illegal. Saigō goaded him "into a rage" by accusing the Chinese of "duplicity" in pretending that they had always claimed authority over southern Taiwan. By the 25th, however, the two sides had agreed to recommend to their governments that China would reimburse Japan for the cost of the expedition and that it would police southern Taiwan in order to prevent "outrages upon strangers," while Japan would withdraw its troops as soon as China had met those promises (164–69). Eleven days later, on July 6, House left Sheliao, eager to send home detailed news of all that had happened.

From Amoy, the *Herald* reporter sent the following cable on July 9: "The Japanese war operations are virtually ended. A conference has been held at Formosa. China agrees to pay the expenses of the expedition, and guarantees the safety of foreigners. Japan accepts and retires." Its appearance the following day created a sensation in America. As in the *Maria Luz* case two years before, few Westerners believed the Japanese capable either of a quick victory or of persuading China to sign such an agreement. Doubts about the settlement persisted throughout the fall. But a series of multicolumn stories by House in the *Herald* that summer, most of which served as the core of his book, convinced all but the most skeptical of the completeness of the victory—and the competence of Japanese soldiers. When negotiations in Beijing that fall resulted in a Chinese admission that the expedition was "a just and rightful proceeding" and pledged China to pay half a million taels in compensation once Japan had withdrawn her troops (with 100,000 taels to go to the survivors of the murdered Ryūkyūans), House probably had a right to gloat.[14] Ever the partisan, he said Japan "had done a good work . . . for the whole community of nations," then added:

> Twice within the past three years Japan had rendered a service to humanity, in defiance of the combined and threatening hostility of the authorized delegates from almost every Power that holds relations with its government. In 1872, it fought the fight against the coolie trade so gallantly that the infamy of that barbarous traffic no longer darkens the earth. And now it had cleared the highway of the Pacific of a danger and a dread which had hung over it for a quarter of a century. Thanks to Japan . . . there would at least be no more "rover" massacres. (184–85)

Historians' views of the episode have been more mixed. Most scholars are far less sanguine about Japan's motives: critical of the arbitrary assertion of control of the Ryūkyūs, prone to focus on the role of domestic politics in prompting the decision to send troops, and unwilling to accept

Japan's claims that it had no colonial designs. Most historical accounts also make the difficult diplomatic talks more central to the narrative than House does, particularly the struggles over issues of sovereignty and responsibility in Taiwan and the Ryūkyūs. In the latter case, Chinese officials are held to have blundered, failing to grasp the fact that the final agreement implicitly recognized Japanese suzerainty in the Ryūkyūs. On the matter of control in southern Taiwan, historians see China's belated admission that sovereignty entailed the acceptance of administrative responsibility as marking a monumental shift in its broader approach to international affairs. The new Taiwanese situation forced China to shift its defense priorities away from the interior and toward the coastal regions, and it led the Chinese to regard Japan, for the first time, as a serious military and political threat. The historians also have observed a good deal more complexity in Japan's domestic reactions to the expedition than House's account reveals: widespread criticism over the cost of the mission (3.5 million yen), and enough anger about the meagerness of the indemnity that Ōkubo decided to have the troops return quietly to Nagasaki rather than bringing them to Tokyo for a grand reception.[15]

If House's perspective was biased, however, the facts he conveyed were unassailable, and even the arguments, which demanded no little courage since they defied the international community's common wisdom, were powerfully made. Japan, he showed, had taken on an international project in the face of active opposition from the strongest Western powers and triumphed. No matter how one evaluated the rightness or wrongness of the expedition, Japan had played the imperialist game successfully, and in so doing had changed Asia's status quo. One student of the press sees the episode as a "watershed in the image of Japan conveyed by the foreign newspapers."[16] From this point on, he says, "Both the country itself and its people had to be taken very much more seriously." The important thing to House was that this underdog nation, with whose causes he was coming to identify, had demonstrated that Asians need not always bend to the imperialist powers. House applied what he thought of as the highest values of the day—equal application of international law to all countries, protection of international waters from terrorist attacks, and punishment of those who murdered the innocent—and was convinced that Japan had acted nobly.

When House returned to Tokyo, he continued to cover Japanese news for the American press, but the tone of his work changed. He spent more time now advocating Japan's case directly (though never uncritically), and he did so more often through nonjournalistic media. Just why he moved in this direction is not wholly clear from the documents available. We know that he continued to interact intimately with Ōkuma, sometimes at public functions, often at work, sometimes at parties at House's Tokyo residence. We also know that he became a soul mate of foreign ministry advisor LeGendre, who had pushed hard for Japan to colonize Taiwan. And it is likely, though I have not found documentation to prove it, that House was paid for the materials that he wrote.[17] The most important factor in House's new position, however, lay in his own intellectual and emotional evolution. He had loved Japan from the moment of his arrival, defending it against the barbs of other foreign journalists. He also had a lifelong habit of fighting for underdogs, a label that fit Japan's experience with the imperialist powers (though hardly with China and Taiwan!). Four years of interacting with Japanese officials, enjoying the Japanese lifestyle, admiring the government's handling of crises, and resenting Japan's treatment by the European powers: all of these had made him more and more a partisan. Now, two months of living with Japanese soldiers in a tropical camp had clinched his emotional attachment to this new homeland. He would continue to write as an American patriot; that will be abundantly clear in the chapters that follow. But by the time he arrived back in Tokyo in July 1874, he had become Japan's champion, in heart as well as in the works he produced.

After finishing his manuscript on the expedition, he turned to accounts of two 1860s episodes in which Japan had received short shrift from the imperialist powers. The first, titled *The Kagoshima Affair: A Chapter of Japanese History*, was intended to correct a distorted historical record. The episode had been precipitated on September 14, 1862, when retainers of the lord of Satsuma, Saigō's home domain, fatally stabbed the British merchant Charles Richardson for not showing proper respect when he encountered their lord on the Tōkaidō, Japan's most important highway. England demanded an apology, execution of the assassins, a 100,000-pound indemnity from the Tokugawa government, and another 25,000 pounds from Satsuma. Though the *bakufu* agreed to the demands, it could not force Satsuma to do the same, and when the killers remained free and the 25,000 pounds unpaid the following August, seven British ships bombarded Satsuma's capital city of Kagoshima, inflicting massive damage. The local forces fired back, forcing Britain to withdraw, but in December Satsuma agreed to meet the British demands.

The general telling of this story in Western histories depicted the Satsuma leader, Shimazu Saburō, as a chauvinist out to "immolate the Europeans"; Richardson as an innocent victim; and Great Britain as an aggrieved party, seeking recompense for a heinous deed. The British diplomat Ernest Satow constructed a typical narrative, claiming that "a most barbarous murder was committed on a Shanghai merchant named Richardson." He showed Richardson and his men "wheeling their horses in obedience" when the Satsuma procession ordered them to turn back and talked about "poor Richardson" being "hacked at . . . with their sharp-edged heavy swords."

He said the terrified foreign community in Yokohama would have lynched Shimazu if British diplomats had not intervened. That account, wrote House, fit the "substance of the original event like a sort of comet's tail of confused and disconnected particles." He showed that Lord Shimazu actually had tried hard to avoid altercations, that Richardson had provoked the assault, and that Great Britain's "immoderate and excessive" response "was not an endeavor to establish . . . sound principles of civilization" but "a sordid intrigue for the benefit of British Trade."

House's narrative, although polemical in tone, is persuasive, based on a careful reconstruction of the episode and meticulous use of sources, particularly American and British diplomatic records. His attempt to show that Richardson was hardly an innocent victim illustrates his approach. After several pages of depicting the lengths to which Shimazu went to avoid confrontation with the foreigners, he turns to Richardson, noting that the fourteen-year resident of China had "gained a certain notoriety for violence in dealing with the inhabitants" there and that he was contemptuous of Japanese customs. Then House explains the Japanese custom whereby everyone, official and peasant alike, was expected to move to the roadside and dismount when "a dignitary of high station" rode by, and notes that "most visitors in strange lands recognize the expedience . . . of conforming to the established public customs." Richardson, by contrast, ignored all of this when the Satsuma procession approached and insisted that his four-person company stay on the road, two abreast. It was this refusal to shift to a single column at the edge of the road that provoked the lord's retainers. They would have overlooked the arrogance of not dismounting, House explains, but to refuse even to get off the roadway was beyond forgiveness. According to the survivors' depositions, one of Richardson's companions begged him to turn aside when he saw the retainers' mounting anger; another shouted, "For God's sake, let us have no row." But Richardson retorted: "Let me alone; I have lived in China fourteen years, and know how to manage these people." "A moment later," says House, "the blow fell."

House does not exonerate the Japanese, nor does he suggest that Richardson's attackers should have escaped punishment. He argues rather that the Satsuma men were provoked by a flagrant disregard of Japanese custom and that error-laden British accounts of the incident exaggerated both the victim's innocence and the attackers' crimes in order to justify their nation's harsh retaliation. The purpose of the heavy penalty demanded by Great Britain, he contends, was not to seek justice but to improve England's commercial position in East Asia. "The perpetual cry is money, more money, forever money. . . . To extend her trade, under conditions prosperous to herself and ruinous to Japan, is now the chief if not the only object of her efforts."[18]

House's other 1875 booklet, *The Simonoseki Affair,*[19] also sought to correct an inaccurate narrative but went further, urging the United States to make monetary amends for its role in perpetrating injustice. House's hope, which he said was "most unlikely" to be realized,[20] was that the U.S. Congress would return America's portion of a $3 million indemnity paid by Japan after the western tip of Honshū island was bombarded by Western ships in 1864. As in the Kagoshima document, he began by pointing out what he took to be errors in standard accounts of the event, but this time, instead of simply analyzing each error, he took readers through the episode chronologically, constructing a lawyerly account that was as tortuous to read as it was damning for the accepted version of events. He worried that even a restoration of the indemnity would be ineffectual, since so much damage already had been done to Japan's standing in the international world. "The pound of flesh has been hewn away, and many drops of blood have fallen with it. . . . What art could hide the ineffaceable scars left by years of humiliation and oppression?" (33).

The booklet began with a defense of Japan's claim to sovereignty over the Inland Sea, based on international law, and with an explanation of how the country's domestic troubles in 1863 made it difficult for the Tokugawa government to control a contentious domain like Chōshū, which governed Shimonoseki, the western entrance to that sea. Then House described three episodes in June and July of that year, in which ships from France, the United States, and the Netherlands drew Chōshū fire by sailing into Shimonoseki harbor. He also described the Western powers' retaliation, which inflicted major damage in terms of property and life, and argued that: 1) the Western ships' entry into the Shimonoseki straits was illegal under the Western treaties with Japan; 2) any losses suffered by the Westerners were more than redressed by the punishment meted out at the time; and 3) no British ship was involved in the incidents, despite the wide impression "that English craft suffered equally with those of the three other countries" (11).

This is followed by an account of British minister Rutherford B. Alcock taking the lead early in 1864 in putting together a *four*-nation expedition to punish Japan for the 1863 shellings—despite Britain's lack of involvement the previous fall. "Perhaps it is too much to expect that Ministers in the East, when pursuing a cherished design, should be trammeled by mere considerations of fact," House wrote (15). And again: "He bore himself not as a minister of peace and goodwill to a harrassed, distressed, and tottering government, but as a messenger of wrath and vengeance" (16). House explained that Foreign Minister Earl Russell specifically forbade the use of British force against Japan, writing to Alcock on July 26: "Her Majesty's Government positively enjoin [sic] you not to undertake any military operation whatever in the interior of Japan" (16). But the prohibition arrived in Tokyo too late to forestall a four-power squadron, which on September 5 began a three-day attack on Shimonoseki. Negotiations afterward required that Japan split an "exorbitant" $3 million indemnity evenly among the four nations.

What was the justification for this British-led "retaliation," when retribution already had been meted out in 1863? According to House, there was a single motive. As in the Kagoshima affair, the bottom line was commercial. He quoted documents in which the foreign diplomats agreed to set the indemnity higher than Japan's "ability to pay" (and above the losses their ships had sustained) as a negotiating tool to pressure Japan to open another port to trade (26). The Japanese officials, however, were worried more about the threat of domestic opposition to opening additional ports than about the massive indemnity, so they agreed to the $3 million. They sued several times during the next decade for postponement of payment installments, but in 1874, when the British, French, and Dutch pushed hard for an immediate opening of the whole country to trade and foreign residence, the Japanese decided to pay the final portion and end the episode.

"The history of the Simonoseki Affair ends here," House concluded (33). But he was not ready to drop the issues that surrounded it. He was distressed at the failure of a move in Washington to write off America's portion of the final installment, despite support from Bingham and many members of Congress. Even before the Formosan expedition, his *Herald* articles had begun demanding restitution for the Shimonoseki fiasco.[21] And within months of the appearance of his new booklet, he would launch a new crusade for the United States to return its entire share of the indemnity—with interest. He would write articles; he would lobby influential friends along the eastern seaboard; and when a movement got underway in Washington to return the indemnity with a stipulation that it be used for education, he would insist that America had no right to attach strings to money obtained illegally. He even would make a secret diplomatic trip to Washington to lobby for its return.

All of that activity constitutes a story for later, though. When his booklet appeared in mid-1875, he appeared discouraged. The work itself may have "brimmed with an intense belief in justice and love of Japan," as a Japanese scholar says. But just then prospects looked dim. The previous year's triumph in Taiwan had left him temporarily exhilarated, convinced that Japan would win international respect. But reflection a year later on how little really had changed in the way the Europeans treated Asians left him muttering about a "diplomacy which rests on a solid substratum of force." Justice in an imperialist world seemed far off. And once more his own career had plateaued. Teaching lacked the sense of influence that writing provided; yet neither the *Herald* nor the *Tribune* had agreed to his demands for a *regular* foreign correspondent's contract. House was not one to brood long, however. Gloom goaded him to search for fresh outlets. So he began working on several schemes, and when the chance came a year later to begin publishing a newspaper, to commence writing weekly articles and editorials about Japan, he decided to take the biggest leap of his life. At forty-one, he would become an editor.[22]

NOTES

1. *Japan Weekly Mail* essay, February 24, 1883; "the" was misspelled as "they" in the original.

2. See Edward H. House, "Carnelian: A Romance of a Sleeping Car, in Two Parts," *Overland Monthly and Outwest Magazine* 12, nos. 6–7 (June 1874): 501–10, and 13, no. 1 (July 1874): 9–17. His business affairs are discussed in House to Elisha Bliss, November 25, 1873, EHC, University of Virginia. The House contributions that did appear in the *Tribune* tended to be almost identical to those in the *Herald*.

3. Usui Chizuko, *Joshi kyōiku no kindai to sendai*, 191. The school's name was changed to Tokyo Jogakkō toward the end of 1872; it became a forerunner of the high school of Ochanomizu Joshi Daigaku. General school data come from Shiga Tadashi, *Nihon joshi kyōiku shi*, 336. Useful information on the school also is found in Takase Sōtarō, *Kyōritsu Joshi Gakuen nanajūnen shi*, 7; and Monbushō, *Gakusei hyakunen shi*, 212–14. One Takebashi student was Taga (later Hatoyama) Haruko, who became a prominent educator and mother of the prime minister Hatoyama Ichirō; see Sally A. Hastings, "Hatoyama Haruko," in Anne Walthall, ed., *Human Tradition in Modern Japan*, 83.

4. Aoki Koto's recollections come from her student essay, "The Story of My Life," June 20, 1874, WEG, Rutgers University; the tales of her walks to school were recounted to the author by her son Kuroda Masao, in a Tokyo interview, June 17, 1971; and Margaret Griffis's journal entries and the discussion of suicide are found in Henshū Iinkai, ed., *Za yatoi*, 144. The empress's visit, recounted in *Shimbun zasshi*, no. 175, in Nakayama Yasuaki, ed., *Shimbun shūsei Meiji hennen shi*, vol. 2, 93, was called to my attention by Takashima Mariko. House's recollection of Koto's "griefs" is recounted in his letter to Edmund Clarence Stedman, May 28, 1883, ECS, Columbia University. Adoption of adult children has a long tradition in Japan, though typically only males were adopted in order to carry on a family name; I have found no records to determine whether House made the adoption official through legal action. "Worthless scamp," "unspeakable wretchedness," and "save her from" are in House to Henry Villard, May 20, 1897, HVP, Harvard University. I have not found records to ascertain Koto's birthdate, either. Some secondary sources give 1857, but House said Koto was married at age fourteen (which means that she likely would have been born in 1859), and family recollections list her birth as 1859 (see Kuroda Hatsuko, *Ikiiki kyūjūsai no seikatsu jutsu*, 98); I have thus opted for 1859 as the most likely year.

5. "Long disease" is House's phrase for a traditional Japanese marriage, in "The Women of Japan," *Tokio Times*, November 29, 1879. China's reference to barbarians

is cited in Grace Fox, *Britain and Japan,* 287; Japan's plans for colonization are discussed in Robert Eskildsen, "Of Civilization and Savages," (2002): 396–97; as well as in Leonard Gordon, "Japan's Abortive Colonial Adventure in Taiwan, 1874," (1965): 173; and one of the best overall treatments of China's attitude is in Chang Lung-chih, "To Open up the Mountains and Pacify the Savages," 6–12. The evaluation of the Yokohama press is found in Olavi Fält, *The Clash of Interests,* 111–42, especially 115. An indication of how worried the government was about the foreign press's attitudes is given in the twenty-three volumes of translations into Japanese of the Yokohama papers' articles on the expedition found in the Ōkuma papers at Waseda University (OM, A125).

6. For Henderson's ultimatum, see House, *The Japanese Expedition to Formosa,* 273. LeGendre's arrest is described in cables from LeGendre to Ōkuma Shigenobu, August 6, 7, 1874, in Charles LeGendre Papers, Library of Congress. A full year after the episode, on April 7, 1875, Ōkuma wrote LeGendre, promising two months' salary plus $400 as a present of thanks to both Cassel and Wasson; see LeGendre Papers, Library of Congress. One Japanese reporter, Kishida Ginkō of *Tokyo Nichi Nichi Shimbun,* also accompanied the expedition. House described his promise of payment by the *Herald* in a letter to Mark Twain, November 13, 1874, MTP, University of California. He may have received compensation from the Japanese government too: on April 2, 1874, Saigō authorized LeGendre to "employ a foreign secretary during the expedition to Formosa" at a monthly salary of $150, plus $75 expenses; see LeGendre Papers, Library of Congress. Surviving records do not make it clear whether or not this sum underwrote the work that House did, but the chances are that it did since LeGendre often urged that House's skills be employed to win favor for the Japanese government, a fact that will be discussed in chapter 8. The historian Ōtani Tadashi ("Edowādo Hawādo Hausu senkō," *Senō Hōgaku Ronshū,* September 24, 1988, 243) supports the view that House was paid. The other lengthy English-language report on the expedition, James W. Davidson, *The Island of Formosa,* 122–69, is almost wholly "constructed from [House's] narrative," 122.

7. House, *Japanese Expedition,* 22. Subsequent quotations from this book are given in parentheses in the body of the text.

8. Romanizations for the group vary, with Mudan being the standard *pinyin* rendering today. I have chosen to use Botan, however, because scholars from the region say that it most closely approximates the pronunciation used by the group itself.

9. The figures were put together after extensive interviews with tribesmen by Douglas Cassel. They are given also, with comments on the "character" of each tribe, in James R. Wasson, *Report on Formosan Expedition,* Tokio, 1875, 101, in Charles LeGendre Papers, Library of Congress.

10. "Thoroughly aroused" is from Wasson, *Report,* 50. Other quotes about the Stone Gate battle are from House, *Japanese Expedition,* 119–25. Wasson's report agrees almost wholly with House's account, except that he reported one and a half or two hours of fighting before the cliffs were scaled. Like House, he was not with the troops at time of the battle.

11. Tokutomi Sohō retold this incident years later as an example of the singular tenacity House repeatedly showed in his approach to journalism; see his "Hausu sensei no omoide," 112–13.

12. The only map of the region of any authenticity at the time was a rough one drawn up by LeGendre after the *Rover* incident six years earlier. House himself prepared another map, based partly on LeGendre's, in writing his book. See *Japanese Expedition,* 114–115.

13. *Tokei Journal,* June 20, 1874, cited in Fox, *Britain and Japan,* 297.

14. Long stories about the Formosa expedition appeared in the *Herald* on June 24, 1874, and August 17, 19, and 20, 1874. Shorter items and editorials were run on June 24 and 28, July 10 and 12, and August 9, 19, and 25, 1874. The terms of the October 31, 1874, agreement concluding the affair are translated in House, *Japanese Expedition,* 204–06.

15. The total cost of the expedition is from Davidson, 167. The results of the negotiations on China are discussed in Chang, 27–29.

16. Fält, *Clash of Interests,* 368.

17. Examples of social invitations back and forth between the two men are found in June 12 and 15, 1875, letters between House and Ōkuma: OM A4410, Waseda University. LeGendre's views on colonization are discussed in Eskildsen, 396–97; House's continuing LeGendre connection will be discussed in chapter 8.

18. For "immolate," see House, *The Kagoshima Affair,* 14. Satow's account is found in *A Diplomat in Japan,* 51–52. House's other comments are in *Kagoshima Affair:* 2–3 (overall appraisal of errors), 14–17 (Richardson's behavior), and 35 (British goals).

19. The standard romanization is Shimonoseki; House, however, used Simonoseki until his later years.

20. House, *The Simonoseki Affair,* 33. Subsequent quotations from this booklet will be indicated in parentheses in the text.

21. See, for example, his article in the *New York Herald,* April 4, 1874, describing the "whole Simonoseki affair" as "a movement solely for the purpose of exacting commercial concessions."

22. "Belief in justice," Nakamura Shōmi, "Beikoku no Shimonoseki shōkin hensen ron ni tsuite," 71; and "substratum of force," House, *Simonoseki Affair,* 33.

7

Japan, 1876–1881: Growing Pains

> The orderly movement of the past has been awaiting this day. . . . It is time to convene a convention and adopt a constitution.
>
> —*Tokyo Nichi Nichi Shimbun,* March 17, 1880

Edward House had barely taken up his new job as an editor in January 1877 when rumors from southern Kyūshū began inundating Tokyo. An "outbreak of some magnitude" had occurred; that much everyone knew. But there were endless whisperings about the nature of the uprising, particularly about who was behind it. Some gossipers said that Saigō Takamori was involved, but most regarded that idea as unthinkable; Saigō might have resigned from the government in a fit of indignation three and a half years ago, but he was too loyal to Japan, too intimate with the country's leaders, to head a rebellion. "Saigo is certainly not a participator," wrote House in his new paper, the *Tokio Times,* reflecting the established view.[1] He was wrong, however. Just two weeks later, the *Times* was reporting that Saigō had been stripped of his official ranks. He had given his full support to what would become modern Japan's largest, and last, military insurrection, a war known in Western history books as the Satsuma Rebellion and in the Japanese accounts as the Seinan Sensō or War of the Southwest.

The rebellion was both centerpiece and symbol of the years from 1876 to 1881, a time when growing pains wracked the new body politic, even as the government's responses removed any doubt that the Meiji administrative structure was here to stay. The period's most obvious problem was what to do about the two million ex-samurai, called *shizoku,* whose old-fashioned attitudes proved a frequent obstacle to the official modernizing policies. One of the most serious difficulties posed by the old warriors was economic. They were expensive. For centuries, all samurai had lived off government stipends in return for running the country. But the Restoration in 1868 had changed the structure; government was no longer based on status, no longer dependent on samurai manpower. The stipends, however, had continued, forcing an outlay of millions of yen annually to men who no longer had any particular public function. Each year in the early 1870s, the government spent a full quarter of its income on these stipends.

The leadership's consensus solution was to abolish the *shizoku* class, a process begun in 1871 with regulations allowing samurai to give up their special hairdos and stop wearing swords. Over the next five years, decree after decree gradually blurred the status distinctions. Commoners were allowed to take surnames, their daughters were permitted to marry into samurai families, and the *shizoku* right to kill commoners for showing disrespect was abolished. When the Council of State in 1873 offered cash-strapped samurai a one-time, final payment equivalent to several years' stipends, about a third of them took the offer. But the majority of the stipends continued, pushing the government toward financial disaster. The culmination of these acts came in 1876, when sword wearing was banned and stipends were abolished by fiat. The blow was softened by a large final payment in government bonds, like that others had received in 1873, but for most of the old warriors the impact was crushing. It was a costly move for the government, too, requiring nearly 175 million yen—almost triple the annual government budget—to pay off some 310,000 families. No one doubted, however, that the short-term expense would pay off in the long run.

Most worrisome to the officials was the question of how the eradication of samurai status would affect the country politically. For the samurai themselves, the 1876 decrees hit at both the symbolic level, undermining their prestige, and the pocketbook, since few knew anything about working for wages. The upper- and middle-level *shizoku* saw their yearly income levels drop between 47 and 74 percent, while the poorer experienced annual income losses of up to 98 percent.[2] An 1883 study in Hiroshima found more than half of the former samurai now living in poverty. The result was a season of serious discontent. In three southwestern provinces—Hagi, Kumamoto, and Fukuoka—October of 1876 brought uprisings and scores of deaths. And the following January the Satsuma Rebellion broke out, plunging Japan into a nine-month war that would involve more than 80,000 troops, result in 16,000 casualties (including 6,000 deaths) on the government side alone, and cost 42 million yen—four-fifths of the government's annual budget.

The war was instigated by Saigō's followers, who had congregated in a network of *shigakkō* or "private academies" across southern Kyūshū after he left the government in 1873. When they heard that government officials were going to remove a weapons deposit from Kagoshima, the Satsuma capital, they seized the weapons themselves and rose in revolt. Saigō himself actually had been cool toward the idea of rebellion, but now, according to his biographer, "personal loyalty to his provincial countrymen proved stronger than his sense of abstract loyalty to the government," and he took the leadership of the 22,000 rebels. Facing him on the government side was the commoner-based army of Yamagata Aritomo, one of Saigō's closest friends before the Korean crisis. The fighting focused first on the rebel castle at Kumamoto, where government forces held out for fifty days before breaking the rebel siege. Then it raged for months across the southern island, until the government's superior numbers, as well as the "strong showing of its green conscripts," finally destroyed Saigō's stand. On September 24, the old warrior committed suicide on the battlefield. When Yamagata was given Saigō's head, he reportedly had aides wash it, then said: "Alas, your face looks serene. For your sake I have not been at ease for half a year. Now I am at peace." And it was a peace that would last. There would be individual acts of violence—the May 1878 assassination of Ōkubo Toshimichi, for example—but never again would an armed *shizoku* rebellion threaten the government. The opposition henceforth would make its case on the speakers' hustings or, eventually, at the ballot box.[3]

The difficulties of the Satsuma Rebellion were intensified by the country's financial condition. When the Meiji officials took power, they inherited a disunified, agrarian economy that had only "isolated islands of modernity." The Japanese people were well educated, and there were national markets, but 60 percent of all production was in agriculture, and the feudal domains' combined foreign debts totaled 10 million yen. Convinced that Japan could not resist the imperialist threat without a modern economy, the leaders threw their energy into commercial and industrial development. Under the guidance of Ōkubo and Finance Minister Ōkuma, the government drew up an efficient land tax system, designed a budget process, and devised unified currency and banking structures. It also built railroads and telegraph lines, created a postal system, supported a quasi-private shipping fleet, established model spinning mills and silk plants, built coal mines, spent major sums on land development in Hokkaidō, and set up experimental factories for producing beer, woolens, tile, cement, and chemicals. In 1880 it helped establish the Yokohama Specie Bank for foreign exchange. And it encouraged private individuals to create wealth. The leaders were imbued, in historian Kenneth Pyle's phrase, with the "catch-up vision."[4]

One result was a period of impressive growth. Large-scale railway construction was carried out in the Tokyo and Osaka regions in the 1870s, laying the groundwork for a full 2,000 miles of railway track by 1889. Similarly, by the end of the 1870s, telegraph lines connected towns across the entire nation. And although the balance of payments in trade remained a problem, the government's encouragement of silk and cotton production led to an 80 percent improvement in Japan's overall trade situation between 1865 and 1880. Private wealth grew, too, as businessmen like Shibusawa Eiichi and Iwasaki Yatarō created model institutions such as the Daiichi Bank, the Osaka Spinning Mill, and the Mitsubishi shipping company, dedicated to efficiency and high profits. Indeed, surprising numbers of wealthy peasants and local businessmen quickly became "cold, ruthless, competitive profit-maximizers . . . in the tradition of Andrew Carnegie, Cornelius Vanderbilt, and John Rockefeller."[5] And although their workers may have suffered (as we shall see in a later chapter), the national economy profited.

One unfortunate result of this rush toward modernity was a serious struggle with government deficits and inflation. When the sums required for fighting the Satsuma rebels and buying off the *shizoku* were added to the costs of priming the economy and running the government, the pressures on the public purse approached disaster level, particularly after rural agitation led the government to cut the land tax in 1877 from 3 to 2.5 percent, resulting in a revenue decline of nearly 5 million yen. The *Tokyo Nichi Nichi Shimbun* said the government should cut spending, suggesting a curtailment in the construction of "useless" government buildings.[6] Instead, the government borrowed from the national banks and issued 27 million yen in notes to pay for the Satsuma Rebellion. From 1876 to 1879, the value of notes in circulation grew by more than half, to 164.4 million yen. The inflation that resulted helped some landowners, whose property became more valuable, but it hurt almost everyone else. Rice prices doubled between 1877 and 1880; gold and silver flowed out of the country; interest rates soared; and the value of paper money plummeted. House wrote in *The Atlantic Monthly* early in 1881: "The government is in straits which may almost be called desperate, for lack of funds requisite to the conduct of public business. . . . The outlook offers nothing but bankruptcy and national ruin."[7]

No one in power would have given him an argument. What they did debate was how to deal with the situation. Intellectuals such as Fukuzawa Yukichi joined many officials, including House's friend Ōkuma, in urging that Japan continue to concentrate on growth, borrowing cash from Great Britain if necessary. Others, led by Ōkuma's rival Matsukata Masayoshi, advocated an austerity policy of spending cuts and increased taxes that would lay a foundation for later growth, even if it triggered an economic downturn in the short term. When Matsukata took over the Finance Ministry in 1881, the deflationary policies led to years of depression, placing major financial stresses on most Japanese citizens. They hit the rural areas especially hard, sending rice prices plummeting, causing one farmer out of five to lose his land, and producing hundreds of cases of starvation. At the same time, they did end inflation and increase government revenues, undergirding an economic upswing in the late 1880s.

These military and economic challenges pushed the Meiji leaders to increased activism in several other areas in these years. For one thing, the rebellions convinced them of the necessity of bringing people from all social strata into the national community, of creating structures that would encourage farmers, workers, and fishermen in every locale to begin thinking of themselves as *Japanese.* Second, the samurai outbursts made it clear that some kind of constitutional system, which would give a voice to outsiders, was necessary for political stability. Third, the economic difficulties strengthened the argument that Japan must get rid of the unequal treaties and take control of its own tariffs. Without more income from trade, even the modernizing programs already underway would wither.

The need to give all Japanese citizens a sense of nation-consciousness seemed especially pressing. Even though the lenses of the twenty-first century make it easy to think of loyalty to emperor and nation as having ancient roots, the reality was that few commoners had even a modicum of attachment to something called Nihon, or Japan, at the middle of the 1800s. The pre-1868 class and status structures deprived all but the elites of concepts such as "public" and "state." As the scholar Maruyama Masao has commented, commoners in the Tokugawa years "were permitted to exist only to serve the samurai and to feed the samurai." Most had no higher ties, either institutional or emotional. And the feudal domain structure, fortified by Japan's mountainous terrain, meant that the frame of reference for most people was their own village, plus a nearby market center in the same valley. Nothing more. Fukuzawa put it this way: "Many millions of people throughout Japan were sealed up in many millions of separate boxes, or separated by many millions of walls."[8] These divisions did not matter much in the era of seclusion, but now, in the age of imperialist threats, such local-mindedness would not do.

For that reason, the new structures and programs of the early 1870s all were designed, in part, to encourage national cohesion. Prefectures took the place of the feudal domains; the social class structure was abolished; a military draft made peasant boys think of themselves as "Japanese"; schools, required for all children now, taught national values; uniform land taxes were imposed; and a national currency sent the message that everyone belonged to the same system. The government even sent Tokyo newspapers to each prefecture. But the officials quickly became aware too of the need for symbols and rituals to reinforce the new structures, for what Takashi Fujitani calls "mnemonic sites" to make people *feel* Japanese. They decided for that reason to refurbish many of the old national symbols—and, just as often, to create new symbols that looked old. Shintō shrines, which for centuries had been purely local sites for venerating village spirits, were linked now in a national network that promoted ceremonies to honor emperor and nation under the direction of a government department of Shintō affairs. The Great Food Offering (Daijōsai) marking the accession of an emperor to the throne was reinstituted as an "ancient ritual" in 1871, even though it had not been used for centuries. Ten new holidays were created between 1873 and 1878 to encourage people to celebrate together, including an Empire Festival (January 3), National Foundation Day (February 11), the Emperor's Birthday (November 3), and the Rice Harvest Festival (November 23). A national flag came into use, and in 1880 "Kimi ga yo" was selected as the unofficial national song. The impact exerted by these programs was suggested late in the era when the novelist Tayama Katai declared, "Philosophically, I am a 'freethinker,' but in my soul I am one of the Great Japanists." Indeed, a few left-wingers had begun asking by then whether the reforms had created too much nationalism. In the 1870s, however, Japan's leaders, worried about disunity, would have been delighted to know their programs would have such an effect.[9]

The government's interest in the second goal, the development of a constitutional system, was more reactionary than progressive, prompted by the surging influence in the late 1870s of Itagaki Taisuke's "freedom and people's rights" (*jiyū minken*) movement. The motives of movement leaders were, as we already have seen, as diverse as Japan's landscapes, ranging from the conservatism of Itagaki, who only wanted "rights" for the elites, to the democratic spirit of Ueki Emori who argued: "All people are created equally by Heaven. . . . If you cannot have freedom, die and be done with it!" But the very diversity of the movement meant that its impetus was toward ever wider participation in the public sphere. The movement members' professions ran the gamut: journalist, educator, farmer, political activist, housewife. And by the late 1870s its participants increasingly represented local elites who were more populist than the original leaders. Two things made the officials listen to them. First, their voices were amplified by a growing press, many of whose writers were political activists themselves. People in almost every village were reading newspapers by the late 1870s (or at least listening to them read aloud in the village square), and even the most pro-government of these sheets carried reports about the *jiyū minken* movement. Second, despite differences, the activists joined together on the need to create a popular assembly within a constitutional system. A *Kōkai Shinpō* writer said in 1876, "Government is the joint property of the people, not the exclusive property of the officials," and an 1880 petition in Nagano asserted that a majority of "Japan's more than seven million households support the opening of a national assembly."[10]

From the vantage point of the twenty-first century, the popular rights advocates posed little threat to the Meiji leadership; their demands were peaceful and moderate. But the officials worried about the precedents of the French Revolution and their own pre-Restoration activism. So they took measures, both repressive and constructive, to prevent disruption of any sort. On the repressive side, they issued press and assembly laws in 1875, prohibiting speech that might disturb public order. They also restricted participation in political organizations. On the constructive side, they set up several quasi-representative bodies: a fairly powerless prefectural governors' assembly as well as prefectural and city assemblies. And the emperor called in 1879 for leading officials to prepare memoranda on what kind of constitution Japan should have. None of this satisfied the popular rights advocates; it seemed too slow and cautious. But the course toward broader participation in the political process was set. And when two crises rocked the government in 1881, the meandering path to constitutionalism turned into a straight road.

The first crisis was caused by the constitutional memoranda. By late winter, all of the junior councilors but Ōkuma had prepared drafts proposing a system in which a weak legislature would answer to a powerful emperor; they also argued that Japan should move slowly in creating the new structure. When Ōkuma finally turned in his response to the emperor in March, he shocked his peers by urging a more liberal, British-style system with a strong parliament, with elections to be held the very next year. The councilors' astonishment turned to alarm in July, when the press precipitated the second crisis by reporting on a government scandal. The Colonization Bureau, which had poured millions of yen into Hokkaidō land development, had decided secretly to sell off land and property in the northern island to a group of bureau insiders at less than a thirtieth of what the development had cost. For a month, editorialists and speakers damned the government, arguing that the lack of a constitution rendered officials unaccountable and thus susceptible to corruption. Fukuchi Gen'ichirō, known until then as a pro-government editor, shouted to a crowd of 4,000 at Tokyo's Shintomi Theater on August 26: "It is shameful that a national assembly has not yet been formed. . . . The people may want to deliberate, but they have no way of preventing this sale, either by rational debate or by passing laws."[11] The intensity of the uproar paralyzed the official world for nearly a month. Then, on October 12, a decree announced that the ranks-breaker, House's patron Ōkuma (who was whispered to have leaked the land development scandal to the press), would leave the government and that a constitution would be granted within a decade. The promise of a constitution quieted the furor, and government work returned to its normal state, but not before the leaders had learned that they could ignore the demands for popular participation only at their own peril.

We have commented before that every domestic problem was linked at least in part to some foreign threat or pressure. The issue that made national strength and tranquility seem so urgent in the late 1870s was treaty revision. Since 1858, when Japan signed its first commercial pact with the United States, all of the treaties had sharply limited the tariffs that Japan could impose on imports, and had imposed extraterritoriality, a system under which foreigners accused of crimes in Japan were tried by their own country's consular court. Despite a promise that the treaties would be up for revision in 1872, the system had become solidified long before then, and both the tariff limits and extraterritoriality served as constant reminders of how weak Japan's claims to sovereign status really were. Extraterritoriality was particularly galling at the psychological level, since all but Britain's consular courts were run by men with limited legal experience, sometimes by downright incompetents or "frank adventurers" whose "antics . . . were matters to marvel at."[12] This meant that thieves and opium smugglers occasionally went free; brawling, drunken sailors were left unpunished; and an American who took the Japanese trains without a ticket in 1873 remained untouchable. In a serious episode that drew House's fieriest editorial wrath, the captain of the German ship *Hesperia* ignored Japanese efforts to quarantine his cholera-infested ship in Yokohama harbor in 1879. The Japanese officials, robbed by the treaties of jurisdiction, looked on helplessly (though not quietly) when the ship's crew debarked and an epidemic broke out. America's former president, Ulysses S. Grant, who happened to be in Japan at the time, reportedly suggested that the Japanese blow up the *Hesperia*. Even when consular court decisions were fair, as they usually were, the system insulted Japanese sovereignty.

And the tariff limits were an even more serious problem. Their impact was not just psychological. They threatened the nation's economic viability, limiting the customs rates that Japan could charge to less than 4 percent, on average, in a day when the Americans were charging duties of nearly 50 percent, and they held Japan's tariff income to a mere 1.5 percent of the government's annual revenue. For that reason, Foreign Minister Terashima Munenori and his colleagues made a decision in the mid-1870s to delay discussions of extraterritoriality and focus, for now, on the tariff issue. They argued in negotiations with the Western powers that tariff autonomy was a sovereignty issue: to be denied the right to set one's own duties was not only inequitable, but it also infringed on the rights that came with being an independent nation. The only reason Japan had bound itself by such treaties in the 1850s was that it had been weak and uninformed about international practices then.

Negotiations over tariff autonomy continued without letup during the late 1870s, with the Japanese showing flexibility on peripheral issues such as the opening of new ports and the elimination of export duties. They also tried a host of innovative approaches, including quiet efforts to get favorable treatment of their position in the press, the holding of separate negotiating sessions with different countries, and the sending of representatives to lobby in foreign capitals. At times, they stood on the brink of success. Indeed, by 1876, U.S. minister to Tokyo John Bingham had begun to write home that Japan's "proposition is so reasonable, so just, and . . . in no sense hurtful to the rights of any one of the Treaty Powers." He argued that it was in America's interest to "be the first to say that this proposition is acceptable."[13] By 1878, even the State Department had come around, and on July 25, a new treaty actually was signed between Japan and the United States, granting Japan tariff autonomy. Unfortunately, the treaty's final clause stipulated that the other treaty powers would have to agree to similar pacts, and they refused to do that. As a result, the 1870s ended with Japan still bound by unequal, unfair treaties that bound it to second-class status. But with every year, its leaders were growing more determined that that situation could not continue.

Nervous exhilaration had been the dominant mood in Tokyo's official circles in 1876 when House began discussions about becoming a newspaper editor. The government's hold on power was shaky, the Meiji system's very existence challenged by ex-samurai in the southwest. Even the peaceful opponents in the freedom and rights movement evoked images of revolution for men like Ōkubo and Ōkuma. Yet it would have been hard to find a single leader who was not hopeful, or an official who did not see the blend of progress and challenge as invigorating. Japan was on the move; optimism prevailed. By the time Ōkuma was ejected from the leadership clique in 1881, by contrast, the situation had reversed itself. The government was much more secure than it had been in 1876. No one doubted any longer that the regime was here to stay; what Marius Jansen has called Japan's "political and social separatism"[14] was gone. But the energetic optimism had vanished along with the violent opposition. The economic crises and political infighting had combined with the intransigence of the European powers to cast a pall over politics. It had not, however, dimmed House's conviction that Japan was well along the road to modernity, or that it deserved better treatment by the rest of the world—two themes he would use a newspaper to trumpet consistently across the last third of the 1870s.

NOTES

1. *Tokio Times,* February 17, 1877.
2. Mikiso Hane, *Modern Japan: A Historical Survey,* 93.
3. For Saigō's decision to head the rebellion, see C. L. Yates, "Saigō Takamori in the emergence of Meiji Japan," in Peter Kornicki, ed., *Meiji Japan,* 196. For "green conscripts" and Yamagata's reaction to Saigō's death, see Roger Hackett, *Yamagata Aritomo,* 81.
4. "Isolated islands" is from Kazushi Ohkawa and Henry Rosovsky, "A Century of Japanese Economic Growth," 52, quoted in Hane, *Modern Japan,* 98; "catch-up vision" is from Kenneth Pyle, *The Making of Modern Japan,* 98–101.
5. Trade improvement is from Yasuba Yasukichi, in Nishikawa Shunsaku and Saitō Osamu, "The Economic History of the Restoration Period," in Nagai Michio and Miguel Urrutia, eds., *Meiji Ishin, 175;* and "profit-maximizers" is in Pyle, *Making of Modern Japan,* 111.
6. Translated in *Tokio Times,* February 10, 1877, 71.
7. Edward H. House, "The Martyrdom of an Empire," *The Atlantic Monthly* (May 1881): 611.
8. Maruyama Masao, *Studies in the Intellectual History of Tokugawa Japan,* 328, 331.
9. Quotations are from Takashi Fujitani, *Splendid Monarchy:* "mnemonic sites," 9, and Tayama Katai, 15.
10. Ueki is quoted in Okano Takeo, *Meiji genron shi,* 54; the *Kōkai* article is from Miyatake Gaikotsu, "Meiji hikka shi shiryō," no. 7, 21; and the petition is discussed in Irokawa Daikichi, *Culture of the Meiji Period,* 106.
11. *Tokyo Nichi Nichi Shimbun,* August 29, 1881, in Uchikawa Yoshimi and Matsushima Eiichi, eds., *Meiji niyūsu jiten,* vol. 2, 114.
12. Harold S. Williams, *Tales of the Foreign Settlements in Japan,* 57.
13. Despatch 328, January 19, 1876, in Payson J. Treat, *Diplomatic Relations between the United States and Japan,* vol. 2, 2–3.
14. Marius Jansen, ed., *Cambridge History of Japan,* vol. 5, 23.

8

The *Tokio Times*—"That Naughty Yankee Boy": 1877–1880

Mr. House . . . neither sneers at Japan nor scorns the Japanese. That makes him unusual among foreigners.

—*Tokyo Nichi Nichi Shimbun,* December 18, 1876

He was . . . not a favorite with the worshippers of muddle.

—*Kobe Weekly Chronicle,* December 24, 1901

The *Yūbin Hōchi Shimbun,* a leading Tokyo daily, reported on Wednesday, December 12, 1876, that Tokyo soon would see the birth of another newspaper. Come the new year, the item stated, "the American E. H. House will begin to publish a weekly Western-language paper named the *Tokio Times.*" The following Tuesday the city's most powerful paper, *Tokyo Nichi Nichi,* ran a long piece on the promised appearance. It described House as a man who "pays close attention to Japanese affairs and praises what is praiseworthy while deploring that which should be deplored," a man "known by everyone" in America, a man who had "hiked personally to the battle sites" of the Taiwan expedition in order to disprove the foreign press's "false reports." And it described both his impact on students at the Kaisei Gakkō, and his "behind-the-scenes influence" in the *Maria Luz* affair. "This gentleman," the writer said, "empathizes with us when foreigners hold us in contempt; and he works hard for Japan's well being."

The reports were correct. On Saturday, January 6, a fourteen-page inaugural edition of the *Tokio Times* announced that "for at least a year" this weekly would provide news and opinion about the East for English-language readers in Japan, China, Europe, and America. And it would do it for the sake of assisting, "with what influence it can exert, in the advancement of all honorable effort toward progress in this country." In appearance, the paper resembled Japan's other English-language journals. It contained ads, as they did, for fire insurance, for pharmaceuticals, for tailors, art, gold, silver, bronze, crystal, ivory, hotels, restaurants, silk paintings, life insurance, and "coatings, trowserings, vestings, etc." It listed seventy-one pieces of unclaimed foreign mail at the Tokyo post office, along with the names of ship passengers who recently had left or entered Japan. After noting that "news for the opening week of the year is not abundant," it ran stories on Methodist missionaries in East Asia, the empress's trip to Kyoto, new documents about a Japanese mission to Rome early in the 1600s, and Japan's development of a postal system. One thing that set it apart was the quality of its prose; the essays were written by a man of obvious journalistic training, a man who had entered journalism as a writer, not as a businessman. But in format—and even in the news it covered—it did not seem all that different.[1]

So why start another paper? The region hardly wanted for newspapers in 1877. On the vernacular side, Tokyo had seven lively newspapers when the *Times* appeared, ranging from "prestige papers" (*ōshimbun*), which "ruled not only Tokyo but the press of the whole nation" with their erudite editorials on political issues, to cheap "petty papers" (*koshimbun*) filled with stories of murder, sex, and miraculous healings. The largest of the *koshimbun*, the sensational *Yomiuri Shimbun*, had a daily circulation of almost 21,000, and between them Tokyo's papers reached more than 67,500 homes a day. Across the country, as many as 225 dailies or weeklies now were being published. On the foreign language side, although the numbers were much smaller, the saturation was even greater. Yokohama alone had one French- and five English-language papers, including the fifteen-year-old *Japan Punch*, which pricked egos of prominent foreigners with a monthly dose of sarcastic essays and cartoons. This in a community with only 1,200 foreign residents. And they were lively papers, covering the news at least minimally, running both long and short editorial paragraphs in each issue, providing a venue for reams of daily ads.[2]

These papers did not, however, provide several things that House thought Japan needed. For one thing, they were all based in Yokohama, where issues were refracted through the lens of European trade. For another, they were too expensive for many readers, particularly for educated Japanese who wanted to read an English-language paper. For still another, all but *L'Echo du Japon* was British-owned, and interpreted the world from an unabashedly British perspective. Paid about the same in formal salaries as tea testers, the editors of the three leading Yokohama papers—the *Herald,* the *Gazette,* and the *Mail*—were feisty businessmen driven first by a desire to make money and second by a determination to maintain Britain's dominance in East Asia. J. H. Brooke, the *Herald*'s editor, was referred to as "the mouthpiece of 'John Bull' in Yokohama and Japan," though a pecuniary offer was known occasionally to soften his stance. Grace Fox, in a sympathetic history of British diplomacy, comments that these editors were sufficiently "interested in the growth of English commerce and the welfare of the merchant class" that they sometimes would express "irresponsible and uninformed opinions." A British minister's wife, Mary Fraser, said in the 1890s, "I have stopped reading these rags. . . . I can stand intelligent abuse, or good-natured ignorance; but the two nouns in unqualified conjunction make me tired."

The thing that irritated House most was the papers' constant criticism of Japan and their skepticism about Japan's ability to modernize. The *Mail,* which received Japanese government subsidies for several years and was more moderate than its counterparts, said that it was "sheer nonsense" to talk about Japan ever being able to emulate British "commercial freedom." The *Herald* wrote that "the Japanese are a happy race, and being content with little, are not likely to achieve much." And when it came to specific policies, the papers were consistent and predictable: convinced that the Taiwan expedition would fail, persuaded that foreigners could not live safely in Tokyo, skeptical about Japan's ability to create an efficient postal system, unalterably opposed to any revision of the unequal treaties. Nor did they express their opinions mildly. Fox commented that the ferocity of the Yokohama editors' criticisms "would not have been tolerated by their own government in London," and the American minister to Japan, John Bingham, thought the Yokohama papers ought to be punished for their sins "against the peace and dignity" of the Japanese government. It was little wonder that the Japanese newspaper *Chōya* wrote in 1882 that the British papers "despise Japan, looking down on it from a haughty position of arrogance, conceit, and rudeness . . . deceiving their readers with a mixture of truth and lies."[3]

Fortunately for House's career, he was not the only one troubled by the Yokohama papers. Many Japanese officials also were disturbed—and worried about the impact the journalists' criticism had on Western policies toward Japan. As a result, several powerful men started to talk in the mid-1870s about ways to communicate better with the English-reading public. Actually, the idea of massaging public opinion through the press was not new to them. The Tokugawa rulers had worked hard at information control. And early in the 1870s, the Meiji government had begun giving sympathetic Japanese editors special access to news sources and purchasing major papers for circulation in the provinces. Several officials also had begun discussing, as early as 1871, the creation of a government newspaper. And beginning in 1873, the Finance Ministry had lubricated its relationship with the least antagonistic of the foreign papers, W. G. Howell's *Japan Mail,* by paying 5,000 yen a year to send 500 copies of each issue to opinion leaders abroad. In return, Howell had agreed to publish articles on "the progress of Japan." The agreement fell apart two years later, when the increasingly anti-Japanese Howell demanded more money, but it illustrated how eager officials were to get their own perspectives across to their Western critics.

The officials' ideas about communicating with the foreigners were pushed in more concrete directions after 1874 when House returned from Taiwan and Charles LeGendre, the adviser to the foreign ministry, jumped on the issue. After his fight with Bingham about going to Formosa in the spring of that year, the general had begun thinking about how the Western community could be brought to support Japan more, and on July 8, he wrote a fifteen-page memo to Ōkuma Shigenobu, urging the creation of a government-supported, English-language paper. No developing state could make genuine progress without the confidence (and the assistance that flowed from such confidence) of the imperialist powers, he wrote. He thought Japan was particularly hindered by poor communication, because European and American ignorance was overwhelming, and because the Yokohama papers worked so hard to portray Japan as "a country . . . on the eve of rebellion and disintegration." To win the foreign leaders' confidence, Japan's government should create "an organ of its own," to be edited by "a man of experience, who has been brought up to the profession, and has learned it in the best journals of England and America." Such a project, he said, would cost about $4,000 in start-up costs, plus a thousand dollars a month in salaries, contributors' fees, "and other expenses."

LeGendre followed up in December with a massive memo to Ōkuma on Japan's relations with other countries, reiterating his view that the "malicious efforts of the foreign newspapers of Yokohama" were undermining Japan's prospects in Europe, because "these journals, though feeble in ability, are nevertheless the only channels through which intelligence concerning Japan has reached Europe for many years." He pointed out specific inaccuracies that had been reported abroad (including a *New York Times* report that a "tyrannizing" Japanese government had banned the use of *tatami* mat flooring!) and gave examples of how corrective reporting had improved attitudes toward Japan during the Taiwan episode and how a pamphlet on the Shimonoseki bombardment had fostered American sympathy toward Japan. Once again he declared that the government needed to create an organ that "shall, by sufficient distribution in the capitals of Europe . . . create a new interest in, and a more complete comprehension of, the Japanese situation." He wanted this journal to have two parts: an official section for which the government would be responsible, and an unofficial section devoted to relatively free debate and discussion. He also insisted, once more, that the paper be edited by a person "of integrity and ability" who would "view the political situation and necessities of Japan with sympathetic eyes."[4]

LeGendre did not use House's name in these memos, but Ōkuma could not have had any doubt about who was intended for the job. House was a friend of both men; he had written the pamphlet on Shimonoseki; he was the only man in all Japan then who fit the general's description of what kind of journalist was needed. What is more, House himself had proposed a similar project to officials soon after his return from Taiwan. Early in 1875, LeGendre invoked House's name directly, suggesting to Ōkuma that he be hired at a salary of $11,000 a year; in April he recommended that House and *Tokyo Nichi Nichi* editor Fukuchi put out a joint, twenty-four-page English-Japanese weekly at an annual cost of $14,280, and in 1876, he called for the government to buy the *Japan Mail* for $15,000 from Howell (who was planning to return to Europe) and put it under an investment company, with House as editor. Ōkuma apparently liked this last proposal, but House, knowing that the *Mail* was not making a profit these days, demurred.[5]

The only big question remaining by 1876 seemed to be what form the envisioned paper should take. The *New York Herald* reporter always had been an independent spirit, no more willing to bend to the will of editors like Horace Greeley and James Gordon Bennett, Jr., than he had been to accept the domination of his schoolteachers. He seems not to have been worried about the ethics of accepting pay from the government. This, after all, was an era when ties between journalists and government were common. Indeed, many of the editors and reporters he admired most—Greeley, John Hay, and John Russell Young—traveled easily back and forth between journalism and politics. And Fukuchi, the powerful Japanese journalist to whom he was closest, saw newspapers not as independent media but as levers for influencing opinion, as "movers of humankind." Moreover, House's sympathies with Japan were of such depth and long standing that he welcomed a chance to trumpet them more effectively. As he himself would put it later, he already had spent half a career fighting for this country; so he was not worried that he might be forced to write anything against his will. What he sought was a mouthpiece, a promise of reasonable editorial independence, and adequate pay. Once those things were assured, he would have no problem accepting a government contract.[6]

Thus it was that on October 11, 1876, House agreed to become an editor and a Japanese government employee, even as he discontinued his work for the *New York Herald*. He signed a confidential agreement (*naimitsu gian*) that day, stamped by Ōkuma, Ōkubo, and the powerful Iwakura Tomomi, providing him with 15,000 yen over a twenty-eight-month period, or nearly 6,500 yen a year, to put out a weekly newspaper. The restrictions on what he could publish were twofold: he would print any articles sent to him by Ōkuma and Ōkubo, and "all essays and editorials on Japan will be written truthfully and impartially, with the well being of the government in mind." The contract provided that the government would send 500 copies of each issue to opinion leaders in Japan and abroad and that if House were to become ill or die, the subsidy would continue only at the government's discretion. A separate agreement stipulated that Fukuchi's company, Nippōsha, would print the paper. The contract was renewed in 1878, with a 1,000 yen increase in postal and printing fees, after Ōkuma's colleague Hirai Kishō reported that the *Times* was "commanding great respect abroad" and assisting in the treaty revision struggle.[7]

House would be at the *Tokio Times* for only three and a half years, but those years would change his life course. He would go into the era healthy and come out incurably ill; he would begin 1877 as a American who loved Japan and enter 1880 as a transplanted Japanese who felt forgotten by his homeland; he would start the period pressed financially and end it comfortable. The financial change was perhaps the most surprising. Never impoverished, House had nonetheless struggled over finances throughout his career, haggling with editors and agents for a bit more cash to support his reportorial lifestyle, returning to his room early on many days to dash off a small piece that would net another fifty dollars. The *Tokio Times* salary of more than 500 yen a month was luxurious by the standards of the day: double that of Fukuchi, Japan's premier domestic editor, and ten times that of most editors; it left him by the late 1870s with enough money not only to rent a spacious home overlooking the Sumida River in the foreign quarters at Tsukiji but to purchase several rental lots in Yokohama. And after his stepmother, Candace House, left him with a $1,500 estate in 1879, he was able to launch a charitable educational project, which will be discussed below. The economic comfort would not last forever, but the affluence of the late 1870s would provide a cushion for the early 1880s, when reverses set in.[8]

House's place in Tokyo's elite circles also changed in these years; as editor of one of the region's most influential papers, he now became a "name." He did not think of himself as sociable, although his correspondence in these years is full of exchanges with dignitaries about dinners and receptions, both hosted and attended: an evening with Ōkuma, a toast at the farewell banquet for the *Mail*'s Howell, a note to a friend about missing a dinner party thrown by Yokohama Consul General Thomas Van Buren ("I keep aloof from half of his spreads because I can't bear them"), an outing with pioneer zoologist Edward S. Morse, an 1877 visit from British author W. B. Mason, who described him as "tall in stature, inclined to corpulence, and of sallow complexion." "When you had the good fortune to find him hospitably disposed," Mason wrote, "an intellectual treat awaited you. The suave manner, the caustic wit, the voice musical and well modulated, the ready repartee—all revealed the man of the world." One sign of his new stature was the appearance of nearly twenty cartoons about him—"that naughty Yankee boy"—in the *Japan Punch* during the late 1870s. The fact that former president Ulysses S. Grant's sole private appointment during his 1879 visit to Japan was with House also says something about the status the editor had achieved.

The new prominence did not make House immune to what he called the normal "downs and ups" of life. We will have more to say later about the illness with which he began to struggle in these years, and the barbs of expatriate rivals that endangered even his physical well being. He also had two encounters with fire. A mere three weeks after he had launched the *Times*, a wooden beam in the chimney of his apartment caught fire early on a Saturday morning. Fortunately, it was discovered quickly and the main damage was done by the firefighters, who cut away the roof and sprayed "plentiful streams of water." Far more serious was a wind-whipped Tokyo blaze in December 1879, which "took off a slice of the city," razed 11,464 homes along sixty-eight streets, and left thirty dead and 40,000 homeless. House's *Times* described a world of "shivering crowds" left in its wake: "half naked, shelterless and hungry, crouching . . . before the biting, pitiless, breeze: mothers searching for their offspring, children weeping for their parents, persons . . . raking the bare and blackened soil where once their houses stood." It did not tell its readers that the flames had destroyed House's own home, as well as a set of buildings in which he had just launched a new school "for poor girls . . . a pet project of mine . . . for educating young girls of too humble a station to get a chance in the usual way." The school, which marked the culmination of an ambition that House had nurtured ever since his teaching days at Takebashi Girls School, had consisted of a schoolhouse, an office, and teachers' lodgings, all paid for by House himself. He had had high hopes for the school when the fire struck, because it had attracted the kind of attention in high circles that "would have produced fruitful results in various quarters." Unfortunately, it was not adequately insured, and House feared "a long postponement."[9]

That the school should have attracted high-level attention so quickly was, of course, the result of House's high profile as editor of the *Tokio Times.* The first issue, on January 6, made it clear that this would be an *intellectual* journal. It was dignified, the format was neat and clear, and the visual effect was serious. The paper had a full complement of news items, but no one would have mistaken it for a popular weekly. Artwork was wholly missing, even in the advertisements. The prose was sophisticated. And after three pages of news-oriented "editorial paragraphs," the reader found a full-page essay on the vibrant state of Japanese society, three pages on Japan's seventeenth-century relations with Rome, a two-page review of Russia's status in Japan, and a page of short news items. These were followed by a section of excerpts from papers abroad, mostly relating to trade and diplomacy. The focus, in other words, was on politics and diplomacy. There was more opinion than news. And there was nothing sensational.

This did not mean that the *Times* would be dull. Readers surely did not think so. By the middle of its second year, the paper had achieved a circulation within Japan of about 350, double that of the *Mail* and the *Gazette.* Again and again across the next two years, House boasted in the paper that it had twice, or even thrice, the number of readers that its competitors had, and though precise circulation figures are unavailable, he appears to have been telling the truth. One reason for this may have been that he kept the subscription rates at about half those of the other foreign papers: $12 a year, or twenty-five cents an individual copy. Another may have been that the *Times* was the only English language paper in Tokyo. A third was that it had government backing, a detriment in the eyes of Yokohama merchants but a sign of authority for many other readers—particularly for Japanese readers of English. The most important reason though was the nature of the paper itself: its contents, its writing style, its breadth, its wit, its reliability.

From the first, both friends and competitors commented on the weekly's erudition. The missionary educator Guido Verbeck (and House's former fellow teacher) called it "a most excellent journal conducted by a trained journalist." Mason talked about "the sure touch of the accomplished man of letters, the polished diction, the apt phrase and allusion." The competitor *Mail* said the *Times*'s writing was "smooth and easy, and of excellent texture." And years later the journalist Tokutomi Sohō would say: "Not many people today could put out that intelligent a journal." House's prose had a tendency toward overkill; Tokutomi thought it was sometimes like "murdering tofu with a kitchen knife." But it always was clear, always intelligent, and invariably filled with the colorful phrases that attracted readers who cared about diction.[10] The fact that House wrote most of the paper's essays and news stories personally meant that lucidity was consistent across the columns too.

The breadth and authority of the articles also attracted readers. Even though House focused on issues of state, he also covered every kind of news imaginable. Economics ranked high in the paper's priorities, with reports on trade running alongside analyses of government budgets and population reports. The foreign legations were described in detail. When Japanese officials were promoted and demoted, *Times* readers knew about it. Health news also received wide coverage, particularly the cholera epidemics that broke out far too often. So did the East Asian struggle with opium; House reported frequently on China's struggles with that drug, and on Japan's determination to keep it out. There were reports on sheep farming, railway openings, school exams, wine brewing, Tokyo's poorhouse, sumo wrestling matches, Japanese toilets, the emperor's birthday, cremation, extortion by rickshaw runners, the opening of the baseball season, Tokyo gardens, the best libraries, volcanic eruptions, and ways to make travel more enjoyable. The paper serialized books on topics such as political economy, the 1860 assassination of Ii Naosuke, and LeGendre's argument that Japan was "progressive"; and it also contained weekly translations of Japanese editorials, and was unusually rich in articles on literature and the arts: theater and book reviews, summaries of Japan's "periodical literature," translations of Nō plays, descriptions of Tokyo's theaters, restaurant reports. The fact that it published most of the government's important notices, as well as endless statistics on disease, finances, trade, and population made it particularly useful to foreigners in governmental or diplomatic work.

One other thing that made the *Times* attractive was its wit. When House used his verbal stiletto, the effect was hilarious for all but the victims. But he did not have to be engaged in direct combat to be witty. On March 3, 1877, he wrote about the *ayu* (sweetfish), "that dainty and delicious article of food . . . which Dr. Hepburn dismisses, in his dictionary, with the cold and unfeeling remark that it is 'a kind of river fish.'" "A kind of fish!" House writes, then devotes a column to the sweetfish's "tender and engaging qualities." Once, he related a story that made the rounds after an unpopular foreign attaché left Japan. The Japanese bureau with which the diplomat had communicated most often had hung his portrait on the wall now. "And a fine stroke of policy," House had a bureau clerk say; "the portrait will be just as active and efficacious as the original ever was, and will cost nothing beyond the first outlay." He told his readers still another time that Eve must have played tennis well in the Garden of Eden, because she was unencumbered by clothes. When he heard that an American had fallen into a Tokyo canal, he wrote: "This is all wrong. Canals are built for traffic, not for falling into. . . . If foreigners are determined to fall into canals, although this is certainly not one of the rights guaranteed by Treaty, they will doubtless have a canal built expressly, where Americans can go and fall in all day long." When it was pointed out to him that the gentleman had fallen into a moat, not a canal, House retorted: "This does not, in our view, better the case." Moats were not "to get into" but "for getting into people's eyes, for the inspection of brothers who are ocularly subject to beams."[11]

The first major news story after the birth of the *Tokio Times* was the outbreak of the Satsuma Rebellion in Kyūshū late in January, and the paper's handling of it told any reader who had missed the fact: Japan now had a foreign newspaper of a different kind. Like the other papers, the *Times* covered the episode aggressively, giving it two to four pages an issue. But the tone was different. The accounts were more reliable, thanks to House's sources and to his dedication to accuracy. They also were more sympathetic to the government. And though the paper could be sarcastic in its debates with the Yokohama papers, the approach generally was thoughtful and cautious. On February 17, the day the insurrection broke in the weekly press (and just six weeks after the *Times* had written about the danger of rebellion: "all is clear now, and the outlook is equally clear"), House reported: "An outbreak of some magnitude has occurred in Satsuma. . . . To what extent the insurrection at Kagoshima may prove formidable, we have, thus far, no sufficient grounds for forming an opinion." A week later, he said: "We have hardly any more authentic intelligence than could be given last week, when there was virtually nothing of value to place upon record." Even on September 29, when other foreign papers were reporting dramatically on Saigō's suicide, he introduced the prevailing versions of what had happened with the note that "a degree of obscurity" beclouded the rebel leader's fate.

House's coverage was characterized by unwavering confidence that the government troops would win, balanced by concerns about the effect war would have on the march of progress—and puzzled anger at Saigō's treachery. He expressed faith often in the generals' wisdom and the soldiers' skill, then worried about the financial impact of the war. On March 3, for example, he reprinted a *Nichi Nichi* editorial that claimed: "The treasury becomes empty; the national debt is increased. . . . A civil war is disastrous." Six weeks later, on April 14, he reported that the government already had spent 5.7 million yen fighting the rebels. And since Saigō was the rebellion's leader, he tended to blame him most frequently for the troubles, though as often in tones of sadness as of fury. Once it was certain that Saigō was leading the rebellion, the *Times* ran a moving piece, recalling the dignity with which he had served in the government and lamenting: "The destruction of an illusion so earnestly and universally maintained is a national affliction." An accompanying reprint from *Nichi Nichi* suggested that Saigō's "brain must be in some way affected to cause him to act as he now has." Throughout the spring and summer, House continued that tone; Saigō should be grieved rather than hated, but as a traitor he must be punished. On October 6, after Saigō was dead, House reprinted a vernacular paper's summary of his career, with a reference to Shakespeare: "When Brutus murdered Caesar he said: 'As Caesar loved me, I weep for him; as he was fortunate, I rejoice at it; as he was valiant, I honor him; but, as he was ambitious, I slew him.' And the same may legitimately be said of Saigo Takamori."

House's final analysis of the rebellion was that its unexpected length, while "a national calamity" in financial and human terms, was a political blessing, because it had eradicated the opposition and provided a new degree of stability. "What Saigo could not achieve," House said, "no imitator will presume to attempt." The irascible editor could not resist a gibe then, in that final analysis, at the other foreign editors who had so consistently foretold national disaster. Noting that only his *Times* had predicted a government victory from the start, he wrote: "We do not hold that this is proof of superior clearness of vision on our side; but it stands as incontestable evidence of the dulness, or wilful blindness, or deliberate malice of the others."[12]

Once the war was over, House turned the *Times*'s columns to those goals that had prompted him to accept the editorship in the first place: explaining Japanese progress, combating the imperialist powers' inequitable treatment of Japan, and reporting the news. If that formula made the *Times* appear polemical, House was not bothered. Journalism meant fighting for causes, and Japan had become his crusade. The *Japan Punch*'s first cartoon of House showed a dapper man with a long, thin nose, full sideburns, and a moustache, wearing a hat marked *Tokio Times* and carrying an American flag with Japan's rising sun in the middle of it;

Japan Punch, *the Meiji era's leading English-language humor magazine, highlighted House's pro-Japanese approach nearly a year after he began editing the* Tokio Times *(November 1877).*

the caption read: "The new flag of Japan—a la Tokio Times & Co." Years later, the journalist Tokutomi would say that House stood out from other journalists because he "took Japan seriously, empathetically, at a time when the Japanese themselves, influenced by the West, still were demeaning themselves." He said House was able to "look beyond the present, to the future. Indeed, he did more than just look at that future; he told others what he saw. And he told them boldly."[13]

One result was that the Bostonian wrote often about Western oversimplification of, and condescension toward, the Japanese. In the very first issue of the *Times*, he recalled the way Westerners attributed every positive Japanese development to "luck," giving no credit to the "force of national character." Four months later, he wrote about the widespread use of the term "Asiatic" as a "neat, effective and sufficient method of estimating the character of these hundreds of millions of beings, comprising scores of dissociated and antagonistic races, and covering a space that stretches from the pole to the equator." He speculated that London's writers would "instantly fly to arms" if someone tried to make similar generalizations about Europe. Another four months after that, he lamented the inability even of Japan's friends to write respectfully about "a people and a country which for ages they looked upon solely as material for caricature and diversion." And he was still at it in 1879, agreeing with the Japanese complaint that Americans, "calling themselves Christian, and Japan heathen," typically asserted "the right of Christians to command and the heathen to submit; for the heathen to give and Christians to take." In the final edition of the *Times*, he asked Westerners to stop using the "senseless vulgarism . . . Jap."

The converse of this was that the *Tokio Times* took Japan's progress seriously. "What transformation more strange, more startling . . . could the most vivid imagination picture forth," his inaugural editorial asked, than what had occurred in the last dozen years? In the mid-1860s, Japan had been "lapsing into frail decrepitude"; today it "stands in friendly and respected intercourse with the powers of the earth." He wrote—and acted—as if he genuinely respected the people among whom he lived, whether he was setting an example by printing his journal on paper made in Japan or describing a Japanese mail system that delivered letters more efficiently than the foreign post offices had, whether he was reporting on the first ship with a Japanese flag to sail up the Thames (the *Niigata-maru*) or commenting on the twenty national banks that had been founded since 1872. When a new central telegraph office opened in 1878, the *Times* called it "one of the most successful structures, in the foreign style in Tokio." And he often contrasted Japan's energy with the "heavy," "idealess," and "soulless" Chinese approach to change.[14]

Nothing illustrated his respect for the Japanese more than the way he engaged them in debate and criticized those things he disliked. He supported the establishment, but he was no sycophant. Nor was he patronizing. Rather, he discussed issues with the vigor of one to whom the alternatives really mattered, contending regularly that Japan should be more forceful in taking treaty relationships into its own hands, and calling for more "intellectual independence" in dealing with China. Often his criticisms related to specific news items: the "economic absurdity" of a scheme to sell silk worms to Italy, the extravagance of officials who built ostentatious residences, the harsh enforcement of press laws in 1877 without "sufficient reason nor necessity." In June 1877, he gave the better part of a column to the firing of the Kaisei Gakkō teacher Horace Wilson, who had introduced baseball to Japan, so that a Japanese could be hired. He sympathized with the desire to fill posts with Japanese but asked why officials would dismiss those "who know their work and do it zealously and well," while retaining arrogant and less competent workers.

Just as often, House's criticisms were ongoing. For months in 1877, he lambasted officials for failing to regulate rickshaw pullers' charges. He also expressed endless bafflement at Tokyo's outdated firefighting methods, dashing off an editorial note after every serious fire on the need for change. On March 23, 1878, he was particularly perturbed, writing: "The present absurd practice of squirting water on the attacked buildings through wooden syringes, and standing like dumb effigies in dangerous places till the eyelashes are scorched, shows a most unworthy conservatism and should be abandoned." He said "a dozen good hand-machines, well equipped with suitable hose and manned by persons whose paid business it is to extinguish fire, would stop an outburst of this nature." And after the December 1879 fire that destroyed his own home, he was withering, calling the fire fighting department "useless," hopelessly conservative, and "utterly dishonest and corrupt." He concluded that three things were needed: less flammable construction materials, better fire fighting equipment, and a sound insurance system.[15]

Nor did House hesitate to critique broader social practices. Much as he admired the Japanese generally, he was contemptuous of certain practices—and said so freely. Nothing illustrated this candor better than his articles on the way the Japanese treated women. His first lengthy treatment appeared on March 2, 1878, in response to a letter in which the progressive educator Fukuzawa Yukichi urged families not to put their daughters in Westerners' schools, lest nonutilitarian learning make them poor marriage candidates. Expressing surprise at the letter's appeal "to a selfish and retrogressive sentiment among the elders of the community," House accused Fukuzawa of implying that women had no purpose but to be "assistants in their husbands' households." He suggested that as modern education made Japanese men more broad-minded, there would be "nothing but wretchedness in future unions" if the women were not similarly educated. And he wondered if the real reason for Fukuzawa's conservatism lay in a male fear that educated young women might "become intractable and insubordinate, and resolve themselves into an element hostile to the welfare of the state." House derided that fear as "ludicrous," but added that if men could not keep pace with women in an equal educational system, then "the interests of the nation would be best served by as speedy a transfer as possible of all sorts of control to those who may prove themselves better entitled to leadership." He promised to publish a later review of "the whole question of the condition of women in the empire."

That review did not come for a year and a half, but when it did appear, in successive November 1879 essays, it was more hard-hitting still. House began, on the 22nd, with a statement that no nations treated women in a truly civilized fashion, though Americans came closest to the ideal, while Africans were worst and Japanese and Europeans shared the middle ground. The faults of others did not, he said, excuse Japan for perpetuating the "worst and meanest relic of human barbarism": a tendency of husbands to treat their wives as servile beings. House was disdainful of men who acted enlightened during sojourns in the West, then, on their return to Japan, confined women to domestic roles and denigrated their intellectual leanings. "To our mind," he said, "the profoundest lesson of foreign culture remains untaught until the sentiment of cold and selfish disregard for the rights" of women "has been burnt out of their souls."

A week later, House focused on the marital difficulties of educated women, particularly those who had studied abroad. "Marriage, for them," he wrote, "means a weary and hopeless sorrow, a 'long disease,' the crushing out of all brightness from their hearts." He blamed several groups and social forces: husbands, in-laws, extended families, a social milieu that precluded equality. Everything conspired against the educated bride to "grind her spirit away by menial degradations, and crowd excesses of vulgar toil upon her," to eradicate any "recollection of her little scholarly attainments." Even if a husband wanted to treat his wife with respect, House said, relatives would "nullify" his instincts "by introducing concubines into the home." Lest anyone think he was describing only the worst cases, House estimated that Japan had no more than "a score" of homes, primarily those of middle-level officials, where a woman might find life decent. He offered two anonymous examples of girls school graduates who had been abused by prominent families. About one, he wrote: "Four years ago she was an expert linguist, with talents and endowments not inferior to what are seen among the best foreign classes. At this day, she is nearly unintelligible in any tongue but her own, and the bright ambition and mental activity of her youth are dead, if not forgotten." About the other: "From the moment of marriage, her life was made a burden by the cruel impositions of her husband's family," leading her to take the "almost unprecedented step" of leaving her husband and finding her own work. House concluded by urging two reforms. First, "it must be known and felt that the man who defiles the purity of his home, debases his wife, or imposes infamy on his daughter, smites his own honor with a blow from which it can never recover." Second, schools for women must be opened. Japan could not "claim the full fruits of civilization" until "mothers as well as fathers, have enjoyed the utmost benefits of broad and catholic education." Seven months later, in the last issue of the *Times*, he called an "improvement in the position of the women" the "most important" reform Japan could make.

House's views on women were remarkable. They would not have been thought radical a century later; indeed, his patronizing language about "little" and "dainty" women would have given offense, as would his acceptance of the home as the woman's proper sphere. But several things made the articles exceptional at the time. They demonstrated, for one thing, House's unvarnished candor, what Bingham called his "independent fashion of declaring his faith with characteristic frankness and courage." The objects of his attacks were not limited to outsiders or even to low-level officials; he chastised the very men who were subsidizing the *Times*, and did so in explicit language. The articles also took the discussion of gender reform beyond what would have been advocated by any but the most radical writers. Westerners in Japan called often for "better treatment" of Japanese women, but their arguments rarely touched on political rights, or the kind of broad, equal education that House had in mind. They condemned prostitution and concubinage; they despised arranged marriages; they advocated love between husband and wife; but they had little to say about public roles for women. Similarly, Japanese "progressives" such as Fukuzawa and the diplomat Mori Arinori sought an end to concubinage and demanded more humane treatment in the home, but they made it clear that they were *not* advocating equal rights. As Mori wrote in 1875, after another scholar had suggested that he favored equality: "I indeed said that wives and husbands should be honored without distinction. . . . I absolutely did not touch on equal rights, however." When the Shikoku activist Kusunose Kita demanded in 1878 that women household heads be granted the right to vote, Mori and Fukuzawa dismissed her as an extremist. Thus, House's call, in a government-supported journal, for "broad and catholic education" and for women to take leadership positions in society bordered on the revolutionary, as did the fact that he backed up his views by encouraging his own daughter, Koto, to live a visible public life and by creating his own school for girls from poor families.[16]

House's other central crusades at the *Tokio Times* were more in tune with mainstream Japanese ideas—and thus appeared even more radical to his fellow foreign editors. Most of these campaigns dealt somehow with imperialism. Indeed, no issue so thoroughly aroused House during the *Times* years as the way the Western powers had appointed themselves to be world arbiters, devising rules that benefited themselves even as they spoke the language of justice. In the eighth issue of the paper, House reprinted a stinging *Tokyo Nichi Nichi* analysis of the imperialist system, which argued: "We cannot arrive at an equality with foreign powers, because they maintain their conduct not by reason or on moral principles, but depend upon force." The writer maintained that "equitable principles have been discarded on the European continent, and each nation has to preserve its peace by being well prepared for war. . . . This is not the golden age in which morality controls force."

House's attacks on the imperialist system went in many directions. Frequently, trade was the culprit: the fact that diplomats cared more about their own countries' profits than about fairness or anything else. Other times, he wrote about the ineptitude of diplomats, particularly those from the United States. Sometimes, he talked about the imperialists' ignorance of Asia, and the blithe way they employed derogatory stereotypes. And in almost every issue, he had something to say about what he saw as the chief imperialist villain: British arrogance and hypocrisy. He was so consistent, in fact, in his attacks on the British that a twentieth-century ambassador, Hugh Cortazzi, would write (without citing evidence) that House had been "employed to write anti-British propaganda." Cortazzi also would call House's *Times* "a largely anti-British newspaper," even though its mission was far broader, and more nuanced, than that evaluation suggests.[17]

House was particularly hard on British trade policies. Over and again, he charged that *nothing* mattered to the British except profits. The British championed "free trade," he said, because they already controlled the seas and had the resources to flood a country's markets until competitors had been driven out, after which they could raise prices at will; an absence of tariffs simply ensured the British advantage. "No man's pie is free from her ambitious finger," House wrote in one issue. The merchants provoke quarrels among East Asian nations, he wrote in another, "with the object—we can think of no other—to make money by selling arms to these countries." And again, as a warning to the Japanese, he quoted a British citizen who had said that "Africa must be filled with English goods before the local inhabitants had time to discover how destructive this would be for them." He also attacked British involvement in the opium trade, in more than thirty *Tokio Times* articles. He described the "transfer of over a score of millions from Chinese coffers to those of England," quoted a Chinese scholar to the effect that "opium is one of the worst of our poisons, and its presence . . . the sorest of our evils," and railed against a consular court's decision not to punish British citizens for importing opium into Japan, as long as it was called "medicinal opium," even though treaties forbidding the import of opium made no distinction between "medicinal" and "smoking" opium. The motive behind the decision, House declared, "is trade—trade again—always trade." The fact that the *Gazette* and *Herald* occasionally advocated the import even of nonmedicinal opium proved the point for him.[18]

The personification of the trade-first policies, in House's mind, was Harry Parkes, British minister to Japan from 1865 to 1883. House did not write as often about Parkes as he did about trade, but his attacks were scalding. Actually, House was a supporter of Parkes when he launched the *Times*, calling him a man whose "repose, when the time for it comes, will have been more laboriously earned than that of many public servants." But Parkes's view of diplomacy ran counter to House's, and the diplomat's tendency to patronize and scold the Japanese irritated the editor more each month, until by late 1877, he had become a frequent critic of the British minister.

The first strong attack in the *Times* appeared in September, when House accused Parkes of a "meddle and muddle" policy for attempting (unsuccessfully) to obstruct Japan's entry into the Universal Postal Union. When the *Japan Mail* accused House of writing in spite, he responded with a fulsome attack, finding Parkes guilty of "almost a mania" for "interfering with such affairs of administration as he can find a pretense for intruding upon." He said the envoy's "temper was too imperious to be controlled" and speculated that the Japanese would have him recalled were it not for their "generosity . . . and a cordial readiness to overlook injuries." Postal issues inspired another *Times* attack two years later, after Parkes demanded $10,000 when Japan took over the Yokohama buildings in which the British consular post office had operated. House said the buildings had been appraised at $500 and called Parkes's demand "too outrageous for even the submissive temper of Japan." When Parkes suggested that in lieu of payment the Japanese deliver packages addressed to the British consulate free of charge, and without inspection, House exploded, accusing the English of trying to avoid paying any tariffs at all. He said Parkes had a "devilish propensity to exasperate."

Most exasperating to House was Parkes's single-minded pursuit of British commercial interests. When the minister asked his fellow Englishmen in Japan to comment on potential treaty revisions in the spring of 1879, House wrote that "the minister knows perfectly well what he intends to do. . . . He will consent to no changes that shall interfere, even in the remotest degree, with the advantages of his countrymen." He said Parkes would "resist, to the utmost," any change in the treaties "unless he can secure some special benefit by way of compensation." Parkes's "sole idea of revision was," he said, "renewed and increased benefits for England," adding: "This may be insolent and harsh, but there is nothing to prevent him from being as insolent and harsh as he likes." The editorial said that the Japanese government ought to confront Parkes forcefully, since logic did not work with a man who "always has said, in plain words: I stand here to maintain the interests, chiefly commercial, of my country, and I will listen to nothing that tends to abridge those interests." When Parkes left Japan temporarily in the fall of 1879, House joined many Japanese officials who preferred privately that he not return, because "he has—as we have often had occasion to lament—made the name of his nation hateful and abhorrent throughout this land."[19]

Although some observers later would write that the *Times*'s raison d'être was "to write that indefatigable Minister Sir Harry Parkes out of the country," and although *Japan Punch* called House "the naughty Yankee boy who would throw coals at the British Lion,"[20] the truth is that Parkes only ranked among House's secondary issues in the late 1870s. The matters that really engaged him, the problems that consumed the greatest quantity of his paper's ink, week in and week out, were just two in number: the biased journalism of the Yokohama papers, and the in-

Japan Punch *captured House's antipathy for the British Minister Harry Parkes (left) in this February 1878 cartoon.*

equities of the treaty system. If the fight with the Yokohama press gave the *Times* its wit and color, the treaty revision crusade showcased House's debating skills.

When House took over the *Tokio Times,* he was interested less in making money than in articulating carefully reasoned positions. His tone, once he actually began editing, however, turned caustic, and his editorials soon were filled with as much wit and name-calling as a night at the Pfaff beer cellar. At the heart of the shift was his rivalry with the editors of the *Japan Herald,* the *Japan Mail,* and the *Japan Gazette*—a rivalry that produced what House called a "blood and thunder" style of writing that "isn't journalism, but . . . has to be done, just now and just here, or I could not make myself heard."[21] Actually, petty sniping had typified Yokohama journalism since its inception, even when the editors shared a common ideology. Now, with a peer to challenge their anti-Japanese views, the snipping gave way to snarling. "If you take sides with the eastern nations, in this far east," wrote the journalist Young, "you bring upon you the rancor of the foreigners. . . . You are bribed, bought, corrupted. You are possessed of the devil." Surely, that was the way the Yokohama editors saw House. They called him "pharisaical," "venomous," a "hack-writer," a "mendacious ruffian." When House criticized the editor of the *Mail* in 1877 for suggesting that LeGendre favored compromise with the Satsuma rebels, the *Mail* accused him of adopting a "mode of warfare . . . to which no English gentleman can condescend." And after House censured Parkes in 1878, the *Gazette* mocked the *Times*'s "'damnable iteration' of insult, its simulated indignation for wrong never inflicted, its venomous malice, its false suggestions, its garbled, distorted, and untrustworthy narrations." As for House's actual allegations: "We will not descend to discuss the specific charges. It is enough to deny them. . . . Faugh!"[22]

One reason the Yokohama papers' attacks were vicious was that House gave what he got. *Japan Punch* said in February 1878 that his language had "a modern Bismarckian manner of putting things bluntly, just as they were, without any niceties." And he himself wrote that "nothing could be effected by adhering to the milder method first contemplated." To use "gentle persuasion or moderate debate," he said, "would be a senseless affectation. . . . Courtesy and soft speech . . . would be mistaken for timidity." He recalled that William Lloyd Garrison, "on being told that he was 'all on fire,' answered that he 'had need to be on fire, for he had mountains of ice to melt.'" So House coined invective as though he loved it. He whaled away at the issues: the *Herald's* "rudeness" for wanting to deny Japan the right to earn customs revenue, or the smug arrogance of the *Mail* in doubting that legal disputes "between foreigners and foreigners will ever be entrusted to even a partly Japanese jurisdiction." And he defended himself vociferously, particularly when accused of inaccuracy, because the loss of a reputation for reliability would "be seriously, perhaps fatally, injurious." Moreover, he pointed out each of his rivals' mistakes. Near the end of 1879, when the press was in a dither over tensions between Japan and Korea, House wrote that his "contemporaries in Yokohama" were creating stories out of whole cloth: "This minister has been deposed, that one suspended in disgrace, the other sent into political exile. . . . All this, and more, day after day;—and what does it come to? . . . Not one prediction verified nor a single alarm realized."[23]

The *Times*'s attacks sometimes were humorous, as when House laughed at an opponent who attempted to have him attacked with a "loaded cane," or when he accused the *Gazette* of trying "to shed a little obscurity" on an issue. Sometimes the editorials were snide, as in an observation that the *Mail* had contradicted itself by saying first that 1876 was a bad year, then that it was a "period upon which both the government and people . . . may look back with pride." Sometimes House was simply pithy, as in his April 19, 1879, reference to the *Gazette* as "the British minister's new organ." Sometimes, he was thoughtful, noting in the fall of 1877 that while papers in the West trivialized Japan, they still treated it more fairly than the Yokohama journals did. And always, House was meticulous. After a Yokohama paper had reviewed his booklet on the Kagoshima Affair, he wrote that the writer either was a fool (if he had not read the booklet) or a knave (if he had read it), then pointed out thirteen of his "conspicuous and flagrant lies."[24]

The vitriol flowed until House closed down his paper on June 26, 1880. In the last issue, House wrote that the *Herald* editor, J. H. Brooke, had "venom . . . in his fangs" and "wants to see Japan an English dependency." Of the *Gazette*, he said: "Its shrill, unnatural voice now excites only pity mingled with derision, when lifted in lamentation over its lost virility." Not to be outdone, Brooke gloated over the *Times*'s demise: "Like a tallow candle burned down to its socket, it has gone out with a stink, and society is well rid of a weekly and nasty nuisance." He referred to House as an "unconscientious writer who prostituted his intellect" and judged the paper "a ghastly, ludicrous, and conspicuous failure." The bitter farewell said more about Brooke than about House; indeed, when the *Herald* died in 1914 the respected Frank Brinkley wrote that "its methods have been the methods of the thug." It also illustrated the level to which invective had fallen. House probably was right; he would have been devoured had he not answered in kind. But if the language made for lively reading, it also undermined the force of many arguments.[25]

The issue that drew the *Times*'s most incisive coverage was treaty revision. As we already have seen, the treaty issue already had a two-decade history when House launched his paper. The Japanese had made repeated efforts to end the tariff limits and extraterritoriality, but the only real revisions, in 1861 and 1866, had left the consular court system untouched and had reduced the tariff limits even farther, with the average falling below 4 percent. "Sad to say," wrote the *Tokyo Nichi Nichi,* "in the last days of the Bakufu administration, foreigners by dint of contention and threatenings succeeded in getting the charges cut down to the present insignificantly low rates." No revisions at all had occurred since the Meiji Restoration.

By the time House shut down the Times *in 1880, the foreign press in Yokohama had come to hate his defense of Japanese causes so much that* Punch *no longer even included American stripes on his flag.*

House raised this issue in his very first edition. His longest editorial paragraph on that January 6 argued that Japan was too advanced to be treated like China and Turkey on the extraterritorial question, and that protective tariffs, which had "brought the natural resources of America to a state of mature development," would do the same for Japan if it were given the right to set its own duties. Two of the issue's four sets of reprints from other papers also dealt with treaty revision. The longer of the two excerpted articles from several papers in England, the bastion of "free trade" (i.e., low tariff) ideologies, which admitted that protectionism had left the Americans "on the point of becoming our most dangerous rivals." A writer in *The Graphic* put it this way: "The Protective system, though, perhaps, economically fallacious, has been practically successful." In the months ahead, House would call often for protectionism; if an emerging nation could not safeguard its infant industries through tariffs, its domestic economy would not thrive.

All told, House ran more than a hundred editorials and articles on the treaties, and discussed them peripherally in at least that many more essays. His underlying principle was that while weakness had forced Japan to sign unfair treaties in the 1850s, its present strength made equal treaties both just and mandatory. To regain dignity and achieve prosperity, Japan had to find a means, by force if necessary, to throw off the old accords and sign equal agreements with each of the imperialist powers. Otherwise, it could not be called a sovereign state. House was not naive about what it would take to accomplish treaty revision; he agreed with Fukuzawa, who said that "foreign relations are governed, not by reason, but by passion," and he never held much hope that the British would give up the advantages of the unequal system without a great deal of pressure. But that did not daunt him. He never doubted the justice of his position, and he felt sure that there were means to bring it to fruition, particularly once the government decided in the fall of 1877 to negotiate directly with officials back in America and Europe rather than in Tokyo, where foreign representatives usually acted as a bloc.[26]

The largest number of House's treaty articles concentrated on the tariff question. He launched that discussion in a March 17 editorial on Japan's trade statistics from the previous year, arguing that "a higher duty" would improve Japanese commerce. Then, on March 31, the American economist Henry C. Carey began a series of eight long letters, advocating protectionism as a source of prosperity for any country, advanced or otherwise. And on April 21, House ran his first major *Times* editorial on tariffs, showing how the treaties enabled British steamers to transport more than 330 million pounds of coal a year, duty free, at a loss to Japan of more than $21,000 in tariffs—or a full fifth of what the customs house took in each year. One of the points that House pounded home constantly was that Japan desperately needed this revenue for its modernization program. He pointed out that even Great Britain, the "declared exponent and advocate" of free trade, took in more customs revenue than Japan did. And he lauded the value of protectionism in building native industries. Typical was what House called an "admirable" essay, reprinted from the *Penn Monthly* on May 17, 1879, which showed "a sweeping wave" of protectionism in Europe. Bismarck's Germany had committed itself to protective tariffs; protectionists had become a majority in France; even Switzerland, "*the* free trade country of Europe," was putting high tariffs on certain goods. A later piece showed how America's growing silk industry had been helped by 60 percent tariffs, while the absence of duties in England had enabled the French to invade the British silk market. Once the British had eliminated protective duties, "destitution followed wherever silk was manufactured."[27]

House also employed the language of justice, arguing that the refusal to grant Japan tariff autonomy amounted to a denial of sovereignty. When the *Mail* urged Japan late in 1877 to exhibit "a fair and liberal spirit" in a treaty revision conference, House huffed that the Japanese surely would be fair and liberal—they always were—but were not "'bound' to approach it in any spirit excepting that which pleases them. . . . The truth should never be lost sight of, that the regulation of a customs tariff is a national right." He said the "fetters" of tariff limits had been "imposed in her hours of extremest weakness"; now that she was a healthy participant in international affairs the restrictions should, by right alone, be removed. Several months later, House described tariff autonomy as "an independent right which is enjoyed without dispute by every state—the feeblest and the mightiest alike—in Europe and America." He pointed out that in the West, no nation "is under trade obligations to another unless a reciprocal advantage is enjoyed at the same time" and that such obligations always were specific and limited, whereas "in Japan, the tariff regulations are comprehensive to the extremest breadth," and nothing is reciprocal. Japan's quest for tariff autonomy, he added, "is an open, straightforward and honorable effort to assert a sovereign principle of national independence."

House's trump card on this argument came from Townsend Harris, negotiator of the first U.S. commercial treaty with Japan. House had written Harris about the limits in 1875, since the former minister's name often was "quoted in a sort of defence" of the treaties. Harris responded two months later, saying that tariff restrictions had been needed in 1858 because of "the ignorance of the Japanese," but that he had intended them to be temporary. For that reason, the treaty explicitly stipulated that rates could be revised in a few years, at Japan's initiative. And Harris thought they should have been. As House quoted him in the *Times*:

> *I constantly told the Japanese commissioners that before the time came around for revising the Treaty they would have gained such experience as would enable them intelligently to deal with this matter themselves;* remarking that while ten years was an important part of a man's life it was as nothing in the life of a nation. *I never, for a moment, claimed a right to interfere in matters which purely belong to the municipal affairs of every nation. Such interference is the result of absolute conquest, and not of any international right.*

House followed with a comment that Harris's alleged support for the treaties had been used often by the anti-reform forces "in justification of the claim" that the tariff system should not be changed. Now, he said, we "see what the motives that influenced Mr. Harris really were." He added that Harris's memory was in error about the "ten years"; the agreement actually had stipulated that revision could come five years after the Kanagawa port was opened (i.e., 1864). The Harris letter, which was reprinted in *Tokyo Nichi Nichi* for Japanese consumption, created a stir. Bingham was upset by what he saw as a predecessor's attempt "to steal my thunder" in the treaty reform campaign; and Harris's thoughts kept rippling through the journalistic and diplomatic community for years to come.[28]

The *Times* expressed elation in 1878 about the improved prospects for tariff reform, thanks to the support that Bingham and the U.S. State Department now threw behind it. House began writing often about concrete alternatives to the present system, even if the British would not go along. At one point, he recommended that Japan simply renounce the treaties and set whatever tariffs it pleased. No one would go to war over that, he said. All of the negotiations, "the endless iterations of conference, negotiation, correspondence," had "brought forth nothing—not even a mouse." Japan should be bold. "One sturdy breath of independence, and the swollen bubble so long blown by diplomatic arrogance and assumption tumbles back into the froth of which it was composed." A more realistic kind of "diplomatic ingenuity," he suggested later, would be to form an alliance with one other power, preferably the United States, but possibly France, Germany, or Russia, in which both would grant concessions, such as the mutual elimination of duties on imports. He did not see this as a permanent arrangement, since it violated his protectionist principles, but it might break the log jam. Trade between the two countries would soar, and the other treaty powers, including England, would be forced to negotiate new agreements. "To gain 'a great right,' it might be necessary to sanction 'a little wrong.'" He also held out hope for the unilateral negotiations then underway between Japan and the United States.

House's optimism soared when the Japanese and Americans reached tentative agreement in mid-1878 on a treaty returning tariff autonomy to Japan. But the hope turned sour when the Japanese, misperceiving American desires, made the bilateral agreement effective only when the other treaty powers had agreed to similar treaties. The impact of that mistake was to render the new pact meaningless. House called it "the most deplorable diplomatic blunder committed by Japanese agents since the original surrender of sovereign rights, twenty years ago." To ratify it now "would be just as useful" as "to submit the document to flames and ratify the ashes." He said the draft treaty had been excellent; it restored to Japan the right of "regulating customs duties and controlling foreign commerce." But with the added clause, the treaty became hostage to the British. "A whole agreement is carefully put together, like a child's toy structure, only to be knocked into fragments by the final touch." Years would pass before House would show optimism again about treaty revision. When the issue came up in 1879, he would write: "When Japan is prepared to say, 'This I want and this I will have,'—she will get it, and not before."[29]

House's editorials on extraterritoriality also quoted Harris. On this issue the aging diplomat had said: "*The provision of the Treaty giving the right of ex-territoriality to all Americans in Japan was against my conscience.*" He explained that the secretary of state at the time, W. L. Marcy, had condemned extraterritoriality "as an unjust interference with the municipal law of a country which no Western nation would tolerate for a moment," but had insisted that Harris include it anyway, because Congress would not ratify a treaty with an Asian nation without it. "I fear," Harris said, "that I shall not live to see this unjust provision struck out of our treaties, but I fondly hope that others may see it fully abrogated."[30] After establishing the ethical argument, House took a different tack on extraterritoriality, arguing that it was a less immediate problem, because the Japanese government had decided to let the consul court issue ride until tariff autonomy had been secured. For that reason, House's subsequent editorials on the topic had less to do with revision strategies than with the abuses the system caused. That did not make the essays milder, however. In article after article, the *Times* described iniquitous verdicts that issued from the consular courts, building in the process a powerful case against the system as a whole.

One of the first episodes to attract House's pen was a pair of nearly identical cases in the fall of 1877 that produced contradictory results in different courts. Two residents of the Tsukiji foreign quarters, one British, the other American, had refused to pay their rent. When the Japanese government sued, the British court ordered the woman to pay her back rent, while the American court ruled that, due to legal technicalities, the defendant owed nothing. Noting that the cases illustrated the "absurdity of the ex-territorial system," House ran a piece from *Hōchi Shimbun*, which asked: "How are foreigners justified in saying that their methods of dispensing justice are the only trustworthy ones?" The following May, House talked about the "growing scandal" of Yokohama sailors—"a notoriously ignorant, irresponsible, and, when vinously excited, quarrelsome class"—who got into violent scrapes and went away with little or no punishment. Following an 1880 case in which a British seaman named Ross murdered the officer of an American ship, House published a list of extraterritoriality's abuses: poor policing of the treaty ports, a woeful licensing system for bars and saloons, jurisdictional disputes over who should try the accused and who should administer punishment. The inconsistencies encouraged crime, House wrote; even though Ross had been sentenced to death, debates over who had jurisdiction meant that he might never be punished—"all because of that ever patent absurdity which still grows a luxuriant perennial crop of abuses—the distorted phenomenon of extraterritoriality."[31]

The episode that drew House's angriest attack followed the arrival of the German ship *Hesperia* in Yokohama's outer harbor in July 1879. The vessel had spent most of the previous month in Kobe, where a cholera epidemic had broken out; so the Japanese quarantined it, as they had all arrivals from the Osaka-Kobe region. The German minister Karl von Eisendecher objected, however, saying Japan had no jurisdiction over German ships. After a German doctor and the Yokohama consul general inspected the vessel, he ordered it to sail into the inner harbor and unload its passengers and cargo, even though a Japanese officer, aghast, "absolutely forbade the captain to leave the station." Bingham was convinced that the German defiance helped to spread the epidemic, which had taken more than 100,000 lives by December. As he wrote to the State Department: "I cannot resist the conviction that this toll of death would not have been nearly so great if the Government of Japan had been aided and not resisted, as she was by certain foreign powers." Former president Grant, visiting Japan at the time, fumed that "no European power would dare to do such a thing in the United States" and suggested that the Japanese fire at the German ship.

House published numerous articles on the episode, using phrases such as "outrage," "diplomatic law-breaking," and the "utter poverty" of the Germans' attempts to explain their actions. He contrasted von Eisendecher's insolence with the "lavish generosity" that Japan had heaped on German Prince Heinrich during a visit two months earlier. In December, House wrote that the *Hesperia* episode had touched off a debate in Germany and England that actually betokened an end to the extraterritorial system, perhaps within a decade: "The doors of debate have at length been thrown open, and . . . we may now look for that publicity which, in England, heralds the death blow of any system of unprincipled oppression and arrogant injustice." He predicted that Parkes, the man he blamed for goading von Eisendecher into defiance, would be recalled, if only the Japanese government would suggest it. House was naive about the possibility of the British minister's recall, but he was right in his revived dream about ending the consular court system, although fifteen years, rather than ten, would pass before it actually happened.[32]

Two visitors to Japan during the summer of 1879, one British and one American, helped to raise House's hopes that his fight for fairness was not futile. First came John Pope-Hennessy, the British governor of Hong Kong, on a June trip to examine the land about which he had heard such conflicting reports. Even though the trip was personal, Pope-Hennessy was hosted as a dignitary. He was received in Yokohama harbor "with ambassadorial honors and a salute of seventeen guns," given a sword by the Meiji Emperor, and lodged at the residence of Industry Minister Inoue Kaoru. From the first, the governor and House got on well, for they were soul mates. A former governor of West Africa, the Bahamas, and Barbados, Pope-Hennessy was a rarity among colonial officials, a man who treated subjects with respect and, in the sneering words of traveler Isabella Bird, harbored "known sympathies with coloured people." Since arriving in Hong Kong in 1877, he had set colonial precedents by clamping down on the opium trade, refusing to let Chinese be coerced into emigrating to Australia, and putting Chinese and Indians on the colony's legislative council. The Japanese paper *Yūbin Hōchi* said his policies were in direct contrast to the "active principle of the English in the far east," which was "to suck out the last drop of blood from the people."

Like House, he was adored by a minority and hated by most of his compatriots. One Hong Kong resident said his empathy for the Chinese caused "a sort of panic" among the British. His own foreign minister was amazed at his "eulogy of the cleanliness of the Chinese." A Chinese newspaper wrote that he had a habit "of treading upon a continuous series of official and communal corns," while a German journalist observed that his colonial work was "by no means in good odor." And when he arrived in Japan, the Yokohama editors accused him of ignoring the wishes of the Hong Kong British, slighting England's commercial interests, and being pro-native. They also hated the fact that he, like House, was critical of Parkes's treatment of the Japanese, though they hardly could have known just how critical. After returning to Hong Kong, he wrote home to former (and future) prime minister William Gladstone that Parkes's "bullying" and "acrid policy" had enabled "the Russians and the United States ministers to gain a position in this Empire they are not—according to Board of Trade returns—entitled to hold."

It was not surprising then that House covered Pope-Hennessy often in the *Times*, even after he returned home. He called him "liberal, generous and humane . . . the foremost officer of his country in this part of the world," and said that "malice alone, and a very low order of malice at that," motivated the clamor against him. In December, the *Times* devoted more than three pages to the governor's success in ending public flogging in Hong Kong. And the following winter House vacationed in Hong Kong, sending home a number of articles, including a March 13 essay showing Pope-Hennessy's efforts to wipe out the "trade in human flesh," a "simply enormous" industry in which teenage girls were bought, at an average of $350 each, to be sent as sex slaves to places like Singapore and San Francisco. In June, he thanked Pope-Hennessy for an "indefatigable" and effective campaign "to obtain for Japan that equitable and amicable consideration that is her due."[33]

House found even more succor in the summer's second visitor, Grant, whose world trip brought him to Japan on June 21. It was the last stop on the former president's odyssey. He had visited more than two dozen countries, and in many ways this was the journey's culminating triumph. During the ten weeks on the Asian rim, Grant met several times with the emperor, visited the Tokugawa shrines at Nikkō, enjoyed a dance by a hundred women wearing kimonos made of U.S. flags, and rode in a procession to Ueno Park along streets lined by "a multitude that might have been computed by the hundreds of thousands." The city of Tokyo alone spent more than $50,000 on his entertainment, and the nine-page list of gifts he received from scores of donors included silk pictures, two boxes of honeysuckle liquor, a bamboo bird cage, thirty cups, seventy-three volumes of Fukuzawa's writings (given by Fukuzawa), three seal furs, and three dozen handkerchiefs. In his final meeting with the emperor, he said he would "leave Japan greatly impressed with the possibilities and probabilities of her future."

In some ways these weeks were as grand for House as they were for the general. Like Pope-Hennessy, he was House's kindred spirit; unlike Pope-Hennessy, he was a fellow American. House and the former president met several times: with a small group of Americans on July 4, the day after Grant arrived in Tokyo; at the Finance Ministry during talks with Ōkuma; when Grant went to the Hakone mountain resort outside Tokyo late in August; when the general came to House's home for a private visit in Tsukiji near the end of the trip; and again when Grant was leaving Yokohama harbor on September 3, for the trip back to America. House also was invited on the excursion to Nikkō, but did not go because of physical problems, and because he had to write "the whole of the *Tokio Times* himself that week." Grant's secretary (and House's friend from the *Tribune* days) John Russell Young wrote after the Hakone visit that he had been eager to have Grant learn House's views "about the East" and that the general "told me he had a most pleasant talk with you." The luncheon at House's "pretty little house near the American Legation, looking out on the sea," was rendered more satisfying, in an ironic way, by the fact that

Grant had turned down an invitation from the British minister, claiming that the press of the schedule had forced him "to decline all private hospitalities."[34]

The friendship that formed between House and Grant probably had as much to do with the similarity of their views as with the fact that they moved in similar circles back in America. In his first Japanese speech, in Nagasaki, Grant toasted "the prosperity and independence of Japan," and as he traveled through the country, he constantly talked about how impressed he was by Japan's progress. He pronounced Tokyo's engineering education as equal to any in the world. He judged the treaties unfair and urged the Japanese to announce to the world that they were "at an end" and that "she was prepared to sign the most favorable conventions that could be devised, provided the treaty powers recognized her sovereign, independent rights," adding that "England is in no humor to make war upon Japan for a tariff." The former president also criticized the harsh European treatment of Asians generally, fuming in a July interview with the emperor that he had "seen things that make my blood boil, in the way the European powers attempt to degrade the Asiatic nations." Imperialist policy, he said, "seems to have no other aim than the extinction of the independence of the Asiatic nations. . . . It seems incredible that rights which at home we regard as essential to our independence and to our national existence . . . are denied to China and Japan. Among these rights there is none so important as the right to control commerce."

House discussed these views in a deluge of Grant-inspired articles that summer and fall. After a "little group of Americans" met with the general upon his arrival in Tokyo, House wrote: "He belongs to us. . . . He represents the best of what is common to us all." He reported on each of the general's movements, and when the trip drew to a close he wrote that no friend of Japan ever had evidenced "a sincerer determination to respect and encourage its efforts in the direction of real progress and independence." He said Grant had influenced the Japanese to insist on their international rights more forcefully, and he expected the former president, on his return to America, "to aid her in every meritorious step she may take toward the realization of her hopes as a free nation." Ten days after his departure, House announced that a new international organization, Friends of the East, was being formed to espouse Japanese independence. Two of its founding members would be Ulysses S. Grant and John Pope-Hennessy.[35]

By June 1880, rumors about the demise of the *Tokio Times* were rife; so it took few by surprise when the June 26 issue announced the paper's suspension "for a period of at least six months, and perhaps one year" because House had to make a trip to America. The issue's contents were much like those of other weeks: a description of "domestic and other slavery" in Hong Kong, a call for Japanese villages to spruce up their buildings, a report on Japan's national railway system, several ads (in one, "E. H. H. Tokio, Tsukiji" sought to rent a piano), and a host of "personal intelligence" items, including an announcement that a new Russo-Greek bishop had been appointed in Tokyo. House reported that friends had urged him to turn the paper over to someone else while he was gone, but he had rejected the idea because the *Times* was uniquely "the vehicle of expression for the views of a single person." He said that "to make it the medium for the sentiments of another . . . would break up an association upon which the efficacy of the publication has, in a good measure, been felt to depend."

There were nearly as many accounts of why the paper was closing as there were rumor mongers. The Yokohama papers said that its readership was too small and it was no longer viable. Some thought dissension within the government had undermined support for the paper's subsidy; others suggested that House had alienated powerful backers with his harsh attacks on certain policies and customs. The rumors were pure speculation, however; the real reasons were quite different. His decision had nothing to do with the financial status of the paper, which still boasted the largest circulation among the English-language papers. Nor does it seem to have resulted from any loss of backers, or of the subsidy. All the evidence supports House's report in the last issue that the *Times* "was never a prosperous paper, in the ordinary sense, and was not expected to be," but had "paid its way, and a little more," which "was quite enough."

The reason House gave for shutting it down was that he had to go home for business reasons, which clearly was true. He had not been to America for seven years; his uncle and business agent had died unexpectedly (and in debt) the previous winter, leaving House without close relatives and plunging his financial affairs into "a serious confusion"; the calls for him to come home and straighten things out were "loud and earnest." There also was a matter of health. House's early revelries—the heavy drinking, the battlefield recklessness, the devil-may-care mountain climbing—had begun to take their toll on his body. During 1879, occasional attacks of the gout left his joints inflamed and wracked with pain. Not long before the closure of the paper, he wrote to his friend Young that he would have to keep the letter brief, because he was in bed "with rivets of red hot iron around my ancles [sic]." His physical problems were not widely known, since he did most of his writing at home, but he hoped to find medical assistance back in America. There also was an even less public reason for his leaving. The treaty revision fight had lost steam at the end of the 1870s, and Ōkuma decided that it might help to have House do quiet lobbying abroad for revision. So it made sense to shut down the paper for a few months, so that he could get things in order back at home, and fight his crusades in a different venue.[36]

When the *Times*'s end came, House felt pleased with what he had accomplished. "The work built up since 1877 by conscientious and honest, if not always powerful or skillful, hands can never be pulled down," he wrote. His crusade had "progressed too far to be in peril of undermining by any process its enemies can apply." He had testimonials to the paper's influence beyond counting: letters from friends like the Hartford clergyman Joseph Twichell saying "you have made a good deal of a Japanese patriot of me," Bingham's constant use of *Times* articles in his despatches to the State Department, the *Tokyo Nichi Nichi*'s designation of a staffer to translate *Times* pieces for the Japanese public, the constant translation and collection of his essays by Japan's government offices. Even the denunciations of the Yokohama papers made it clear that he was taken seriously, and the fact that one of them, the *Mail*, had begun by 1880 to soften its opposition to tariff autonomy suggested that his arguments were having an effect.

It would be a mistake to give House too much credit for changes that occurred in the imperialist nations' policies toward Japan. But it would be an equal mistake to ignore his influence. At the very least, he gave voice to a pro-Japanese view that, until 1877, had been absent from the journalistic discourse; by 1880 he had helped to make that view a part of the mainstream debate. And his name carried much weight in Japzan itself. Young, the colleague from those old days when House had been "envied among men" in New York journalism, said his Tokyo friend had "given himself to Japan with a spirit that I might call the missionary spirit of self-abnegation. He has fought her battles. He has defended her name. He has endeavored to win her a place among the nations. . . . His name is a power in Japan." House was suffering an attack of gout so severe when he left for America in August that servants had to carry him aboard ship. But his spirits were high, buoyed by the knowledge that he was making a difference, and by a conviction that the assignment just handed to him would allow him to exert new influence back home. It also would give him a chance to show America and Europe to Koto.[37]

NOTES

1. For House's career, see *Tokyo Nichi Nichi Shimbun,* December 18, 1876.

2. Japanese press statistics are based on Yamamoto Taketoshi, *Kindai Nihon no shimbun dokusha sō,* 402; and the power of Tokyo's "prestige papers" is noted by Tokutomi Sohō in Chikamori Haruyoshi, *Jinbutsu Nihon shimbun shi,* 90. For the foreign press and population information, see James E. Hoare, *Japan's Treaty Ports and Foreign Settlements,* 181–85; and Ebihara Hachirō, *Nihon Ōji shimbun zasshi shi,* 73.

3. For the description of Brooke, see Ian Nish, ed., *Britain and Japan: Biographical Portraits,* 22; for Fox's comments, Grace Fox, *Britain and Japan 1858–1883,* 455;

Fraser's evaluation is in her *A Diplomatist's Wife in Japan,* vol. 1, 200; the *Mail* and *Herald* comments are found in Olavi Fält, *The Clash of Interests,* 218 (*Japan Weekly Mail,* "nonsense," May 23, 1875), and 362 (*Japan Herald,* "happy," April 9, 1881); Bingham's remarks are found in his Despatch to Secretary of State W. M. Evarts, no. 1206, November 15, 1880; and the *Chōya* essay is reprinted in Ebihara, *Ōji shimbun,* 95–97.

4. The subsidies to the *Mail* are discussed in Yamamoto Fumio, *Shimbun hattatsu shi,* 166–67, and Ebihara, 81–86; Howell's promise to publish news on Japanese progress is found in a letter to Ōkuma, November 19, 1873, in the National Archives, Tokyo, Yakukō shūsei, series 1, no. 6. Howell's demand for more money is found in a memo from Charles LeGendre to Ōkuma Shigenobu, July 8, 1874 (OM, C462, Waseda University). The LeGendre memos are in OM C462 (July 8, 1874) and OM C479 (December 23, 1874, with 83–95 dealing with the creation of a paper). The Japanese translation of a similar LeGendre memo to Ōkuma on July 12, 1874, is found in the Japanese National Archives, Yakukō shūsei, series 2, no. 5; it argues that without a good reputation in Europe, Japan will not be able to secure much needed foreign loans. It is significant that by 1873, Japan was using Howell's agency to subscribe to five London papers, including the *Times* and the *Saturday Review;* letter from Hashidrumé to Howell, September 8, 1873, in Yakukō shūsei, series 1, no. 4, National Archives.

5. For House's early contract talks, see his correspondence to unnamed official, item 153, August 15, 1874, in Yakukō shūsei, series 2, no. 8, National Archives, Tokyo. LeGendre's 1875–1876 memos to Ōkuma about using House (OM, Waseda University: LeGendre memos of January 1 and April 5, 1875 and March 5, 1876; and Ōkuma memo to LeGendre, September 9, 1876) are detailed in Kasahara Hidehiko, "Rujiyandoru to seifukei Ōji shimbun," 208–09.

6. Fukuchi's ideas are found in *Tokyo Nichi Nichi Shimbun,* July 28, 1875. House's comments about his own consistency are in *Tokio Times,* July 7, 1878, 2.

7. The contract is in OM A1115 (October 1, 1876), Waseda University. The extension (June 24, 1878) and Hirai's discussion (April 24, 1878) are found in OM A1116; both are discussed in Kasahara, 211–12.

8. The terms of the Candace House estate are discussed in a series of letters between John Child, House's uncle and American financial manager, and Washington Hobart, June 6 to July 14, 1879; also see Hobart to House, January 20, 1879; all letters are in EHC, University of Virginia. House lived in these years at Plot 9, in the Tsukiji area, about two blocks from the American legation.

9. Van Buren's "spreads" in letter from House to John Russell Young, undated, JRY, Library of Congress; Mason comments in W. B. Mason, "The Foreign Colony," 244; apartment fire report, in *Japan Weekly Mail,* January 27, 1877; Tokyo fire description in *Tokio Times,* January 3, 1880; description of House as a "chief" sufferer in *Japan Weekly Mail,* December 27, 1879; fire statistics in *Japan Gazette,* December 29, 1779; and report on the girls school, in letter from House to Young, February 5, 1880, JRY, as well as in *Japan Weekly Mail,* July 24, 1880.

10. Circulation figures and subscription rates are discussed in Hoare, *Japan's Treaty Ports,* 142; and Nish, *Britain and Japan,* 21. Also see *Tokio Times,* July 6, 1878, 2, and January 3, 1880, 14. Only fifteen of the *Times*'s 350 subscriptions were taken by the government. The evaluations of House are found in Mason, "Foreign

Colony," 243; W. E. Griffis, *Verbeck of Japan,* 289; *Japan Weekly Mail,* January 6, 1877; Tokutomi Sohō, "Hausu sensei no omoide," 116–17.

11. See *Tokio Times* for literature summaries, May 26, 1877; for *ayu,* March 3, 1877; for diplomat's portrait, January 30, 1877; and for toppling into the canal/moat, February 10 and 17, 1877.

12. "Destruction of an Illusion," *Tokio Times,* March 3, 1877. For House's overall analysis, see *Times,* September 29, 1877. Several sources, including Shōwa Joshi Daigaku, ed., "E. H. Hausu," 386, say House followed the government troops to Kyūshū. Nothing in House's papers, or in the *Tokio Times* coverage, supports that claim, however.

13. The cartoon is in *Japan Punch* (November 1877); for Tokutomi, see his "Hausu sensei," 120.

14. All articles are from the *Tokio Times:* "Asiatics," April 28, 1877; Christians and heathen, March 15, 1879; "senseless vulgarism," June 26, 1880; Japan's transformation, January 6, 1877; purchase of Japanese paper, June 26, 1880; *Niigata-maru,* September 22, 1877; national banks, July 7, 1877; telegraph office, March 30, 1878; and Chinese approach, August 10, 1878.

15. *Tokio Times:* "intellectual independence," October 10, 1877; silk worm exports, June 16, 1877; press law enforcement, January 27, 1877; firing of Horace Wilson, June 2, 1877; the Kaisei Gakkō had become Tokyo University that April, but the *Times* still referred to it as Kaisei Gakkō; squirting water on fires, March 23, 1878; and "useless" fire department, January 3, 1880.

16. Bingham's comment is in his Despatch to Secretary of State W. M. Evarts, no. 760, March 30, 1878. Mori's remark is found in *Meiroku Zasshi,* March 1875, in William Braisted, trans., *Meiroku Zasshi,* 399. Kusunose is discussed in Sharon Sievers, *Flowers in Salt,* 29–30.

17. Nish, *Britain and Japan,* 17.

18. See *Tokio Times,* February 24, 1877 (critique of imperialism); November 30, 1878 (not using force in Korea); January 5, 1878 ("no man's pie"); September 6, 1879 (arms sales); January 12, 1878 (African trade); December 29, 1877 (transfer of money due to opium); April 10, 1880 (Chinese scholar's view of opium); and April 13, 1878 (import of opium to Japan). Articles supporting opium imports are found in the *Japan Herald,* April 10, 1878; and the *Japan Gazette,* January 7, 1880.

19. *Tokio Times* editorials: April 14, 1877 (Parkes's "industry and energy"); September 8, 1877 ("meddle and muddle"); September 15, 1877 (Parkes and postal union); July 26, 1879 (purchase of postal building); April 19, 1879 (treaty revision); and November 8, 1879 (Parkes's departure). For a private Japanese view of Parkes's departure, see Yoshida Kiyonari letter to U. S. Grant, October 11, 1879, USG, Library of Congress.

20. For writing Parkes out of Japan, see *Japan Weekly Mail,* January 4, 1902, as well as Harry Emerson Wildes, *Press and Social Currents in Japan,* 266–67. There is no evidence for any agreement with the government to attack Parkes, nor do House's editorials at the *Times* support the idea that this was his main goal. The *Japan Punch* description is from February 1878.

21. House to John Russell Young, March 27, 1880, JRY, Library of Congress.

22. For the quotation from Young, *Tokio Times,* December 27, 1879; "hack-writer," *Japan Gazette,* July 30, 1881, cited in Fält, *Clash of Interests,* 260; "mode of

warfare," reprinted in *Tokio Times,* August 18, 1877; and "damnable iteration," *Japan Gazette,* January 4, 1879.

23. *Tokio Times:* December 27, 1879 (House's explanation of his method); January 27, 1877 (*Herald*'s rudeness); January 24, 1877 (*Mail*'s arrogance); February 10, 1877 (reputation for reliability); and November 30, 1878 (false rumors).

24. *Tokio Times:* June 26, 1880 (attack); December 13, 1879 ("obscurity"); January 20, 1877 (*Mail* contradictions); August 4, 1877 (trivializing Japan); and February 2, 1878 (*Kagoshima* review).

25. House's last issue, *Tokio Times,* June 26, 1880; *Herald* diatribe, *Japan Daily Herald,* June 26, 1880; and Brinkley's comment in Harold S. Williams, *Tales of the Foreign Settlements in Japan*, 163.

26. *Nichi Nichi* on tariff reduction, translated in *Tokio Times,* November 24, 1877; and Fukuzawa's view of foreign relations, *Tokio Times,* December 14, 1878.

27. *Tokio Times:* British income from tariffs, October 20, 1877; and British silk industry, April 24, 1880 (emphasis in original).

28. *Tokio Times:* July 28, 1877 ("a national right"), and November 24, 1877 (Japan's "independent right" and Harris's letter; italics in *Tokio Times* but not in letter itself). House's letter to Harris was written January 17, 1875; Harris's reply was sent March 22, 1875; both, marked "copy," are in Charles LeGendre Papers, Library of Congress. The reprint in the *Times* is verbatim from the letter, except for minor punctuation changes and the addition of a sentence saying that Harris attempted to set a tariff limit, on the one hand, to provide enough revenue to "show the Japanese the benefits of foreign trade, and on the other hand to . . . avoid such excessive taxation as would amount to prohibition." It is not clear whether the addition results from an omission in the LeGendre copy or an addition to the *Times* version; it does not materially change the letter. For Bingham's response, see Payson J. Treat, *Diplomatic Relations between the United States and Japan,* vol. 2, 33. Treat doubts that Harris intended his letter to be published, but the fact that he responded specifically to a request from House, a journalist, suggests that Treat was mistaken.

29. *Tokio Times:* July 27, 1878 (unilateral renunciation of treaty); August 10, 1878 (alliance with a strong nation); February 1, 1879 (the fatal clause); and April 19, 1879 (useless "spectacle").

30. From *Tokio Times,* November 24, 1877, Charles LeGendre Papers, Library of Congress, emphasis in the *Times* but not in the letter. The last line of the letter said, "I fondly hope that you [rather than "others"] may see it fully abrogated"; otherwise the quotations follow the Harris letter precisely.

31. *Tokio Times:* September 8, 1877 (Tsukiji cases); May 18, 1878 (violent sailors); and June 12, 1880 (Seaman Ross).

32. *Tokio Times:* August 9, 1879 (general account of *Hesperia* episode); July 19, 1879 ("diplomatic law-breaking"); July 17, 1879 (German prince); and December 13, 1879 (discussion in England and Germany). For Grant, Bingham comments, see Treat, *Diplomatic Relations,* vol. 2, 88.

33. The salute on Pope-Hennessy's arrival is described in James Pope-Hennessy, *Verandah,* 213; Bird's comment, from *The Golden Chersonee,* is in Sir John Pope-Hennessy Papers, Box 8–2, Rhodes Library, Oxford University; *Yūbin Hōchi* quote from *Tokio Times,* July 14, 1879; "sort of panic," Pope-Hennessy papers, Box 8–1, 19;

"treading on corns," from *China Mail,* in *Verandah,* 197–98; bad "odor," from *Allgemeine Zeitung,* in *Tokio Times,* December 27, 1879; "bullying" and "acrid policy," Pope-Hennessy to Gladstone, August 24, 1879, in William Gladstone Papers, British Library; "liberal, generous," *Tokio Times,* June 21, 1879; and "utterances of John Hennessy," *Tokio Times,* June 19, 1880.

34. The Ueno parade is described in John Russell Young, *Around the World with General Grant,* vol. 2, 572–75; the gift list, Ulysses Grant Papers, series 10, box 24, Library of Congress; farewell to emperor, August 1879, Grant Papers; Hakone meeting, letter from Young to House, August 22, 1879, EHC, University of Virginia; Nikkō excursion, House to Grant, July 31, 1879, Grant Papers; declining Parkes's, meeting at House's home, Young, *Around the World,* vol. 2, 590–92.

35. Young, *Around the World,* vol. 2, 481 (Grant's toast), 582–83 (renouncing the treaties), and 543 ("blood boil"). From the *Tokio Times:* "belongs to us," July 5, 1879; Grant will aid Japan, August 30, 1879; and Friends of the East, September 13, 1879.

36. Letters from House to John Russell Young, JRY, Library of Congress: business demands, March 27, 1880; and "red hot iron," June 18, 1880. The fact that House could not secure a like-minded American to take his place at the *Times* also may have played a role in the decision to close the paper; see House to Young, March 27, 1880, and Young to House, December 1, 1879, EHC, University of Virginia.

37. "Work Built Up," *Tokio Times,* June 26, 1880. For influence on Twichell, see Twichell to House, June 9, 1879, MTP, University of California at Berkeley; for *Tokyo Nichi Nichi* translator, see *Japan Chronicle Weekly,* February 16, 1922 (I am indebted to Peter O'Connor for this piece of information); and for Young's evaluation, see Young, *Around the World,* vol. 2, 591–92.

9

Japan, 1881–1885: The Outsiders

> Boys to the army, Girls to the factory.
> Reeling thread is for the country too.
>
> —Female silk reelers' song[1]

Edward House traversed the Pacific once, and the Indian and Atlantic Oceans three times each in the 1880s, and his life course took more traversals still. The decade's early years pushed him to new peaks of influence, while the later gave him fresh understandings of pain and torment. The last half of 1882 found him searching for a different niche in Tokyo following Ōkuma Shigenobu's fall from power, whereas 1883 provided dramatic evidence of his influence. And if this was a tumultuous time for House, it was equally so for his Asian homeland: partly because of the political convulsions that followed the 1881 government change and partly because the drive toward modernity had begun to pull new groups into the national discourse, groups whose experiences challenged not only the evolving state structure but the established ways of seeing the world. The middle-aged men who shaped policy still worried about the traditional elites, but by the early 1880s they were thinking more and more about the newly visible segments of society: women, farmers, businessmen, even novelists and artists. It is a good time, thus, to pause in our examination of the Meiji evolution and look at what was happening to those outsider groups whose lives were influenced as much by the gales of modernity as the old elites' had been.

By now, nearly every sector of urban society was awash in changes that balanced Japanese traditions and modern ideas. In business and industry, for example, the 1880s saw the emergence of private enterprises run by profit-oriented businessmen who combined old-style government ties with a keen sense of markets and a cold-headed (often cold-hearted) commitment to efficiency and profit. In shipping, the fledgling Mitsubishi company of Iwasaki Yatarō from Shikoku used the government contracts it had won during the Taiwan expedition and Satsuma Rebellion to create a company which, after an 1885 merger, would dominate Japanese shipping throughout the twentieth century. Iwasaki also purchased the Takashima Coal Mine in 1881, and by mid-decade was running warehouses, lending money, and operating currency exchanges. Other businesses took hold in the 1880s when the government sold off more than twenty of the unprofitable model factories that it had created in the 1870s. And the official-turned-businessman Shibusawa Eiichi used the early 1880s as his launching pad for a remarkable career as Japan's first "venture capitalist and promoter for hundreds of new enterprises." In 1883, he opened the Osaka Spinning Mill, on the premise that a modern company needed three things: large capital investment, technological and technical expertise, and efficient production. Among other innovations, he purchased the best and largest machinery, introduced electric lights, and experimented with nighttime shifts. Rapidly soaring profits made the company a model; they also served as a base for Shibusawa to organize more than fifty other firms over the next fifteen years. Japan's industrial takeoff would not occur until late in the nineteenth century, but by the mid-1880s, the class of private, government-connected entrepreneurs that would make the takeoff possible had emerged.

A similar eruption occurred in journalism. The 1870s had seen the birth of a modern press, with all of the prestige papers tied, like House's *Times,* to political factions. They were small in size; their circulations rarely reached 10,000; their pages were erudite but dull. Financial pressures and political tumult began to change that in the early 1880s, however, giving birth to respectable commercial journalism. The pioneer was Murayama Ryōhei, who took charge of *Osaka Asahi Shimbun* in 1881 with the declaration that a newspaper was "not merely a vehicle for . . . political discussions" but a tool to "describe the mysteries of society" and to make money. The very next year, the influential Fukuzawa Yukichi launched *Jiji Shinpō* with those same goals in Tokyo. He deplored the partisanship of the elite papers and made it clear that neither news nor a solid balance sheet was beneath his dignity. He also went after ads, declaring that "advertising is as important to a business as weapons are to an army." As in business, these pioneers would not see their new ideas become the industry norm until the 1890s, but by mid-decade *Asahi* had become the biggest, richest daily in the country, and *Jiji*'s circulation had surpassed that of all the old elite papers.[2]

Similar stirrings were occurring in literature and the arts, where the rampant westernization of the 1870s was producing new ways of envisioning reality. In 1885, for example, Tsubouchi Shōyō attacked the didacticism of traditional fiction in an influential essay, "The Essence of the Novel," lambasting writers' tendency to "consider the novel as an instrument of education" and "to stop at nothing to squeeze in a moral." He called for them to write about real people living real lives and experiencing real emotions. He was not good at writing that kind of fiction himself, but by the turn of the century, a number of skilled writers had turned Japanese fiction into an innovative, exhilarating arena.[3] A reverse twist of this process occurred in painting, where the same social and intellectual forces were at work. Although the *bunmei kaika*, or enlightened civilization rage of the 1870s, had sent traditional Japanese painting into a sharp decline, the eighties saw the trend reversed, and the pioneer this time was an American, Ernest Fenollosa, who had come to Tokyo in 1878 as a teacher, at the invitation of House's friend Edward Morse. Fenollosa fell in love with traditional Japanese art and went everywhere arguing that the native arts were as good as anything in the West. He and his famous student, Okakura Tenshin, founded the Tokyo Art School with government backing to push their ideas, and by the end of the 1880s Japan's art establishment was promoting the effort to combine Western and Japanese styles, an effort that gave birth to Japanese impressionism. The 1880s were thus a time, in almost every sphere, when the seeds of modernity, planted hastily in the 1870s, emerged as healthy Japanese hybrids, a time when most evolving institutions combined native and foreign elements to create something newly, and uniquely, "Japanese."

Life was dynamic for society's outsider groups too, but usually not in such positive ways. The Tokyo leaders may have worked wonders at the national level in handling economic challenges and taking Japan through the waters of imperialism. But they cared less about the impact of change on the non-elites. Someone had to pay the bills, to fill the ranks of the new army and factories, to follow the "modern" laws and customs imposed from the top, to grapple with the loss of friends who moved away to the towns and military training camps. As in most modernizing societies, it was the *minshū* or common masses who had to pay up most often. These groups included both the villagers and the growing urban underclasses: fishermen, miners, rickshaw pullers, prostitutes, charcoal sellers, farmers, factory workers, and most of the country's women—in other words, about 90 percent of the population. Not all were victims. Indeed, the rich farmers' (*gōnō*) class took much of the initiative in the rural areas until the middle 1880s, setting their own agenda for change, profiting off of government policies, and growing ever richer. But the underclass tended to be heard only if they made trouble; their concerns were addressed "not as a matter of justice or right," but "because they would strengthen national cohesion."[4]

The experiences of two groups in the early 1880s, the women and the farmers, illustrate just how high the costs of change were for most Japanese. Farmers constituted 80 percent of the population at the end of the Tokugawa era, and while Japan's 60,000-plus villages were seen by the samurai simply as sites where people should behave themselves, produce goods, and pay taxes, they actually were complex places. Indeed, the traditional social and political divisions, reinforced by an increasingly commercial economy, had provided villages with enough autonomy and income by the 1800s for the richer farmers to live well. They also had divided village life into distinct strata, with a few affluent families dominating local life, handing out gifts, and providing baths to poor neighbors, while a few held poorly paying but respectable jobs and the majority worked dawn to dusk to scrape out a living. The villages' relative autonomy meant that despite official restrictions (no fine food, no silk garments, no smoking, no conspicuous spending, little tea or alcohol), most villagers actually wore, ate, and did whatever their incomes would allow, so long as they did not call attention to themselves by riots or loud complaints.

Our belief in progress tempts us to assume that life got better for farmers in the Meiji era. The truth, however, is more complex. While the income of some improved, the centralizing policies of the new government were, by the 1880s, taking away much village autonomy and making agricultural life even more difficult for great numbers. Several of the era's new laws fell most heavily, or sometimes just most irritatingly, on the farmers. The endless official admonitions to wear Western-style haircuts, to avoid public nudity and urination, and to stop blackening teeth galled most villagers, and the 1873 switch to the solar calendar disrupted their agricultural rhythms, prompting one critic to grumble: "The cherry trees bloom in the sixth and seventh months, and the summer storms come in the tenth. . . . Nothing is the way it should be." More fundamentally, compulsory education and universal conscription forced young people to school and to military camps when their labor was needed in the fields. It is no wonder that the military draft was referred to as a "blood tax," particularly after rich *gōnō* began buying exemptions for their sons.

Indeed, mountain and seaside villagers alike found almost every area of life constricted by the new regulations. And they did not always accept the rules passively. As Scott Schnell's study of Hida in the Japan Alps shows, when twenty-seven-year-old Umemura Hayami from far-off Mito was appointed governor in 1868, the villagers objected. He set out at once to overturn the region's "backward" practices: removing Buddhist images from Shintō shrines, replacing fire brigades with national security troops, requiring that taxes be paid in cash, publicly humiliating girls who had sex with married men. But the villagers resisted, and when he forced compliance, they rose in a bloody though unsuccessful rebellion that left Umemura dead and the reforms in limbo. The whole episode, says Schnell, was "a clash between two distinct value systems—that of the local mountain peasant versus that of the centralized administrative bureaucracy."

Most serious for the farmers was the land tax. As in the Tokugawa era, government assessments were based almost exclusively on land holdings; there were no income taxes and few levies on other kinds of wealth. But after 1873, the nature of the land tax changed. No longer would it be based on crop yield, but on land value alone, which meant that farmers received no relief when crops were bad. The system also was administered in a less personal way after the early Meiji years, with land values determined more often by officials who lived far away. Although protests led to a slight loosening of the system in 1877, and a lowering of the tax from 3 to 2.5 percent, the burden remained heavy, with land taxes accounting for a full 80.5 percent of government revenue in the last half of the 1870s. One result was rural anger, with each of those years producing at least a dozen local tax revolts. The situation got even worse for farmers early in the 1880s, due mainly to the Matsukata deflationary policies discussed in chapter 7, which put national development ahead of ordinary citizens' well-being. Government and industry may have been helped by the curtailment of spending, but "what benefited industry," says Stephen Vlastos, "hurt agriculture, particularly the small and marginal producers who produced cash crops." Rice prices plunged between 1881 and 1884, to a third of what they had been, raw silk prices to half. And taxes kept rising, so that they consumed twice as much of most farmers' income in 1884 as they had in 1877. Bankruptcies more than tripled in two years, passing the 108,000 mark in 1885.

For the very poorest families, the impact of all this was marginal (though even margins could be fatal). Like farmer Kanji in the Meiji novel *Soil* (Tsuchi), they were too poor for inflation or recession to make much of a difference. The pattern, says the schoolteacher Nagatsuka Takashi, was about the same as it long had been: "At the end of the harvest season," they simply "withered up like the vegetation around them. . . . While the frogs and insects hibernated peacefully, farmers had to consume their meager stores of grain just to keep themselves alive from day to day. Inevitably a time would come when they had nothing left to eat." For those at the village's middle level, however, the recession of the early 1880s was dire. And unlike those at the bottom, they were not always content to curse officials or sabotage creditors. As a result, the early 1880s produced the largest commoner uprisings of the century. In the fall of 1882, more than a thousand northern farmers rioted in Fukushima, when police tried to break up their protests against being forced to leave their fields and build roads. Two years later, a small cadre of farmers not far away, at Mt. Kaba in northern Ibaraki Prefecture, gave their lives attempting to assassinate officials responsible for the Fukushima crackdown. And in November 1884, more than 5,000 Chichibu villagers, who had seen silk prices fall by almost 50 percent, rose in a highly disruptive and widely publicized rebellion west of Tokyo, seizing debt records and demanding tax reduction, as well as government protection against harsh creditors.

None of these rebellions, or nearly a dozen others like them, achieved their goals. They did, however, illustrate two important things about Japan's villagers in the 1880s. First, they showed how dire conditions were. Pushed to the limit by government taxes, and by creditors who took advantage of misery, villagers were willing to put their lives on the line by the thousands. They had little to lose from violent uprisings. And beside, when things had gotten bad in earlier, more Confucian centuries, benevolent officials (at least in nostalgic retellings) typically had come to the farmers' aid. Second, the rebellions show us how politically sophisticated many of Japan's villagers were. Many rebel leaders had ties to the freedom and rights movement; indeed, quite a few actually were members of the Jiyūtō, or Liberal Party. Roger Bowen has shown that if economic destitution was one motivation for participants in these incidents, political ideas were another, especially for the leaders. Many used words like freedom and democracy, and they often cared more about such ideas than ex-samurai party members did. As one commoner song went:

> We are free; we have rights.
> The people of Japan must claim their rights;
> If we do not, then our companion is shame.

This political sophistication even pushed farmers in some villages to write model constitutions and form debating societies. The Chichibu "uprising was not just an expression of debtor discontent," says the historian of popular movements Irokawa Daikichi; it reflected a "revolutionary transformation in values" that allowed farmers to say, "Justice is on our side and not on the government's."[5] Unfortunately, he also shows, poverty and emperor-centered "conventional morality" combined to prevent most farmers from imbibing those new values.

If poverty and despair characterized the lives of most farmers in the early 1880s, powerlessness and disaffection shaped the consciousness of that other large outsider group, the Meiji women. This group was both smaller than the farmers (only half of the nation's population, as opposed to 80 percent) and more diverse, representing every social status and economic class. But women also had much in common with the farmers. They too were expected to live lives of self-abnegation, to contribute to the task of state building without making major demands. They were admonished to perform their work invisibly and to stay off the public thoroughfares and out of the limelight, unless duty demanded otherwise. They were asked to provide the nation's moral foundation and much of the labor to run the factories and farms. And like the farmers, many of the Meiji women found their situation *more* restricted, not less, than it had been in earlier centuries. In some areas, the limitations they had to endure were greater even than those imposed on male farmers. Early Meiji women were expected, for example, to accept a spouse's lovers without complaint. And they were banned from leading political meetings, from receiving an equal education, and from initiating divorce proceedings, except in unusual cases.

The restrictions did not, however, keep all women out of the country's expanding political life. The people's rights movement may have been overwhelmingly male—certainly, its early leadership held little sympathy for women's issues—but its promise of democracy attracted several of Japan's pioneer female activists. We already have seen how Kusunose Kita created a stir during the late 1870s by insisting on voting rights for some women. By the time of House's return to Japan in 1882, other women were taking to popular rights platforms across southern and western Japan. Kishida Toshiko, a former tutor of the Meiji empress, packed lecture halls with women sympathetic to her demands for political rights; sent to jail for eight days in 1883 for denouncing the patriarchal family system, she never muted her insistence on gender equality. One member of Kishida's audience in the Inland Sea town of Okayama in 1882 was Fukuda Hideko, a teenage teacher whose mother had tutored her in ideas about individuals and rights. Fukuda was so moved that she decided to reject a marriage proposal and open her own school for girls; two years later, deciding that more effective work could be done in the capital, she traveled to Tokyo and joined a group that had decided to take weapons to Seoul, where they would help pro-democracy progressives overthrow the autocratic Korean government. It was a bizarre plan, and the sixty-odd plotters were arrested, tried, and jailed, but it made Fukuda famous as dramatic evidence of how determined some women were to transcend traditional roles. The press hailed and damned her as "the first woman jailed for a political crime."

These popular rights activists did not, however, typify most Japanese women in the early 1880s. While they were important as a vanguard, the vast majority led quieter, usually grimmer lives. The view that women should remain at home, rearing children and maintaining "the family's fortune and reputation," dominated conventional thought just as it had in the Tokugawa era. But while a decentralized political system allowed Tokugawa women much freedom and variety in actual practice, the Meiji government's increasing efficiency meant that women's lives actually grew more restrictive. "State attention to women's roles," write Sally Hastings and Sharon Nolte, "was a product of the sweeping political and social reforms of the Meiji Restoration," and the state now defined "good wives and wise mothers" as valuable, even while it condemned political activity by women. Gender replaced class and status as the dominant way of separating groups. A "cult of productivity" became normative. Even a girl's education focused, after the 1880s, on subjects that would help her run a household. It would take most of the Meiji era for the new norms to be codified. Not until 1889, for example, would women be barred explicitly from political activity, and only in 1898 would a new Civil Code make the subordination of wives to husbands a matter of law. But by the early 1880s, the state was moving determinedly toward the gender-based orthodoxy that angered Kishida.[6]

For large numbers of women and girls, even the restrictions of the traditional household would have seemed a paradise in the early 1880s, however—partly because the power that women exerted at home was extensive, and partly because the government's policies were now forcing thousands of young women into excruciating work in the nation's factories, mines, and brothels. Like soldiers, these women and girls were defined as servants of the state, instruments in the effort to create a strong nation capable of resisting the imperial powers. But more even than the farmers and the "good wives," they were forced to give their very marrow to the modernity machine, receiving in return neither respect nor enough money to eke out a decent daily existence.

Thousands of women became, in effect, indentured servants in the prostitute trade. During the Tokugawa period, most but not all major cities had had licensed brothel quarters; now, with the advent of a new era, the licensing policy became universal. Although the government issued a decree banning the buying and selling of prostitutes following the 1872 *Maria Luz* affair, the prostitute trade actually had become robust by the second Meiji decade, regardless of the polite terms agents used to mask what they were doing. The officials simply winked. Indeed, when the powerful Itō Hirobumi (a notorious womanizer, married to a former geisha) was asked in 1896 what he thought of the public prostitution system, he said it was an excellent way for loving daughters to help fill the family coffers; he also said his favorite pastime was "a geisha companion to entertain me after work." As the process typically worked, agents would visit the villages and offer sizeable loans to parents who agreed to send their girls off to the city, where they supposedly would pour sake, eat rich food, and wear stylish kimonos; if they wished, they would return home in a couple of years. The reality, of course, was different. The girls thus recruited, some of them as young as ten, would be paid so little after the brothel owner took out his fees that repayment became impossible. And their living and working conditions were deplorable: two meager meals a day, poor health care, and long hours, serving one customer after another each night. Most women could not quit because their loans had not been paid off. They were slaves.

The inhuman conditions did not, however, stem the tide of girls and women to the cities' entertainment quarters. By 1883, Tokyo had 400 houses of prostitution, with 3,156 licensed prostitutes; a dozen years later, the number was up to 5,456; and by 1904, Japan as a whole had 43,143 licensed prostitutes. One reason many parents were willing to give their daughters to the system was that they did not realize how bad the conditions at brothels were. While most urbanites understood the situation well, villagers frequently were ignorant, particularly in the first half of Meiji, and thus susceptible to the agent's "sweet talk." Another reason was poverty. When an agent promised a fat loan, and the possibility of outside income, it was hard for a starving family to resist. Asked why she had sold her daughter, one mother replied: "We sold her in order to pay our debts, so we feel we needn't be ashamed."[7]

Even more young women were forced into difficult work situations by Japan's growing silk and cotton industries. Driven to make Japan competitive, Meiji officials threw a great deal of energy into encouraging textile factories, and by the end of the 1870s, the silk industry was challenging the silk centers of Europe. To run the machines in the increasingly modern factories, employers turned to the nation's young women, first to samurai daughters and then, by the end of the 1870s when the labor supply was insufficient, to farm girls. As a result, by the late 1880s, between 60 and 90 percent of the nation's industrial workforce was female, and women produced 60 percent of Japan's foreign exchange. As Sharon Sievers notes: "Without the work of Japan's women the apparent miracle of Japan's economic growth might not have been possible." That fact did not, however, lead to decent working conditions. The officials may have called the work "patriotic," but their reality was as grim as that of the prostitutes. Agents combed the valleys and river sides, promising wonderful lives to the girls, nearly a fifth of whom were under fifteen, offering parents bonuses or advances, then getting them to sign sham contracts that protected employers but gave no rights to workers or parents. A typical contract ran for five years, promised wages at the firm's convenience, and forbade the employee from giving away company secrets. Sometimes a calculating, financially stable family used the advance to build a new home; more often, the parents accepted the deal because they could not put enough food on the table; the subtraction of a mouth and addition of a few yen meant the difference between survival and starvation. One daughter recalled her mother's joy when she sent back her pay. "I don't know how many times I thought I would rather jump into Lake Suwa and drown," she said, but "whenever I thought of my mother's face then, I could endure any hardship."[8]

And the hardships were numberless: pittance wages (typically less than twenty yen a year in 1880), confinement in fenced-in dormitories with two dozen girls per room, fourteen-hour work days, censorship of letters and reading material, inadequate food, shared bedding, and constant problems with lice, beriberi, tuberculosis, pneumonia, and cholera. Stories abounded of supervisors who slapped inattentive or sleepy workers. Girls guilty of theft sometimes were stripped naked and marched through the factory as examples to the others. Those who tried to escape were fined and beaten. And managers, with keys to the dormitory rooms, abused their charges sexually. One workers' song went: "In Suwa geisha get thirty-five sen. / Common prostitutes get fifteen sen. / Silk reelers get one potato." Although the majority of girls and women put up stoically with the conditions, surprisingly large numbers resisted. Figures are scarce, but many escaped, jumping over fences, taking back routes and forest paths to avoid the boys hired to catch them, and defying the threat that their parents' harvest would be confiscated to make up for the advance that had not yet been paid back. "The day may come when the cock ceases to crow," went one proverb, "but never the day when the factory girls stop running away." Some girls committed suicide. And some staged work stoppages. When new rules at the Amamiya plant in Kōfu in 1886 cut the lunch break from an hour to thirty minutes, reduced wages by almost a third, and took away permission for workers to go to the toilet, more than a hundred women walked out. They returned to work only after the employers had agreed, four days later, to several demands, including a maximum work day of fourteen hours. The work action there was followed by strikes at four other factories in the region that summer.[9]

The strikes did not bring great improvement to the workers' lives, but they did make it clear that there was a limit beyond which some would not be driven. They also highlighted the priorities that drove Japan's leaders in this second Meiji decade. Scholars may argue over the motives of men like Itō and Matsukata. But none dare deny that they gave priority to the national institutions and large businesses. As David Howell says, "The demands of national integration always prevailed over the interests or indeed the futures of the dispossessed, be they former samurai, small-fry local notables, the urban masses, or impoverished peasants." And the efficiency of the new regime meant that, in contrast to the Tokugawa years, the state now intruded regularly into individuals' lives, "telling them not just how to behave in the public realm but how to think like subjects of a modern nation-state."[10]

The results of this intrusion could be mildly melancholic for some of those who lived in the countryside: for the young Sugimoto Etsubo, for example, who returned from school one day to find the household Buddhist shrines papered over so that the gods would not have to watch the family eat meat. More often, they were devastating: for the silk reelers in Kōfu, or for the 556 homeless who died of starvation and sickness in the Osaka-Nara region in 1886, thanks largely to Matsukata's economic policies.[11] Edward House may have seen himself as a champion of the underdog when he laid down his *Tokio Times* cudgels and went off on a foreign trip to seek equal treatment of Japan by the imperialist powers. But sincere as his righteous vision was, it also was myopic. His preoccupation with the victimized *state* left him largely oblivious to the commoners who bore the brunt of that state's modernizing policies. It was perhaps an understandable oversight, given the nature of the times, and the circles in which he moved. But that fact did nothing to mitigate the miseries experienced by millions of Japan's commoners.

NOTES

1. Patricia Tsurumi, *Factory Girls: Women in the Thread Mills of Meiji Japan,* 92.

2. For Shibusawa as "venture capitalist," see Gary Allinson, *The Columbia Guide to Modern Japanese History,* 21; for Murayama, *Asahi Shimbun,* July 1, 1882, in Iwai Hajime, *Shimbun to shimbunjin*, 69; and for Fukuzawa, Yamamoto Fumio, *Shimbun hattatsu shi*, 129.

3. Donald Keene, ed., *Modern Japanese Literature,* 57.

4. Kenneth Pyle in Marius Jansen, ed., *Cambridge History of Japan*, vol. 5, 707.

5. For calendar critics, see Mikiso Hane, *Peasants, Rebels, & Outcastes*, 63; for Hida insurrection, see Scott Schnell, *The Rousing Drum*, 186–93 (quote, 192–93); see Jansen, *Cambridge History*, vol. 5, for effects of Matsukata deflation (419–20) and Chichibu uprising (421–23); the plight of the peasant Kanji is in Nagatsuka Takashi, *Soil*, 48; the song, by Ueki Emori, is in Roger Bowen, *Rebellion and Democracy in Meiji Japan*, 206; and Irokawa's comment is in his *Culture of the Meiji Period*, 166, 168.

6. Fukuda's jailing is in Hilary Conroy et al., eds., *Japan in Transition*, 284. For "family's fortune," see Gail Lee Bernstein, ed., *Recreating Japanese Women*, 4; and for Hastings and Nolte, see Bernstein, *Recreating Japanese Women,* 151 ("state attention") and 154 ("cult of productivity").

7. The general description of prostitution is based largely on Tsurumi, 181–86; Itō's comments are in Tsurumi, 182, and Oka Yoshitake, *Five Political Leaders of*

Modern Japan, 37; figures on licensed prostitutes are from Hane, 208–10, and Tsurumi, 184; and the quotation of a farm mother is in Hane, 212.

8. Workforce figures, Bernstein, 153; "work of Japan's women," Sharon L. Sievers, *Flowers in Salt*, 56–57; and daughter recalling mother's face, Sievers, 55.

9. The material on working conditions and resistance is from Tsurumi, 52–55 (Kōfu strike) and 90 (sexual abuse, running away).

10. David Howell, in Merle Goldman and Andrew Gordon, eds., *Historical Perspectives on Contemporary East Asia*, 108.

11. Goldman and Gordon, *Historical Perspectives*, 112.

10

A Change in Course: 1880–1885

Japan wants just such a friend as you to be in this country.

—Yoshida Kiyonari, Washington, D.C., to House, 1880

Life is getting to be a very dreary thing with me.

—E. H. House, November 2, 1882[1]

The gout attack that forced House to let servants carry him aboard the *Oceanic* when he left Yokohama at the beginning of August 1880 continued to plague him on and off after his return to the United States. But neither the pain nor long absence from New York had diminished his eagerness to influence opinion makers on Japan's behalf. He reached California on Thursday, August 19, imbued with a mission. If he had headed for Tokyo ten years earlier as an opinionated reporter, he had come back as an advocate journalist, determined to see how far a facile pen and influential connections could go in winning Western sympathy for treaty revision. After a few days at San Francisco's glass-roofed Palace Hotel, he headed east, for six frenetic months of visiting friends, writing essays (and a book), caring for family affairs, and arguing Japan's case. After that, he would give half a year to quiet diplomatic work in Europe before returning to New York, and then to Japan. The private record shows him struggling with pain in these months. The public record reveals a man afire, a partisan energized by renewed friendships and new campaign venues.

The sixteen-day boat trip across the Pacific seemed to reinvigorate House. He would tell people in later years that the seas always treated his body gently, and the comfortable conditions aboard ship heightened the comfort. His daughter, Koto, was seasick for several days but House did just fine. Our knowledge of the shipboard conditions comes from the fact that Koto, twenty-one years old now, decided to keep a daily journal about "the way men and women are, how men love and treat women, and the relationships between parents and children," in order to "promote the equal rights of men and women in my mother country" and to "make my stepfather House happy." Her first observations, however, had less to say about gender than about the pampered life of the fifty-one *Oceanic* passengers (including, she wrote, three missionaries, one prostitute, one Japanese merchant, and "one Japanese woman—Koto"). The dining room was adorned with a chandelier "shining like silver," mirrors, a piano, and books; beyond it was a smoking room "where women are not allowed." Breakfast included two or three varieties of meat each day, plus eggs and vegetables, and elegant evening diners feasted on "many meats and fishes." Koto was particularly struck by the way that couples, married and unmarried, "held hands." On the night the ship entered San Francisco harbor, she "could hardly sleep," so thrilled was she to be in "this land of humanity and invention (*ningen to hatsumei*)," this place "I have anticipated for twenty years."

The trip across the continent took House and Koto to Chicago, then to Galena, Illinois, for a three-day stay at the Ulysses Grants ("Mrs. Grant . . . used to call me 'dear,' and when I was leaving her, she gave me a gold ring . . . and a precious kiss"), thence to Niagara Falls ("so wonderful and remarkable that I wished I could show them to my folks at home"), to Buffalo for a visit with House's friend David Gray (it plunged House into "dead gloom"), and finally, in early September, to Boston ("the best city of all"). There, Ned and Koto settled down for a few weeks, making side trips to the White Mountains, "brightly illuminated" with fall foliage, and to Plymouth and "the pilgrim's rock" for another rendezvous with the Grants. These were tense days in America, with the country still engulfed in North-South animosities and an evenly divided electorate in the midst of a presidential campaign. It was a grand time for Koto though, and it was the beginning, for House, of one of his most direct campaigns to gain justice for Japan.[2]

House spent his fall months reconnecting with former associates, sometimes with frustration over a decline in the "frankness and openness which I think used to prevail in the circles where I belonged," but more often with the joy of renewing old friendships. When an early October spell of gout prevented him from visiting Thomas Bailey Aldrich's countryside Pankapog home, he met him instead at the Houghton Mifflin publishing offices in Boston. The meeting was strategic as well as convivial, since Aldrich was about to become editor of *The Atlantic Monthly*, a journal that would provide some of House's most tumultuous moments during the next decade. He went up to New York later in the month, for talks with *Herald* editor James Gordon Bennett, Jr., and the paper's star reporter, John Russell Young, to whom he had become close during Grant's Japan visit. He also called on his Civil War confidant Clarence Edmund Stedman, now a famous poet and wealthy Wall Street financier. And he renewed his friendship with Mark Twain.

House and Koto made their first call on the Twains in Hartford late in October. Early the next month, the humorist wrote a note to House, thanking him for setting his mind at ease over whether some unrecorded remark during Grant's campaign visit to Hartford had offended the general. And in December, an amused House wrote from New York, saying he had had a "dreadful scare" when a respected journalist passed along rumors, "on the absurdist grounds you ever heard of," that Twain was "very ill, *in fact deranged*, etc. etc." House had run all over town "in a pelting storm" to make sure the charges were not true. It was during these months too that House's impish side, so long dormant in Tokyo, resurfaced. One of Twain's notebooks for this period says that House put gun powder in the meat of a constipated dog, "then filled him up with water.—Imagine the result." The two men's correspondence in these months reveals the souls of comrades: chatty, witty, sarcastic. When House could not visit Hartford early in 1881, Clemens wrote: "Lord, you *are* such a disappointing lot. . . . And I did *want* to show you my book so bad." The physical proximity clinched a friendship that had been spasmodic until now, setting the stage for one of the most intimate relationships, and the bitterest estrangement, of House's life.[3]

When not seeing people, House usually was writing, or negotiating writing contracts. He put quite a lot of energy into the relationship with Bennett at the *Herald*. His formal connections with that paper had ceased when House began working on the *Tokio Times*, but Bennett, unable to hire a replacement, had pressured House early in 1880 to begin helping again with stories from eastern Asia. House had obliged several times by finding men to cover crises, and in May, when tensions between China and Russia soared to fever pitch over the remote Ili River valley, he had agreed to do some writing himself, because the news seemed too important to be ignored. He complained often, however, about Bennett's unwillingness to come up with "some distinct understanding as to the duties that might be required," and his slowness in paying the reporters House engaged. In September, after House's return to the States, Bennett wrote or cabled as often as three times a week, asking for advice on "Eastern matters" as well as for articles on the theater. When in Newport, Rhode Island, in the middle of the month, Bennett begged House to take a morning train from Boston so they could have a working lunch about the paper's coverage of naval movements in the western Pacific. "Will send carriage to station if you let me know when train arrives," he cabled. House (like everyone else) remained unhappy with Bennett's erratic approach to business, but he wrote for him several times that fall.[4]

Although he published a few things on the arts, House gave his pen—and voice—primarily to diplomatic issues. He aimed at four things, all of which were familiar to his audiences in Japan but fairly new to American readers: broader American sympathies for Japan, the return of the U.S. portion of the Shimonoseki indemnity, revision of the treaties, and the recall of British minister Harry Parkes. And he preached his messages endlessly. No sooner had he reached the Pacific shore in August, for example, than he wrote an article for the California press on the need for America to support Japan's causes, and he wrote similar articles for other papers across the country. Early in 1881, he did an interview for the *New York World,* arguing that Japan had a "very strong feeling of friendliness for" the United States that must be reciprocated if America were to realize its trade potential in Asia. He pleaded for the return of the indemnity as a matter of simple justice, commenting: "I do not think so much of Japan in the matter as I do of the United States. I have plenty of sympathy for Japan, I hope, but my chief concern is for my own country's character." About the treaty, he argued, America debased itself by following the British. Were the Americans to agree to unilateral revision, Asia's Pacific nations would begin "transferring to us much of their trade with England." In other words, justice would be done, and the United States would profit.

House spelled his views out most vividly in "Martyrdom of an Empire," which ran in *The Atlantic Monthly* the following spring. His first concern was the tariff limits, which allowed Japan to meet only one seventeenth of its annual government budget through customs revenues, in contrast to the United States, where "the entire cost of carrying on the government business is defrayed by the customs," and England, where "the customs supply nearly half." The system had placed Japan "in straits which may almost be called desperate." The second half of the article focused on House's desire to see Parkes removed. After criticizing most of the foreign envoys—the American ministers for incompetence, the Germans, Italians, and French for being British lackeys—he zeroed in on the British minister, a man known for "irascibility and hatred of Asiatics." He detailed more than a dozen specific abuses Parkes had heaped on the Japanese, everything from "the furious smashing of a glass" publicly as an illustration of how Japan could be "dashed in pieces," to an effort to get Japan to allow opium sales. He accused him of negotiating by "beatings of tables with rulers, inkstands, and other available implements." And he said Parkes worked only "for the glory of England generally, and more especially for the benefit of its trade."

House also criticized the minister in British journals such as the *Pall Mall Budget*, as well as in his communications with political leaders—and in the process stirred up considerable heat. The *Japan Weekly Mail*, in particular, took House to task no fewer than three times during July of 1881. It called him "histrionic," accused him of "diatribes," and said he was from a class of men for whom "a grain of truth is speedily cultivated into a full crop of extravagance and defamation." Curiously, however, when the *Mail* editorialist examined House's specific accusations, he came up with no errors. He admitted repeatedly that House's writing was "not without a grain of truth" and concluded that a balance needed to "be struck between the exceptional services Sir Harry Parkes has rendered . . . and the sometimes ill-advised harshness of his methods," adding that the tariff system had "been kept in existence very much longer than is either just or expedient."[5]

House did more than merely *write* about Japan's relations with the West in these early American months, however. He also lobbied both officials and well-placed friends on behalf of "the chief object" that Ōkuma had assigned him: winning support for Japan and securing "the repayment of the Simonoseki Indemnity." His overriding goal, he wrote to the Japanese statesman, was to make Americans "active friends of Japan (as they already are passive friends)," and he would do that by keeping in mind "that Americans are vain, like the rest of the world, and that, in order to secure the quick attention and interest of readers, I am obliged to adopt a tone that will please their self love." At the beginning of December 1880, he talked about Japan once more to Grant, whose trip to Asia had convinced him that it was time to "put a stop" to "the indignities the people there are subjected to by foreigners." Then, with the general's support, he went to Washington on December 6, where he stayed for a month, calling on Japanese minister to the United States Yoshida Kiyonari and several high-level officials, including his Civil War friend, John Hay, who now was assistant secretary of state. After an initial period of skepticism over House's real intentions, Yoshida praised House's ability "to reach the tender spot of the people in awakening . . . interest regarding the relations of the two countries," and President Hayes and Secretary of State William Evarts promised to urge that Congress return the indemnity. The results were even more encouraging than he had hoped, and House was able to write a private letter to Ōkuma, saying that "the conditions of all matters connected with Japanese interests are as favorable as could be reasonably expected by any person."[6]

One reason for the ebullience may have lain in the unfolding of a small episode that promised for a short period to take House's life, once again, in new directions. About this time rumors began to circulate that important people were urging President-elect Garfield to nominate House to be the

U.S. consul general in Yokohama, responsible for trade and the consular court in one of Japan's most important locations. It would have been a remarkable appointment, given House's views. Indeed, the *Japan Gazette* reacted to the rumors with near panic, sneering that "these are not times when the interests of foreigners in Japan . . . can be entrusted to a literary toady . . . to a person whose reputation, both among Japanese and among foreigners, is notoriously bad." In the end, the nomination stalled and the episode proved only a diversion, but the flurry deserves retelling, if only because it illustrated how far House had moved from the world of pure journalism.

We already have seen how deeply House felt about the need for competent American representatives in Asia. As a result, when he heard hints in 1880 that his friend Young might be appointed minister to Japan, he rejoiced. And when other rumors began circulating that House himself might have diplomatic prospects, he was, at the least, intrigued. The discussions came into the open the following February. On the eighteenth, Grant wrote to Garfield that his time in Asia had persuaded him "that there was huge opening in that direction for an extension of our commerce" and that the president would be wise to appoint Young as minister and House as consul general. Beside speaking the language and enjoying the confidence of the Japanese, he said, House was "an able writer" who "would keep the Minister, and the Department at Washington, better posted in regard to all Eastern matters than any other man could." The next day, Twain informed House that he had heard about Grant's recommendation after writing to Hay himself, with a recommendation that House actually be named minister to Japan. Grant, he added, thought the ministership would be politically impossible, since House had been out of the United States so long—and besides: "the Consul Generalship is of infinitely more importance, both for us and for Japan."

Discussions of the nomination bubbled up repeatedly across the next year. In March, C. O. Shepard, with whom House had lived during his first Tokyo months, wrote from England to urge House to let his name go into nomination. That same month, House wrote to his friend (and Ōkuma's secretary) Hirai Kishō, at great length, quoting Grant's view that he "could swing a much greater force toward the building up of commerce" as consul general than as minister and saying that while he preferred private work, perhaps "publishing the Tokio Times again," the one "thing that could move me to take it would be to feel sure I could be *very* useful to Japan." He added: "I care absolutely nothing for the distinction or the dignity. I do not care very much for the money it would bring me. . . . I have almost a horror of it. If I *do* accept, you may be sure it will be one of the greatest sacrifices I have ever made in my life."

He made it clear in an April letter to Young, however, that while such a post surely would not be awarded to "a recluse like myself," he was not rejecting the idea, since "there is truly a large field for valuable work, and . . . important practical results are attainable." He also noted "Greeley's sound maxim—never to decline anything before it was offered." By June, he had decided to drop the whole idea, he told Hirai, in a letter from Paris. But when Grant started pushing his appointment again in the fall, House was conflicted. He wrote to Ōkuma early in October that the job was "too insignificant" to consider; then, when he learned a few weeks later that the statesman had resigned from the government over the Hokkaido land scandal, he began having second thoughts. "You know," he wrote to Hirai on October 31, "that Mr. O. was the only high officer with whom my relations were confidential, and as none of the others know me so well, I might find myself almost alone. . . . Under these circumstances, it might perhaps be better for me to go back with some power and authority in my hands." He said he detested the idea of working with Western businessmen in Yokohama but promised to "reflect deeply upon the subject, and decide with great care." When Young thought House's nomination likely in December, the Bostonian was ready to accept. "Not long ago I was more than indifferent," he wrote, "but as the subject grows and shapes itself in my mind, I see its more favorable aspects, and it would now be somewhat of a mortifying disappointment if nothing should come of it." He delayed his return to Japan to be available for Congressional hearings. And when he heard in January that Shepard was seeking the post, he expressed irritation.

House had to settle in the end for mortification—and appreciation for "General Grant's good opinion and favoring words." The whole idea died without a formal nomination, partly because of House's controversial views, but mainly because the incumbent consul general Thomas Van Buren, a House nemesis, contrived to stay on. It is, of course, interesting to speculate on the impact such an appointment would have had. Could a man so hated by Western traders, a man who had recently worked as Japan's publicist and agent, have survived in that diplomatic post? Would American trade, or Japanese-American relations, have improved materially, as Grant and Young thought they would? Or would his appointment simply have proved that systems dwarf men? We will never know, but the mere asking of such questions highlights the unique position that House occupied at the beginning of the 1880s as a journalist and American patriot on the one hand, as an activist and Japanese advocate on the other.[7]

An even more dramatic indicator of the complicated role House had taken on was the six-month mission across the Atlantic that he undertook for Ōkuma and the Japanese government during 1881. When he sailed for London on February 24, his ostensible reason was to show Europe to Koto. And he did that in full measure, introducing her to the literary and political leaders of England, taking her to the Grand Opera in Paris, and riding with her up an Alpine cable car in Switzerland. In Paris, they ran into *Herald* editor Bennett, a "poor devil" who smiled "a sort of sickly smile," perhaps because he had not paid House for his recent articles. And in Italy, House bought Koto a ring, which her descendants still show to guests. One could hear the envy when his old friend, the loner novelist Charles Reade, wrote to House from London in May: "You have done well to adopt Koto. In youth our hearts are india-rubber . . . and we can live alone. But it is not so in old age. I can well understand that many things you and she are enjoying together amuse you only by reflection from her naif delight."

Much of the trip's joyous tone sprang from the renewal of literary and theater friendships. In London, he stayed with Reade, who had turned reclusive after the death in 1879 of his longtime companion, Laura Seymour. Having House as a guest seemed to invigorate him, particularly when the American brought Reade together with Edwin Booth, the famous American actor whose British appearances had evoked mixed reviews from critics but raves from the public. Booth was bound down by a "very, very sick wife" and went out little except to perform, so when the actor agreed to visit Reade in April, House's satisfaction was palpable. He would recall years later how his author-friend's "long-dormant energies" returned as the three talked about Dickens, Thackeray, and the London press, which Reade called "an ass." When House and Koto left for the continent, Reade's depression came back, and he wrote: "I cannot work. I have no one to work for who loves me enough to compensate my trouble. . . . I sleep—I wake. I vegetate—I exist."[8]

House, by contrast, throbbed with life now, because he had both a companion and a mission. He was out to change Japan's place in the world by working as a behind-the-scenes diplomat. He actually had two goals in England, one general, one specific. The first was to effect a change in attitudes, to get the British public to look more favorably on Japan and thus hasten the day of treaty revision. To that end, he made calls at London's major newspapers, particularly the anti-Japanese *Telegraph* and *Spectator,* held a dinner party for a dozen leading citizens who "had lately discussed Japanese topics in rather an ignorant spirit," and made at least two evening visits to Parliament. The second goal was "to weaken or destroy the influence of Sir H. Parkes." Reiterating themes he had been trumpeting for several years now, he talked to anyone who would listen. "To wish well to Japan has become identical with wishing destruction to Parkes," he wrote to Ōkuma following the trip. For that reason, "a great part of my labor . . . has been to discredit and cast shame upon Parkes in his public capacity." He talked with several members of Parliament and spent time at the country home of the Liberal MP Edward J. Reed, who had been granted a private audience with the emperor during an 1879 visit to Japan.

Unfortunately, the times were not propitious for House's endeavors. While he told Ōkuma that some "sound and advantageous opinions" had been planted, the British public was largely indifferent and Parkes appeared invulnerable, so his reports to Tokyo were pessimistic. One of the problems lay in the British tendency to deal "with Japan as a conquered province"; a more serious one resulted from the fact that Japan's minister to London, Mori Arinori, had made public statements defending Parkes. House wrote to Mori, saying that a discreet word from him would ensure the end of Parkes's tenure, and when Mori wrote back that the minister's position required that he "remain scrupulously aloof," House exploded. "I leave your Excellency to imagine the annoyance—I may almost say the consternation which this intelligence caused me," he wrote to Ōkuma. "For the first time since I left Japan, I began to feel that I was engaged in a task which no energy, devotion or ability on any part could bring to a successful conclusion." He was even more frank in letters to Hirai, where he talked of "this pompous showing off of uniform in the palace drawing rooms, this lusting after titles of European nobility, this wasting of money in rents of useless mansions fit for dukes or princes—and at the same time this cool indifference of the things of real interest and anxiety." He told Ōkuma that while some regarded Mori's stance as a diplomatic nicety, he himself had other suspicions, unprintable in a letter.[9]

House's approach in France was similar, in approach and in results. He met several times with Japan's acting minister to France, Suzuki Kan'ichi, and had private talks with Premier Leon Gambetta; he also spent time with opposition leader Georges Clemenceau, who had been a fellow reporter in the U.S. Civil War. As in Britain, he sought both to increase general interest in Japan and to counter the anti-Japanese approach of French diplomats. And he found the people he talked with sympathetic but equally unencouraging. Gambetta told him the French were so heavily focused on domestic affairs that "neither he nor any person . . . could pay any great attention to Japanese subjects." And while he was impressed by Clemenceau's "intelligent appreciation of our affairs," the conversation was "equally fruitless." The lessons to be drawn from this, House told Ōkuma, were that "it is hard to get Europeans and Americans to take Japan seriously," and that the "old and (to me) detestable theory" still held: "*strong* nations must look exclusively to their own interests, and cannot allow any consideration for the affairs of such as are less powerful."[10]

It was thus a chastened House who returned to the United States at the end of August, a more cynical man than the one who had shut down the *Tokio Times* a year before. He did not, however, show any evidence of second thoughts about having undertaken the mission. Observers of a later period might question the legitimacy of a journalist serving in what was undeniably the role of secret agent, accepting a paid, confidential assignment from officials in another government, in order to help that government win a better position internationally. But if that issue bothered House, it never showed up in his writings, either private or public. His payments were modest, just enough to cover travel and an assistant, along with funds for entertaining politicians and opinion leaders.[11] And everything he did (except for the fact of accepting the assignment) seems to have been transparent. While his meetings with opinion leaders were discreet, there appears to have been no effort to keep them secret. And he stated his positions overtly, to anyone who would listen. In part, his lack of concern suggested an era in which the boundary between advocacy journalism and personal diplomacy was not so sharply drawn. In another part, it revealed, again, that House the journalist was made of the same cloth as House the man. He was a crusader for fair international treatment of Japan. Period.

If House was disappointed on his return to the United States, he also was eager to get back to Tokyo, but there were promises to keep and business to wrap up, so it would be another six months before he and Koto could leave. Like the previous year, his time was divided between writing and socializing, and when he was not doing one of those, he usually was in bed, with the gout. Actually, his first weeks back were consumed by the need to finish editing his first general interest book on Japan, a little volume of essays and stories called *Japanese Episodes*. The proofs were ready soon after he got to Boston, and he tackled them early in September with the attention to detail that had marked his earliest reporting. He liked the swinging Japanese figure that editor Benjamin Ticknor had put on the title page; he wondered if *Japanese Diversions* would be a better title; he worried about large chunks of space on page three, wondered whether to use the period after his middle initial, and thought the type for one essay's title was "rather heavy." He also caught inconsistencies in capitalization. When the book appeared, he was equally careful to send copies to all of his friends, who proclaimed it "delicate" and "perfectly lovely."

The 247-page, four-by-six-inch volume, purporting to show "the inner life of the Japanese," included four pieces: a romantic tale of love between a rural innkeeper's daughter and a rickshaw puller, a description of House's climb up Mt. Fuji, and two accounts of life among the Japanese elite. The pages brimmed with House's admiration for Japan, and the detail was rich and more accurate than that found in most contemporary accounts. He described the impossibility of swearing in Japanese ("the language contains nothing in the way of violence"), the rude behavior of the foreigners he so loved to loath ("graceless wretches who made the region hideous with their obscene excesses"), the beauty of the shoreline at Ienoshima ("rugged sides, riven by volcanic convulsions, and channeled by the action of the waves"), the skill of Japanese male actors playing women's roles ("astonishingly clever in their feminine airs and graces"). While not a best-seller, *Japanese Episodes* was as well received by the critics as it was by House's friends. A reviewer for *The Nation* praised House's "playful humor, and kaleidoscopic vocabulary," and said he cast everything "under the spell of moonlight."[12]

House's social schedule was more intense than it had been the previous fall, and every bit as convivial. He was in touch with Aldrich over a series of writing schemes, including an effort to get *The Atlantic* to publish Charles Reade's next romance. He rejoiced that John Hay had returned to journalism, because it would give him a chance to visit the *Tribune* offices, that place of "hard tussles and narrow scrapes" where he now would explain some of Japan's "*realities,* which are better than the enchanted romances of other regions." House's visits with Stedman were times of "pure friendliness and sentiment."[13] And with Young, he balanced pleasure and business. That the two men enjoyed each other's company was obvious. In November Young threw a bash that brought out House's old bacchanalian side, perhaps for the last time. "What delightful—but what dangerous—festivals yours are!" he wrote to Young. "Imagine an established invalid plodding his homeward way at 3 a.m. after a social blaze like that of two Sundays ago, and looking forward to the penalties of such indulgence. Henceforth I live in the past—as far as such revelries are concerned." But as much as they reveled in each other's company, their communications more often dealt with diplomatic business. Young pushed House's candidacy for the consul general's position throughout the fall, and House plumped for Young to become minister to Japan. He had no doubt that Young could have the post, and went so far as to advise him about housing in Tokyo. When he heard rumors in February that Young might take an editing post at the *Herald*, he expressed distress. And when Young accepted the Chinese legation instead of Tokyo, House was distraught. "I am terribly afraid you cannot content yourself in that dreary isolation," the Japanophile wrote. "I now see myself doomed to a companionless series of years."[14]

The most active friendship that fall was with the Twains—and Koto was central to the relationship. Gifts and cards, as well as the tidbits of life, flowed back and forth. When it looked as if House would return to Japan before the end of 1881, Twain wrote that he thought they could have remodelers out of the house by mid-November, so that the Tokyo pair could come for a visit: "We have all talked of this visit, and anticipated it, and hankered after it, ever since you and Koto vanished out of these doors." When gout and the consul general discussions delayed House's departure into the new year, Clemens wrote that he and "the madam" were "mighty glad . . . for that makes the visit here next to absolutely *certain*. . . . I am sure we shall have possession of the essential

When the Houses visited the Twains in Hartford, Koto stayed in this third-story bedroom just down the hall from Twain's poolroom. The space came to be known in the Twain household as "Koto's room." (Courtesy of The Mark Twain House, Hartford, Conn.)

parts of the house by the middle of December." When a January date for the visit finally was set up, the humorist begged House and Koto to stay until mid-April, if possible: "We want as much of you as we can get."

In the end, the Twains may have gotten more than they really wanted. Almost as soon as the twosome arrived in Hartford, House was felled by an "attack of gout—so fierce as to keep me in bed here for three weeks." It was not the period's first attack of the disease; in November he had written from bed that the malady made him "a prisoner more than half the time, at this season of the year." By the third week of February, however, he had improved enough to go back to New York. And by mid-March, he and Koto were en route to Yokohama, aboard the same luxurious *Oceanic* that had borne them to California eighteen months before. The contrast between the highly social activities of those Western months and the concentrated, private work at the *Tokio Times* in the late 1870s hardly could have been greater. House had become an American insider again, and Koto had become a sophisticate, admired for her charms and artistic skills as much as her father was for his writing. At the same time, both of them were yearning for Tokyo. Koto had had enough, for now, of the exotic West; House wanted "the repose and tranquillity" of "my home at Tokio"; some said "he could not survive apart from Japan."[15]

They sailed east to Japan this time, on an uneventful voyage across the Atlantic, through the Suez Canal, past India and China. Repose and tranquility were not to be found, however, for Tokyo was a changed place when the *Oceanic* arrived in Yokohama on April 9. The day was rainy and windy, with temperatures in the upper 50s, and a seer would have found the weather an omen—for both House and his adopted country. The most apparent problem for Japan itself was a political tempest, with three political parties that had been formed after the 1881 constitutional crisis fighting viciously over who would shape Japan's future. Indeed, just three day's before House's return a rural schoolteacher from Gifu had made headlines by stabbing Liberal Party leader Itagaki, after reading a newspaper report that Itagaki had belittled the emperor. Prices were falling; farmers and women were entering politics; miners and laborers were protesting or striking. Most ominous to House personally was the fact that Ōkuma had been forced from the government in the 1881 constitutional crisis. "From all that I could learn," the Bostonian recalled in a later letter to Ōkuma, "you wished to remain in complete retirement." And that deprived House of his major source of information and influence—and destroyed his plans to reopen the *Tokio Times.*

The inability to resume publishing was a devastating blow. From the day he left Japan in 1880, he never doubted that he would restart the paper. Already in January, before he left New York, the Japanese press had him "planning to publish a daily, English-language" paper again. And in mid-March, while he was on the seas, the papers reported rumors that he was back and about to "take up writing" at his "old newspaper." But it was not to be. He talked with several officials and even discussed private financing with bankers. The officials, however, would not promise him the money or independence he demanded: the country was in depression, the government was strapped for cash, and the Ōkuma faction was out of power. Nor were the bankers able to work out financing. So his hopes for a new *Times* died, never to be revived.[16]

Instead, he accepted an offer to begin teaching again at Tokyo University on September 1, in addition to doing freelance articles for Associated Press, the *New York Herald,* and other American and Japanese publications, including his old nemesis, the *Japan Weekly Mail.* He needed money, after all, to put food on the table, not being a wealthy man, and few jobs had brought him more satisfaction than working with students. The teaching assignment was limited, just four hours a week at a salary of 80 yen a month. But Tokyo University was Japan's premier institution, and House's position was prestigious, teaching English literature to the university's

"Upper Students" as a replacement for the redoubtable William Houghton, who had returned to America after five years at the school. So he expressed excitement in a letter to Young (now in Beijing) about returning to "my old love." At the same time, he wondered if his body was "strong enough for even that little labor." And as it turned out, it was not. Almost as soon as he took the post gout felled him again, and by late autumn he was missing classes often; so in January 1883 he requested a leave, and on July 15 he resigned.[17]

Indeed, the major story of his first months back surely had to be the gout, which ravaged his body with new fury. Attacks recurred periodically during his first months in Tokyo, much as they had in New York. Then in September, following a trip to the Hakone mountains, the illness came with a new force, making travel impossible, taking away the use of his legs (forever), and making it impossible to write "without sending streams of perspiration all over me." The disease, which inflames joints, makes the skin peel, and causes high fever and severe pain, was fairly common in these years, especially among men in stressful positions who had been heavy drinkers or workaholics. One friend wrote in 1884 that House was fortunate to have "nothing more serious than gout." But there was nothing common about House's case. While most people's attacks lasted a week or two, he was laid prone for nearly half a year now, and the pain was excruciating.

He wrote to Young in November: "While still in bed all the time, I am going through new courses of drugs—drugs on waking up—drugs before each meal—drugs after each meal—drugs at night,—with potions, lotions and notions innumerable. And my diet now excludes fish, most meats, tea, coffee, eggs, pastry and some other things." Life, he said, had become "a very dreary thing." In mid-January, he wrote that he had been prone for five months, but there seemed "a chance of my getting lifted out of bed to a table" soon, in which case he might at last have his Christmas meal. He began to experience longer periods of relief after that, so that he was able to do more writing, but the inflammation kept spreading to new joints. By May, the disease had reached "my right hand, which was the last member to surrender." And in July 1883, he would write to Twain that the gout "has now got the best of me entirely." He said he had "not put my feet to the ground" for ten months and had largely "lost the use of the upper part of my arms." His hands were "pretty wrenched and distorted," though he could "use them after a fashion."

Pain was not House's only concern, frightful as it was. At least as frustrating was the isolation, and the inability to work. "Can anything more horrible be imagined for an actively disposed man?" he wrote to Stedman. "Six months, in fact, have been taken out of my life, for I have nothing to show at the end of them but a few light trifles in the way of sketches and essays." And for a while, the idleness threatened his financial security too. "Experience," he declared, had shown him now "the imperative need of having a substantial pecuniary sheet anchor at command, in case health declines, friends (so designated) fail, or malignants betray. It takes a deal of soul-grinding to teach the awful truth that there is almost nothing to be trusted in this world but hard cash." Years later when he came across a note from this period in which Frank Brinkley had chided him for ill temper, he wrote in the margin: "No doubt I was in error—but Good God, how I was strained by pain and worry in those days."

The physical trials, combined with the disappointment of having his *Tokio Times* dreams dashed, also made House cynical about Japan itself. The officials running things now were all "marionettes, who 'don't dare' this or that, lest the frown of European diplomats should overshadow them." They did not seek his advice now, probably being "afraid to come . . . taking their cue from high authority." Even Saigō Tsugumichi of Taiwan expedition fame had become corrupt, he opined, and the ambitious Foreign Minister Inoue Kaoru—who "is the government, all by himself"—had grown rich beyond imagining through "wild speculative operations." It was all a sad contrast to Ōkuma who maintained "decorum in public business" and scrupulously "declined to take anything" from private men, even if "he may not have been the most high-minded of men." House was not even sure he wanted the Shimonoseki indemnity to be returned in the current situation, since men like Inoue were involved in "big money making conspiracies" that might dilute its effect. Indeed, he wrote in a letter to Grant, word was about that an Inoue business associate named Irwin was promoting the use of "bribery, and nothing else" to get Congress to return the money. "I am very cold upon Japan just now," House sighed, in a letter to Young in Beijing. "They have played 'last feather' with me. . . . I can thrive on misuse for perhaps a dozen years, but by the thirteenth, my stomach begins to reject that sort of nourishment."

There were a few bright rays. Pain and personal disclaimers notwithstanding, he produced a surprising number of essays, including character sketches of famous people he had known (Charles Dickens, Richard Wagner, Franklin Pierce, British playwright Tom Robertson), as well as articles for the American and Japanese press. His correspondence with friends continued. And most important, his relationship with Koto deepened in extraordinary ways. His letters referred often to her assistance as a translator and transcriber, and to her constant care. "I should never have known to what extent human patience, gentleness, affection and untaught wisdom can go," he wrote to Stedman in New York. And to Twain: "Koto sustains me through it all with more than a daughter's tenderness." The bond was intensified by the fact that Koto was not always well herself. She was given to undiagnosed seizures, "often so sudden that she is initially paralyzed."

The attacks never lasted long, but they terrified House, particularly when they occurred in another room and he could not get to her. But they also brought out a tenderness that he would have hidden in earlier days. "If I had married and had children of my own," he reflected in the summer of 1883, "I could not have had such a daughter. . . . I fear I should have been a bad head of a family, and not the best of fathers."[18]

Although the paralysis of the legs was permanent, the pain grew more manageable as winter waned in 1883, and House's productivity levels increased so much that those who knew him only by his writings would not have suspected his troubles. Medical experts today suggest a link between a person's mental state and gout attacks, and House's experiences support their analysis, since the return of his health coincided with the renewal of his journalistic crusades. The precipitating event was a series of late-January, early-February articles in *Jiji Shinpō* and the *Japan Weekly Mail* discussing new talks about the return of the U.S. share of the Shimonoseki indemnity. Both papers' articles contained what House saw as factual errors about the Shimonoseki episode, and he felt compelled to set the record straight. It was imperative, he said in a series of detailed letters, "to correct certain mistakes" that might confuse the discussions.

His first response, on February 10, detailed five important mistakes in the *Jiji* and *Mail* accounts, errors that had become part of the imperialist narrative. First, the American ship *Pembroke*, which had been fired on initially by Shimonoseki troops, was not simply "passing the Strait" when it was attacked in 1863; it had entered the harbor and dropped anchor, in violation of treaty restrictions. Second, the Dutch and French ships that were attacked by Shimonoseki guns a few days later were not merchantmen, but gunboats and warships. Third, the four-nation retaliation against Japan in 1864 was uncalled-for, because Japan had neither made "murderous attacks," as alleged, nor violated the treaties. "The truth is," he wrote about Japan's 1863 attack, that "one American merchant ship was driven away from a place where she had no right to anchor; and one French gunboat and one Dutch ship of war were assailed while passing through the Strait. That is the whole." Fourth, even if there had been a Japanese violation in 1863, the French, Dutch, and Americans had wreaked more than enough havoc in their immediate retaliation to have more than repaid any wrongs.

House's fifth—and most damning—point was that the 1864 "retaliation" was a "scheme of unjust vengeance," led by the British, to "create new Western trade opportunities in Japan." The $3 million indemnity, he explained, drawing on diplomatic correspondence, was intended merely to pressure Japan into opening more ports. A spirited debate over these points ensued between House and *Mail* editor Brinkley, and on February 24, Brinkley capitulated, admitting that the American and European ships had "had no right to force the passage of the Strait" and that London had "explicitly interdicted" the use of force in 1864. The four-nation attack and subsequent indemnity, Brinkley agreed, were "disgraceful," the work of "agents of Lynch law."

If Brinkley's editorial capitulation eased the pain of House's illness, events of the next month must have boosted him even more, because complaints about gout largely disappeared from his letters. On February 25, Congress voted to return the indemnity, and on April 23 the full $750,000 was delivered by U.S. Minister to Japan Bingham. House was quiet that spring about the congressional decision, but later he would write several times to Ōkuma about his pleasure over the return. He reminded him in an 1887 letter that the return of the indemnity had been "the chief object of my labors" during the 1880–1881 visits to Washington and that "the money was restored to Japan within six months after my return." Three years later, he wrote in another letter:

> You cannot know that the result was brought about directly by my endeavors;—that I received a promise from the highest authorities in the United States that the Indemnity money should be restored at a certain date; and that I communicated to you what that date would be, the conditions under which restitution would be made, the channels through which it would pass, and a variety of other particulars which I take pleasure in believing would have been of no slight importance to you if you had retained your position as leader of the national administration.

House's memory may, by 1890, have made the connections between his efforts and the outcome a bit more precise than reality warranted. Certainly other prominent Americans, including the 1860s Yokohama businessman Francis Hall, had long opposed the indemnity too. But the core of his recollection was accurate.[19]

His personal situation improved even more, late in 1883, when the foreign ministry decided to give him a pension. Inoue sent notification in December that, beginning on January 1, House would be granted a seven-year, annual allotment of 2,500 yen in thanks for "many years service done by yourself for the interest of this country." Whether the beneficence was intended as payment for his *Times* crusades and the return of the indemnity, or as compensation for the refusal to underwrite a new paper, it certainly showed that House's friends had not lost all of their influence. The government had no formal obligation to assist him now, but there obviously were officials who still appreciated what he had done for the country and wanted to retain his support. House himself was touched by the gesture. He wrote to Inoue that his own country would not have treated him so well, and that he regarded the pension as "proof of a rare and, I believe, a wholly exceptional magnanimity, on the part of the Government that manifests it."

Truth be told, it surely was more than mere government magnanimity that touched House; the pension's size had to impress him too. Decades later, the writer Lafcadio Hearn would observe that one could live comfortably in Japan for 1,250 yen a year. Now, in 1883, Japanese editors seldom received more than 150 yen a month. House would tell friends that Tokyo "is the most absurdly cheap place to live in that I ever knew or heard of," a place where his own "pretty cottage upon Yedo Bay" rented for fifty dollars a month, a place where he and Koto could have a pony, a carriage, a row boat, and five servants for $100 a month. Even with the "boisterous . . . little luncheon or dinner or croquet parties" that Koto loved to throw when House's health permitted it, expenses were low. A government pension of more than 200 yen (roughly $170) a month took away most of the financial worries that had plagued him during the previous year.[20]

House's productivity also increased as his health returned, and he threw himself again into his two passions: writing about Japan and helping people in need. The latter involved a resuscitation of the school he had begun for poor girls before leaving for the United States. Although the late 1879 fire that destroyed his first school left him pessimistic about a revival, he somehow secured funds and in the summer of 1880 started it back up in Yushima, not far from the University of Tokyo. The school offered training in math, reading, writing, and sewing—all without cost—under the instruction of a single teacher, Aoki Tatsu. It appears to have struggled along during House's time abroad, then to have flourished after his return, when it was renamed the Hausu Gakkō (House School). City records from 1882–1884 show thirty-eight girls in attendance, for a demanding 290 days a year. The intent of the school, said House, was to give "a chance for those who can afford nothing to get a bit of education for their daughters"—all for the purpose of "elevating in some degree" their "position in life." As he put it:

> I have between 30 and 40 scholars, from 5 to 13 years old. I clothe them, give them in winter a little substantial food when their poor frozen stomachs need it, and have them taught just enough to enable them to rise one or two or possibly three grades in their social lives. More than this I can't undertake, at present, for, cheap as everything is in Japan, schoolhouses, teachers, garments and the rest cost *something*. However, the small concern prospers, and will do its share of good—in fact, it *has* already.

He also provided a "gratis distribution of simple medicine" for the girls.

There seems little doubt that House's support of the project was inspired as much by Koto's interest in women's issues as by his own lifelong passion for helping the needy. He had seen the opportunities that education had opened for her, and he and she had felt together the pain that ignorance could inflict on woman and girls. Now, House wrote to Young, Koto was "even more concerned in the school than I am, and glories in the idea of anybody taking an interest in it." She helped out with the teaching too—in addition to running the House home, managing her father's business affairs, and working at a "dispensary for the sick," which she had founded in her old neighborhood. The school did have its detractors, particularly some Protestant missionaries who objected to its secularism. "The way that harmless honest school enterprise was bullyragged and hooted at," House wrote to Twain, "would have made you think . . . that it was a college devoted to the inculcation of vice and crime." He said the missionaries would have preferred that the girls "would never have had that chance to better themselves" than that they be taught English without "the superstitions of the Christian faith."[21] Most observers, however, praised the schools for its innovations and principles.

House's primary salvation after mid-1883 came from his resumption of steady writing. In addition to doing new sketches of famous acquaintances (the actor Henry Irving, Abraham Lincoln),[22] he returned to newspaper journalism, lending his pen regularly now to the *Mail*, which had been taken over in 1881 by Brinkley. An Irishman who had been in Japan since 1867, Brinkley was in many ways House's antithesis: a religious conservative, conciliatory by nature, a clumsy writer, a former math teacher. But the two also had much in common. Both had come to Japan for a brief visit, then stayed for a career. Both had become related to Japanese women, House by adoption, Brinkley by marriage. Most important, both had been impressed sufficiently by Japan's progress to become its champions.

House's decision to become a *Mail* writer, and sometime editor, was eased by the fact that Brinkley had transformed the paper into a supporter of Japanese issues. That was not enough to make House respect its journalism. He sneered at the "amateur fashion" of its editing and told Young late in 1882 that the *Mail* "meant no more to me than the Skowkegan Clarion." He also accused its editors of sloppy reporting. But the new philosophy enabled him to contribute to the paper with a clear conscience, once his health improved. The four dollars per column salary helped too. And Brinkley was delighted to secure his assistance. As he told House late in the summer of 1883, "With your writing in the Mail I really do feel that it is a paper." And in September, he told him that his drafts were so well done that no editor "ever thinks of touching your work."[23] It is impossible to determine precisely which articles House wrote, because neither news columns nor editorials contained bylines. The content and writing style, however, made some of his pieces obvious. On October 6, for example, the paper ran a long story on New York journalism, including the salaries paid during House's years at the *Tribune* (Horace Greeley made just $5,000 as editor of the *Tribune* in 1861, Young $15,000 a year at the *Herald* in the

1870s), and several issues contained House-style attacks on extraterritoriality. On October 13, the paper blamed foreign behavior for irregularities in the treaty port judicial system, and on October 20, an essay said that the only reason that system persisted was the Westerners' "prejudices of race."

House's new role as *Mail* correspondent initiated a House-Brinkley friendship that never would wither. Brinkley's letters took on an increasingly personal tone in the winter of 1883, suggesting locales that might be better for House's health, offering bottles of imported wine, discussing whether Koto had time to care for the Brinkley children. By the summer of 1884, he was asking House to edit the *Mail* during his trips away from Tokyo. In mid-August, about to leave for a weeklong trip to a hot springs, Brinkley explained what the editing would entail. At 7:30 each evening, proofs of that day's "original matter . . . including translations" would be delivered at House's Tsukiji home from Yokohama. After checking them, House was to have the proofs back to Yokohama, by train, the first thing the next morning. Brinkley said House might have to correct, or even reject, some essays, particularly those of the dentist-turned-writer (and later newspaper editor) F. W. Eastlake, whose work, "between you and me," could be "superficial and flighty." House also was to write a news summary on Thursday for the weekly edition.

Brinkley was so pleased with House's work that he wrote, on returning, that "the best thing I could have done for the 'Mail's' sake would have been to stay away a month." He traveled again in October, declaring that the paper's readers "will regret my return." And in the new year, Brinkley put House in charge for an extended time, while he traveled in China. House could be difficult to deal with. He always had been touchy about his work; now, the gout made him cranky. He complained about *Mail* editors who changed something he had done; he accused Brinkley of "unwillingness to give displeasure to this or that class of foreigners"; and he fumed that Brinkley edited his copy freely because he knew House was too frail to "come and demand apologies or explanations." But Brinkley generally ignored the complaints. "I miss you terribly," he wrote after House left Japan in the summer of 1885; "there is not a soul here who can write me a note which does not require as much labor to correct as to compose."[24]

Editing and writing buoyed House's spirits for a time, but by late 1884 he was restless again, perhaps because the gout was back, perhaps because the wanderer's muse seemed to visit him every few years. His letters home began expressing apprehensions, with those to Twain taking on a particularly wistful tone. Throughout 1883, the House-Twain letters had been witty and chatty, full of news about friends, or stories about how the Twains had eaten some of House's incense tablets, mistaking them for candy. After the fall of 1884, however, House's letters turned melancholy. He was sick again, and the doctors had "done their best to frighten me."

He was longing for his American friends. He wished Twain would seek appointment as minister to Tokyo. And he began worrying about what would happen to Koto if the gout should kill him. In a December letter, he pointed out that he had thought of turning property over to Twain, so that the novelist could provide for Koto in the case of his demise, but instead he had made other arrangements "by virtue of which she would have as much control over the houses and lands as I myself now have."[25]

It was thus no surprise, after another attack of gout in the spring of 1885, that House and Koto decided to head back to New York. His last three years had been successful by most standards. He had seen the Shimonoseki indemnity returned to Japan; the Japanese government had recognized his service with a large pension; he had edited and written for the area's best English-language newspaper; he had provided a school for three dozen needy girls. And he had seen Koto blossom into a companion, an accomplished translator, a recognized hostess, and a competent businesswoman. But sickness and the contrast to earlier days made it hard for House to see the positive side of this ledger. He no longer could get about without a wheelchair; often he could not leave home at all. More and more, he felt cut off, conscious not only of aching joints but of diminished influence. So early in August he paid $800 for three tickets to New York via the Suez Canal and Europe, one for himself, one for Koto, and one for a Japanese servant.[26] He would not arrive until the following spring, because this time the gout attacked en route. The departure itself refurbished his hope, however, both for renewed health and for the revival of American friendships. Had he known what would happen to those friendships in the next few years, he might not have embarked.

NOTES

1. "Such a friend," letter from Japan's minister to the United States, Yoshida Kiyonari, to House, October 2, 1880, in EHC, University of Virginia; and "dreary thing," House to John Russell Young, November 2, 1882, JRY, Library of Congress.

2. For the ship and arrival in San Francisco, see Koto House, "Seiyō kakkoku ryōkō ki," August 1880. The diary, which is held by the Kuroda family, is unpublished and only fragments of the first days of the trip remain; copies of the same fragments are in the Ōkuma monjo at Waseda University Library. Material on the trip to the east is from letters in the Kuroda family holdings from Koto to "my dear teacher" (unnamed, but possibly Margaret Griffis, since she writes in English and refers to lessons she took under her back in Japan), October 18, 1880; and to Mrs. Gray (apparently David Gray's wife), October 13, 1880. "Dead gloom" of Buffalo in House to Twain, September 13, 1880, MTP, University of California. The visit to Galena also was recorded in the *Galena Gazette*, September 3, 1880, which

mistakenly called Koto's biological father the "Chief Justice of the Supreme Court of Japan." I am indebted to Aaron Lisec for this information.

3. "Frankness and openness," House to E. C. Stedman, November 5, 1883, ECS, Columbia University. For the story of the dog, see Frederick Anderson et al., eds., *Mark Twain's Notebooks & Journals,* vol. 2, 382; this section includes July 1880 to January 1882. Twain's expression of disappointment is from his letter to House, February 4, 1881, EHC, University of Virginia (emphasis in original). The other material on Twain comes from letters in MTP, University of California at Berkeley: invitation, Samuel Clemens to House, October 6, 1880; Grant's attitude toward Twain and inference of late-October visit, Clemens to House, November 9, 1880; and rumors, House to Twain, December 30, 1880.

4. House wrote Bennett on February 5, March 27 (need for "some distinct understanding"), March 30, May 12 (helping with China story), and June 4, 1880, JRY, Library of Congress. Bennett offered to send a carriage to the station in a cable to House, September 16, 1880; he also wrote to House, September 2, 12, 20, and 25: EHC, University of Virginia.

5. House's early articles ran in the *Alta California* (August 23, 1880), the *Chicago Times* (September 5, 1881), and the Brooklyn *Eagle;* see his letters to Ōkuma Shigenobu, August 23 and September 6, 1880, and to Hirai Kishō, January 30, 1881, all in Waseda University Library. For the interview, see *New York World,* February 16, 1881, 2. "Martyrdom" ran in *The Atlantic Monthly* (May 1881): 610–23; see especially 615 (budget portions), 611 ("desperate"), and 619–21 (Parkes). The *Pall Mall Budget* essay ran on June 9, 1881. The *Japan Weekly Mail* attacks came on July 9 and July 30, 1881; the July 9 *Mail* was equally harsh about Edward Reed's similar attacks on Parkes. It bears noting that Frank Brinkley, who became *Mail* editor in 1881, wrote to House on August 29, 1883, just after Parkes was transferred to China: "So Sir Harry is off at last! . . . It is a weight off my mind too. My personal liking and esteem for the man made it almost impossible for me to write of his policy as I really felt about it," EHC, University of Virginia.

6. House describes the indemnity repayment as his "chief object" in a letter to Ōkuma, October 7, 1887, OM C336, Waseda University; his discussion of how to reach the Americans is in his letter to Hirai, September 22, 1880, Waseda University. Grant's attitude about treatment of Japan is described in his letter to Samuel Clemens, April 1, 1881, MTP, University of California; Yoshida's evaluation is in his letter to House, October 2, 1880, EHC, University of Virginia; and Grant's promise and House's description of his own work in Washington is in his letter to Ōkuma Shigenobu, December 8, 1880, OM C332.

7. For the *Gazette*'s pique, see *Japan Gazette,* December 16, 1881. A cryptic cable from House to Mark Twain, October 16, 1880 ("With General Grants Party. You know one single phrase may start and spread a splendid movement") suggests early discussions of the consul general possibility, MTP, University of California. For Grant's recommendation, see Grant to James A. Garfield, February 18, 1881, JAG, Library of Congress; for Twain's recommendation, Clemens to House, February 19, 1881, EHC, University of Virginia; and House's discussion of pros and cons is in House to Hirai (emphases, House's), March 10, 1881, Waseda University Library, while his self-appraisal and his April deliberations are in House to Young, April 10 and 25, 1881, JRY, Library of Congress. For his decision to drop the idea,

see House to Hirai, Waseda University Library, June 13, 1881; for the job's insignificance, House to Ōkuma, October 10, 1881, OM, Waseda University; and for his revived interest, House to Hirai, Waseda University, October 31, 1881. From House to Young, JRY, Library of Congress: House's fear of mortification, n.d. (context suggests December 1881); House's irritation at Shepard, January 7, 1882; and Grant's supportive words, December 15, 1881.

8. Reade's comments on Koto and Paris life, as well as his depression are in his letter to House, May 17, 1881, Princeton University Library; the encounter with Bennett is in House to John Russell Young, September 4, 1881, JRY, Library of Congress; the meeting with Booth is in House, "Edwin Booth in London," 270–76.

9. House recalls his desire to "weaken or destroy" Parkes in a letter to Ōkuma, October 7, 1887, OM C336, Waseda University. The rest of his London experience is described in his report to Ōkuma, September 3, 1881, OM C333. Mori's need to remain aloof is in his letter to House, June 10, 1881, while House's comment about "pompous showing off" is in House to Hirai, June 13, 1881, Waseda University Library. House had written favorably of Reed's pro-Japanese views at the *Tokio Times* (July 26 and December 13, 1879). They are discussed disparagingly in Stanley Lane-Poole, *The Life of Sir Harry Parkes,* vol. 2, 301. The "conquered province" phrase comes from James Bingham's diplomatic despatch to James G. Blaine, November 21, 1881, D-USMJ, National Archives.

10. The trip is reported in House to Ōkuma, September 2, 1881, OM C333, Waseda University.

11. House discusses payment in a secret memo to Hirai (Kishō), Honyaku shūsei, no. 6 (May 11, n.d. [apparently 1880]): 29810–9 (9)–186/143, Kokuritsu Kōbunshokan, Tokyo. He suggests slightly over 1,000 yen a month as the likely cost of the trip. I have found no response from Hirai.

12. House's editorial comments are found in his letters to Benjamin Ticknor, September 9 and n.d., 1881, BHT, Library of Congress; the friends' evaluations come from Edmund Stedman to House, November 1, 1881, ECS, Library of Congress; quotations from *Japanese Episodes* are on 3 ("inner life"), 56 (no swearing), 153 (Ienoshima), 154 (rude foreigners), and 233 (female impersonators); the review is from *The Nation,* November 3, 1881, 360.

13. For Aldrich correspondence, see House to Thomas Bailey Aldrich, September 8, 1881, Houghton Library, Harvard University; for Hay, House to John Hay, September 5 and 8, 1881, Brown University; and for Stedman, Stedman to House, October 22, 1881, ECS, Library of Congress.

14. Young's party is described in House to Young, November 22, 1881; House's distress is found in his letter to Young, February 18, 1882. Both in JRY, Library of Congress.

15. See a series of 1881 letters from Samuel Clemens to House: October 8 ("vanished"), EHC, University of Virginia; November 21 ("mighty glad"), MTP, University of California; and December 27 ("as much of you"), MTP. The "fierce attack of gout" is in House to Young, February 18, 1882, JYP, Library of Congress; and House's feeling of being a prisoner is in his letter to Stedman, November 20, 1881, ECS, Columbia University. House's desire for "repose" is in his letter to Ōkuma, September 3, 1881, OM C333, Waseda University. House's need for Japan is in Ebihara Heihachirō, *Nihon Ōji shimbun zasshi shi,* 124.

16. Ōkuma's retreat is described in House to Ōkuma, January 1, 1886, OM C335, Waseda University; Japanese press reports are from *Meiji Nippō,* January 18 and March 16, 1882; discussions of his efforts to revive the *Times* are in Ebihara, *Ōji shimbun,* 125, and Shōwa Joshi Daigaku, ed., "E. H. Hausu," 388.

17. House's teaching is discussed, among other places, in UNESCO Higashi Ajia Bunka Kenkyū Sentā, *Shiryō yatoi gaikokujin,* 346. His comments about the position are from his letter to Young, September 14, 1882, JRY, Library of Congress.

18. For perspiration, see House to Young, September 14, 1882, JRY, Library of Congress; for "nothing more serious," Joseph W. Harper to House, September 19, 1884, EHC, University of Virginia; for course of drugs, House to Young, November 22, 1882, JRY, Library of Congress; for life's dreariness, House to Young, November 2, 1882, JRY, Library of Congress; for Christmas dinner, House to Young, January 17, 1883, JRY, Library of Congress; for "right hand," House to E. C. Stedman, May 28, 1883, ECS, Columbia University; for "got the best of me," House to Samuel Clemens, July 12, 1883, MTP, University of California; for enforced idleness, House to Stedman, February 25, 1883, ECS, Columbia University; for need for cash, House to Young, October 15, 1882, JRY, Library of Congress; for "strained by pain," Frank Brinkley to House, September 8, 1884, EHC, University of Virginia; for marionettes, House to Young, June 30, 1882, JRY, Library of Congress; for the lack of visits, House to Young, November 22, 1882, JRY, Library of Congress; for discussions of corruption, House to Young, November 2 and 14, 1882, JRY, Library of Congress; for Inoue's control of the government, contrast to Ōkuma, and ties to Irwin, House to U. S. Grant, November 6, 1882, USG, Library of Congress; for "cold upon Japan," House to Young, October 15, 1882, JRY, Library of Congress; for Koto's patience and House's reflections on marriage, House to Stedman, May 28, 1883, ECS, Columbia University; for "daughter's tenderness," House to Clemens, July 12, 1883, MTP.

19. Letters from House to Ōkuma, October 7, 1887, April 28, 1890, C336 and C342 respectively, OM, Waseda University. Circumstances surrounding the actual return are discussed in Nakamura Shōmi, "Beikoku no Shimonoseki shōkin hensen ron ni tsuite," *Ōkuma Kenkyū.* The *Japan Weekly Mail* debate is discussed in my "Edward H. House: Questions of Meaning and Influence," *Japan Forum,* 21–24. For Hall and indemnity, see F. G. Notehelfer, ed., *Japan Through American Eyes: The Journal of Francis Hall,* 57; Hall argued that the attack on the *Pembroke* was illegal but that indemnities undermined the growth of commerce.

20. House's pension is discussed in letters between House and Inoue Kaoru (December 1883, January 14, 1884, and January 4, 1884, respectively) in "Beikoku 'Hausu' e nenkin oyobi teate kane kyūyo ikken, "Gaimushō Gaikōshiryōkan, Tokyo. Hearn's recollection is in his 1903 (n.d.) letter to Mrs. Wetmore, Tokyo, in Elizabeth Bisland, ed., *Life and Letters of Lafcadio Hearn,* vol. 2, 497. For Tokyo living costs, see House to Stedman, May 28, 1883, ECS, Columbia University; for the rent House paid, Koseki Tsuneo and Kitamura Tomoaki, trans., *Kunippingu no Meiji Nihon kaisōki,* 180.

21. For restarting the school, see *Japan Weekly Mail,* July 24, 1880, citing material from *Tokyo Nichi Nichi Shinbun;* for Hausu Gakkō records, see Tokyotō Kōbun Shokan documents: *Gakuji nenpō* (1882): 16–17 and (1883): 29–34; *Shiritsu shōgakkō kyōin shorui* (1884): 205–10; and *Shiritsu shōgakkō shorui* (1885): 487 (closing of the school). For House's account of the school and Koto's interest, House to Young, June 18, 19, 1882, JRY, Library of Congress; for Koto's assistance with the young

girls, Frank Brinkley to House, May 17, 1885, EHC, University of Virginia; for the dispensary, see House to Edmund Stedman, May 28, 1883, ECS, Columbia University. House's description of the missionaries' reactions (and his account of providing medicine) are in House to Twain, May 1, 1888, MTP, University of California. Another account of House providing assistance to orphans is found in *Yomiuri Shimbun*, January 15, 1885, 2.

22. The sketches are discussed at great length in correspondence between House and Edmund Clarence Stedman, between May and November 1883, in ECS, Columbia University. He says he could write sketches of (among others) Alexander Dumas, Leon Gambetta, Fanny Ellsler, Horace Greeley, Jenny Lind, John Brown, Artemus Ward, Henry Raymond, the composer Gioacchino Antonio Rossini, and Charles Reade; see House to Stedman, May 28, 1883. He feared (House to Stedman, July 10, 1883) that his two sketches on Lincoln would not be publishable because they were too honest about Lincoln's preelection mediocrity and about that "curse of Lincoln's life, his unhappy mad wife"; like most of the others, they appear not to have been published.

23. House's evaluations of the *Mail* are contained in his letters to Young, October 15 and November 22, 1882, JRY, Library of Congress. For "it is a paper," see Brinkley to House, August 29, 1881; for "touching your work," Brinkley to House, September 21, 1883, both from EHC, University of Virginia. The *Mail* published both a daily and a weekly edition; House's contributions ran in both.

24. All from letters from Brinkley, EHC, University of Virginia: editing duties, August 15, 1884; "stay away a month," August 23, 1884; "regret my return," November 1, 1884; "unwillingness to give displeasure" and "demand apologies," September 8, 1884; and "I miss you," October 28, 1885.

25. The Twain-House letters here are from MTP, University of California: incense, Clemens to House, November 12, 1883; Twain and Tokyo legation, House to Twain, December 20, 1884; and Koto after House's death, House to Twain, December 9, 1884. The description of doctors trying to frighten House is in House to Stedman, December 5, 1884, ECS, Columbia University.

26. See Captain H. Longley to Dr. Tripler, August 7, 1885, EHC, University of Virginia.

11

Japan, 1885–1892: Imperial Constitutionalism

> If the Japanese people are indecisive in following the world's general trend, the blue eyed, red haired peoples will invade Japan, like billowing waves. They will drive us to the islands of the sea.
>
> —Tokutomi Sohō, 1886[1]

In the summer of 1885, Mark Twain described Japan as a "darned old dreamy and beautiful . . . Land of Dead Issues." He said he admired Japan for that: "Gott im Himmel! I would delight to live in Japan; for my idea of heaven itself is a place where all the issues are dead ones, and no man, not even the angels, cares a damn."[2] His patronizing compliment was misinformed, however; if Japan appeared quiet from abroad, distance or disinterest must have been the culprit. Its political life, close up, was aquiver. This was the period when so many of the ideas and forces introduced by the Meiji Restoration reached fruition, particularly in the realms of politics and intellectual discourse. It also was the decade when assertive nationalism and support for continental expansion began to emerge, the time when many features of that aggressive Japan that would challenge Western dominance early in the next century began to come clear.

The backdrop for this period can be found in the political debates of 1882 and 1883, when the new political parties discussed in chapter nine provided Japan's expanding public with a season of vigorous debate about what kind of political structure Japan needed. All of the "prestige papers" supported one or another of the parties in this discussion, as did large numbers of intellectuals and businessmen. Farmers and schoolteachers sat around village fires, discussing constitutional theory. Citizens of Shikoku crowded local halls to hear popular rights orators and screamed, "Kill him!" when they suspected a government informant in their midst. Nearly every journal in the country published its own constitutional draft and sneered at partisan rivals as illiterate, corrupt, or disloyal. And the thinker Nakae Chōmin declared in a popular essay that any constitution worthy of the name would enfranchise the masses: "Constitutionalism is to be respected but democracy loved," he wrote. The historian Irokawa Daikichi calls this "a unique period in our history," a time when sixty villages in the Tokyo region alone formed groups to discuss what kind of constitution Japan should have.[3]

By the time House had begun writing for Frank Brinkley's *Japan Mail* in mid-1883, this popular political frenzy had largely subsided, unable to sustain itself in a milieu where elections would not be held for another six or seven years. By 1884, even Ōkuma, the founder of one of the new parties, had grown disillusioned by the bickering and quit the party movement, as had the other major party founders, Itagaki and Fukuchi Gen'ichirō. But that had not meant a cessation in political activity—just a shift in its locus, from the village squares to the state councils. So by the time House arrived back in New York, the center of political activity had gravitated to a coterie of officials occupied with the task of with drafting both a basic law of state and a broad system of constitutional support structures.

Their work had started in 1882, when Itō Hirobumi left for Europe to study constitutional theory under German and Austrian scholars who believed in "strengthening the foundations of the imperial sovereignty" and avoiding the "extreme liberal radicals of England, America, and France." After returning to Tokyo in 1884, he and fellow officials Inoue Kowashi, Kaneko Kentarō, and Itō Miyoji gave themselves to crafting a document that would balance constitutional limits on authority with the absolute imperial sovereignty that they considered the core of Japan's historic tradition. To help them in the effort, they employed another German advisor, Hermann Roesler, known for despising popular government. Itō may have been a reform-minded activist when he was younger, but years in power had taken away any penchant for liberalism. He distrusted commoners and was determined that the constitutional system leave as many prerogatives as possible to the men around the emperor.

His suspicion of popular government was shared by the quintessential bureaucrat Yamagata Aritomo, the diplomat-turned-educator Mori Arinori, and nearly all of the other central leaders, who threw their energies into buttressing the constitution with organizational structures that would keep the state in control and the foreigners at bay. The aloof but brilliant Yamagata, like Itō a native of the old Chōshū domain, focused on the local government edifice, and on the military system. As minister of home affairs, he believed that the "best preparation for a future constitutional system" would be the creation of an efficient system of local administration to replace the chaotic village and town government structures long in existence. Easy communication with—and control of—local government, he maintained, was crucial to national strength in an imperialist world where the "assets and resources of the East are like meat before a pack of tigers." For that reason, his Home Ministry drew up a series of codes in the run-up to the constitution, standardizing local administrations and subordinating them to Tokyo. An 1884 regulation provided for appointment of local government heads by higher officials, and gave prefectural governors veto power over many local assembly actions. Four years later, the Municipal Code and the Town and Village Code required that all city mayors and prefectural governors be central government appointees, and that Tokyo control the expenditure of most local taxes. The Home Ministry also dramatically reduced the number of "localities" in these years, amalgamating 80,000 towns and villages into roughly 15,000 administrative divisions by 1889 so as to provide easier coordination from the center. And the number of police posts was more than tripled in the last half of the 1880s, to 11,357. As a result, says Yamagata biographer Roger Hackett, "an authoritarian political system was made more rigid and efficient." Local officials would be beholden to Tokyo bureaucrats for their jobs, as well as their ideas.[4]

Yamagata took a different tack with the armed forces, pushing policies that would keep the military free from governmental interference. The army and navy, he argued, needed unity, discipline, and, above all, independence from civilian officials. He tried to assure spiritual unity with the 1882 Imperial Rescript for Soldiers and Sailors, which urged military men to be loyal to the emperor and stay out of politics, declaring: "Duty is weightier than a mountain, while death is lighter than a feather."[5] At the institutional level, he worked with a rising young military star, Katsura Tarō, to shift Japan's organizational pattern away from the French model toward the more centralized German style. As a result, an independent General Staff Headquarters was created, and the army and navy chiefs were placed directly under the emperor, with no responsibility to the civilian government. Katsura also revised the army's organizational structure in the late 1880s, creating a divisional system designed for tighter control. And he maneuvered the Getsuyōkai, an influential group of young officers who advocated a limited defense system, out of existence. The conscription law was revised too, to make it more difficult for affluent young men to get out of the draft. The reason the Yamagata-Katsura camp gave for these changes was that they wanted to prevent the military from interfering in civilian government. Their real motive was quite the opposite: to keep politicians from participating in military decisions. They succeeded so fully that the military would, in time, become immune to most constitutional checks.

Other constitutional preparations centered on the structure of the central government. In 1884 the groundwork was laid for a legislative upper house by giving peers' titles to more than 500 family heads, including eleven as princes, twenty-four as marquises, and 323 as viscounts. Although most of these men came from the ranks of the traditional elites, almost 14 percent were businessmen, religious leaders, and officials from society's lower ranks. A year later, the clumsy Council of State was replaced by a cabinet with an emperor-appointed prime minister presiding over departments such as commerce, home affairs, education, and foreign affairs. Even more important was the creation of a bureaucratic structure designed to attract bright men who would see themselves as "slaves of the emperor,"[6] independent of party influence. Members of this bureaucracy, from vice-ministers on down, would be admitted only by passing rigorous civil service exams. One positive result of this reform was that Japan developed one of the world's most highly trained, respected bureaucracies; less positive was the fact that the civil servants became fairly impervious to political, or public, influence—sometimes even contemptuous of it.

Nowhere did the rulers' determination to immunize the constitutional state from popular contamination show up more vividly than in a set of measures adopted to restrict political speech. In 1882 and 1883 new assembly and press laws, aimed especially at the popular rights movement, made it more difficult to state opinions publicly, either in meetings or in print. The former required permits for public gatherings and forbade several groups, including police officers and teachers, from holding meetings at all, while the latter eradicated more than sixty newspapers at a swoop by requiring owners to deposit a large security fee before publishing; it also "pulled out the people's tongues and hearts," said one critic, by censoring many types of writing.[7] Even more heavy-handed was a Peace Preservation Law (*hoan jōrei*) issued on Christmas Day, 1887, that proscribed secret assemblages, laid down penalties for people who incited unrest, allowed police to break up meetings, and—most dramatically—banned "dangerous" people from living within seven and a half miles of the palace. By the next day, police had labeled more than 570 Tokyo residents dangerous, including such popular rights celebrities as Nakae and Ozaki Yukio. Within the week, those "dangerous" ones had been sent home to the provinces. The coming constitution might create a legislature and give the "people" a voice. But the drafters were determined that that voice should be as quiet as possible.

The actual writing of the constitution, carried out secretly under Itō's guidance after 1886, produced few surprises. The document was promulgated on February 11, 1889, with enormous hoopla and ceremony. Newspapers vied to be the first to get texts of the constitution to their readers. Mountain villagers celebrated by building monuments and holding feasts. The journalist Kuga Katsunan chose the day to inaugurate a new paper named *Nihon*. And thousands of Japanese rejoiced with fireworks that night, even as they mourned the death of Education Minister Mori, who had been assassinated on his way to the promulgation ceremonies by a Shintō nationalist who thought Mori had not shown enough respect during a recent visit to the imperial shrines at Ise.

While some popular rights advocates rued conservative features of the constitution, hardly anyone escaped the excitement. Japan had become the first Asian nation to adopt a constitution, the first to create a national legislature, the first to have an independent judiciary. Sovereignty may have rested with a "sacred and inviolable" emperor who had "given" the constitution to the people, and freedoms of speech and religion may have been circumscribed by the phrase "within the limits of the law," but the fact that Japan now *had* a constitution, and that freedoms were promised at all, was a great step forward. Similarly, the creation of an assembly, however limited, gave a voice to hundreds of thousands of people who never had had one before. The state, moreover, was subject now to the same kind of fundamental law that governed most of the Western powers. The pride and rejoicing were universal. As the Mito widow Nishimiya Hide put it: "I had never experienced anything like this since the day I was born. It really showed how much the world had changed."[8]

One reason for the pervasive pride lay in the fact that Japan, by 1889, had become a far more nation-conscious place than it was at the time of the Meiji coup. In 1868, most residents had identified primarily with their regions, or their families, with little sense of being "Japanese." But the Restoration leaders had worked hard to change that, fearful that a weak sense of nationhood would make Japan vulnerable to imperialist aggression, and convinced that commitment to the nation would increase support for government programs. It was that conviction that had produced many of the early-Meiji reforms: bringing the emperor from Kyoto to Tokyo, requiring universal school attendance and military service, creating new holidays and the national Yasukuni Shrine. Above all, the Meiji rulers had struggled to instill popular loyalty to an oracular emperor who would serve not just as sovereign but as the warm and embracing heart, parent, and *kami* of the land. All of these efforts had mixed results in the first Meiji years; the farther one went from the cities, the less loyalty one saw. But their impact increased as time passed, and by the late 1880s nationalism was being described as "the main trend in Japan's press and intellectual world."[9]

This rising nationalism was propelled by a new generation of intellectuals, men like *Nihon* editor Kuga and House's admirer, Tokutomi, who had come of age since the first encounters with the West. Born in the pre-Restoration world, these men belonged to the torn generation: educated in science-based curriculums, released from the status rigidity of the Tokugawa era, yet confronted with endless cultural conflicts. Theirs was the first generation to be taught by Western teachers, to learn foreign languages, to study European philosophy—and to be confronted daily with Japan's scientific and technological shortcomings. The result, for many, was cultural disorientation and embarrassment. As Kenneth Pyle, the pioneer student of this group, notes: "Though national consciousness thus permeated the thinking of the new generation, national pride did not." The result was the emergence of a discourse in the 1880s aimed at carving out an intellectual and spiritual niche for Japan, a discourse that has been labeled cultural nationalism.

Cultural nationalism took various forms. Some of the young journalists' mentors agonized over the excesses of Westernization, particularly the pursuit of self-interest, and called for a return to Confucian emphases on self-sacrifice and public mindedness. The Tokutomi camp, by contrast, said Japan should take pride in the speed with which it adapted to the "universal" principles of the "civilized" the West. His 1886 best-seller, *The Future Japan,* written when he was just twenty-three, saw Japan utilizing Spencerian principles to become a democratic and industrial (but not military) giant. A third group, who followed Kuga, sought a middle way between East and West, arguing that Japan must hold vigorously to its own "national essence" or *kokusui,* even as it embraced what was best in the Western tradition. At the heart of each position was a conviction that the Japanese people must believe in themselves and their own traditions. As Tokutomi wrote in *Kokumin no Tomo:* "The reason the English are a great nation is not only that they are a great people, but that they believe they are a great people." The lesson for Japan was obvious.[10]

The force that shaped this rising nationalism most insistently was Japan's continuing ill treatment at the hands of the imperialist powers. We already have seen the endless international difficulties this archipelago nation experienced in the 1870s and early 1880s: the dashed hopes for treaty revision, the frustration over trade imbalances, the apathy House faced when he pled Japan's case in London and Paris. Now, in the late 1880s, as every fresh effort at treaty revision dramatized Japan's weakness, the public lost patience. In 1887, for example, when Foreign Minister Inoue Kaoru proposed ending extraterritoriality by letting Japanese and foreign judges sit together in expatriate cases, the popular uproar forced his resignation. The mere suggestion of allowing foreigners on Japanese courts was taken by many as an admission that Japan was not sovereign in its own land. When Ōkuma took a similar tack a year later, having returned to power as foreign minister, a right-wing zealot threw a bomb at his carriage, shattering his leg and ending his second term of political service.

Two episodes involving foreigners particularly stirred up nationalistic passions in the latter 1880s. The first, the wreck of the British vessel *Normanton,* showed extraterritoriality at its worst. When the ship sank off the Kii Peninsula on October 21, 1886, the British captain saved his twenty-six crew members but allowed all twenty-three Japanese to drown. Three weeks later, when the Kobe consular court found the captain innocent of wrongdoing, the Japanese public erupted. "Foreigners treat their Japanese passengers like luggage," wrote *Tokyo Nichi Nichi Shimbun,* calling for people to rise up in opposition to the unequal treaties. The public was little appeased a few weeks later when the shocked court reconvened and sentenced the captain to three months in jail but again found his crew innocent.[11]

Even more explosive was the Ōtsu incident, which occurred near Lake Biwa in May 1891, during a visit by Russia's Crown Prince Nicholas. This time, a nationalistic policeman stabbed the prince—to "protect" his own beloved emperor from foreign contamination. The episode typically is discussed by historians for its role in establishing judicial independence (the courts resisted cabinet pressure to try the policeman under laws written only to cover violence against the *Japanese* emperor) and the press's right to freedom from prepublication censorship. But it was just as important for illustrating the nationalistic fevers then at large. Fear of foreign pollution stirred the policeman to violence; apprehension about a Russian military response led officials to seek the death penalty for the officer, even though he had not hurt the crown prince badly; and concern about national dignity fueled the press's coverage of the event. In demanding that the courts not bend the laws, *Kokumin Shimbun* proclaimed: "We should shed tears of sympathy and grief, but we dare not forget the dignity and standing that go with being a great Eastern nation."[12] It was no longer enough to avoid foreign attacks; Japan's reputation mattered, too. The fact that Russia, in the end, accepted the emperor's simple apology served as proof to most cultural nationalists that Japan could act as a sovereign nation ought to act: proudly and from principle.

The rising nationalism also developed a more aggressive side in these years, as opinion leaders began moving toward what Akira Iriye has called an "ideology of Asianism." One sees this in the military in the triumph of the Yamagata and Katsura factions, who wanted an armed force that was ready not just to defend the archipelago but to fight overseas. In 1886, Katsura and his peer Kawakami Sōroku wrote a letter arguing that the ability merely to defend one's self was "the goal of second-rate nations," and by 1890, Yamagata would be ready to say in his first speech as prime minister that Japan's security depended as much on developing a "line of advantage," or buffer zone, as it did on protecting its "line of sovereignty." Creating that line of advantage, he asserted elsewhere, meant that Japan should become dominant in Korea. One also sees the shift to a more aggressive nationalism in the writings of Tokutomi, who so recently had been the country's most celebrated internationalist. Increasingly convinced that the trend of the world was toward imperialism and that the unequal treaties were "our shame . . . our disadvantage," the young journalist began calling in the early 1890s for Japan to "solve the problem of national expansion without delay" and to "embark upon great adventures abroad."[13]

Perhaps the most telling evidence of the changing national mood came in the 1890 Imperial Rescript on Education, a document that would be repeated daily by Japanese schoolchildren for the next half century, much like the pledge of allegiance in the United States. The conviction that schools should be instruments of nationalism had been nurtured by Mori, who argued as education minister that the only way for Japan to maintain prestige was to inculcate "military education" in the schools "because military education makes people serious." And the decision to have students express their patriotism by daily recitation of a sacramental document was made after Yamagata became prime minister in 1890. It was no coincidence that he argued in the Diet that year that "there are two indispensable elements in the field of foreign policy: the armed forces first, and education second."

From one perspective, the imperial rescript reflected the resurgence of Confucian morality by locating the source of education in the "Imperial Throne coeval with heaven and earth" and by admonishing children to "be filial to your parents," to "bear yourselves in modesty," to "promote common interests." From another perspective, the document illustrated Japan's commitment to modern legal systems, with its calls to "respect the Constitution and observe the laws." And from still a third, it raised the new military theme by urging students to offer themselves "courageously to the State" in cases of national "emergency." But in all ways, it made education the servant of the nation, urging students to see themselves as part of a greater Japan, children of a benevolent emperor who ruled through a constitutional system. Education had traveled a great distance since 1872, when the education law had defined learning as "an investment for success in life."[14]

Japanese still looked to the West in the early 1890s, but they no longer followed the imperialist nations slavishly. Why should they, after what Japan had accomplished? Ad hoc rule had been replaced by constitutionalism. The government had become secure. A legislature met regularly to debate laws and budgets. Schools in provinces and cities alike were attracting a higher and higher percentage of eligible children. Asian nations looked increasingly to Japan for leadership. And the army had become a major force in national life, poised to take the Japanese model abroad. As a result, the sense of inferiority had evolved into pride, tinged with a bit of doubt. The self-abnegation of the early Meiji years had given way to the cultural nationalism of a people not yet satisfied with their place in the imperialist world, but convinced of their own abilities and their right to equal treatment by the Western powers. The rulers' reasons for having moved Japan in this direction—for creating an emperor ideology designed to give the people a national identity, and for building a military-economic base strong enough to make Japan competitive—are not hard to divine. Without popular commitment to the national good and a strong military-economic foundation, Japan might not have survived in the imperialist world. Within a decade or two, as the world climate changed, people might begin to question whether nationalism and the strong military were unalloyed blessings. In the middle of the third Meiji decade, however, there seemed no alternative.

NOTES

1. Tokutomi Sohō, *Shōrai no Nihon,* 182.
2. Samuel Clemens to House, May 23, 1884, MTP, University of California.
3. Quotations from Itagaki are from *Chōya Shimbun,* October 30, 1881, in Uchikawa Yoshimi and Matsushima Eiichi, eds., *Meiji niyūsu jiten,* vol. 2, 314–15. Nakae wrote this in 1887, but used similar language throughout the early 1880s; see Nakae Chōmin, *A Discourse by Three Drunkards on Government,* 76. Irokawa's evaluation is in Irokawa Daikichi, *The Culture of the Meiji Period,* 108.
4. Yamagata's fear of imperialists, Stewart Lone, *Army, Empire and Politics in Meiji Japan,* 26; increase in police posts, Marius Jansen, *The Making of Modern Japan,* 401; and Hackett's evaluation, *Yamagata Aritomo in the Rise of Modern Japan,* 108, 114.
5. Translation in Arthur Tiedemann, *Modern Japan: A Brief History,* 107–12.
6. Quote in Peter Duus, *Modern Japan,* 122.
7. Cited in Midoro Masaichi, *Meiji Taishō shi: genron hen,* 135.
8. Anne Walthall, "Nishimiya Hide," in Anne Walthall, ed., *The Human Tradition in Modern Japan,* 56.
9. Nishida Taketoshi, *Meiji jidai no shimbun to zasshi,* 151.
10. Quotations are from Kenneth B. Pyle, *The New Generation in Meiji Japan*: "national consciousness," 19; and British pride, 147 (from *Kokumin no Tomo,* May 23, 1891).
11. *Tokyo Nichi Nichi Shimbun,* November 7, 1886, quoted in Haruhara, *Nihon shimbun tsū shi,* 61.

12. *Kokumin Shimbun,* May 17, 1891.

13. For Iriye, see his "Japan's Drive to Great-Power Status," in Marius Jansen, ed., *The Cambridge History of Japan,* vol. 5, 757; for Katsura/Kawakami, Lone, 21; for Yamagata, Hackett, 138–39; and for Tokutomi, John Pierson, *Tokutomi Sohō 1863–1957,* 227–28.

14. Mori's comments are found Yamaji Aizan, *Essays on the Modern Japanese Church,* 157; and Yamagata's speech is in Irwin Scheiner, *Modern Japan: An Interpretive Anthology,* 179. The rescript is reprinted in Ryusaku Tsunoda et al., eds., *Sources of Japanese Tradition,* vol. 2, 139–40. For the 1872 ordinance, see Mikiso Hane, *Modern Japan: A Historical Survey,* 102.

12

Interesting Times: 1886–1892

> How you keep up your powers of work and clearness of brain after all you have suffered, it puzzles me to think.
>
> —Frank Brinkley to House, 1889[1]

Dreams of New York drew House and Koto powerfully when they left Yokohama on August 11, 1885, but they barely made it to Hong Kong, and once there, months passed before they knew if they would be able to go farther. The friendly seas betrayed House this time. A dreadful heat struck eastern Asia, and House became "so ill and weak" en route that he had "to refuse every kind of norishment [sic]" for two full weeks. Warning that a few more days aboard ship "would surely have killed him," the Hong Kong doctors commanded the journalist to stay put until he was in better health. It was a frightening order, for Hong Kong was anything but hospitable to sufferers: tropical, with late summer temperatures ranging into the nineties, humidity levels rising to the upper eighties, and thunderstorms threatening well into the autumn. Frank Brinkley wrote that he had "never heard of any invalid finding recovery in Hong Kong." And if the weather was wretched, social life was almost nonexistent. House's friend John Pitman, who had worked for Ōkuma's finance ministry in the 1870s, was in Hong Kong now and called often, bringing "cheerfulness." Friends like Brinkley wrote about how much they missed him. And he was able on better days to pen a few letters, including one to Ōkuma recalling "the consideration and the confidence which you were always kind enough to show me" and predicting a day "when you will possess even a greater degree of strength" in government. But mostly he just suffered, awaiting the day, which did not come until late February, when he could continue to New York.[2]

When he did arrive there, in May, his plans were less concrete than they had been in 1880. As he told his old *Tribune* editor Whitelaw Reid, he had returned "in obedience, I suppose, to the grip of home feeling which fastens upon every man when he discovers that his gear is getting so rusty as to threaten to go to pieces." Six years earlier he had been afire with diplomatic goals, but this time only his joints were inflamed. He expected to use those "few fragments of my machinery" that still worked to continue publicizing Japanese issues. As for concrete goals, however, he had none, except to find relief from pain. And even that seemed pointless when his illness got much worse the "very night" of his return. It was a repeat of his arrival in Tokyo four summers earlier. "When health goes, all goes," he wrote to Edward Morse, his zoologist friend from Tokyo days. And Reid was convinced that House really had lost everything. "I went to see poor House," he wrote to John Hay early in July, "finding him in a deplorable condition indeed, and stayed with him an hour or so. . . . His knee-joints were kept bent so long by gout that they have solidified. It has been years since he has stood on his feet and he can never hope to move about, even on crutches. It comes the nearest to a living death of any case I have ever seen, and is most pitiful. Yet his mind seems perfectly clear and his ways and talk have even more than their old gentleness." He added that his old friend's visage made it almost impossible to recall "the old escapades when he was crazed with drink and the mischief he wrought."

One result of the illness was that Koto became the public figure in the family. In addition to nursing her father, she settled them into their 2123 Sixth Avenue lodgings, reestablished House's business and personal connections, and entertained his guests. She also set out to create an American life of her own, making calls on several of her own friends, including Julia Grant, and beginning painting lessons with a Mrs. Nicholls, an "artist of no little distinction" who helped her gain admission that fall to the New York Art League after she had produced the required "charcoal drawing of the Venus of Milo from a cast." And early in June, Koto made a short trip by herself to the Twains in Hartford, prompting Mark to gush that she had left "freighted as usual, with everybody's hearts." He reported overhearing Olivia comment to their children: "O, she's the dearest child in the world."[3]

House himself found relief only in friends and letters these days. Fortunately, there was an abundance of those. Reid came from time to time, and made him feel like "a released prisoner suddenly brought into contact with active life." So did Hay, and Edmund Clarence Stedman. Thomas Bailey Aldrich, the *Atlantic Monthly* editor, wrote frequently, as did Morse, and

Aldrich's publishing rival Joseph W. Harper. Mark Twain came too. He visited twice during House's first month back, then continued to call when business took him to New York. And he wrote a great deal, as did Olivia and the Twain daughters. The girls seemed to stimulate House's spontaneous side, as no others had been able to do for years. In July, they sent him a "lingo-letter," written in what Mark called an "infernally ingenious and original" language that "we can't make head or tail of." When House figured it out, fourteen-year-old Susie wrote back thanking him for "not revealing our secret to Mamma and Papa" and adding naughtily: "But Mr. House I must triumphantly say that there were a great many mistakes in your nice little note." In August, Twain wrote to describe the typesetting machine that he had developed for newspapers and to relay Olivia's fondness for House ("Why, hang it, man, I'm *always* trying to undermine Mrs. Clemens's good opinion of you, but I have grown tired of it at last and given it up."). In November, he invoked a darker mood, describing House's plight as "simply hell" and reporting that Olivia thought Mark too irresponsible to accede to House's request that he become executor of his estate. "She wants to see Koto well protected," Twain said, and proposed his own executor, Franklin G. Whitmore, a man who "saves me a raft of money which I should otherwise lose."[4]

The November letter suggested just how dark House's mood was now. With the approach of winter, his condition had grown graver, in Koto's estimation, than "at any time in his life," so serious in his own view that "the skiff came very near touching the opposite shore." Fortunately, the darkest hours also betokened the end of the siege, and in mid-December things brightened. He wrote to Stedman on December 15 to "signalize my restored power over my right hand." And two days later he was feeling well enough to consider an invitation to spend Christmas with the Twains. He was not able, in the end, to go to Hartford, but he was ready to accept another Twain request—to dramatize *The Prince and the Pauper.* On the twenty-sixth, Twain wrote that he had "ordered a couple of P+P's to be sent to you," aware surely of how much this new project would lift House's spirits, but blind to the tortuous events the project eventually would set in motion.[5]

House's correspondence during the latter half of 1886 contains only the briefest mentions of Japan, and even less of public life in general. If he was writing anything serious, he did not mention it. By the next spring, however, the old passions were stirring again. In March, he wrote some pieces for Reid's *Tribune,* in April for other New York papers, and by May he was working on articles for *Scribner's Magazine* and *The Atlantic Monthly,* in addition to trying his hand at a new field that would become important to him in the next few years: children's stories. One of the *Atlantic Monthly* articles—a squib, actually—recalled the witty repartee of several authors around the Charles Dickens dinner table one evening in the 1860s, while the *Scribner's* contribution indicated that his return to free-lancing was serious. Titled "The Sacred Flame of Torin Ji," it brought him back to romantic fiction, one of his fortes as a young man. It also brought his pen back to Japan, for the first time in nearly two years—and earned him a substantial $325.

A tale of jealousy, tragedy, and love, "The Sacred Flame" contains most of the themes that had dominated House's interactions with Japan. There is an idealistic American benefactor: a young Mr. Halithorne who collapses of heat prostration while hiking in the hills around Kyoto. There is a talented young Japanese woman: Ina, a maiden as beautiful as "a fountain dancing in the sunlight," who nurses Halithorne back to health. There is the abused Japanese wife: Teishin, who has fled a miserable marriage and become the abbess of Torin Ji, where Halithorne is taken to recover. There also is jealousy (from nuns who resent having a foreigner on the grounds), fire (when Halithorne falls asleep smoking a pipe), and romance (as Halithorne and Ina fall in love and secure permission to marry). In the end, Halithorne rebuilds the temple and settles down in Kyoto, where he and Ina create schools for young people. The story is vintage House, dividing both Japanese and foreigners into stereotypical groups, with connivers and idealists on both sides. As Charles Wordell puts it: "The voice House used . . . was knowledgeable, respectful, critical, and yet prejudiced in favor of the quaint." To have written about Japan in a more nuanced way would not have sold well in the New England of the 1880s, nor would it have reflected House's view. He rarely dealt in subtleties.[6]

House's other major writing effort that spring was a pair of long essays for *The Atlantic Monthly* on the British novelist Charles Reade, with whom he had lived during his London stays. Aldrich, the *Atlantic* editor, considered Reade's recent biographer (and nephew) Compton Reade "an ass," and was eager for House to correct the reverential tone of his work. The pieces showcased House's descriptive skills, portraying Reade as a man whose genius lay in his egomania and irascibility as much as in his writing skills. His discussion of Reade's relationship with Laura Seymour, with whom he lived, unmarried, for many years, combined candor and sympathy. The articles also made it clear that the vigorous House was back, ready to put his mental and social skills to use once more, as did his decision to leave New York in mid-May for a lengthy stay in Hartford. Twain wrote him on the fifth, telling him they were "warming up the climate" and "shoving out the leaves" for his arrival. Two days later, he told him to "ship the wheel chair" and trunks. And on the ninth, Twain wrote Charles Webster that he expected "Ned House to arrive here (on his back with gout,) the 16th."[7]

It took something of an act of faith for a sick man to visit the Twains, because their home was no place for the passive. The house itself, built at great expense in 1873 and remodeled in 1880, was as lively in style, as packed with spectacular surprises, as was Twain himself. In the first floor bedroom where House likely stayed, for example, a tube-on-the-wall precursor to the intercom allowed guests to summon servants by blowing, then speaking. Everywhere, there were extravagant chandeliers, huge folding fans, Tiffany wall stencils, grand fireplaces, and rich mahogany furniture. On the third floor, down the hall from Koto's pink bedroom, was the billiard room, where Mark and his male friends drank beer and ate hardtack, shot pool, and spun yarns into the night, "laughing, you know, and having such a good old time." To be a guest at the Twain home was to participate in a conviviality that accepted few bounds. Twain's girls recalled sitting on the stairs outside the dining room and whispering to each other, "Father is telling the beggar story; they must have reached the meat course." One visitor told how "the ale, wit, and parlor tricks captivated the company until daylight."

House and Koto stayed with the Twains for six weeks, watching spring pass into summer; then in late June, when their hosts left for vacation in Elmira, New York, they rented quarters at the homes of neighbors, first the Robert Yosts, then the Twain's close friends, the George Warners, where they would remain until the following spring. The weather bothered House in the early summer weeks, but not enough to keep him from getting "up, and writing to the dear little girls." As the summer passed, he felt better and better, until he could write to Twain early in September that he would not recognize him when he got back. "I am so changed that I think of getting naturalized, and perhaps christened," he wrote. "I have twice been out to dine." On Monday evening, September 5, Koto threw him a surprise fifty-first birthday party that left him in "a state of such high excitement that I do not know whom I conversed with, or what I said." It was, he said, "such a thing as never happened to me before in all my life." The previous year doctors had told him that he would have to leave the Northeast before another winter came, "without a chance of ever returning." But now, reinvigorated, he decided to stay. The Warners were pleased, finding "the Houses . . . easy and most agreeable people to have in one's house."[8]

This meant that House's correspondence recovered its old vibrance that summer and fall. There were numerous interchanges with H. Moss, his barely literate business agent in Yokohama, who was glad that "the exchange is a trifel better" and sorry that House did not have the funds to "purchas" a building that had come up for sale. House and Brinkley were back in touch again, with House complaining once more about careless editors who chopped up manuscripts. He resumed his letters to Ōkuma, begging Japan to take "a bold, resolute and determined position" on treaty revision. And he and the Twain daughters wrote constantly: about a "beautiful" fire in Elmira, which the girls had watched with opera glasses; about the nuisance of insects in both Hartford and Elmira (bigger in Elmira, the girls claimed); about Grandma Langdon's seventy-seventh birthday ("that is quite aged I think"); about House's suggestion of substitutes for profanity. "I am sure Momma is very grateful to you," Susie said about those suggestions, "for hitherto mine have been of my own invetion [sic], and a great source of displeasure to her." Once the Twains returned, the new sociability resumed, with Koto showing up at Twain dinners in Japanese garb even when House was too tired to go, and Mark learning some Japanese phrases.[9]

Most significant for his public life, House also began writing vigorously again, initiating his most prolific, powerful season as an advocate of Japanese causes for U.S. readers. As he wrote to Ōkuma in October, his goal was, once again, "to keep the facts of Japan's condition before the public of America, and to convince all intelligent readers that Japan is warranted in denouncing the treaties . . . to create such a state of feeling as will make it essential for the Government at Washington to take notice of the affairs of Japan, and to proffer aid and encouragement to your nation." To that end, he published a fourteen-page December essay in *The Atlantic Monthly*, "The Thraldom of Japan," which took apart Western abuses with the vigor of earlier years. The general approach was not new, but it updated his materials and pulled together his thoughts in the most concentrated way yet.

Using the controversies triggered by his dissection of Harry Parkes six years earlier as a launching pad, he focused once again on the injustices of imperialism, asking his fellow citizens if they could imagine giving European rulers the right to set U.S. tariff rates or to set up "European tribunals in the seaports of the United States." He updated his figures, pointing out that Japan in the 1887–1888 budget received a minuscule one-thirtieth of its income from customs duties, while in the United States the national "expenditure is entirely defrayed from this source." He called the standard argument for maintaining the consular courts—that Japanese could not be trusted to judge foreigners fairly—absurd: "There is probably no one among the diplomatists now in Tokio who is not profoundly convinced that justice would be more surely, more rapidly, and more equitably administered than it now is, if . . . the Japanese jurisdiction extended over all alien residents." He then listed many areas in which Japan had become a leader among civilized nations: the "excellence" of the army's organization, the high reputation of Japanese sailors, the "precision and regularity" of Japan's commercial shipping, the country's "elaborate and thorough system of education," the safety record of Japanese railways, the "magnificent" lighthouse system, the mint that showed "artistic taste as well as mechanical dexterity," the language skills of Japan's telegraph operators, the efficient and profitable postal system, the "scrupulous integrity" of the courts, and the lack of crime. He attributed the country's safety in part to the fact that the "laws are moderate, and are never known to be enforced with undue harshness."

After criticizing minor nations that insisted on extraterritoriality even though they had few residents in Japan (Spain had just three, Peru none, and Russia twenty-one), House reviewed the recent efforts to revise the treaties and offered two potential solutions. One approach harked back to his 1881 *New York World* interview, calling for a "friendly government" such as the United States to "disregard the remonstrances of the great mercantile nations" and revise its Japan treaty unilaterally. Since America nearly had done that in 1877, he pointed out, a draft already was in place. His second suggestion, also repeating a standing theme, was that Japan simply "notify the powers that the treaties are no longer endurable, and that upon a fixed date they will be declared null and void." He was convinced that no country would use force to oppose Japan. "Her restoration to such complete and untrammeled authority as is exercised by other civilized states cannot come a day too soon." The language was vintage House, overstated perhaps, but carefully researched and argued. Aldrich called it a "vindication of Japan," and published it "with pleasure."

The timing of "Thraldom" turned out to be fortuitous. Less than two months after its appearance, Inoue Kaoru resigned in frustration as foreign minister and was replaced by Ōkuma. Whether Ōkuma actually read the article is not known. But House wrote him a confidential letter summarizing its arguments, particularly his belief that European nations were too wrapped up in their own issues to object seriously if Japan were to renounce the treaties unilaterally. No direct connection can be drawn, but the fact is that with the ascension of Ōkuma Japanese officials began talking about the possibility of unilateral denunciation. It also is a fact that Ōkuma took the lead in those discussions, sometimes so aggressively as to worry more cautious officials.[10] And it is a fact that once House began, he would not stop writing about Japan for a year. He took the treaty revision crusade to academic journals such as the *New Princeton Review,* gave interviews to reporters, wrote newspaper articles, penned his first (and only) novel about Japan—and did it all with the passion that caused Tokutomi Sohō to liken him to a sumo wrestler.

The provocation for his most vigorous 1888 crusade came in mid-February, in a *New York Evening Post* essay criticizing the Japanese government for the peace preservation law that had removed political activists from Tokyo the previous Christmas Day. The article was inflammatory by any reckoning, characterizing the Japanese system as "despotism tempered by assassination," charging inaccurately that the law had "turned Tokio into a camp" and that the authorities had found it "necessary to do considerable beheading among the troops." The "blood-pit was well moistened," the anonymous writer said; "the prospect of Japanese absolutism becoming a constitutional monarchy" had grown "exceedingly remote," the hope of ending extraterritoriality an "idle dream."

House responded furiously, arguing that the ordinance had been necessary "for the preservation of social order," and was issued only after "physical assaults had been committed upon officials, and murderous threats openly directed against members of the Imperial Council." Its impact, he said, had been to send "some four hundred restless rustics" guilty of "illegal demonstrations" back to "their provincial homes." What concerned House most were the charges that the government had executed people and made a "camp" of Tokyo. He derided these as "the wildest rhapsodies of a distorted imagination." He also chided the writer for suggesting that beheading was practiced in Japan: an "amazing accusation" for which there was "not the shadow . . . of justification." Eight days later, on February 29, House wrote again, demanding evidence from the anonymous essayist that "changes of Government are accompanied by acts of violence," or that "any person has been 'beheaded' of late years in Japan."

The exchange touched off six weeks of discussion in the New York press—in the *Times,* the *Commercial Advertiser,* the *Christian Intelligencer,* and *The Nation,* among others—with neither side giving more than a nod to the other's position. Although the public rhetoric was generally polite, it had a bitter, and personal, subtext for House. Rumors circulated that the original essay had been written by William Elliot Griffis, his old friend at Kaisei Gakkō and one of the most respected U.S. interpreters of Japan. House dashed off a series of letters and telegrams to Griffis, asking whether he knew of any evidence of "extensive executions" or beheadings, and whether he had had reason to reverse his plea for treaty revision in the January 1888 issue of *The Congregationalist.* When Griffis responded that, indeed, he did not know of any such acts of cruelty and that the "information upon which the attacks were based was probably sent to the newspapers . . . by a gentleman now residing in Japan," House responded on March 1 with a somewhat disingenuous letter of assurance that he rejected the rumors about his friend's culpability. On March 6, House thanked Griffis for providing him with "direct reasons for denying that the arraignment in the *Post* is your handiwork." And on March 31, when rumors continued to circulate, House advised him to disavow the article publicly, "with proper indignation."

It came out late in 1888 that Griffis was indeed the offending writer, a fact that House appears to have suspected all along. Griffis's reasons for criticizing the Japanese government so harshly probably lay in his close tie to the missionary movement, since many victims of the peace preservation regulation were Christians. Less clear is his reason for misleading people about his authorship, though acknowledgment would have tarnished his reputation as a Japan sympathizer. He had written harsh pieces before, but they usually had appeared in Christian publications rather than in the mainstream press. What is absolutely clear is that House was stunned both by his friend's defection and by his dishonesty. He already had been irritated by Griffis's penchant for speaking authoritatively on the basis of limited knowledge. Now, House decided that the Reformed minister was a hypocrite and a threat to Japanese progress. His future comments on Griffis always would have an acid edge.

The Griffis flap was a foretaste. Within a year, House would be engulfed in an even more acrimonious dispute with the American Christian community, which would make him hate everything Christian for the rest of his life.[11] We already have seen how his early Tokyo experiences turned him cynical about Christians, particularly after pressure from religious organizations kept Reid from printing some of his material. And when a religion professor at Oberlin College, James King Newton, plagiarized a House article in 1887, House's thoughts about Christian hypocrisy seemed confirmed. The feature of Christianity that angered him most was the "false and injurious" missionary system. Not only did the evangelizers threaten Japanese culture, they violated their own principles: "Their angry quarrels, in which they often invite publicity . . . their frequent fondness for gain . . . their sharp dealings with the poorer class of tradesmen and laborers, which are notorious wherever they dwell; these and other unpleasant features of their life in Japan are by no means calculated to endear them to the populace."[12]

Until 1888, however, House's quarrel with Christians usually was carried on privately, in sarcastic quips to Twain, or Morse. With the appearance of his novel *Yone Santo, A Child of Japan,* serialized in *The Atlantic Monthly* from January to August of that year, the struggle became personal, public, and petulant. He had begun working on the novel in late 1886, during his days of physical crisis, and by the time he went to Hartford in the spring of 1887, Aldrich had pronounced the tale of a Japanese woman's sad struggle against both Christians and traditional prejudices "thoroughly lovely," a must for his magazine. He wished "that the narrative did not end so sadly," but when House asked if he should change it, Aldrich said no, recalling how he had brightened the ending of his own *Queen of Sheba* ten years before to boost sales. "It ceased to be a work of art," Aldrich said. "I never think of it without regret." So House retained the ending, and reviewers praised the story, *The Critic,* for example, calling the "study of Japanese life from the insider point of view . . . the best yet made in fiction."[13]

Critical approval did not make the book a commercial success though; the churches saw to that. Before looking at the New England Christians' efforts to undermine the novel, however, we must glance at the story itself, and the themes that upset them so. The heroine of the tale is a poor, brilliant Japanese girl named Yone Santo, who is allowed by the reluctant grandparents with whom she lives to attend a missionary school. There, she surpasses her classmates academically but is mistreated by teachers for refusing to convert to Christianity. The teachers are among the novel's most vivid characters: single women for whom nothing matters but reclaiming their charges from heathendom, zealots who expect to pay less than fair prices because of their "clergy" status, who attribute each of life's problems to being "in Japan," and who think dyspepsia in a Christian building "preferable to good digestion elsewhere" (3). It is not missionaries alone who use Yone badly, however. Her own high-bred family regards education as superfluous for women and marries her to an illiterate boat maker who despises her schooling. And a romantic young American, Mr. Milton, takes advantage of her naïveté about romance, then drops her when things became complicated. Through it all, Yone's one benefactor is an American agnostic, Dr. Edward Charwell, who rages against her teachers' lack of compassion and persuades her husband to grant her a weekly day off from domestic duties. In a powerful conclusion, cholera sweeps the community when a German ship ignores an official quarantine, and Yone nurses her former missionary teachers back to health, then dies herself, still unappreciated—because she is a heathen.

Nearly all of House's themes show up in *Yone Santo,* in concentrated form. The novel's language is prolix yet compelling. The story line, while riveting, never transcends polemicism, even though House later claimed that he wanted only to write a romance. Most of the characters are familiar to those who know House's biography: a heroine reared by grandparents and condemned to a lifeless marriage, a German captain who defies a quarantine, a young American womanizer, and an atheist American intellectual who supports the education of women and is detested by expatriates.[14] And the ideas are those that had shaped his writings for two decades. Unequal treaties bring suffering to the Japanese; talented women are condemned to dreary lives by bigoted parents and husbands; narrow-minded missionaries cause more harm than good; Japan benefits from modernity but is victimized by Western self-centeredness. As Wordell puts it: "The Japanese were not the real subject of this book. *Yone Santo* was both a denunciation of mission activity in Japan and an attack upon the international abuses that had damaged the Japanese economy."

An even more dramatic story was the ruckus *Yone Santo* raised. Although nothing that House said could have been new to anyone who had read his articles, the ideas provoked bitter controversy when they appeared in fictional, humanized form. Neither Aldrich nor the *Atlantic* publishers—nor House—predicted the row. Almost as soon as the first installment appeared, Aldrich was urging House to talk with Henry Houghton about publication as a book. And on March 26, House signed a book contract with Houghton Mifflin, agreeing to 10 percent royalties. Even then, both House and Aldrich worried occasionally about how the Christian faithful would react to the harsh portrayal of missionaries. House wrote to Morse in February that "the missionaries will do all they can to tear down my work. How they do buzz and sting!" And in April, Aldrich, having heard rumors of a church effort to spread "an unfair and harmful idea of your purpose," suggested that House write a preface to the book, explaining that he did not mean to "attack *all* missionaries and *all* missionary work, but only that special group of missionaries introduced in your fiction." No one thought the threat very serious, however, and when the *Atlantic* installments drew favorable responses, plans for the book proceeded apace, with the publishers announcing on April 28 that composition would begin within three weeks.[15]

Then came May, and House's sharpest attack on the missionaries. In that month's segment, Charwell confided to a young woman teacher, more open-minded than the others, that he had conducted an investigation for many years to find missionaries "whom I could hold in honor, whose characters I could unqualifiedly respect, whose methods of dealing with the Japanese seemed to me worthy of approval," but the search had been fruitless. "Do you mean," she asked, "that no single one of them equaled your hopes and wishes?" "Not one," he replied. "Once or twice, indeed, I have believed myself approaching a point of contact with individuals who seemed fashioned in a nobler mould; but they shrunk before such tests as I felt bound to apply, and their falling masks revealed . . . selfishness, or cowardice, or conceit." It was a harsh indictment, admitting no exceptions. And its sweeping nature, wrote Aldrich, "brought down upon H.M.& Co. *an avalanche of letters of protest*." It also triggered articles in Christian publications, damning House's entire approach to Japan. And it chilled the atmosphere between House and the publishers, who began worrying about *Yone Santo*'s commercial prospects.

Aldrich never wavered in his support of House, though he asked him several times to soften his language ("What an exquisite story this would have been if you had left out the missionary business entirely!") in order to avoid the wrath of what he called the Christian "idiots." The same was not true of the publisher. By the end of the first week of May, Aldrich was worrying about having placed too much confidence in Mr. Houghton's "firmness"; a week later, he was advising House not to "hold them to their contract" if they decided to withdraw it; and on May 24, the publishers asked House to tone down the story. House wrote in the margin of that letter: "First intimation of Missionary Influence." And he wrote to Morse: "The missionaries are on the war-path, screaming for my scalp. . . . But I certainly will not haul down my colors in this affair, and the Reverend Griffis and his brotherhood are curiously mistaken if they fancy they can intimidate me."[16]

A flurry of letters filled the mails early in June. The editors wrote on the fifth that if House remained "unwilling to modify the book to the extent we are constrained to think it should be modified," perhaps he should "withdraw the book from our hands." They never mentioned that both sides had signed a legally binding contract "drawn by themselves, at their own request." House refused to make the changes they demanded, and the following week, on Thursday, Houghton Mifflin sent him a long letter laying the groundwork for breaking the contract. The publishers claimed to have informed Aldrich early on about their concerns over the antimissionary passages, and to have been "gratified to learn that you had acceded to our request" for modification of those sections. Since then, they said, other concerns had arisen, but House had shown "an entire unwillingness further to modify the work"; so the book "is not what in good faith we had taken it to be." Seeing no chance for reconciliation, they asked: "Is it not better that we should separate amicably at this point? No publisher can publish, to advantage, a book in which his confidence of success has been shaken." House decided that "further persistence would have been a waste of time and energy," and Houghton Mifflin officials marked their copy of the manuscript "cancelled by mutual consent."

Angry and disappointed, House sent the novel to other major publishers, including Scribner's and Harper and Brothers, but they too turned him down, doubtful about the books' commercial success. He also contacted the Robert G. Ingersoll law office, which had supervised publication of the well-known agnostic's works, and received back an indignantly sympathetic letter from C. Farrell, decrying Houghton Mifflin's "lack of moral fibre" and recalling his own experiences with publishers: "I have gone through similar experiences again and again, and I know how dishonorable, unscrupulous and deceitful so called Christians and religious organizations can be, and to what extent business men and business firms, will cringe and crawl to propitiate their favor." He reminded House that "the day has gone by for successful suppression of free thought and free expression," and suggested two less influential houses known for their willingness to "proudly brave the flack": George Putnam's Sons, and Belford, Clarke. In the end, House turned to Belford, Clarke, which published an attractive edition near the end of 1888. He expressed deep disappointment in private letters to friends. The Belford, Clarke people were good-hearted but weak on the business side, he said. The "shameful carelessness" of the printers resulted in typos, even after

House had "worked like a steam engine over the proofs." Publicly, however, he focused on appreciation for Belford, Clarke's courage in standing up to the Christian establishment. As he wrote in an angry epilogue to *Yone Santo,* he owed to that publishing firm "the rescue of his book . . . from the oblivion to which the members of that fraternity, and their instruments, would have condemned it."[17]

No one came out of this fiasco looking good, except perhaps Aldrich, who put his position at some risk to publish all eight installments of *Yone Santo* without alteration. Certainly House's reputation was tarnished by the many attacks, and his tendency toward hyperbole was criticized in several journals. Houghton Mifflin had no compunction about breaking a contract for the sake of profit. And although the Christian establishment may have gained what it sought in the struggle with House, it is hard to find anything kind to say about the way church leaders used "a flood of denunciation and invective" to suppress free expression. Indeed, the most disturbing lesson of the episode was just how quickly opinion leaders of many stripes cast off their commitment to free expression. House's polemical approach may have been irritating, but it was not dangerous, nor did it attack individuals. His positions were carefully argued and rooted in fact. But questioning the missionary approach and arguing that the Japanese were as civilized as their American counterparts went beyond the pale for many in the establishment. Not only would they denounce him, they would deprive him of a voice. Indeed, a year later, when *Japan Mail* editor Frank Brinkley pronounced *Yone Santo* "simply a delightful story," he added that he "dared not reproduce it" because "I have too many friends among the missionaries."[18]

One thing that seems to have sustained House during this episode, beyond the expressions of support from *Yone Santo* admirers, was the intellectual and social life of the Twains' Nook Farm community. In the spring of 1888, he invited Morse ("a fine fellow, for all the alphabetical tags to his name") to visit him in Hartford, and took a "somewhat eccentric," ten-day steamboat excursion to New York, spending nights "on the water, which I am extremely fond of," and days seeing city friends. He also practiced the piano at the Twain home, and played logomachy, a form of anagrams, with Mark. One day after Twain had cheated to win, House allegedly got so angry that he "suddenly pushed his wheel-chair back . . . and began to wheel himself toward his room," saying "things to me which would have been hard to bear if they had come from an undersized well person." House also advised Olivia on the benefits of what was, for Americans, an experimental treatment for pain, massage, explaining that he had used it daily during the bad days in Japan, often for an hour or more, and had never experienced it "without being benefited." He also entertained the thought that Koto's paintings might make Japan "intellectually and morally known to

Americans, particularly after she had a successful month-long stay at the New York Art Students' League in May. And the summer provided another burst of chatty exchanges with the vacationing Clemens daughters: talk of baseball, "harmony lessons," horseback riding.

When autumn came, however, House and Koto began talking of another move. They had been in Hartford for a year and a half, sometimes at the Twains, most of the time at the George Warners. In many ways, these had been the best days in a decade, a time full of intellectual stimulation and witty repartee, a time for Koto to come into her own socially and professionally, a time for House to write, free for months on end from gout's ravages. But his illness took a bad turn in the fall of 1888, and his doctors urged him to move to the city for "treatment by more skilful [sic] experts than could be found in the smaller town." Koto also wanted to be closer to her art teachers, and House began finding Hartford's remoteness an obstacle in cultivating friends for Japan. So in October, they moved to 211 East Fourteenth Street, a second floor apartment so close to the heart of New York that "the smallest boy could throw the largest stone from Union Square to my door."

For Koto, the move back was a leap into a whirlpool. In addition to settling in, running the house, and caring for her father, she had to give endless hours to the art league, where she was expected not only to take classes but to participate in constant exhibits and receptions. She loved the work, but not the load. Soon, she began to feel like Yone in her father's novel, captivated with learning but so burdened with chores that she could neither sleep nor concentrate. "Papa," she wrote to Olivia Clemens, "makes fun of the contrast between his quiet existence in Hartford and the constant liveliness which surrounds us here," but she doubted that she could maintain the schedule for long. She was often sick in these months, dropping ten pounds from her usual weight of just over 100 and leaving House with "more anxiety than I am disposed to let her know." He wrote to the Twains in February that "our main domestic occupation, now a days, is taking care of one another," adding: "It is all wrong that people have to grow old—young people, that is. Old people may grow old; there is no great harm in that; but young people—it is a shame."

If he was not abed or taking care of Koto, House was busy writing, and renewing connections with people who might help Japan. When Mutsu Munemutsu, Japan's minister to Washington, came to New York during Christmas week, House arranged for him to meet influential journalists and businessmen. He also set about contacting people about U.S.-Japan trade possibilities, sought out a publisher for Frank Brinkley's writings, talked to the Japanese consul in New York about American merchants interested in buying Japanese sardines, and wrote to Ōkuma about other export opportunities, including "the preparing of goat skins, for gloves, etc., from the Bonin Islands." He reported diplomatic prospects to Ōkuma too, noting that nearness to the press would help him look out better for Japan's interests. When he found errors in articles about East Asia, he arranged interviews to set things straight. And the Japanese officials took note, writing in January 1889 that his pension would be continued once the earlier installments ended, though at a 20 percent reduction to 2,000 yen a year ($1,490 at the day's exchange rate). The award letter called on him "to promote the interests of Japan whenever a suitable opportunity presents itself, in the same satisfactory manner as you have done hitherto."[19]

Despite occasional setbacks, most of 1889 seems to have been good for House physically, allowing him to entertain dinner guests occasionally, to go out "walking" (i.e., riding) in the park on weekends, to travel once or twice to the beach, even to attend the theater. In September, he wrote to Augustin Daly asking permission to be "carried by my servants to the orchestra stalls" of Daly's Theater because the doctor was permitting him to attend plays "for the first time in many years." He assured Daly that he would arrive early and not cause "inconvenience to anybody."[20]

House's emotional life, on the other hand, took a plunge, because his relationship with Twain soured. Warm interchanges between the two families continued until the end of February, with Mark promising on the 26th to visit House soon in New York. But after that, it became clear that two innocent letters of earlier months were going to create problems. The first was Twain's request in December 1886 that House turn *The Prince and the Pauper* into a play, the second a December 4, 1888, letter from Abby Sage Richardson to Twain, asking permission to do her own dramatization of the novel. A widow whose second husband had been shot in the *New York Tribune* offices by her first spouse, Richardson had little playwriting experience but was so impressed by the child actress Elsie Leslie that she proposed doing a script in which Leslie would play both prince and pauper. Twain suggested that she seek House's advice, but gave her the go-ahead. When she said that she preferred to work alone, Twain agreed, and on January 3 signed a memorandum of understanding. It did not take long for Twain to regret the agreement, finding that he had partnered with a writer whose dreams exceeded her talent. But the distress of working with Richardson was a drizzle compared to the torrent of troubles it caused with House.[21]

That House was upset when he heard about the Richardson contract should not surprise us; he thought the dramatization rights were his alone. Making matters worse, he had felt more of a bond to *The Prince and the Pauper* than to any of Twain's other works. The humorist had talked with House frequently while writing it and had consulted him when he attempted his own early dramatization; he also had given Koto one of just six copies printed on special India paper and had autographed her volume: "With the affectionate regards of The Author." Most important,

House had played a minor but important role in preparing the novel for press. Reading the proofs for Twain in the fall of 1881, he had discovered a historical error—"a peculiarly cussed little blunder," Twain called it. Having made Miles Hendon, one of the central figures, a baronet "some sixty years before Baronets were invented," Twain's inclination was to add a footnote saying he had made a mistake. But House disagreed, saying the novel had "so thorough an air of coming right out of the sixteenth century, that I hate the idea of acknowledging a blunder." An admission of error, he added, sounded like a "'Mark Twain' device," and this book might be "by the author of Mark Twain's books" but it was more serious; it was by Clemens. So House spent "a day's search among authorities" at the New York Public Library, followed by "an evening of rumination" and "a morning . . . of reperusal" of the manuscript, which resulted in ten minor changes, plus this footnote when the baronet title appeared: "He refers to the order of baronets, or baronettes—the *barones minores,* as distinct from the parliamentary barons;—not, it need hardly be said, the baronets of later creation." Twain responded effusively, thanking House for the "great sacrifice" of "getting out of bed to go and ransack the libraries, in bodily pain, and hunt out that mass of information." The footnote remains in the novel to this day.[22]

House appears to have been moving along in his own efforts to turn the novel into a play when he heard about the Richardson-Twain agreement. So he responded in two ways. He sent the five acts that he had finished to the Library of Congress early in 1889, for copyrighting. And he wrote to Twain, seeking an explanation. On February 26, Twain wrote back, expressing surprise that House still was interested in dramatizing the book and saying he would come to New York soon to talk about it. Then on March 19, Twain responded in detail to a more urgent House inquiry. He said it all was "quite simple: I have lately made a contract for the dramatization of the Prince and Pauper. I must live up to it unless there is an earlier contract in existence. If you have one send me a copy of it, so that I can take measures to undo my illegal action, and I will at once proceed in the matter." He wrote that he recalled House's interest in the work "two years or more ago," that he remembered that his friend had sketched out "a part of the first act," but that he assumed House had "gradually abandoned the matter" since he stopped talking about it. When someone else offered to dramatize the book, it seemed sensible to accept. "I would naturally have preferred you," Twain added, "who I knew *could* write plays; I still hankered after the benefit of your experience, and suggested in my letter to Mrs. Richardson that she try to get your help." He ended by commenting that his memory could "be all astray," but that "I supposed I had a full right to make that late contract and I made it." "If you have a previous one," he added, "I beg you to send me a copy, and I will come as near getting things exactly right as possible."

That letter was the last civil communication House and Twain ever had. House turned now to the Ingersoll law office, asking counsel and pointing out that he still had in his possession the 1886 letter, in which Twain asked him to write the drama "for 1/2 or 2/3 of the proceeds," as well as a copy of his own December 24 response: "I should . . . be well pleased to undertake the dramatization." On March 29, Ingersoll informed Twain that House claimed to have "made a contract with you" and felt that "he has not been treated with fairness, and that his rights have been and are being wholly disregarded." He asked Twain to give him his own version and wrote the same day to House: "Undoubtedly you have a claim against Mr. Clemens." Twain in turn turned to his own attorney, Daniel Whitford, who told him: "There is always a cripple or a woman or some one in these entanglements of yours." He suggested that Daniel Frohman, who was producing the Richardson play, approach House "and get rid of him for five hundred dollars or as much less as possible." The offers were made, though Twain later denied to a reporter that he ever "offered him a penny," but House was not interested, even when the amount was doubled. The case moved next to the courts, and by early 1890, New York's literary world was abuzz with one of the "most widely publicized and most troubling" of Twain's endless legal entanglements.[23]

House applied for an injunction on January 11, 1890, to stop production of the Richardson play, which had opened in Philadelphia on Christmas Eve and in New York at the beginning of January. On January 27, the day Judge Joseph Daly of the New York Court of Common Pleas heard the case, *The New York Times* ran a long piece laying out House's charges and Twain's defense. House, it reported, claimed to have originated the idea of having a single child play the roles of both the prince and the pauper. He said that he had reported to Twain on May 7, 1887, that he had finished "the complete scheme of the play," that he had read the first act to him on June 13, and that by the end of August he had finished most of the script. House also asserted that during the June reading, Twain had responded with phrases such as: "That's a play," and, "I see that on the stage." Twain denied that there had been a formal agreement for House to dramatize the play and contended that the June reading had been an experimental effort only, "something in the way of a skeleton." He denied that House ever had suggested that the manuscript was nearly complete, and said House's silence about the project after June had convinced him that he had lost interest. The *Times* writer ended by portraying House as the victim of a greedy literary prince. "Twain," he said, "had been growing rich, while the poor writer, now confined closely to his room . . . had no resources except in his pen. To see months of labor thrown away at such a time was about as serious a thing as could happen."

Judge Daly issued his ruling on March 8, declaring that while the contradictions in the two writers' accounts made it impossible to ascertain the whole truth, House was the more believable, because his accounts were carefully thought out and often documented, while Twain's memory was persistently vague. The decision did not depend on whether House had completed most of the manuscript, the judge ruled. The key issue was that the 1886 letters constituted a legal contract, and that Twain had deprived House of income that would have accrued to him if that contract had been honored. For that reason, Daly issued a temporary injunction, halting the Richardson-Frohman production until the case could come to trial. A March 9 headline on page one of the *Times* declared: "Mark Twain Is Defeated: Judge Daly Upholds Playwright House and Says His Dramatization or None Must Be Presented." The article said there had "not been a theatrical lawsuit for years that has awakened the general interest that this case has." And it called Daly's decision "a great victory for Mr. House and a personal vindication of his honor."

The play did not actually stop, however, because on March 11, House, satisfied with this vindication, agreed with producer Frohman to suspend legal proceedings in return for a percentage of the play's profits, with the remainder of the proceeds held in an escrow account until the trial against Twain had run its course. Undoubtedly helped by the notoriety, the Richardson play proved more successful than the poor reviews—or Twain's and House's contempt for it—would have led one to expect. It took in more than $5,000 during a seven-week New York run, then moved on the road for the next two years: to places as distant as Washington, D.C., Detroit, Memphis, New Orleans, and Atlantic City.

In the end, House's victory proved Pyrrhic. In addition to destroying a friendship, it touched off a tangle of legal, personal, and business problems that left him distraught and embittered, eager to get away from the United States. House tried to produce his own version of the play in September, apparently misunderstanding the royalty agreement he had signed with Frohman, and was stopped after two weeks by an injunction issued by the same Judge Daly. Following the stoppage, he quarreled over salary payment with the actors who had been in that production, and at one point secured a warrant to have the home of the lead actor's parents searched for the script to the play—which was found under one of their mattresses. He also engaged in several acrimonious disputes with his attorneys—first Ingersoll, then the Morgan and Ives firm, then Charles E. Le Barbier—and tried to have Frohman enjoined from continuing his own production of *The Prince and the Pauper*. Eventually, the case against Twain, which had started all of the difficulties, was simply dropped, House having left for Japan before it came onto the docket. In January 1894, Twain's attorney moved for dismissal, and the episode came to an end.[24]

Much worse than the legal difficulties was the estrangement that the episode engendered between Twain and House. It was not unusual for

Twain to turn against friends; Samuel Charles Webster said the Hartford don "wanted a lawsuit started against somebody" almost weekly. Twain himself quipped that "a man has *got* to make an ass of himself once a year anyhow." And his daughter Clara called his temper "a raging flood of waters that tore away puerile dams." But the level of invective this time was startling, even for Twain. He marked up his old friend's letters with acid comments, including the following on an envelope accompanying one of House's notes to Olivia: "This man never had an interest of the trivialest kind . . . that he didn't smother everybody under avalanches of twaddle about." He wrote to his sister not long after the trial: "Let the dog bark till his teeth drop out; it will do him no good; . . . A year hence nobody will be able to remember what cur it was that barked." He used the canine metaphor again with a *New York World* reporter, calling House a "dog-in-the-manger."[25]

Twain became so obsessed, in fact, that he wrote a forty-nine-page screed, "Concerning the Scoundrel E. H. House," summarizing his relationship with the Boston reporter. On the first page, he described him as "a man who does overmuch crying . . . and doubtless . . . will go on dripping his tears on me through the press." In one of many errors, Twain said that House's claims to having helped with the *Prince and The Pauper* proofs were concocted out of thin air, perhaps as a result of drinking opium for his pain:

> He makes it appear that he conferred on that book a laborious and very valuable amount of editing. He may really and honestly have thought that that was so, for at intervals his gout so tortured him that he drank laudanum in startling quantities, and that sort of a beverage probably assists the imagination; and he may still honestly think that it was so, for he has continued his laudanum drench these nine years, now, and so his imagination has probably improved all the time. Nevertheless, the truth is that he suggested only one correction—a verbal one.

That suggestion, Twain wrote, was that the word "entreated" had been used incorrectly—but it was House who was wrong (11–12). Twain also disparaged House's claims to have written parts of Boucicault's *Arrah-na-Pogue,* accused him of "being diffusively palaverous and ornamental" (an affliction he got "in the Orient, where they always go the longest way around instead of the shortest way through" [22]), and charged him with being "so methodical that he even keeps a diary, now, of things that ought to have happened in 1887" (25). The Hartford bard said his only reason for inviting House and Koto as guests in 1887 was that Ned "was a friendless and forsaken cripple. . . . I was the only friend he had in the world" (27–28). He reported too that House was an "exploiter of . . . violent language," saying he "used it very frequently toward that patient, and willing, and harmless and humble little Japanese slave that he brought with him" (34) and that he "brutally insulted one of the first ladies in Hartford in her own house" (40). And he sneered that House used his illness shamelessly, pumping "the public for sympathy" (42). His onetime friend, he concluded, had "a heart sodden with malignity" (44). At the end of the document, Twain penciled in the following: "House's motive? 1. Malignity; fury at himself for having thrown away a handsome chance; desire to see his name in print, article-accepting notoriety. But he will be forgotten a month after he lets me alone. This advertisement is worth $10,000 to him" (49).

House may not have given as much as he got in invective; he certainly forbore to write a document about Twain. But what he did say was equally bitter. Little more than a month after making sure that Twain had indeed signed a contract with Richardson, he began reconstructing his relationship with Twain. "He is not my friend," he wrote to Stedman, "and never was." House talked to reporters about Twain's "absolute and almost unqualified forgetfulness," commenting that he never had known the humorist to remember "anything whatever with literal accuracy." And when Twain called him a "dog-in-the-manger," House responded with a letter to the *Times*, quipping that "the distinguished humorist is happier in the manufacture of modern fictions than in the application of ancient fables." "Who," he asked, "is the offending cur in this performance?" then answered: "Mark. . . . It is his habit to snarl contemptuously at all literature except his own precisely as he snaps his teeth in scorn at courts of law which do not decide cases in his favor."

The mutual railings make for lively reading, but they are ultimately disheartening. These men had shared so much for twenty years: a hard drinking, devil-may-care approach to youth, a rare ability with words and stories, skepticism about religion, love of children, a childlike willingness to see the world in fresh ways. House had introduced Twain to New York's celebrity world in the 1860s; Twain had promoted House's candidacy for a diplomatic post in Japan at the beginning of the 1880s. House had asked Twain to be responsible for Koto if he himself died prematurely. Twain prized gifts House sent from Japan and took Japanese language lessons from Koto. They also shared a deep cynicism about the very establishment of which they were so much a part, a skepticism about what Twain called the "loyalty of unreason." Unfortunately, they also shared thin skins and volatile personalities. Both men could sniff out personal slights as easily as missionaries found sin in *Yone Santo.* As long as the slights came from others, they helped bond House and Twain. But now, with each convinced that the other was selfish and hypocritical, there was no ground for compromise. Neither could apologize. A second-rate dramatization made spiritual paupers of them both. House made one benign reference to Twain in one of his later children's stories. But they never spoke again.[26]

How does one maintain sanity in times such as House experienced in the late 1880s and early 1890s? The religious establishment hated him. A publisher dropped him. He lost his friends in the Hartford community. Conflicts with attorneys, producers, editors, and actors proliferated like lakeside mosquitoes in August. And the weeks-long gout sieges kept recurring, once or twice a year. How did he cope? One answer lay in the impact of the troubles themselves. It would be wrong to say House thrived on troubles; his writings make it clear that he despised conflicts, even though he was incapable of the compromises that might have ended them. At the same time, the fights gave him focus. Never, in these days, could he have gone mad from boredom.

A second answer appears in the fact that he maintained enough of the routine, enough involvement in his precrisis pursuits, to keep life structured. He kept on writing: revising the *Prince and the Pauper* script (of course!), dashing off a letter to the *New York World* to reiterate one more time that the Westerners' 1864 attack on Shimonoseki had been a "cruel and wanton outrage," penning recollections of his youthful encounters with the German composer Richard Wagner and the American editor James Russell Lowell, writing an article for *Scribner's Magazine* on the Ise shrines, which remain unchanged "to all appearance, from the original edifices" before Christ's time. He also continued to dote on Koto, particularly the way she cultivated friends and made progress in dancing and painting. And he kept up his correspondence with those friends Twain had said he did not have. He heard once from Saigō Tsugumichi, the Taiwan expedition leader who had become a force in Japan's government, once from Foreign Minister Aoki Shōzō with word that his annual 2,000-yen stipend was being continued, and once from a cousin, John Howard Child, who was putting together a family genealogy. He chatted with Joseph Harper about old friends "like Herman Melville and Charles Reade." He also kept writing to Ōkuma, and wrote to the statesman's secretary on a "new and somewhat unfamiliar" typewriter, suggesting that "a large and profitable enterprise might be founded" if the Japanese were to invent a typewriter for their phonetic syllabaries. And eclectic as ever, he wrote to Morse, decrying the U.S. press's inattention to an 1891 earthquake in which 400,000 Japanese were left homeless, and discussing an article he had drafted on the origins of the world. "Why shouldn't the universe have been built in . . . the way I describe?" he teased. "It's as good a theory as the Biblical, anyway."[27]

It may be, however, that the most important source of House's sanity in these years was the introduction of two new elements into his life, both of them tinged with the interests of earlier years. One of these was music. House never had given up his love for piano or composition. Even in his *Tokio Times* years, he had sometimes arranged or composed pieces for public performance. But music had received short shrift for many years. In the summer of 1892, however, he had another fling with composing. Stedman had written a poem, "The Lark," which he wanted put to music, and House obliged with what Stedman called a "perfectly exquisite composition" full of "rare strange chords" that "grow upon me the oftener they are heard." The important thing about composing, House wrote, was for the music to jibe with the song's ideas. Composers "should never seek for effects which are not wholly consistent with their poem." He said the "simplicity and delicacy of your stanzas . . . would have been affronted by any attempt at brilliant or profound treatment." House left New York before his renewed interest in music could mature, but the work on "The Lark" signaled a revived talent that would enrich his later years in Tokyo.[28]

Children's literature provided House's other new outlet. He had begun working on some pieces for young people during the dark days of 1886–1887. In 1889, he wrote a series of syndicated newspaper stories on topics such as Japanese acrobats, jugglers, and fireworks. Now, whether as respite from the Twain fight or because he needed money, he turned to youth literature more seriously. In 1891, he published six pieces in *Harper's Young People*, for which he was paid $585, and the following year he came out with *The Midnight Warning and Other Stories*, a 299-page, illustrated volume of seven stories, each connected somehow with his lifelong passion about justice. "Gracie's Godson" told the tale of an urchin, won over to the value of hard work by a young woman's goodness. In "Natty Barton's Magic," sincerity overcame class pretensions, and "A Patriotic Pianist" described the courage of New Orleans pianist Louis Gottschalk, who shocked a Civil War audience by playing "Yankee Doodle" when they requested "Dixie."

The signature story of the collection, "Midnight Warning," had been rejected several times as too controversial for a youth magazine. Based on an actual incident, it related the experiences of the teenage children of a southern plantation owner named Claiborne who supported the North during the Civil War. While Claiborne was off serving in the Union army, his children were challenged by both Union and Confederate troops, and before it was all over, one of the sons had become a Union spy, while the daughter, Jennie, had fallen in love and married a Confederate officer. As the editors of *The Youth's Companion* wrote, "Midnight Warning" broke two rules of youth magazines: it took sides—which "in a paper of national circulation . . . is unwise," and it contained a love story. A book was different. There, House could give full range to his northern patriotism, as well as his penchant for romances and complex story lines.[29]

By late 1891, House and Koto were talking about a return to Tokyo. Although gout attacks continued, his health had been stable enough for a couple of years to make travel feasible. His spiritual condition, by contrast, had been tumultuous. He had accomplished much in these years: the completion of two books, publication of dozens of articles in leading journals and newspapers, the successful introduction of Koto into New York's social and artistic world, a good deal of effective lobbying for Japan. But the pains exceeded the joys. There had been too many fights: with clergymen, with editors, with friends, with his own body. And by the summer of 1892, he still was mired in legal sloughs too numerous to allow easy sleep. So he and Koto decided the time had come to return to the East.

Before leaving, he turned to two of his friends from Civil War days, asking one to go along to Japan and the other to help him get there. To the former, the poet-financier Stedman, he wrote that Japan was a "land of inspiration," a "tranquil and idyllic" spot where "a poet may surrender himself entirely to the control of the imagination." House knew that Stedman would decline the invitation, but he said his friend would be a poorer poet as a result. "Pack your trunk, my dear Stedman, and start with us, three months hence." Then he turned to Henry Villard, now head of the Northern Pacific Railroad, for help in setting up the rail trip to Tacoma, Washington, from whence he and Koto would sail on September 29. As it turned out, the use of Villard was astute, for House fell ill between Chicago and Minneapolis, and the solicitude of the railwayman's agents not only eased his pain but convinced fellow travelers that they were in the company of someone important. As House wrote: "Rank began to be conferred upon me at Chicago, when I was discovered to be a consul on the way to his post. Before St. Paul, I had blossomed to the proportions of a Minister Plenipotentiary. . . . If you hear it proclaimed that I have been sent from Washington to negotiate new treaties with all the Empires of Asia, you must not be surprised." He added that he anticipated the coming voyage, "for the sea and I are old companions, and always on the best of terms." In Tokyo he would put his troubles behind. He would be home again.[30]

NOTES

1. Frank Brinkley to House, February 15, 1889, EHC, University of Virginia.

2. For shipboard illness and Pitman's friendship, see Koto House to Olivia Clemens, September 22, 1885, MTP, University of California; Hong Kong as a bad place to recover, Frank Brinkley to House, February 20, 1886, EHC, University of Virginia; and appreciation of Ōkuma, January 1, 1886, OM, Waseda University.

3. "Rusty gear," in House to Whitelaw Reid, June 19, 1886, WR, Library of Congress; onset of illness and settling in process, Koto House to Olivia Clemens, May

31, 1886, MTP, University of California; "when health goes" and Koto's entrance into Art League, House to Edward Morse, October 4, 1886, Edward S. Morse Collection, Peabody Essex Museum; House's deplorable condition, Reid to John Hay, July 2, 1886, JH, Brown University; Mrs. Nicholls, House to Twain, July 29, 1886, MTP; and Koto's visit to Hartford, Samuel Clemens to House, June 5, 1886, MTP. On May 25, 1886 (EHC, University of Virginia), Twain sent a long, witty letter to House, detailing, word for word, a conversation in which Olivia responds with a profane outburst when told that Koto would not be coming at once to visit; Twain added: "I have not reported merely the spoken words . . . but also those which were uttered secretly in the heart."

4. For Reid's visit, see House to Reid, June 26, 1886, WR, Library of Congress; Twain's visits are discussed in Robert Browning et al., eds., *Mark Twain's Notebooks & Journals,* vol. 3, 234, fn. 26, and 239, fn. 43; and in Clemens to House, October 8, 1886, EHC, University of Virginia. For the lingo-letters (all in MTP, University of California), Clemens to House, July 16 and 26, 1886; and Susie Clemens to House, August 14, 1886; for the typesetter and executor plans (also in MTP), Clemens to House, August 11 and November 26, 1886, respectively.

5. Koto's evaluation of House's condition is in her letter to Olivia Clemens, November 22, 1886, MTP, University of California; for House's view, see House to Edward Morse, December 12, 1886, Morse Collection, Peabody Essex Museum. The renewed use of the right hand is in House to Stedman, December 15, 1886, ECS, Columbia University. Twain's dramatization request is in Clemens to House, December 17, 1886, his remark about sending copies in his letter to House, December 26, 1886. Both in MTP.

6. The dinner conversation is in House's "A Forgotten Literary Phenomenon," *The Atlantic Monthly* (July 1887): 134–36. The Torin Ji stories appeared in two installments, *Scribner's Magazine* (September-October 1887): 332–45 and 420–35, specifically "fountain dancing," 333. "The payments are recorded in *Scribner's* to House, May 10, 1887, EHC, University of Virginia. Wordell's evaluation is in his *Japan's Image in America,* 86.

7. Aldrich's evaluation of Compton Reade is in his letter to House, August 31, 1887, TBA, Library of Congress; the *Atlantic Monthly* articles were "Personal Characteristics of Charles Reade" (August 1887): 145–57; and "Anecdotes of Charles Reade" (October 1887): 525–39. The May 5 and 7 Twain letters to House are from MTP, University of California; his letter to Webster is quoted in Samuel Webster, ed., *Mark Twain, Businessman,* 381.

8. For "having such a good time," Mary Lawton, *A Lifetime with Mark Twain,* 41; beggar story in Clara Clemens, *My Father Mark Twain,* 33; ale and wit, in Kenneth Andrews, *Nook Farm,* 90; writing the little girls, Koto House to Olivia Clemens, June 23, 1887, MTP, University of California; Ned's improved health, House to Twain, September 8, 1887, MTP; doctors' warning, House to Whitelaw Reid, March 5, 1887, WR, Library of Congress; and "agreeable people," Lilly Warner to Olivia Clemens, August 28, 1887, MTP. Koto apparently gave a few Japanese lessons to Mark in the spring of 1887; his journal then includes several phonetic renderings of Japanese words—for example, "sighyenarrah—good night" (*sayonara* or goodbye) and "combangwah—good night" (*konbanwa* or good evening); see Browning et al, 292.

9. Moss's misspellings are in his letters to House, June 30 and September 11, 1887, respectively, EHC, University of Virginia; suggestions about treaty revision, in House to Ōkuma, October 7, 1887, OM C336, Waseda University. Clemens girls' letters all are in EHC: "beautiful" fire, in Clara Clemens to House, July 14, 1887; seventy-seventh birthday, Clara to House, August 9, 1887; and profanity substitutes, Susie to House, August 4 [?], 1887.

10. Edward H. House, "The Thraldom of Japan," *The Atlantic Monthly* (December 1887): "European tribunals," 722; U.S. expenses and customs revenue, 723; Japanese justice, 724; Japan's strengths, 725–27; numbers of foreign residents, 727; United States taking initiative, 729; Japan acting unilaterally, 730; and "restoration to . . . authority," 731. Aldrich's evaluation is in his letter to House, September 6, 1887, TBA, Library of Congress. House's letter to Ōkuma was on February 13, 1888, in OM C338, Waseda University. U.S. Minister Richard Hubbard used House's language when he wrote to Washington about unilateral denunciation on February 20, 1889: "Japan has determined to cut loose from the thraldom of sixteen Treaty Powers, which have heretofore claimed that no change . . . could be made, save by the humiliating permission of all the said Powers," U.S. Department of State, Despatches from United States Ministers to Japan, National Archives.

11. The original letter appeared in the *Evening Post* on February 14, 1888; House's response ran on February 21; for texts, I have relied on a compilation of the major articles in Baba Tatsui, *Baba Tatsui zenshū,* 261–329. House's letters to Griffis are in WEG, Rutgers University. Griffis's eventual admission of authorship is discussed in Ardath W. Burks, "Coercion in Japan," 33–52. Evidence that House knew early that Griffis was the author is found in a letter from Frank Brinkley to House, May 19, 1888 ("I enjoyed your slicing up of that fellow Griffis"), EHC, University of Virginia. For an example of Griffis's more negative view of Japan when writing to fellow Christians, see his "Japanese Buddhist," *The Independent,* April 5, 1888, 3; speaking of the growth of "reformed" Buddhism, he writes: "*They will Buddhaize Christianity. . . . Japan's crisis is at hand!*" (emphasis his).

12. The discussion of church groups blocking publication of House's articles is in House to Reid, September 6, 1871, WR, Library of Congress. The plagiarism was in James King Newton, "Japanese Treaty Revision," *Bibliotheca Sacra* 44, no. 173 (January 1887): 46–70. House wrote to Morse on April 23, 1888 (Morse Collection, Peabody Essex Museum), that the plagiarizer was "a very poor creature," but that he had been punished enough by his own institution. He said Newton was "doing very strange things now," talking widely about "accidental losses of memory, careless copyists, etc., etc."; also see Browning et al., 332, 335. House's criticism of missionaries is in "Missionary Terrorizing," *The Truth Seeker,* February 9, 1889, 86–87; I am indebted to Charles Wordell for calling my attention to this article.

13. Discussions of the nature of the manuscript are in Aldrich to House, May 16 and June 7, 1887, EHC, University of Virginia; letters about the editing of *Yone Santo* continued through mid-1888. According to an *Atlantic Monthly* payment record, in EHC, House was paid a total of $1,405 for the eight installments of the novel. For the review, see "A Pagan Saint," *The Critic* (February 2, 1889): 50–51.

14. For House's avowed desire not to write polemics, see his postcript in *Yone Santo,* 276. About characterization, he wrote to Aldrich during the editing process:

"I took pains to avoid portraying individuals. Every incident is paralleled by some fact within my knowledge, and every trait of character has its prototype but all these are so mixed and distributed that no single figure could possibly be taken (justly) as depicted from life." House said that although Charwell shares his own "good will for his Japanese associates," he differs in significant ways, and "no single girl fits Yone." Indeed, "hundreds are as good, as loyal to duty and as high principled, but they are not my little scholar and sufferer" (May 5, 1887, TBA, Harvard University).

15. "Not the real subject," Wordell, 89; Aldrich urges book publication in Aldrich to House, January 21, 1888, TBA, Library of Congress; for the contract, see March 26, 1888, EHC, University of Virginia; missionaries tearing down work, in House to Edward Morse, February 14, 1888, Morse Collection, Peabody Essex Museum; and recommendation of preface, Aldrich to House, April 13, 1888, TBA, Library of Congress. Aldrich also had written House on June 15, 1887, while the manuscript was in process, saying a Houghton reader worried that "there is too much onslaught on the missionaries," EHC, University of Virginia. Publication estimate is in Houghton Mifflin to House, April 28, 1888, EHC.

16. Charwell's evaluation of missionaries in *The Atlantic Monthly* serialization of *Yone Santo* (May 1888): 629; in the book itself, 145–46. Several letters were from Aldrich to House (all 1888), TBA, Library of Congress: "avalanche" (emphasis in original) and "exquisite story," May 2; "idiots," May 28; Houghton's "fairness," May 7; and "hold them to their contract," May 13. House's "first intimation" is in Houghton Mifflin to House, May 24, 1888, EHC, University of Virginia; "warpath," in House to Morse, May 28, 1888, Morse Collection, Peabody Essex Museum.

17. The following (all 1888) are from EHC, University of Virginia: "unwilling," Houghton Mifflin to House, June 5; definitive letter, Houghton Mifflin to House, June 14; and Ingersoll's experiences, C. Farrell to House, July 9. The other references are from House's epilogue to *Yone Santo*: legally binding contract, 279; House's decision to capitulate and the Houghton Mifflin copy of the manuscript, 281; appreciation of Belford, Clarke, 281–82. On September 28, 1890, Boston dentist Carl Ludwig Barnay wrote House, asking permission to prepare a German translation of *Yone Santo* (EHC, University of Virginia); I have found no records on whether the translation was completed or published.

18. "Flood of denunciation," *Yone Santo*, 278. Brinkley's response is from his letter to House, February 15, 1889, EHC, University of Virginia.

19. Description of Morse in House letter to Twain, February 14, 1888 (year not written, but internal evidence makes it 1888), MTP, University of California. For steamboat excursion, see House to Morse, April 23, 1888, Morse Collection, Peabody Essex Museum. The discussion of the logomachy match is in Twain's bitter memoir following the 1889–1890 *The Prince and the Pauper* dispute, "Considering the Scoundrel E. H. House," 34, MTP. For Koto's prospects, see House to Olivia Clemens, May 2, 1888, MTP; "harmony lessons," Clara Clemens to House, July 19, 1888, MTP; massage, House to Olivia Clemens, April 23, 1888, MTP; "constant treatment," and discussions of Bonin Islands trade, House to Ōkuma, November 24, 1888, OM C337, Waseda University; "smallest boy," House to Whitelaw Reid, November 13, 1888, WR, Library of Congress. For Koto's life in

New York, see her letter to Olivia Clemens, December 22, 1888, MTP; Koto's illness is in House to Olivia Clemens, February 14, 1889, MTP. See *New York Tribune,* November 22, 1888, for an interview setting the record straight. The Foreign Ministry stipend, granted on January 24, 1889, is promised in "Beikokujin 'Hausu' e nenkin oyobi teate kane kyōyo ikken," Gaimushō gaikōshiryōkan, Tokyo.

20. The theater request is in House to Augustin Daly, September 25, 1889, Folger Shakespeare Library.

21. Paul Fatout, "Mark Twain, Litigant," *American Literature* 31 (March 1959): 30–45, gives the fullest treatment of the battle between House and Twain. For the proposal and agreement, see Abby Sage Richardson to Clemens, December 4 and 9, 1888, MTP, University of California. Twain also received dramatization offers early in 1889 from Irving Putnam (January 24) and Thomas Reddy (January 25), apparently also in response to Leslie's performance in *Little Lord Fauntleroy;* see MTP.

22. Twain's gift to Koto is described in Samuel Clemens to Koto House, January 2, 1882, MTP, University of California. The "cussed little blunder" is in Samuel Clemens to James R. Osgood, October 21, 1881, MTP; House's insistence on changes is detailed in House to Benjamin Ticknor, October 23, 1881, BHT, Library of Congress; and Twain's appreciation is in Clemens to House, October 24, 1881, EHC, University of Virginia. Twain's effusive description of House's extraordinary efforts is important in light of his assertions after 1889 that House did nothing of importance on the manuscript.

23. For copyright, see Ainsworth R. Spofford to House, February 12, 1889, EHC, University of Virginia. Also in EHC are Twain's explanation, Clemens to House, March 19, 1889; Twain's request that House dramatize the novel, Twain to House, December 17, 1886; Ingersoll's statement of House's charges, Ingersoll to Clemens, March 29, 1889; and Ingersoll's belief that House had a case, Ingersoll to House, March 29, 1889. House's agreement to dramatize the novel is in House to Twain, December 24, 1886, from Fatout, "Mark Twain, Litigant," 34. Whitford's quip about Twain's cases is in Whitford to Clemens, April 5, 1889, MTP, University of California; his proposal to offer money to House, Whitford to Clemens, March 28, 1889, MTP; House claimed to a reporter that Twain's side offered him $5,000, a claim that Twain attributed to "Mr. House's imagination," *Hartford Courant,* January 18, 1890. For "most widely publicized," see Fatout, "Mark Twain, Litigant," 30.

24. The success of the play comes from both Fatout, "Mark Twain, Litigant," 43; and box office receipts, October-December 1891, in EHC, University of Virginia. Judge Daly was a brother of Augustin Daly, the theater owner House had written for permission to be carried to his seat the previous fall. Twain complained that he never received any royalties from Frohman's production, though both House and Richardson did. He wrote to his attorney, Daniel Whitford, October 16, 1890 (speaking of Frohman): "Am I to be insulted in this brutal way by this son of a bitch and have no recourse?"; MTP, University of California.

25. Twain lawsuits, in Fatout, "Mark Twain, Litigant," 30; making an ass of one's self, Clemens to Charles H. Webb, November 26, 1870; Twain's temper, Clara Clemens, *My Father Mark Twain,* 24; "twaddle," House to Olivia Twain, February 14, 1889, MTP, University of California; "let the dog bark," in Samuel Charles

Webster, *Mark Twain, Businessman,* 393; and "dog-in-the-manger," quoted in *New York Times,* September 7, 1890.

26. "Not my friend," in House to Edmund Stedman, April 26, 1889, ECS, Columbia University; Twain's forgetfulness, in *The New York Times,* January 28, 1890, from Fatout, "Mark Twain, Litigant," 38; "Who is the offending cur," in *The New York Times,* September 7, 1890, 14. The reference to Twain is found in House's "Bright Sides of History," *St. Nicholas for Young Folks* (November 1898): 34. "Loyalty of unreason" is in Mark Twain, *A Connecticut Yankee in King Arthur's Court,* 72.

27. Shimonoseki explanation, *New York World,* June 25, 1890; recollections: House's "Wagner and Tannhäuser in Paris, *New England Magazine* (June 1891): 411–27, and "A First Interview with Lowell," *Harper's Weekly,* September 3, 1892, 850; description of Ise, E. H. House, "Transfer of the Temples of Ise," *Scribner's Magazine* (May 1891): 569–75; typewriter, House to Kato, April 26, 1890, OM, Waseda University; "like Herman Melville," J. W. Harper to House, November 17, 1891, EHC, University of Virginia; family genealogy, John Howard Child to House, August 27, 1891, EHC; and earthquake, scientific theory, House to Edward Morse, December 4, 1891, Morse Collection, Peabody Essex Museum. I have not been able to locate the article.

28. "Perfectly exquisite," Stedman to House, June 21, 1892, ECS, Library of Congress; and reflections on composition, House to Stedman, June 25, 1892, ECS, Columbia University. "The Lark" was copyrighted by the Library of Congress under House's name in 1892, but I have been unable to locate lyrics.

29. The syndicated articles are discussed in a series of at least 10 letters from S. S. McClure to House, January 16 to December 12, 1889, in EHC, University of Virginia. Payment amounts for each *Harper's Young People* article ranged from $15 for "Patriotic Pianist" to $240 for "Gracie's Godson" and are listed in *Harper's Young People* to House, 1891, EHC. For rejections, see A. B. Starey, editor, *Harper's Young People,* to House, November 20, 1891, EHC; "paper of national circulation," editors of *The Youth's Companion* to House, July 30, 1891, EHC.

30. For "land of inspiration," see House to Stedman, June 25, 1892, ECS, Columbia University; and for "rank" being conferred, House to Henry Villard, September 27, 1892, HVP, Harvard University.

13

Japan, 1893–1901: Modernity—and All That Meant

> With what hideous rapidity Japan is modernizing, after all!—not in costume, architecture, or habit, but in heart and manner. . . . Will it ever become beautiful again?
>
> —Lafcadio Hearn, 1892[1]

The seven years that House and Koto had been gone when they returned to Tsukiji in October 1892 must have seemed like twenty, so changed were both material life and the public discourse. Intellectual discussions in particular had taken on a more confident tone, rooted in the constitutional system and the rising nationalism discussed in an earlier chapter. Scholars and journalists wrote as if they owned the political sphere now. Officials worried more constantly, and more publicly, about what the party politicians were up to. And everyone discussed international affairs, defining national defense aggressively and talking about national strengths and rights. When events on the Asian perimeter sent the country into its first modern war during House's second year back, the landscape would change even more, thrusting Japan into the exclusive club of colony holders, making it the unquestioned leader of Asia, and committing its leaders to the development of a military commensurate with its new status.

Many forces propelled Japan toward the Sino-Japanese War of 1894–1895, including a desire for equal treatment by foreign powers and the view that colonies would spur economic growth. Most important, however, were several strategic factors. First was the philosophy, which undergirded Japan's strategic thinking, that only by expanding could

Japan remain competitive in a world where the imperialists controlled the options. "I am not advocating the plundering of other lands," wrote Tokutomi Sohō when war was approaching, "but I insist on war with China in order to transform Japan, hitherto a contracting nation, into an expansive nation." He saw that as the only way to survive. At the more specific, East Asian level, Japanese leaders were worried that a growing power vacuum on the continent would threaten Japan itself if it did not step into the breach. Russia, Great Britain, and even Germany were active in the northeastern region, where the inability to modernize had made Korea vulnerable. China, of course, had been Korea's protector for centuries, but the Middle Kingdom had become what Foreign Minister Mutsu Munemitsu called "a bigoted and ignorant colossus of conservatism," unable to defend its own shores against the imperialist onslaught, let alone Korea. So after the czar decided in 1891 to build a railroad across Siberia, people began talking seriously about what Japan must do to keep Korea "independent" from outsider states and "guide" it toward modernity.[2]

As a result, when Korean officials tried to quiet domestic unrest in June of 1894 by requesting troops from China, the Japanese public reacted strongly, convinced that China was out to compromise Korean independence. It mattered little that China's dispatch of 4,000 troops fell within the provisions of Japanese-Chinese treaties. The movement into Korea was seen by Japanese writers as an act of aggression, designed to keep Korea under Chinese control. When the government did not respond by sending a similar number of troops at once, the press reacted noisily, with the *Ōsaka Asahi Shimbun* declaring: "We should take the lead in recognizing Korea's independence; instead we look on in a daze. This is not the way to preserve the nation's dignity and progress." Fukuzawa Yukichi, the progressive modernizer, demanded war, because China opposed "the progress of civilization." In truth, officials like Mutsu and Itō Hirobumi were only slightly less jingoistic than the public; so, on August 1, Japan declared war against China, launching not only its first modern war, but its shortest and most successful one.[3]

The Sino-Japanese War was a professional boon for House, calling him back into journalism for the last time, as we shall see in the next chapter. For the Japanese public it was a time of chauvinism and pride. The Japanese won every battle in the war. On September 16, they defeated Chinese troops at Pyongyang; a day later they humiliated China's navy in the battle of Yalu; and on November 21, they drove the Chinese out of Port Arthur, in Manchuria. On February 2, they took the Chinese port city of Weihaiwei, not all that far from Beijing itself—at a cost of 700 Chinese lives compared to fifty-four Japanese. And all the while, the press gave its readers stories of Japanese valor, contrasted to Chinese ineptness and Korean squalor. Once, at Port Arthur, there were dark stories, about a massacre of civilians. But the government handled the episode with the public relations finesse of an imperialist power, and the public gave a sigh of relief. When China sued for negotiations in November, Japan deferred, preferring to win more victories and improve its negotiating position before beginning peace talks.

"Every adult," recalled a journalist from a town in the Japan Alps, "every child, every elderly person, every woman, talked day and night of nothing but the war."[4] The same was true of the peace settlement. When it came on April 17, China had certified Japan's place as a colonial power. The agreement, signed at Shimonoseki, gave Japan the extraterritoriality in China that it had so long despised at home, along with navigation rights on the Yangtze River, four new Chinese ports for trade, an indemnity of 364 million yen, and three new territories: Taiwan, the Pescadore Islands, and Manchuria's southern peninsula, called Liaodong. It also affirmed Korea's independence from China. The public exhilaration did not last long, however. Just four days after the Shimonoseki treaty was signed, newspapers reported rumors that Russia opposed parts of the agreement, and on May 14, the government announced that Japan would return Liaodong to China, in return for a modest increase in the indemnity. The reason for this development was what historians call the Triple Intervention; Russia, France, and Germany claimed that the takeover of southern Manchuria would threaten regional stability, and Japan's officials capitulated, not ready to take on Russia. *Osaka Asahi Shimbun*'s May 15 headline read, "Whole Nation in Mourning."

It may be an exaggeration to say that the European intervention was seminal in the evolution of Japan's military policies. Certainly an expansionist definition of national defense had become orthodox in the years before the Sino-Japanese War, as had Yamagata's idea of securing a line of advantage on the continent. It is no exaggeration though to assert that the combination of joy in victory and resentment at Western high-handedness turned jingoism into an unstoppable force. Tokutomi, who was visiting Manchuria when the government's concession was announced, returned home immediately, "disdaining to remain for another moment on land that had been retroceded to another power." The return of Liaodong, he declared later, "dominated the rest of my life. . . . What it came down to was that sincerity and justice did not amount to a thing if you were not strong enough."[5]

The rising nationalism of the late 1880s thus became a torrent after the mid-1890s, demanding strong international policies based on the new phrase *gashin shōtan* (putting one's self through difficulties in order to develop courage). Journalists and politicians expressed what Mutsu called an "exuberance" about expansionism "beyond anyone's power to control."[6] And the official world followed suit, initiating programs that would involve Japan heavily in Asia for the next fifty years. In Taiwan, the Japanese set about creating a hugely costly, and controversial, colonial administration, while in Korea, they supported the efforts of domestic factions to modernize the government. When those factions pushed for radical change, the imperial clan, centered in Queen Min, worked against reform, and a stalemate resulted. Frustrated, Japan's minister to Korea, General Miura Gorō, had the queen murdered, prompting angry resentment and the emergence of a pro-Russian administration. Neither Japan nor Russia had any interest in letting Korea go its own way, however, and in 1898 they agreed to make Korea a joint protectorate. That agreement, in turn, prompted Japan to increase its military presence on the peninsula, which in its own turn led to higher military costs.

The *gashin shōtan* policies thus pushed the military budget rapidly upward in the late 1890s, as Japan sought to take control of an obstreperous Taiwan, maintain a presence in Korea, and counter European activity in China. One could have argued, quite plausibly, that all of this was too expensive, that every move into Asia provoked local opposition, which then demanded new financial outlays for troops and administrators. But no one did respond that way. As Akira Iriye puts it: "If Westerners seemed interested in pushing the Japanese out of Manchuria and if the Chinese, Taiwanese, and Koreans appeared hostile to their schemes, they would respond by affirming, rather than retreating from, their imperialism. . . . This was the standard response of the imperialist powers at that time. The costs were enormous, but it was generally believed that . . . the cost of retreat and retrenchment would be even more devastating." As a result, the expenses of the Sino-Japanese War soon paled against the costs of maintaining Japan's new empire. Each legislative session approved higher expenditures; taxes were increased, and by 1897 the armed forces' budget stood at 110 million yen, more than four times what it had been before the war.[7]

One reason so few people criticized the expenditures was that imperialist ideology had become embedded in the Japanese consciousness by now. Another was that imperialism produced enough successes to take people's minds off its costs. In 1898, Japan forced China to concede special commercial rights in Fukien province, opposite Taiwan, just as the other powers were doing in the rest of China. In 1899, Japan succeeded in ending extraterritoriality, House's great Satan, and partially restoring tariff autonomy. In 1900, Japan joined the imperialist countries in putting down the Boxer Rebellion in Beijing, receiving both respect and a major share of the indemnity as a result. And in 1902, it signed the Anglo-Japanese Alliance, the first equal alliance between Asian and European countries. The agreement, which committed the two nations to shielding each other from Russian advances in East Asia, would not be sufficient to keep Japan from going to war with Russia just two years later, in a conflagration that made the Sino-Japanese war seem small by comparison. At the time of its signing, however, half a year after House's death, the rewards of imperialism seemed worth the costs to most Japanese. When House had predicted to Stedman that the Sino-Japanese War "might result in a complete political reconstruction of the map of Asia, and change the destiny of one half of the human race,"[8] he was not far off the mark. Japan, by 1900, had become one of the imperialist powers.

And more than the country's international standing had changed; its domestic life had been transformed too. Cities became larger and more complex in the 1890s, as the economy grew and industry began to take off. The Sino-Japanese War was profitable for Japan, in a way that no other war ever would be. Not only did it create new jobs and enterprises, it poured cash into the country, thanks to an indemnity from China that paid half again what the war itself cost. And much of that cash was spent on steel and shipping, prompting what economists have called "a turning point in the evolution of the Japanese economy." One should not overstate the importance of this, since agriculture, fishing, and cottage shops still accounted for the bulk of Japan's economy. But the beginnings of modern industry appeared in almost every sector of the economy now, spurred by both private entrepreneurship and government support for key industries. Railroad companies, for example, doubled from twelve to twenty-four in the six years before the Sino-Japanese War, then rose to more than forty right after the conflict. Shipping tonnage more than doubled to 700,000 tons between 1895 and 1905. The silk industry, which had helped Japan get on its feet economically in the early Meiji years, now mechanized with a fury, shifting from hand to machine reeling, and much of the giant cotton industry was mechanized by the end of the century. Even iron, which had lagged behind other industries, began a fairly rapid growth after the government established the Yawata Iron Works in 1901. And trade doubled in the decade after the war, with Japan importing more raw materials and exporting more finished goods—a sure sign of a maturing economy. The most telling sign of what was happening may be the fact that four-fifths of Japan's factories in 1902 had not been in existence when the Sino-Japanese War began.[9]

Statistics may bore or dazzle, depending on a reader's tastes, but they point to one clear fact: Japan's urban landscape was changing rapidly at the turn of the century. For one thing, the cities were mushrooming in size. The nation still may have been heavily agricultural, but the balance was beginning to change. While Tokyo's population had dropped right after the Restoration, it now was growing at breakneck speed. In 1895, it was home to 1.3 million; a decade later, to just under 2 million. And Osaka grew nearly as fast, reaching 1.5 million in 1916. Indeed, while Japan's farming population decreased by nearly a million in the last quarter of the nineteenth century, the urban workforce grew by 3 million. "The villages," complained Kaneko Fumiko, "have been bled for all they are worth for the benefit of the cities."[10]

One result of this shift was a dizzying pace of change in the nature of city life. And not all of the changes were good. There may have been jobs in the late-Meiji cities, but the working conditions were as bad there as they had been in other early industrial countries. Hours in the textile factories continued to be inhuman; living conditions were terrible; pay was lower than in India. When a crusading journalist, Yokoyama Gennosuke, studied Japan's workers in 1899, he began by pointing out that while a few Tokyoites were middle class and above, "the great majority belonged to the lower classes, where life is not easy." About Osaka, which was better off than Tokyo, he wrote: "Dwarfs, cripples, and the deaf, dressed only in rags, swarm about the slums. . . . Bands of pilferers make a living by plying their trade among the crowds." He counted 104 flophouses in Osaka in 1895, an increase of eleven in a year, and described as typical the sight of "a young woman stark naked except for an apron being used as a substitute for undergarments, and talking in a coarse manner through dark, chapped, and cracked lips." The poor (*saimin*), Yokoyama said, "live in every Tokyo ward." These people may not have been worse off materially than their village counterparts, but their lives were less stable, less connected to social networks.[11] And the establishment showed little sympathy. If workers complained, officials recited platitudes about loyalty or talked about how Japan must compete with the West.

It was not surprising then that worker unrest grew right along with the population in the 1890s. Japan could not be said to have had a labor "movement" per se in those years, because although several groups formed unions late in the 1890s, there was little worker solidarity or interest in striking. Nevertheless, workers were fighting more often now against specific grievances. Tokyo laborers had carried out two disputes a year, on average, in the early 1890s (and two or three a *decade* before that!), but in the last five years of the century, they waged more than eight actions a year. Indeed, Japan as a whole had more than 150 significant labor disputes in the ten years after the Sino-Japanese War.[12] When several labor leaders and intellectuals decided to enter the political arena by creating the Social Democratic Party in 1901, officials shut it down almost immediately, under a Public Order and Police Law that limited the right to organize or strike. As a result, it would take another decade for a full-fledged labor movement to emerge. But it was this period, the late 1890s, which produced labor's first significant stirrings.

Japan had its first serious encounter with social activism in these years too. A small number of intellectuals and journalists joined a few labor leaders, and even some bureaucrats, to discuss Japan's emerging *shakai mondai* or "social problem" at the turn of the century: the prostitutes, cleaning people, dock workers, day laborers, rickshaw pullers, newspaper sellers, and others trapped in poverty by the capitalist system. Led by reporters such as Yokoyama, who coined the phrase *kasō shakai* (lower strata of society), and *Mainichi Shimbun*'s pioneering female reporter Matsumoto Eiko, this group worked hard to raise consciousness about the problems of the powerless. *Mainichi*'s editor-politician Shimada Saburō, for example, crusaded against forced prostitution, and *Niroku Shinpō* sent two reporters in September 1900 to help a woman named Ayaginu free herself from a Tokyo brothel. When his reporters were beaten up, the paper's sales jumped, a scandal ensued, and the Home Ministry issued rules making it easier for prostitutes to quit voluntarily. The period's most talked about *shakai mondai* occurred north of Tokyo, in Ashio, where the Furukawa company's copper mines long had polluted the Watarase River, killing fish in the water and crops along the banks. When the government failed to respond forcefully to floods that left more than 300 dead in 1896, Japan's first environmental protest movement ensued, led by the irascible journalist-politician Tanaka Shōzō. Among the crusaders, Shimada was probably the most thoughtful, describing the systemic forces that bred poverty and rendered officials mute before the status quo. "As individuals, officials are not all evil," he wrote; "nor are public men all backward wolves. But after living for so many years under a system that makes them kowtow to higher officials in order to protect their own positions, they . . . have no sense of responsibility toward, indeed no concept of, the public community."[13]

The scale of social activism was small by late-twentieth-century standards. But it made officials nervous in its own time. They had anticipated the raucous political behavior of the Diet and the rise of political parties under the Meiji Constitution. They even had come to grips with the brief emergence of a political party cabinet headed by Itagaki and Ōkuma in 1898. They were not prepared, however, for the entrance of commoners into the public sphere. To men like Yamagata, commoner activism of any sort—in labor organizations, in prostitute activism, in environmental protest—evoked images of the French revolution. So they reacted harshly, suspending newspapers hundreds of times, sending writers to jail, forbidding many public gatherings, disbanding social organizations. A Civil Code in 1898 "enshrined patriarchy and patrilinealism as the norm for all Japanese families."[14] And the 1900 Police Law, noted above, not only banned labor organizations and forbade political activity by women, soldiers, and minors, it gave officials sweeping powers to prevent unwanted political meetings. Worried that they had failed to make the constitutional system immune to disruption by the masses, the oligarchs instituted control measures even more strict than those of the early-Meiji years.

Not everything about city life was grim in these days, however, even for commoners. One of the era's revolutionary developments was the emergence of popular urban culture, shaped by commoner, or *minshū*, tastes as much as by the elites. This resulted in part from the maturation of the education system. It had taken years for local areas to build the schools needed to make compulsory education a reality. By the mid-1890s, however, 61.7 percent of school-aged children were attending classes (more than three-fourths of boys, not quite half of girls)—and by 1901, the boys' rate had passed 90 percent, the girls' 80. That meant more people able to read, more ready to follow "public" developments, to communicate their own ideas in the civic sphere.

At the same time, several savvy journalists saw the need for simply written, inexpensive newspapers that would appeal to these people. We already have seen how Fukuzawa and Murayama began paying more attention to news and profits in the 1880s. They had remained in the minority until the early 1890s, but by the end of the Sino-Japanese War, even the elite journalists were bending to the demand for readable news of war and politics. The most successful at responding to the new environment was Kuroiwa Shūroku, an inkmaker and translator who launched *Yorozu Chōhō* in 1892 for "people who work in the daytime and pay their oil bills in the evening." A newspaper should possess three characteristics, he said: simplicity, clarity, and pleasure. It also should be cheap. The established press scorned his four-page paper as sleazy and called him "Shūroku the pit viper." But they took notice. By 1895 *Yorozu* had become Tokyo's second-largest daily, and the prestige papers were emulating it by strengthening news coverage and making articles more interesting. And by the end of the century, nearly all of Japan's leading papers had gone commercial, simplifying writing, competing for sales and ads, trying (sometimes viciously) to outdo each other with scoops. Not everyone thought this was a good thing. *Nihon*'s Kuga Katsunan sniffed in 1897 that "newspapers . . . can be used to undermine morals."[15] But readers subscribed to newspapers in record numbers, sending the country's largest papers past the 100,000 circulation mark, ten times the readership of the prestige papers in the mid-1880s.

One of the subjects that interested readers most was the changing quality of Japan's material life. Inundation with "novel things" was not new; we already have seen how change engulfed the lives of the elite in the 1870s. What was different now was the penetration of these objects and forces into the lives of commoners. Newfangled articles continued, of course, to be used first by the well-heeled, but the fact that more and more *minshū* shared the spaces of the elites meant that consciousness of what was up-to-date spread across class lines in these years. And as goods became more affordable, the cheap people's papers began to run ads for all of those symbols of the modern: patent medicines, books, cigarettes, alcohol, stylish clothes, electric goods. The dramatic increase of train transportation (passengers quintupled during the 1890s, to over 100 million a year) spread the new goods and fashions even more widely.

Some of the innovations in these years were revolutionary, things that eventually would transform the lives of everyone. Electricity, for example, was introduced in 1887; the first department store opened in 1888; construction began on Tokyo's city water works in 1891, with the first lines bringing safe and easy water to the residents of Kanda and Nihonbashi wards in 1898. It would take years before these systems became part of most people's daily patterns, but other items began to make *minshū* life more interesting right away. During the Sino-Japanese War, Roppongi emerged in central Tokyo as a new entertainment area, catering to the army barracks located there. In 1896, what is thought to have been the first international baseball game was played between Japanese and American young people. In 1900, picture postcards were introduced, setting the stage for a fad that would inundate the post office just a few years later. The first moving picture was shown in 1897, a vitascope production that filled Kanda's Kinkikan hall at a cost of one yen for first-class seats and twenty *sen* for third-class seats. The list stretches on. Wristwatches, thermometers, elevators, the phonograph, beer halls, safety razors, even the *shōjo,* or "not-quite-female female," who asserted her right to seek pleasure publicly: all of these appeared for the first time on city streets in the decade after Japan defeated China. Some gained popularity quickly; others required time. But they showed a Japan obsessed with modernity, a city closer to Paris and New York than to the Edo of forty years ago.[16]

On April 3, 1901, the *Niroku Shinpō* sponsored a *minshū* event in Mukōjima park north of Ueno that illustrated how dramatically urban society had changed since House's arrival from New York thirty years earlier. When the paper advertised a workers' "friendship meeting," thousands sent in reservations. Nervous police warned *Niroku* that only 5,000 would be allowed on the grounds, but when 20,000 showed up, they relented and let them all in. The revelers had a merry day of feasting, singing, watching sword dances, and listening to labor activist Katayama Sen praise workers "whose sweat-drenched work never ceases."[17] It was all quite peaceful and nonthreatening, and it captured much of Tokyo's turn-of-the-century atmosphere: the horse trolleys, rickshaws, and footpaths by which people came; the emergence of labor as a self-conscious force; the commoners' love of festivity; the deference workers paid to authorities; and the nervousness of officials who banned a similar rally the next year. Historians make much of the emergence of a consumer-oriented mass culture in the 1910s and 1920s. What the Mukōjima rally demonstrates is that the seeds of that culture, nourished by nationalism, urbanization, and education, already had sprouted at the dawn of the twentieth century, in the dusk of House's life.

NOTES

1. To W. B. Mason, August 6, 1892, in Robert A. Rosenstone, *A Mirror in the Shrine*, 234.

2. Tokutomi's comment is in Akira Iriye, "Japan's Drive to Great-Power Status," in Marius Jansen, ed., *Cambridge History of Japan*, vol. 5, 765. Mutsu's remarks are in his *Kenkenroku: A Diplomatic Record of the Sino-Japanese War*, 27–28.

3. *Ōsaka Asahi Shimbun*, June 6, 1894; Fukuzawa's comments in *Jiji Shinpō*, July 29, 1894, in Hilary Conroy, *Japanese Seizure of Korea*, 255.

4. Ubukata Toshirō, "Kenpō happō to Nisshin sensō," in Tsurumi Shunsuke, ed., *Jiyānarizumu no shisō*, 91.

5. Quoted in John Pierson, *Tokutomi Sohō, 1863–1957*, 238–39.

6. Mutsu, *Kenkenroku*, 250.

7. Iriye, "Japan's Drive," 770.

8. House to Edmund Stedman, October 23, 1894, ECS, Columbia University.

9. For "turning point," see William W. Lockwood, *The Economic Development of Japan*, 18. Much of the data in this section is in Mikiso Hane, *Modern Japan: A Historical Survey*, 139–44. Data on factories in 1902 and 1894 are in Sheldon Garon, *The State and Labor in Modern Japan*, 10.

10. Tokyo population statistics are from Ariyama Teruo, *Kindai jiyānarizumu no kōzō*, 20. Kaneko is from her *Prison Memoirs of a Japanese Woman*, 40.

11. Tokyo conditions are in Yokoyama Gennosuke, *Nihon no kasō shakai*, 1, 33. Osaka's situation is in Eiji Yutani, trans., "*Nihon no kaso shakai* of Gennosuke Yokoyama," 169.

12. Tokyo strike data in Andrew Gordon, *Labor and Imperial Democracy in Prewar Japan*, 66; and national data in Uchikawa Yoshimi, "Shimbunshi hō no seitei katei to sono tokushitsu," 67.

13. *Mainichi Shimbun*, January 24, 1902.

14. Ann Waswo, *Modern Japanese Society*, 149.

15. "People who are busy," *Yorozu Chōhō*, November 1, 1892; *Nihon*'s criticism of the new journalism, *Nihon*, June 7, 1897, in Ariyama, 34–35.

16. Material culture is in Yumoto Kōichi, *Meiji jibutsu eigen jiten*, 134–258; and Edward Seidensticker, *Low City, High City*: 141 (Roppongi), 166 (baseball), and 201 (beer hall); and *shōjo* in Anne Walthall, ed., *Human Tradition in Modern Japan*, 160.

17. *Niroku Shinpō*, April 4, 1901, in Uchikawa Yoshimi and Matsushima Eiichi, eds., *Meiji nyūsu jiten*, vol. 6, 800–01; recounted in Huffman, *Creating a Public*, 254–55.

14

Evening Years: 1892–1901

> Do everything to the fullest when young; you have to work at it when you are older.
>
> —Kuroda (House) Koto[1]

House returned to Japan in 1892 to recover tranquility, and for the first time in years he seemed to have found it. After a brief late-October stay in Yokohama, he and Koto moved to Tokyo's Imperial Hotel, where they remained until they could secure a house in the Tsukiji foreign quarters. "It is a delight to be in this pleasantest of all lands," he wrote to Stedman, "where the welcomes begin as soon as you arrive and last until the time comes for saying farewell." The exhilaration was almost as fulsome as it had been on his first arrival, nearly a quarter of a century before. And with renewed spirits came better health "than I ever dared to hope." He even began going out for frequent rickshaw rides, sometimes for ten miles at a time.

One of the reasons for House's high spirits was the distance the move put him from the legal muck of New York. "I have surrendered almost everything to be rid of it," he said, "knowing that it was better to stick to what life I had left, than waste strength defending myself against plunderers." Another was that he was surrounded again by people who respected and loved him. The Japanese press announced his return. And as Christmas approached, he and Koto were "still in the midst of greetings so cordial that they make us forget there is anything but sunshine in the world." Inoue, the former foreign minister about whom he once had penned such critical letters, wrote to assure him that he was "very glad to have you here again." He began a new relationship with the then–foreign minister, Mutsu. And he took up his friendship again with Ōkuma, meeting him in late December and corresponding on the twenty-second about Charles LeGendre's latest doings. Ōkuma also gave House the wheelchair that he had used after the 1888 assassination attack.[2]

House always socialized more than one would have thought from his letters during the dark times, and that was particularly true now. He told Stedman on November 25 that days were "a constant whirl of activity," and the correspondence shows continual social interaction across the next few years: calls on (and from) friends; theater visits; shared dinners with Frank Brinkley, to whom he sold $80.75 worth of claret and white wine in mid-1893; dinners back and forth with Ernest Satow, who became British minister to Japan in 1895; and roses sent to Eliza Scidmore, wife of an American attorney, in Yokohama. House was especially convivial when fellow Americans visited Tokyo, determined that they see the Japan he loved. His correspondence is full of stories about showing off the Ueno cherry blossoms, taking friends' friends to the theater, arranging introductions for *friends* of friends' friends back home.

Sometimes House loved the entertaining; sometimes he endured it as a duty. He relished, for example, the time spent on Valentine A. Blacque, "a good deal of a pagan" whom Stedman declared to be "*one of our own kind*," but he despised that given to Stephen Bonsal, a young diplomat from Boston whom Villard had recommended. This miscreant visitor, he reported, went around treating people rudely, abusing rickshaw drivers, and creating enemies, even after House had tried to "make him feel that my house was the same as his home." Nasty experiences never kept House from befriending visitors, but when his own friends visited, he threw his soul into the hospitality. When *Atlantic Monthly* editor Aldrich and his wife came in the fall of 1894, House and Koto saw them almost daily for a week. "Nothing in the future is *absolutely* done; but it is so nearly sure that after you leave Japan I shall never see you again, that I wish you would give me all the minutes you can spare," House said. When rain detained the visitors in Yokohama one day, Aldrich wrote: "We would rather see you and Koto again 'than to walk in a garden of spice' with the Emperor and Empress of Japan." House was wrong about not seeing them again though; the Aldriches visited Japan once more in 1898, this time with their sons in tow, and House and Koto repeated the hospitality, complete with gifts of "a few roses from our garden."[3]

House was a freelancer at heart, not only as a writer but also as a human being, a man who seldom knew just what he would do for a living when he made a major move. He had planned to write when he came to Tokyo first, in 1870, but had had no assurance of enough work to provide a living. When he returned to the States in 1885, the same was true. Now, in 1892, he knew less than ever where his finances would come from. There was the Japanese government allowance, augmented by a few book royalties. And he received rents from the lots that he owned in Yokohama, as well as some income from limited investments that will be discussed later. But the New York legal skirmishes had left his finances shaky, so the respite he sought in coming back to Japan dared not include retirement. At fifty-six, he still needed writing for more than a sense of fulfillment. He made unfruitful inquiries about reporting on a regular basis for the *New York Evening Post;* drafted a number of magazine articles, none of which sold immediately; and did irregular pieces for the *Japan Weekly Mail,* as well as the *Times* and *Tribune* in New York. None of these, however, produced enough money to stabilize his finances. It thus came as a fortuitous surprise in mid-1894 when the looming conflict between Japan and China offered a chance—the first in fourteen years—to become a regular journalist again.

House hinted about what he thought might happen in a July letter to Villard, while the industrialist was traveling in northern Africa. "There is very fair prospect of a fight," he wrote, "with possible ramifications that may set half a dozen other nations by the ears." He saw it as an "ugly little war prospect," but said that he was "strongly lured to put myself in harness again." It was hardly what one would have expected as House's next move. Not only was he bound to a wheelchair, he feared that his reporting skills had "fallen into stagnation," and doubted that the *Times* could afford him or that the *Tribune* would want him. But obstacles rarely bothered House once an idea entered his head, so he "put aside all scruples" and accepted offers from Joseph Pulitzer's *New York World* and the Associated Press. His real motivation, he declared to Stedman, was to "set in operation all the influences I could command on the side of justice and truth," to enlighten an American public that he regarded as either apathetic about Asia or pro-Chinese.[4]

Actually, House's assessment of American opinion was only half right. That the U.S. press looked down on Asians and underestimated the war's importance is obvious in the very name generally applied to the conflict: the "Pigtail War." But public opinion generally was behind the Japanese, partly because Americans tended to see them as the "civilized" Asians ("the Americans, so called, of Asia," wrote the *Atlanta Constitution*), and partly because the Japanese were good at public relations. Japan's minister to Washington, Kurino Shin'ichirō, whom locals regarded as "a good fellow—very civilized," called almost daily on the U.S. secretary of state, while his colleagues in Washington, San Francisco, and New York sent regular releases to the press. It was not surprising then that after Japan's November victory at Port Arthur the *New York Tribune* would declare, patronizingly but approvingly: "Out of the darkness of the Far East a light shines, and it is the light of civilization evolved from conditions of native progress." Nor was it surprising that House became part of the Japanese image-making effort. It is inaccurate to say that the "Japanese Secret Service hired" him, as one scholar does. His sole connection to the Japanese government was the ongoing allowance, which he had discussed publicly during the *Prince and the Pauper* trial in New York. At the same time, there is no question that his determination to show his fellow countrymen the good side of "this gallant little empire" played into the aims of the foreign ministry, as did his decision to write for the Associated Press, which he mistrusted, in order to reach "something like ten million" readers.[5]

House approached reporting as he always had: by assiduously cultivating inside sources. He set his "editorial offices" up on a Sumida River freight barge, which he had transformed into a houseboat to gain both space and relief from the summer heat, and from there he used assistants and the mails to communicate with highly connected people. His most important source in these months appears to have been Foreign Minister Mutsu. Another was Itō Miyoji, special aid to the powerful Itō Hirobumi. And his letters show frequent communication with other Japanese officials, as well as members of the U.S. diplomatic team, including Minister Edwin Dun, a native of Springfield, Ohio, and the only American legation head in the Meiji era to speak fluent Japanese. Since the *World* was alone among American papers in using full-fledged reporters to cover the early stages of the war—House from Japan and James Creelman from the battle fronts—the House stories were more than usually influential. His was the first full report on Japan's important victory in Pyongyang on September 15 and, a day later, on the decisive naval battle off the Yalu River. The stories were based on items "furnished by Japanese who accompanied the army" and "attributed to a Japanese contributor" but actually written by House.[6]

House received repeated notes from the *World* editors well into 1895, expressing their satisfaction with his coverage. His sources were at the highest level, he wrote well, and his viewpoint rested easily with his superiors in New York. In December, however, he became involved in a minor way in the war's biggest controversy, an event that tarnished the image of Japan's army and raised questions about House's judgment. The episode involved Japanese atrocities at Port Arthur following their November 21 victory. Belying their reputation for discipline, the victorious troops killed hundreds of Chinese civilians in the days right after that battle, for reasons that may never be clear. In the words of one Japanese soldier's diary: "Anyone we saw in the town, we killed. The streets were filled with corpses. . . . Firing and slashing, it was unbounded joy." Initially, the Japanese officers reported only the victory, to great homeland jubilation since Port Arthur was strategically crucial. Three Western reporters had by this time joined the Japanese forces, however—two from England and the *World*'s Creelman—and their reports created a sensation. For a time, there only were intimations: a *World* note on November 28 of an "unconfirmed rumor" that 200 Chinese had been massacred, a London report on November 29 that irregularities had been provoked by "persistent atrocities of the Chinese." Then, on December 11, the *World* ran a sensational report by Creelman that Japan's troops had "massacred practically the entire population in cold blood" and had "relapsed into barbarism."

The story, so contrary to the image of Japan that had been presented until then, provoked consternation in New York, and on December 13, the *World* telegraphed House to "cable straightway" the government's explanation of what happened. He did that, and four days later, on December 17, the *World* ran a series of page one stories under the headline, "Japan Confesses." The lead story quoted Mutsu as saying that Japan desired "no concealment of the events at Port Arthur," that the government was "investigating rigidly" what happened, and that the episode "shocks and grieves both the civil and military authorities." Then it placed much of the blame on the Chinese. Escaping Chinese soldiers had disguised themselves as ordinary citizens, making it difficult to distinguish troops from civilians, and Japan's troops were "transported with rage at the mutilation of their comrades by the enemy." The statement said that while the government deplored "as a national misfortune the unexpected transgression of the principles to which it was and always will be pledged," it also protested press exaggerations. Mutsu's statement was a whitewash, understating the atrocities and focusing on Chinese provocations. And House, long conditioned to seeing Japanese matters through official lenses, clearly participated in that whitewash. It was an effective response, however, playing to American predispositions, and the *World* quickly resumed its support for Japan. It ran Creelman's stories, some of them attacking Japan, but it ran other stories criticizing Creelman himself for sensationalism. The day after Christmas, the *World*'s R. H. Farrelly wrote to House: "Let me thank you very much for all you have done for The World and to say that there will be no difficulty about the cable tolls. Everything came all right and we will pay for them all."

That letter added that the paper did not need House for any "more work . . . at present," but about that Farrelly was mistaken, because House continued reporting for the paper, at a salary of $40 a week, for the next fourteen months. Late in the spring of 1895, after a flurry of scoops and analyses about the postwar negotiations and the Triple Intervention, the *World* sent House a bonus that must have ranked among his prized trophies. "Mr. Pulitzer desires you to accept a draft for $250 (gold)," the letter said, "as a token of his personal appreciation of the excellent work which The World has received from you during these Japanese troubles."

It added: "You have beaten Col. Cockerill constantly, Indeed, he has sent nothing by cable that seemed worth the trouble as it has been not only second to your matter but to the press stuff as well. . . . The matter which you sent regarding the stepping in of Russia proved to be beats in almost every instance." The writer assured House "that the World will, as opportunity may arise, express much sympathy with Japan." Not until February 1896 did the *World* cut its Japanese "news department to a peace footing" and replace House's salary with a fifteen dollars per column ("double space rates") fee. "If the occasion arises for a correspondent" in Japan, the *World* wanted House to be its man.[7]

The success of this last journalistic stint had a profound impact on House. Following on the agonies of his last four years in New York, the opportunity "to be once more 'in the swim,'" to compete successfully with some of the era's best reporters, to see his ideas win wide support, did wonders for his spirits. For more than a year, he "was wholly unconscious of fatigue" and experienced no attacks of gout. He found a "sudden accession of vigor and energy" that he had come to regard as impossible. "The mental restoration was for all my life," he wrote to Villard in the fall of 1895. Even if the job evaporated, "the benefit of what I feel . . . will remain forever. The moral branch of my disorder has been completely cured." Japanese press historian Ebihara Hachirō called this "the end of a brilliant career as a newspaper reporter." A happy end it was.[8]

Unfortunately, once again House proved less astute at predicting his own life course than at analyzing politics or forecasting war. Later in 1895, the gout revisited him, and a few months after wrapping up his service to the *World* new troubles arose, from the most unexpected of quarters: Koto. During the first years back in Tokyo, Koto was as active and loyal as ever. She appears constantly in the correspondence to and from the House household: sending gifts to friends on both sides of the Pacific, translating for her father, hosting lavish dinner parties on the Sumida River houseboat, managing several servants, and helping House get about town. Tokutomi recalled a day when he saw a young woman and an older man come into his journal's bookshop. Inquiring who they were, he was told that Koto had brought House to buy a book on treaty revision. She also devoured news avidly, and had become skilled at calligraphy and the tea ceremony, as well as Western-style painting. Her daughter-in-law, Kuroda Hatsuko, who herself became a famous cooking teacher, recalled that Koto's artistic training made her quite particular about the way clothes were put together. If a kimono sash or a brooch were not just right, she would insist that it be changed.

As all of this suggests, Koto also had a mind of her own. The girl who wore a boy's robes to school as a teenager thought nothing now of speaking to strangers on the street, or, as Hatsuko recalled, of sketching her sons in the nude when they visited hot springs resorts in later years—an altogether unusual practice for a Meiji woman.[9] Things of this sort never bothered House; he delighted in her strength and reputation. At least, he did until she fell in love without asking permission. When she announced in the fall of 1896 that she was engaged to the French teacher Kuroda Takuma, he was aghast. One might have expected him to pleased, since he long had talked about a future marriage for her. After all, Koto was thirty-seven years old. And her husband seemed to have the ideal background, having worked as a youth for the Frenchman Gustave Emile Boissonade, one of the Japanese government's most important advisors. He had accompanied Boissonade to France as a secretary, then had become a language instructor at the Army College. Kuroda was not, however, an adequate spouse in House's eyes. Perhaps because he was several years younger than she, more likely because he was taking her away, House found the marriage a "calamity infinitely harder to bear than any of the bodily ills I have suffered in the last twenty years." And the story of his angst encapsulates so much of the aging House's personality that it needs to be told.

House had not thought Koto capable of actually falling in love, in part because of her first marital disaster, in part because of his own bond with her. "Her devotion and tenderness were such as I never dreamed could be given to me," he confessed to Villard. "Her constant watchfulness and fidelity more than once kept me alive when the doctors had put aside all hope of my recovery. For nearly twenty years her affection for me seemed steadfast and supreme. What mine was for her, I cannot attempt to say." But wooed by Kuroda, she "lost the power of self control." And making it worse, she told the story of her budding romance "with that absorbing infatuation which is so pitiful and pathetic in women." As for Kuroda, House thought him dull, young, one of those "seekers for fortune and position, whose ability is unequal to their aspirations," a man of "colossal conceit and arrogance" who wanted Koto for status and money.

When House told Koto about his misgivings, she, ever filial, "consented to submit without resistance to whatever decision I should make." He forbade the marriage and "thought the worst was over." Compliance was not acceptance, however, and "from that moment, happiness went out of our home. Nothing could shake her conviction that I had rejected her suitor without cause and that my decree was arbitrary and unjust. Though she had given him up, her thoughts were always with him, and her faith in me was destroyed." So House relented, because it was "daily torture" to see her unhappiness. He knew that once he died, she would marry Kuroda anyway. And he was sure that if she did that, all of her friends would reject her for having defied a dying father's wishes. The marriage thus took place in October; Koto moved to Kuroda's home, and for the first time in two decades, House began living alone.

By the following spring, when he finally could bring himself to write about what had happened, he was brimming with worry. He said the foreign community had "shut her out," accusing Koto of rejecting a disabled parent. Even more seriously, he worried about her financial security. He was sure that Kuroda did not have the means to support a family. House gave Koto money but feared that, once he was gone, Kuroda would squander anything that he willed to her. He gave a great deal of thought to how he might create an annuity, so that she would have "a regular income, but no capital." He also worried about what he had done to cause Koto to take this new path. And he rued the loneliness of his new life. Koto came to visit House often, but his home was no longer hers, and he had no regular companions now. "I never had any real friends in Japan," he told Villard in the fall of 1898, "but my circle of acquaintance was large enough, and I was more dependent upon human intercourse than I imagined. . . . Solitude is not good for me, and I fear my isolation has injured me in many ways." He thought about returning to the United States. "I see no light in the darkness of my life," he wrote. "Everything has gone against me."

Like all things, the worst eventually passed. After a year and a half, House and the Kurodas moved together to one of his properties in Yokohama. Life never would be as it once had been; Koto's first allegiance now was to Kuroda and to the infant Masao, who had been born late in 1897, but all parties learned to live with the new circumstances. House kept trying to figure out how to keep Kuroda from getting control of the $20,000 to $25,000 estate that he expected to leave, and he declared, "I cannot make a companion of him." But he began to give the young teacher grudging respect. "I am bound to say that the worst and most painful predictions urged upon me with regard to Mr. Kuroda have not been verified," he admitted. "I do believe that he is willing enough to work, and I am convinced that his intelligence is very far above the average." He still thought the young man a "spendthrift" with a "reckless and prodigal" streak and a "vain, arrogant and overbearing" demeanor. But at least Kuroda was talented, and he and Koto loved each other. Another family move, to Tokyo in November 1898, restored even more of House's equanimity, because he was back in "Japan again;—(for I do not reckon Yokohama as a part of the empire, except by the accident of geography)."[10]

The marriage episode dramatized, once again, House's ability to separate private and public lives. His troubles embittered him personally and provoked renewed attacks of the gout. In public, however, he remained the man he always had been, writing essays on political and literary topics, contacting journalists and politicians on Japan's behalf, squabbling with editors over article revisions and stipends, and penning children's stories, including a virtuoso recollection of the "bright stories" of history

Koto, in her late years, with Kuroda Takuma, the husband House tried to keep her from marrying. (Photo from Kuroda family collection. Used by permission.)

that ran for seven consecutive months (1898–1899) in *St. Nicholas for Young Folks*. But there was one significant difference this time. As if to bring life full circle, he returned actively now to the music that had centered his earliest years. He never had gotten wholly away from the piano, or from composition. He wrote a good deal about Japanese music, and at Christmas time in 1878, while editing the *Times*, he did an arrangement of "Ave Maria" for the Catholic Church in Yokohama—an arrangement praised by the reviewer for its "beautiful dialogues between the violin and cello." After returning to Japan in 1892, he also had written occasional music reviews for the *Mail*, initiating through them a friendship with the German pianist Rudolf Dittrich, who called House "one of my best and truest friends in Japan" and ranked his reviews "among the best trophies which I carry home from Japan."[11]

It was in his last three years, however, that he employed his musical skills with the greatest—and sometimes most controversial—intensity, earning his last major accolade, as a pioneer of Western-style music in Japan. Western music had been introduced to Tokyo in the 1870s and 1880s through military bands and Christian church music. Early on, however, several of the imperial court musicians also developed an interest in Western orchestral music, partly because of its inherent beauty and partly so that they could play familiar music for foreign dignitaries. For that reason, two foreigners, the American L. W. Mason and the German Franz Eckert, had been employed occasionally to teach vocal and orchestral music to several of the court musicians. Then, in 1898, seven of those men formed one of the country's first Western-style performance groups, the Meiji Music Society (Meiji Ongakukai), and in December they asked "that enthusiastic amateur, Mr. E. H. House" to be their first conductor: a surprising move to people who knew the aging Bostonian only as a journalist and publicist; a superb move, it turned out, for music lovers. When the society performed works by Gounod, Haydn, and Rossini, along with Japan's new national anthem at Ueno Music Hall on March 11, the reviewer called House "a true artist," and said that "though he had not a large palette of colors with which to work, he succeeded in producing some exquisite paintings in miniature." The review congratulated the Ongakukai "above all" for "securing the help of their talented conductor, who is devoting his erudition and cultured leisure to their cause."

It was an auspicious beginning of a brief but unusual musical career. Subsequent performances drew similar praise, as the Ongakukai improved. In April of the following year, the *Mail* was particularly taken with the brochure that House had produced for the concert, an eight-page booklet in Japanese and English, providing listeners with background on the composers and musical works, with an "erudition" and "admirable literary style" that few but House "could have carried out." By that time, House's success with the Ongakukai had garnered for him another post, as the first person employed to teach Western music to all twenty-five court musicians. On February 5, 1900, House wrote to Baron Sannomiya Yoshitane, Grand Master of Ceremonies for the Imperial Household Ministry, that to prepare the orchestra "for good and substantial work," he would accept the assignment. "So far as I can judge," he said, "I am now strong enough to do whatever is needed." That meant, of course, teaching and conducting from a wheelchair. A six-month contract was signed committing House to teach nine hours a week, beginning March 1, for 200 yen a month. A second six-month contract went into effect September 1.

When the court musicians presented a concert on May 25, led by a full-bearded, graying House, the *Mail* reported that a "substantial beginning" had been accomplished, though it might have been wise to have waited a bit longer before putting on the performance. Waiting was not possible, however, because the empress herself had "graciously signified that it would be her pleasure to listen to a performance of foreign music by her orchestra." The concert included works by Mozart, Beethoven, Söveh, and Mendelssohn, and at the end, "Her Majesty sent for Mr. House, and graciously expressed her pleasure at the entertainment which the musicians (aided by his skill and instruction) had provided." One of House's innovations as director brought him even wider notice. The orchestra had no horns, and when he needed "a long, soft, holding note," he had an alto trombonist attempt it. To his astonishment, House found that the player was able to make the instrument sound like "the oboe in wood . . . but with a tenderness and richness that my critical sense even now refuses to associate with trombones." Alto trombones had rarely been used in scores until then; so it was possible, said a *New York Times* writer, that House had "made a discovery which . . . may bring the alto trombone into more general use."

Praise for the orchestra continued, but House resigned as instructor at the end of 1900, two months before his contract expired, apparently because he thought the musicians were not working hard enough, though health also may have been a factor. The empress presented him with a lacquer jewelry box, engraved with three children flying kites. She expressed her appreciation for the "great progress" made by the musicians and, with surprising candor, her regret that House had found the musicians' "accumulated bad habits of the past" unacceptable. The box remained in the possession of his granddaughter Kuroda Hatsuko at the start of the twenty-first century, as the family's proudest House memento, ranking slightly ahead of a beer stein that Twain had given to House and the ring that he had purchased for Koto in Italy.[12]

Even in the musical sphere, House was drawn to controversy. In the spring of 1901, he vented his frustrations in print over the directions in which Western-style orchestral music was going under the direction of a German viola player, the thirty-one-year-old August Junker, who was teaching at the prestigious Ueno Music School. The school had made great progress across twenty years, House wrote to the *Japan Weekly Mail*, but under Junker, the "satisfactory condition of things has not lasted." House had several complaints, the most serious being that the school's orchestra was putting on performances without adequate practice. "It is an indignity to art, and an affront to the public, to undertake performances . . . until after they have been diligently and unitedly rehearsed," he wrote on April 6. A week later, he escalated the attack. He had ascertained that Junker had misrepresented himself as "leading violin and *chef d'orchestre*" under Theodore Thomas, the world renowned conductor of the Chicago Symphony Orchestra. With his usual careful approach to issues, he quoted a letter from Thomas, saying that Junker "never did anything for me, nor do I think he has had any training or experience in any other way than playing in the orchestra." The inexperience was less a problem than the lie, House wrote. He said Junker had set Japan's musical progress back by his dishonesty, and by his failure to insist on rigor. Reflecting the frustration he had experienced himself with the court musicians, some of whom now were playing in Junker's concerts, he wrote: "Men who were willing, six months ago, to labour strenuously and untiringly in their studies, are now heard to ask why they should be held to the drudgery of toilsome practice. . . . Spasmodic attempts with patched-up bands, in which the first principles of thoroughness and artistic unity are neglected, can lead to nothing but failure."

The charges touched off a storm, which lasted for weeks. Junker himself wrote that while he may not have had experience as a conductor, "good conductors" typically came from the ranks of players—and "one learns as much about music in an orchestra as in a newspaper office." One of Junker's fellow Ueno teachers, R. Von Koeber, accused House of "malicious mischief," petty jealousy, and musical incompetence. "E. H. H. knows no more about instrumentation, conducting, and musical technique—in spite of his boastful assertions—than does his baton, which swings like a pendulum," he wrote; "he does not belong in the world in which I live." A third wrote that House's "trashy opinions" reminded him of "passing a garden roller over a worm." Others came to House's defense, one noting that Junker's allies had followed the "celebrated *dictum*:—'No case, abuse the plaintiff.'" Even one of Junker's defenders began by bearing "testimony" to House's "love for music" and admitting that House's only motive was "disinterested anxiety for the progress and development of a school with which he has absolutely no connection." And a *Mail* editorial called it a "perversion of the verities" for Von Koeber to accuse House of "gratuitous and malicious virulence." Readers hardly could miss the fact that House's main charge, that of operating under false pretenses, was not addressed by Junker's defenders—a fact that may not have cost the German his job, but certainly gave the debate to House.[13]

Neither music nor family complications took House wholly away from his first love—Japan's place in the world—in these turn-of-the-century years. He continued occasional letters to Ōkuma and other Japanese leaders, suggesting policies and evaluating programs, and he kept writing to opinion leaders in the United States. But his main medium in these years was the *Japan Mail*, which generally was seen as the area's most influential English-language newspaper. He and editor Brinkley kept up constant correspondence, and House wrote on a wide range of issues: the need for Japan to assert its sovereignty over the Inland Sea; ways to pay for the Sino-Japanese War (he suggested selling Japanese government bonds abroad); the need to establish a "fixed and permanent" ratio for setting the relative worth of gold and silver, so that "silver can be safely restored to its former usefulness as a medium of exchange."

The continuing alacrity, and breadth, of his mind was illustrated by a discussion early in 1900 of the practicability of replacing Japan's *kanji* (Chinese character) writing system with the Roman alphabet, or *romaji* system. In response to calls by Westerners, including Brinkley, for a shift to *romaji*, House argued that the *kanji* system was every bit as sensible as English. "So long as there are nations on the other side of the globe which reckon time by obsolete calendars . . . and steadily refuse to amend the absurd defects of their own orthography, Europeans have no spare stones to throw," he wrote. Among the problems with using the Roman alphabet: it did not represent all of the Japanese sounds; it lacked a standard pronunciation system ("the English pronounce them in all conceivable and many inconceivable ways"); it could not be written as swiftly as *kanji*. A shift to *romaji* might be expedient since English dominated the world, House admitted, but not because English orthography was inherently superior. For several weeks, he and Brinkley engaged in intricate, bitter, and erudite sparring over the issue. Brinkley ended the debate with the assertion: "We are glad to be able to agree with Mr. House in one point, namely, that this discussion is fruitless." The debate was vintage House: meticulous care about even the most tedious points, insistence that Japanese methods were as sensible as those of the West, careful use of language, and a willingness to argue vehemently with a friend, even while maintaining a warm private correspondence.[14]

There was more at stake, and far less rancor, in House's other early spring debate with Brinkley, another exchange that harkened back to one of his early melodies. This time the topic was—once more—Shimonoseki. While there was little new in House's views, his argument bore striking evidence to the love an old man still held for Japan, and to the generosity with which he regarded even debating opponents if he thought they argued in good will. After insisting, as in the past, that primary responsibility for the episode lay with America and its Western allies, he explained his fear that young Japanese would grow up without knowing how valiant and principled their own leaders had been back then. When Brinkley chided him for being "somewhat harsh" about the Western diplomats' motives, he said that progress in international relations made it easy to forget how self-serving those diplomats had been, but praised Brinkley's "courage and steadfastness in opposing prejudice and contending for justice." He added that "the foreign world . . . has yet a good many revolutions to make, before it reaches the point of fair equilibrium."[15]

Neither gout, nor government subsidies, nor domestic turmoil ever changed House's view of the world. Japan had not reached equality with the Western powers, either in the way the foreign nations treated it or in its performance. But Japan's performance far surpassed the treatment it received at foreign hands. And he still hated that. He also found it dangerous—as he wrote in his most powerful late-century analyses, a set of long, incisive letters to his old friend, now William McKinley's confidant (and future secretary of state), John Hay. The gist of the letters was that the United States had been served badly by its diplomats in Asia, though House did not say it that concisely. After invoking a friendship that went back to the Civil War, he told Hay that American had had "two, and only two" satisfactory ministers to Japan in four decades of intercourse: Townsend Harris, the first envoy, and John Bingham. Even Bingham would have "left a record of utter failure" if he had not stayed long enough to learn on the job. All the rest had been "fourth or fifth rate men, at the best estimate." And inattention of that sort would "be followed by evil consequences if not speedily remedied," because "there is no part of the world where keener intellects, sounder judgment, or shrewder diplomatic intelligence are required than at these Oriental seats of government."

House argued that China and Japan needed exceptional diplomats, but that talented men rarely sought these posts out, because of Washington's tendency to slight them. He also pointed out, at considerable length, just how much potential former president Ulysses S. Grant had seen in Asia. And he argued that the European nations were working diligently to get the best of the United States: "filling their Legations with picked men,—the very best they can command," dispatching experts "all over Northern Asia, to gather information, as secretly as may be," joining to "uproot American influence and prevent Americans from peacefully participating in the reorganization which we all know is inevitable." The one U.S. advantage lay in the fact "that we have no hidden schemes of conquest" and seek "to encourage the civilization and progress of all races." Without competent diplomats, however, that advantage was squandered. "I want the strong and clever men here for our own sake. The statesmen of Japan . . . are quite on a level with the best of the foreign diplomatic corps. Some of them are so adroit, so tactful, so resolute and courageous that they could beat most of their European adversaries at any game of wits."

All of this was made crucially important, House added, by Japan's changing position in the international community. The end of extraterritoriality would demand more diplomatic skill than American diplomats had possessed until now. More important, Japan was asserting itself on the continent, changing the balance of power. "Eastern Asia will remain in its present confused and unsettled state for only a short time, and if we have not made our position secure before the new order of affairs sets in, we shall be thrown back to the second or third place indefinitely. There is no man too good for the work to be done." He thought China and Korea also were critical posts, but Japan, the "brains" of Asia, was most important—"the lever by which Asia is to be lifted out of stagnation." If Washington continued to send mediocre representatives, "there will be a season of disagreement and altercation more than likely to end in a prolonged estrangement." He ended the tome by repeating how deeply he felt about all of this: "Whether I succeed in impressing you, or not, you will recognize one thing. . . . My feeling is too acute to allow me to do it justice."

Before Hay had a chance to respond, House was at it again, sending another long letter, worrying that he had been "over-scrupulous in keeping silence" about the specific people then serving in East Asia. He found most, but not all, weak. Minister Dun knew "Japan and the Japanese more thoroughly than most Americans" and had a "kindly . . . disposition," but "his mind is not ferile, and the notion of originating any idea . . . would never occur to him. . . . One might easily have a worse Minister; but that we ought to have one far better is too plain for argument." The minister to Beijing, Charles Denby, had "no power to distinguish himself or add to our prestige," and John Sill in Seoul was a disaster who should be recalled at once. He thought one of the lower officials in Japan, First Secretary Joseph Herod, was good enough to be named minister to Korea, while the other men in the Tokyo legation were lazy and incompetent. "The absurdity of an Interpreter who cannot interpret," he added, "ought to be stamped out."

The letters were a tour de force: long, knowledgeable, candid, powerfully argued, and directed to a man of influence. They had behind them decades of thinking about each of these issues. Hay himself obviously found them persuasive. He wrote House that he took the first of them directly to McKinley's office and read "the substance" aloud to him. "He could hardly know how good it was; not having read it, he was somewhat appalled by its length, but I made him listen." Hay could not promise House the results he desired; "it is almost impossible for the best meaning President or Secretary of State in the world to do precisely what they would like in the matters of appointment to office." But he was convinced by the argument; "the interests involved cannot be exaggerated." Unfortunately for House, instead of remaining in Washington Hay went off two months later to London, as ambassador, and the next U.S. minister to Japan was Alfred Eliab Buck, a mediocre Georgia Republican who, in the words of Jack Hammersmith, "confirmed the very tendencies that House so bitterly decried." House took the appointment philosophically, however, writing to Hay that his friend's note had "prepared me for the disappointing intelligence which came soon after by public telegrams. . . . Perhaps none but visionaries will indulge hopes to reformation in the diplomatic service of the Far East."[16]

We have seen that House did not often take things so philosophically. It may be that, on this issue, he knew that he had done his best. Hay's willingness to take House's arguments directly to the president also must have softened the disappointment. Or perhaps he was having intimations that the end was approaching, that he needed to be setting life's matters in order. For a decade and a half House had talked more than most men about his own mortality, particularly during serious attacks of gout. But the talk always had had a fanciful quality to it; one was not sure how seriously he really worried. Now, as the nineteenth century slipped toward the twentieth, one sensed a change in tone. The Hay letters had the spirit of a valedictory, or at least a summation; so did the fight to get Japanese musicians to practice harder, and the eagerness to set the record straight on Shimonoseki. House also spent a great deal of time now setting his financial house in order, so that Koto would be secure when he died. In the spring of 1897, he corresponded with Thomas D. Lowther in Chicago, the man to whom he had dedicated *Midnight Warnings*, about a small sum to be willed to Koto. He also wrote endlessly to Stedman: about one well-meaning friend, now dead, who invested badly and "lost her $4,000"; about a "triple blockhead" who "lost Koto thousands in exchange"; about receiving "a full 4 per ct. above your limit" on the sale of $3,000 in Rio Grande Western bonds; about Stedman's cashier who wrote a bill of exchange to the wrong person "by a piece of ineffable stupidity"; about the performance of Louisville & Nashville bonds in the Panic of 1898. Early in 1901, after a long discussion of whether to sell some bonds, House wrote: "No exile ever felt himself more destitute of home connections than I. . . . Sometimes I . . . think of the whirl and bustle of New York (*quorum pars fui*) as a shadowy dream. But I must keep myself wide awake when railroad bonds are in question." Early that November, he had his last will drawn up by his Yokohama attorney-friend George Scidmore.[17]

House's grandson, Kuroda Masao, recalled decades later that during the last year or two, after House and the Kurodas moved to their final, two-story, moat-side home, famous for its Tokugawa-era gate, House spent most of his time upstairs playing piano and drinking whiskey. Kuroda could not have been quite right in that recollection, given House's productivity in these years. But it is clear that his social interactions now took on the mellower, more sentimental, quality of a man in his evening years. In 1899, he made the friendship of a Yokohama music teacher, Emily Sophia Patton, whose friendship evoked his whimsical side. She usually visited him when she went to Tokyo, and while she found his physical existence "a living death," she thought his mind brilliant and witty. In July of that year, he sent her a gentle note full of evidence of the latter. He wrote: "Extra Morning Glory Bulletin. Total number of blossoms this am 27. Total number of leaves this am 21. . . . I don't believe this record can be surpassed, but if ever a larger number come to view, I shall take pleasure in letting you know."[18] His letters to old friends had a more reflective quality now too. He confessed to Villard his hatred for the "wretched" Spanish-American War, whose "evils will live after it." "It is hard," he said, "when one is nearing the end of his life, to find so little that is hopeful in the future of his native land." To Stedman, who said House had given him "a patient friendship . . . the like of which it has been my lot to obtain from few men, or women," he talked about a therapeutic trip to the "slopes of the living volcano Asama," a region near Karuizawa that had become a retreat for foreigners and the Japanese elite. And there were discussions of the death of House's friend and Beethoven's biographer Alexander Thayer ("How many sorrows of this sort the last year has called upon me to bear!"); of Grover Cleveland's scandals ("I always thought him a mass of ignorant and obstinate vanity, yet largely redeemed by . . . integrity"); of finding a book, *The Iron Game,* that described the Battle of Bull Run, where House, Villard, and Stedman had initiated their camaraderie; of being able to work—"the only solid satisfaction I can have, in these later years."[19]

In mid-December 1901, during what started out as one of his chronic bouts with illness, House took a sudden turn for the worse, and on December 17, the imperial household, hearing that the end might be near, announced that the emperor had awarded him the Second Order of Merit with the Sacred Treasure, a rare honor for a foreigner. He died a day later, at 1 p.m., under Koto's care. The *Kobe Weekly Chronicle* reported that his life had been snatched away by "a complication of disorders"—a phrase more full of meaning, surely, than the writer imagined. Even in death House remained fastidious, and contentious. Determined that the religious institutions he despised would have no part in his passing, he left instructions that neither the funeral nor the burial should include anything religious. The *Tokyo Nichi Nichi Shimbun* reported that he was "a rarity among foreigners, a man of no religion." It quoted a friend who called him "chivalrous" (*gikyōteki*): "If he believed in something, he did not worry about the strength of his enemy. That was the way he fought for Japan."

The funeral procession left the House home three days later, at the hour of his death, accompanied by a military honor guard and a long line of carriages. The mourners made their way to the Aoyama funeral parlor where more than 200 people listened to the court musicians perform House's favorite songs and to friends describe his contributions. American minister Buck was there, as were Viscount (and later prime minister) Terauchi Masatake and Education Minister Kikuchi Dairoku. So were his favorite young student Mitsukuri Kakichi and the former foreign minister Enomoto Takeaki, along with John Griffin, who had defended him in the Junker debate. Ōkuma was prevented at the last moment from attending, but his private secretary delivered a eulogy saying House had "laid this country under a deep obligation by his advocacy of her cause."

Brinkley praised him for "combatting the racial prejudices which are the disgrace of this twentieth century." And attorney Scidmore talked about the "fighting quality that led him to sacrifice himself when he believed that he was in the right." Perhaps the most moving eulogy came from the legal scholar Hozumi Nobushige, who recalled what a demanding teacher House had been three decades before at the Kaisei Gakkō. "We all regarded him as an inflexible parent, and he treated us as loved but not indulged children," he said. "We have never known a teacher possessing such personal magnetism. . . . He is gone, but not his ashes alone will remain in our country. There will remain also the students he educated, some in official positions, some in private, but all serving their country through his aid." At the conclusion of the service, each mourner placed a flower on the bier, and the body was taken away for cremation.

House's ashes were interred in the Buddhist temple Dairyūji on the northern edge of Tokyo, where three decades years later, March 19, 1929, Tokutomi Sohō would come to sprinkle water in remembrance. On the

House's marker at Dairyūji Temple in Tokyo was imposing but lonely a century after his death. Photo by James L. Huffman, Jr.

marker, Koto had an outline of his life etched beneath the words: "He nurtured me in love. . . . I shed tears of blood." Obituaries across Japan remembered House's contributions throughout the next month. *Osaka Asahi* heralded the fact that he had "maintained his positions even when the foreign community nearly banished him." The *Japan Herald*, true to form, called him a paid government lackey. The *Kobe Weekly Chronicle* said "his frankness and forcefulness made for him many enemies, especially among those without the capacity for appreciating intellectual gifts of so high an order." And Brinkley outlined both his strengths and his weaknesses. He talked of the "terrible affliction" caused by gout; he called House "the most brilliant writer ever connected with journalism in the Far East"; he described his "intemperance"; and he recalled House's love of the motto, "they are slaves who would not be, in the right with two or three." The comment that probably would have touched House most was Brinkley's conclusion at Aoyama: "Let it be remembered that he was Japan's pioneer friend, and that he fought her battles in the time when opponents were numerous and allies few."[20]

NOTES

1. One of Koto's personal axioms; Kuroda Hatsuko, *Ikiiki kyūjū sai no seikatsu jutsu*, 103.

2. House arrived on October 22. His comments on the return to Tokyo are in House to Edmund Clarence Stedman, November 25 and December 13, 1892, ECS, Columbia University; for press reports of House's return, see *Yūbin Hochi Shimbun*, October 28, 1892; "very glad," Inoue Kaoru to House, October 26, 1892, EHC, University of Virginia; LeGendre discussion, House to Ōkuma Shigenobu, December 21, 1892, OM C344, Waseda University; and gift of wheelchair, Tsuchida Mieko, "Edward H. House," 40.

3. Blacque, in Stedman to House, April 6, 30, 1896, ECS, Library of Congress; Bonsal, in House to Henry Villard, September 20, 1897, HVP, Harvard University; "nothing in the future," House to Thomas Bailey Aldrich, November 10, 1894, TBA, Harvard University; "garden of spice," Aldrich to House, November 12, 1894, TBA, Library of Congress; and "few roses," House to Aldrich, October 9 [1898], TBA, Harvard University.

4. Hints of becoming a reporter, in House to Villard, July 13, 1894, HVP, Harvard University; "fallen into stagnation," House to Villard, September 25, 1895, HVP; and "justice and truth," House to Stedman, October 23, 1894, ECS, Columbia University. Villard reported to House in a September 17, 1894, letter that his inquiries about House writing for the *Post* had been unsuccessful; see House to Villard, November 9, 1894, HVP.

5. "Americans of Asia," *Atlanta Constitution*, July 26, 1894, in Jeffrey Dorwart, *The Pigtail War*, 92; "good fellow," in Dorwart, *The Pigtail War*, 97; "out of darkness," *New York Tribune*, November 25, 1894, in Dorwart, "James Creelman, the

New York World and the Port Arthur Massacre," 699; "Secret Service," in Dorwart, *The Pigtail War,* 96; and "glory" and "gallant," House to Stedman, October 23, 1894, ECS, Columbia University.

6. The use of the houseboat is described in Tokutomi, "Hausu sensei," 124. House's relationships with Mutsu and Itō are discussed in Ōtani Tadashi, "Edowādo Hawādo Hausu senkō," 249–50; using Foreign Ministry sources, Ōtani speculates, with limited evidence, that House's relationship with Mutsu became as close as it earlier had been with Ōkuma, and that Mutsu used House, along with Brinkely, John Cockerill of the *New York Herald* (after 1895), and others to create Japan's positive image abroad. House talked about the Pyongyang article in his October 23 letter to Stedman (ECS, Columbia University); the style of that article was critiqued in *Japan Weekly Mail,* December 29, 1894, in an editorial criticizing the *World* for sensationalizing the later Japanese massacre at Port Arthur. The editorialist used the Pyongyang story as an example of the way in which the *World* reported material in the first person when the writer had not actually been on the scene.

7. "Anyone we saw," diary of Okaba Mikio, quoted in Stewart Lone, *Japan's First Modern War,* 154. Other materials here come from EHC, University of Virginia: "cable straightway," World to House, December 13, 1894; "let me thank you," R. H. Farrelly to House, December 26, 1894; Pulitzer's gift, R. H. Lyman to House, June 1, 1895; cutting Japan coverage, Lyman to House, February 26, 1896; and "if the occasion," Lyman to House, July 14, 1896. Col. Cockerill was John Cockerill of the *New York Herald.* The massacre and government public relations effort are vividly described in Donald Keene, *Emperor of Japan,* 491–96.

8. House to Henry Villard, September 26, 1895, HVP, Harvard University. The historian's evaluation is from Ebihara Hachirō, *Nihon Ōji shimbun zasshi shi,* 126.

9. Putting clothes together, in Kuroda Hatsuko, *Aji to shizen no sanpodō,* 107; recollections of doing nude sketches, from interview with Kuroda Hatsuko, May 5, 1999. It is said by some scholars that Koto probably was Japan's first woman to do Western-style oil paining, Shōwa Joshi Daigaku, "E. H. Hausu," 417.

10. The material on Koto's marriage comes from three letters from House to Villard (HVP, Harvard University): May 20, 1897, August 31, 1898, and November 20, 1898. The episode also is discussed in Stedman to House, July 29, 1897, ECS, Library of Congress, and Brinkley to House, August 27, 1898, EHC, University of Virginia.

11. The children's stories were "Bright Sides of History," *St. Nicholas For Young Folks* (November 1898–May 1899). "Ave Maria" review, *Japan Weekly Mail,* December 28, 1878; Dittrich wrote a series of letters to House from March 25, 1893, until the July 21, 1894, letter from which these quotations come, EHC, University of Virginia.

12. Three articles are from *Japan Weekly Mail:* "enthusiastic amateur" and review, March 18, 1899; brochure, April 28, 1900; "substantial beginning," June 2, 1900. *The New York Times* discussed House and the alto trombone, October 11, 1900, 6. House's letter to Sannomiya, and the contract, are in "Ōshū ongaku ky¯ oshi yatoinin roku ni," Kunaichō. "Great progress" comes directly from the jewelry box in the Kuroda home.

13. All materials come from *Japan Weekly Mail* in 1901: House's charges, April 6 and 13; attacks on House, April 20; "no case" and "perversion," May 25; and House's "ardour," June 1.

14. In *Japan Weekly Mail:* for Japanese bonds, "The Question of a Foreign Loan," November 24, 1894; gold/silver ratio, "Mixed Coins," November 21, 1896; defense of *kanji*, "The Ideograph Question," February 10, 1900; "discussion fruitless," and "Mr. House on the Romaji," March 3, 1900. For the correspondence, see Brinkley to House, February 28, 1900, EHC, University of Virginia.

15. *Japan Weekly Mail* correspondence and editorials, March 9 and 23, 1901.

16. The analysis of the need for good diplomats is in House to John Hay, February 6, 1897, EHC, University of Virginia; comments on specific people are in House to Hay, February 15, 1897, JH, Harvard University (Sill was recalled as minister a few months after House's letter); Hay's response in Hay to House, March 25, 1897, JH, Brown University; and analysis of Buck in Jack Hammersmith, *Spoilsmen in a "Flowery Fairyland,"* 210, 231. House's reaction to Buck's appointment is in House to Hay, July 25, 1897, JH, Brown University.

17. The Lowther will is discussed in T. D. Lowther to House, May 4, 1897, EHC, University of Virginia; loss of Koto's money, House to Stedman, November 25, 1896, ECS, Columbia University; "full 4 per ct.," Stedman to House, July 29, 1897, ECS, Library of Congress; "stupidity," Stedman to House, October 1, 1897, ECS, Library of Congress; panic of 1898, Stedman to House, April 1, 1898, ECS, Library of Congress; and "no exile," House to Stedman, January 23, 1901, ECS, Columbia University. The final will is discussed in George Scidmore to House, November 11 and 20, 1901, EHC.

18. Piano playing and whiskey from interview with Kuroda Masao, June 17, 1971. Patton friendship in Harold S. Williams, "Two Remarkable Australians of Old Yokohama," 65–66.

19. For Spanish-American War, see House to Villard, August 31, 1898, HVP, Harvard University; "patient friendship," Stedman to House, April 30, 1896, ECS, Library of Congress; "slopes," House to Stedman, November 25, 1896, ECS, Columbia University; Thayer's death, Stedman to House, July 29, 1896, ECS, Library of Congress; and "only solid," House to Stedman, December 11, 1896, ECS, Columbia University.

20. "Complication" and "frankness," *Kobe Weekly Chronicle,* December 24, 1901; "rarity," *Tokyo Nichi Nichi Shimbun,* December 22, 1901; funeral description comes primarily from *Japan Weekly Mail,* December 28, 1901, as well as from *Tokyo Nichi Nichi,* December 22; Tokutomi sprinkling water on House's grave, his "Hausu sensei no omoide," 125; and "maintained his positions," *Osaka Asahi Shimbun,* December 23, 1901; and Brinkley's comments, *Japan Weekly Mail,* December 21 (and 28, for funeral), 1901. Five years after his death, a group of House's friends raised 3,500 yen to be used as an endowment at the University of Tokyo for English and music students; see *Yomiuri Shimbun,* June 27, 1906.

Epilogue

> The flower is crushed but its perfume is imperishable.
>
> —Hozumi Nobushige, at Edward House's funeral[1]

One decade and seven months remained in the Meiji era when Edward House died, a time in which the movement toward modernity reached gale force. Internationally, Japan's advance onto the continent became a rush. When Russia refused to remove its troops from Manchuria following the Boxer Rebellion of 1900, Japanese journalists and intellectuals demanded that they be pushed out. And when negotiations between the two countries stalled and Russia moved aggressively into eastern Asia during 1903—developing mining and lumber interests in Manchuria, and completing most of the Trans-Siberian Railroad—the activists warned that Russia was threatening Japan's continental buffer zone. The result was another war, many times the size, far more costly, and much more difficult than the fight with China in the 1890s. As before, the public gave overwhelming support to the campaign, sending sons off to battle with admonitions to sacrifice their lives for the emperor, cheering each press report of another victory. Even House's daughter, Koto, got involved, serving as interpreter when members of the British royal family toured the military hospitals in Manchuria.

There were no massacres in this war, but neither was there the overwhelming success of the earlier conflict. Port Arthur did not fall until January 1, 1905, eight months after the war began, and then at a cost of nearly 60,000 casualties; Mukden to the north was even more costly, with nearly one in six of Japan's 400,000 troops falling to injury or death. By the time

Japan finished the hostilities in May, with a naval victory in the straits between Kyūshū and Korea, her resources were largely exhausted. Had the war continued, Japan would have been hard-pressed to supply either troops or weapons in the quantities needed for a convincing victory. As a result, the peace treaty, negotiated by U.S. President Theodore Roosevelt at Portsmouth, New Hampshire, gave Japan control of Russia's possessions in Manchuria, along with the southern half of Sakhalin—but no indemnity and none of Russia's maritime provinces. And most of the populace back at home, unaware of just how depleted Japan's resources were and convinced that the negotiators should have secured more, responded in anger, damning a "corpselike peace."[2]

More important than the public opposition was the effect of the Russo-Japanese War on Japan's international position. If the Sino-Japanese War had thrust Japan into the imperialist game, this conflict made it an aggressive player, committed too deeply to pull back. On the one hand, the war made Japan a leader in Asia, as it never had been before. Nationalists in India, China, and Vietnam saw its victory over a Western power as a sign that Asian nations need not bow perpetually before the imperialists. On the other hand, the war changed the balance of power in the western Pacific, removing the Russian influence and leaving Japan and the United States as the only two nations capable of challenging the status quo. And the war pulled Japan more deeply into the continent. With Russia gone, Japan's influence in Korea grew, and in 1910 Japan annexed the peninsula following the assassination of Itō Hirobumi by Korean nationalists. By the 1910s, Japan also was well along toward the development of a colony in Manchuria, with an army guarding its South Manchuria Railway and hundreds of thousands of Japanese citizens working in a host of continental industries: mining, electricity, port management, railways, banking, real estate, and many more. Imperialism had become a Japanese game.

At home, Japan continued modernizing, heading simultaneously in two seemingly paradoxical directions, toward what Andrew Gordon has labeled "imperial democracy." On the democratic side, the early 1900s saw the masses move in ever greater numbers into the nation's public life. During the war itself, the socialists had published the newspaper *Heimin Shimbun* and created the country's first antiwar movement. At the end of the war, tens of thousands of citizens demonstrated, and sometimes rioted, in cities across Japan, cursing their leaders for that "corpselike peace," burning police stations, overturning streetcars, killing seventeen, and injuring more than a thousand. And by the end of the Meiji era in 1912, the urban masses, led by the intellectuals and the press, had taken to the streets at least three more times to oppose rises in taxes or streetcar fares. The years also produced increasing numbers of strikes, sixty in 1907 alone, by workers no longer willing to put up with their conditions. They created a mass press too, with individual papers' circulations passing the quarter million mark. And they gave Japan its first women's movement, heralded by the publication in 1911 of the journal *Blue Stockings,* which proclaimed in its first issue: "In the beginning, woman was the sun. She was the authentic human being. Today, woman is the moon . . . radiant only in others' light." In short, the commoners became a full-fledged part of Japan's public space in the last decade of Meiji, convinced that if they had a responsibility toward the government, it also had a responsibility toward them.[3]

Even as the populace became more involved in the civil sphere, however, it also grew more nationalistic, fueling the "imperial" side of Gordon's formula. One reason for this lay in government's attempts to restrict intellectual diversity by promoting conventional, patriotic ways of thinking. Officials did more than censor wartime news; they worked hard to stifle views and activities that might threaten the state orthodoxy. Socialists and anarchists were sent to jail or executed in the late-Meiji years; "subversive" writings were banned; textbooks were standardized after 1903; and a literary award system was created in an unsuccessful effort to co-opt novelists. The efforts to enforce stability through orthodoxy would become even more intense after the late 1920s, but anyone looking for the origins of World War II "thought control" must take seriously the years right after the Russo-Japanese War, when Prime Minister Katsura Tarō said, "Socialism is today no more than a wisp of smoke, but if it is ignored it will some day have the force of wildfire and there will be nothing to stop it." Dissent had to be made costly.

A concomitant force, patriotism, kept most people from wanting to dissent. We already have seen the rise of nationalism after the late 1880s. Now, in the waning Meiji years, it grew stronger yet, inspired by competition with Russia and the pervasive sense of superiority over the new colony, Korea. Most influential was the constant evocation—in the textbooks, in public documents, in the press, in civic ceremonies—of the emperor's role as father of the nation and the people's responsibility to give him allegiance. Recitation of the Imperial Rescript on Education became so routine and rote-like in the schools that Ōkuma worried that it had become an "empty piety" and journalist Ukita Kazutami likened it to a "sutra."[4] When the government conducted a secret (and unconstitutional) trial of a group of alleged conspirators against the emperor in 1911, very few intellectuals even whispered a complaint. And when the Meiji Emperor died the following year, millions outdid themselves in expressions of grief. Japan, personified in the imperial father, had come to undergird and define most Japanese lives.

Over time, that emperor-adoring, nationalist streak would overwhelm the democratic tendencies, as the insistence on loyalty and stability rendered more and more ideas "unacceptable." And as pluralistic expression declined in the 1920s and 1930s, so would the country's ability to keep militarism in check. At end of the Meiji era, however, both the democratic tendencies and the movement toward nationalist authoritarianism seemed virile—in balance, if in tension. The Japan that House had loved was intact, moving toward democracy and gaining respect on the world stage. The likelihood that the force of nationalistic orthodoxy might someday destroy democracy and propel Japan toward a disastrous war seemed slight enough in the early 1900s that few observers gave it any thought.

The final question to be answered by this study is what House's life tells us about Japan's modern history and about our own day. With the reader's indulgence, I will organize the answers to that question around a series of vignettes drawn from my search for the public and the private House. Since the construction of a biography is an exercise in recovery, each of the episodes relates to an act of uncovering, to a discovery of some fact or feature that once seemed beyond recapturing. And in each of those findings, I experienced an insight, either into House or into a broader facet of the past that made Japanese history fresher and more nuanced.

The first discovery came decades ago, in 1969, when I encountered House as a graduate student and decided I wanted to know him better. After pursuing a score of lines, most of them fruitless, I was told by Roy P. Basler, a meticulous, gracious archivist in the Library of Congress manuscript division, that most of House's papers were at the University of Virginia. When inquiries there produced nothing, I reported my disappointment to Basler, who cleared his throat and suggested that all libraries have things they do not know about. Perhaps, he said, I should check their Samuel Clemens collection. Reporting that conversation to a librarian at Virginia, I was told: "Gracious! There must be a hundred House items in our Clemens materials"—enough to warrant an exploratory trip. When I began to work through the collection, I found closer to 1,000 letters and documents. By luck and an archivist's perspicacity, my study had become feasible.

The question triggered by my experience in Virginia was how a person as interesting and significant as House could vanish so completely from the historical narratives—and what his absence tells us more generally about the act of retelling the past. Explanations for the silence are not hard to find. For one thing, he lacked a constituency among the kinds of people who dominated U.S. and Japanese historical writing in the twentieth century. He died without close relatives, or even contacts, in the United States. His only intimate American friends were old men, not far from the grave themselves. Partly because he had alienated some influential people, but mainly because he died and was interred in Japan, his name was lost to American opinion makers. He had friends in Japan, but Koto was not a writer, his grandchildren hardly knew him, and his prominent acquaintances had other reasons for not writing about him, as we will discuss below.

The scarcity and dispersal of documents also militated against his being remembered. As my experience illustrates, only a single Washington archivist knew of any substantial House collection thirty-five years ago, and the papers there depended for their existence on House's friendship with the more famous Mark Twain. Other papers do exist, but not in a central location. Waseda University in Tokyo holds a few, as do Japan's national archives and the Tokyo city archives. In the West, one finds rich but small holdings at the Library of Congress; the British Library; the University of California; and Oxford, Brown, Columbia, Rutgers, and Harvard Universities, among other places. But the materials are scattered across forty libraries worldwide, from London to Oxford, Tokyo to Taipei, Boston to Princeton. Only by digging, traveling, and spending considerable sums of money could his life be reconstructed.

Even more problematic is the fact that House defied most standard narrative categories. Does he belong primarily to political history, or to literary studies, or to music? And where does he belong geographically? As a purveyor of views and influencer of policies, he should be the property of American history. But American historians have not spent much time on the news media or on people who shaped our ways of looking at the outside world. On the other hand, House's crusades ought to have given him a central place in the Japanese narrative. But in Japan too he has tended to fall outside the standard historical categories. He was an English-speaking foreigner; his advice to the government was informal and largely secret; and his role as a publicist was something of an embarrassment. When it came to telling the era's story, he was easier to forget than to mention, particularly since the paucity of sources made the recovery of his life difficult.

So what does this tell us about the way we construct historical narratives? It takes no great insight to observe that the traditional approach to history has been narrow. Until recently, subjects were noteworthy only if they were connected to politics or economics—or to some facet of the *big* and public picture. Women, workers, children, musicians, gays, journalists, teachers, physicians, and farmers, to name only a few, counted only when their stories had something to tell us about the public political life. So too with those whose activities crossed the geographical boundaries that professional historians have so long used to organize their work. Topics and people who did not fit into a standard geographical or political category had no narrator—and so were ignored. Politically oriented, elite white men of the imperialist nations shaped the narratives, and those who, like House, attempted Asian-oriented revisions of the common wisdom, or those who worked across borders, were typically seen as peripheral, insignificant, or extremist.

On the other hand, it is hardly surprising that people of House's ilk should begin to attract interest in a time when the old historical approaches have come under attack from the advocates of subaltern studies, of feminist theory, of neocolonialist analyses—a time when scholars like James Scott remind us that the "public transcript" rarely tells "the whole story about power relations" and often is "positively misleading." Ironically, House gave his career to creating public transcripts. Indeed, he was relatively insensitive to what Scott calls the "hidden transcripts" of non-elites. But it was the elite propensity nonetheless for defining the "public" narrowly, for creating stories that privileged the Western, the official, and the rich—or, as Benedict Anderson has it, the "imagined community" of nation—that eventually left people like House out. Edward Said has helped us to see that Western narrative builders for the last two centuries have essentialized and trivialized things Asian, that "European culture gained in strength and identity by setting itself off against the Orient." To the degree that people like House fought that stereotyping, to the degree that they struggled to make the Japanese positive, complex, fully human beings, they rendered themselves, in their own day at least, peripheral.[5]

My second moment of recovery evoked paradoxical emotions. It was April 22, 1999, a brilliant day in Tokyo when I was at the Foreign Ministry archives, well along in my research. My purpose was to learn what I could about House's formal relationship with the Japanese government. I had read the Yokohama papers' denunciations of him as a paid hack; I had looked at comments by Frank Brinkley and other friends that he received official assistance. But I needed something concrete, something primary. Was House paid for his writing? Was there a quid pro quo? Was there some vague, undocumented sort of arrangement? I was not prepared for my own reaction when I found the 1882 documents, marked "secret" but now freely available, promising him a government allowance. I would discover similar documents later, for other periods, but this was my first hard evidence of a formal agreement. For a moment, I was thrilled. Conjecture was confirmed. Then, almost immediately, I was distressed; House had lost his purity. While there were only accusations, I still could pretend to myself that he was an untainted prophet. Now he was human, more complex. I would have to explain the complexity, to myself as well as to my readers.

Over time, House's complexity became compelling to me; he became more interesting, as he became more human, as he forced me to deal with the fact that no historical character is pure. Like us, the women and men about whom we write are a mixture of good, bad, and indifferent, a collection of nuances. And House's nuances were multitudinous. He demanded full personhood for women, yet threw a verbal tantrum when Koto insisted on independence in choosing a spouse. He crusaded for Japan to be treated equally by the imperialist powers, but said little when it imposed itself on Taiwan, Korea, and China. He was appalled by the vicious rhetoric of the Yokohama journalists, yet claiming he had no choice, retorted with language just as vile. He despised Christianity, but his favorite works included *Ave Maria* and Handel's *Messiah*. He would have had explanations for each inconsistency, but the explanations would have rested in the nuances, and that is the point. The lives of people are filled with paradoxes and contradictions. To pretend otherwise is to do just that, pretend.

Perhaps the most insistent of House's paradoxes was the one that sent me to the Foreign Ministry, his financial relationship with the people whose cause he championed. House's experiences here raised three questions for me. First, did the money affect or influence him? A short answer would be, "Of course it did." There were times, early in his life, that he needed those funds to survive. Without them, he could not have published the *Tokio Times;* nor could he have afforded the time to crusade so insistently. A sense of responsibility to his benefactors surely made him more active in Japan's behalf at times. And as he grew used to supporting its official position, he grew less inclined to criticize its failures—its suppression of popular rights, for example, or its troops' horrific behavior at Port Arthur. But my second question illustrates how nuanced the issue is: Did the money change House's underlying viewpoints? I am convinced that it did not. His views were consistent across the decades; as he wrote himself at the *Tokio Times,* "an unchanging front through half a dozen years of tolerably active controversy counts for something."[6] He praised Japan and fought for her acceptance long before he received financial support. The primary influence of the money was to give him a platform, to provide him with the means to espouse views that he already held, without having to worry about putting food on the table. And to the end, he criticized Japanese policies and people when he felt so disposed.

The third question is whether the financial support undermined House's effectiveness. Here, the answer is mixed. It certainly gave his enemies ammunition; it could not help but raise suspicions about his motives, even for those who were neutral. After all, the Japanese government gained more than it gave. The return of the Shimonoseki indemnity alone brought Japan more than twelve times the total of what House was paid across a lifetime. And the material benefits were the least of what the Japanese government received. But the other side of the issue is highlighted by the fact that House seems never to have questioned his decision to go on the Japanese payroll. He believed in the causes he espoused, and had no means to espouse them without remuneration. Such arrangements were more widely accepted in that era than they are now. Except when he traveled to Washington, London, and Paris in 1880–1881, he never hid the fact of his support, and even then his motives were quite open. Thus, while the government funds made him a target, he would not have been around to attack without them.

It was not money alone that illustrated House's complexity; so did his responses to imperialism. At the self-conscious level he fought that system mightily, publishing attacks not just on the results but on the *morality* of powerful nations subjugating less developed countries. He criticized the "free trade system" as vociferously as twenty-first century activists do globalization, arguing that the British, for whom "free trade" held the force of belief, controlled the world structures so completely as to deprive newcomer nations of a fair chance. Free trade rendered the powerful nations alone free: free to gouge and squeeze the newcomers and the yet undeveloped. House also argued that the right to set one's own tariff rates and to hold expatriates accountable to one's domestic judicial system were matters of sovereignty; unless circumstances genuinely were exceptional, all nations merited these rights. And he insisted that might did not make right. The fact that he (and several others) argued these positions so forcefully draws attention to the fact that support for imperialism was neither universal nor simplistic, even among colonial officials and foreigners profiting from the international system.

At the same time, House was more of an imperialist than he would have admitted to himself. He spoke in hierarchical terms; early on, he thought the Japanese bright but backward; he proclaimed American superiority in almost all things. And while he fought hard to help Americans see the Japanese as fully fledged, complicated fellow human beings, his novels and stories about Japanese women, for example, were filled with stereotypical (albeit lovely) characters worthy of Said's orientalist marketplace, and his portraits of Chinese and Koreans epitomized imperialist condescension. Perhaps even more troubling was his blindness to many forms of imperialism: to the way in which Japan imposed itself on the Ryūkyū Islands, then on southern Taiwan, and later on Korea and China, or to the way the Meiji government treated its own people, enforcing new systems and demanding ever heavier burdens—all without giving the vast majority of the people any voice. When it came to imperialism as a *system*, or to Japan's mistreatment in that system, he was forceful, but his blind spots were numerous regarding many of the system's preconceptions, and the sites that he knew less well.

Does this inconsistency say that House was insincere? Hardly. That he was full of logical inconsistencies? Certainly. But the inconsistencies indicate only that he was human, that all people, even prophets, live within their times, that language and perspectives are imprisoned by milieu. Not even the visionary can escape the thought and discourse frameworks of an era. While House crusaded for values more noble than those that dominated his age, he was capable of seeing only part of the inequities. He focused so intently on Japan's mistreatment, and accepted so unconsciously the Western-oriented, statist assumptions of his era, that he was unable to perceive the way Japan's rulers adopted those assumptions and, in the process, colonialized their own, and other, people. The fact that House was unable to rise above his times may not excuse his comfort with many forms of injustice; neither does it abrogate the visionary quality of his calls for justice.

No experience thrilled me more, during the years of reconstructing House's life, than the afternoon I spent with Kuroda Hatsuko, the ninety-five-year-old widow of House's grandson. I had dreamed for years of meeting her—if she were alive. Once, in 1971, I had made a brief contact with her husband, Masao, but then had lost touch and repeated efforts to locate the family had born no fruit. Then on a chilly February afternoon in 1999, my son James and I found the spot by the castle moat where House's last home had stood. The present owner invited us into her small apartment atop an eleven-story office building, and said that her family had bought the property from the Kurodas decades ago but that she had no idea what had become of them. James and I gave her our cards and left, disappointed. The very next night she called; she had located Hatsuko, who invited me to her home.

We talked in the living room of the house to which Koto and Takuma had moved when they left the moat-side home, a remarkable room designed to invoke the Palace of Versailles. On one wall hung one of Koto's paintings, a pair of half-shucked ears of corn. On the table was the jewelry box that the empress had given to House. Around us were the wines and utensils that Hatsuko had used in a seventy-year career as a cooking teacher. She was frail, but her mind was as lively, her personality as feisty as House's when he entertained in his wheelchair. She knew almost nothing about the journalistic life of her husband's grandfather; what she did know was that he had been a writer and a man of music, honored by the empress, and that Koto was a remarkable mother-in-law. Hatsuko, I found, was quite a remarkable woman herself. As her own daughter-in-law, Kuroda Mitsuko, told me, she had been Japan's first woman mountain climber, and at ninety-five, she still taught six cooking classes a month. She had published two books in the past six years.

The point that became abundantly clear during that afternoon with the Kuroda women was that House left a powerful human legacy. The pride with which Hatsuko talked of her in-laws would have made the old man smile. Koto never had the public life that House did; that would have been nearly impossible in Tokyo of the early twentieth century. But she moved in the city's influential circles and remained the indomitable personality who had run House's home, translated his English, and made decisions according to her own inner lights. She gave herself, after House's death, to the arts and to creating a cultured home for Takuma and two sons, Masao and Shizuo. She continued to paint and to perform the tea ceremony, became an expert in kabuki, and, when she was seventy, took kimono making lessons. She was well known for her strong opinions about proper colors. Hatsuko tells of Koto snickering that her daughter-in-law "looked like a country girl" once when she wore "deep red artificial flowers on a white evening dress," then "taking a violet and green pansy brooch from her own jewelry box and pinning it to my chest with a satisfied chuckle: 'There, that's just right.'"

When Koto was not rearing children or practicing the arts, she was entertaining. She hated cooking herself, but set a sumptuous table. At 3:30 each afternoon, she would gather the family for tea and candies. If friends stopped by at dinner time, she invited them to stay. And they came often, said Hatsuko, "knowing about our delicious food and lively atmosphere." A family favorite was strawberries in sweetened wine, poured over white bread; another was Boston baked beans, the only dish that Koto would make herself. Once, Hatsuko said, Koto had her prepare dozens of sandwiches for the next day's dinner party, demanding that they be kept perfectly fresh even though the house had neither refrigeration nor an airtight storage facility. Hatsuko also recalled how Koto encouraged (and practiced) a brand of individualism that startled some friends. Asked to interpret for the British royals during the Russo-Japanese War, she left her preadolescent boys at home and headed to Manchuria. Years later, when Masao wanted his wife to climb mountains with him, Koto advised her to forget custom and join him. "It is fine for you to go anywhere with Masao," she would say. "Just be sure you come back safely." Koto's circle of acquaintances included the country's leading news makers, and she was a board member of the Women's Patriotic Society (Aikoku Fujinkai), which included Japan's most prominent citizens. Even in her last years, when she was often sick, she stayed informed. "Whenever you entered her room," said Hatsuko, "whether she was in the hospital or not, she would reach out for a handshake and ask, 'What's the news?'"[7] Her death came on August 8, 1939, following eight years of illness, when she was eighty (she hated the number eight!), just as World War II was breaking out in Europe and Japan's army was getting bogged down in China.

One of my most important moments of recovery was also one of the briefest—and one of the most disconcerting. It occurred as I walked down State Street in Ann Arbor, late in the winter of 1969, after I had finished my first research paper on House. I had just presented the paper to a graduate seminar taught by my mentor, Roger Hackett, and as I walked home, one of my classmates commented: "House is really interesting, but so what? Did he matter?" I was haunted by that question for years. Now I am puzzled that I was so haunted. Now I have a chance to answer my friend. Yes, he mattered.

House mattered for the contributions he made, and he mattered for the issues his life illustrated. The former is easier to describe, though arguably less important. As a young member of Horace Greeley's stable of brilliant *New York Tribune* writers, he helped to shape U.S. images of the zealot John Brown and introduced the first Japanese visitors to U.S. readers; he also played a pivotal role in sending Mark Twain's national career into orbit (and he gave us that *Prince and the Pauper* footnote!). During his early years in Tokyo, he was among the most important of what one scholar has labeled the "teachers of the American public," helping his fellow countrymen form positive views of Japan with articles that challenged the strange-inferior-Oriental narrative. In this regard, Japan's early image as an advocate of justice resulted in part from his accounts of the *Maria Luz* episode, and his book on Japan's 1874 expedition to Taiwan still shapes the standard narrative of that episode. Within Japan itself, House was a pioneer in the development of Western orchestral music and sent his students off into a stunning array of public posts. And in his most important role, as crusader, he more than anyone else induced Congress to return the Shimonoseki indemnity to Japan and articulated, like no other writer in English, the case against the unequal treaties. Foreign Minister Mutsu Munemitsu called House the "one who laid the groundwork" for treaty revision, "the one we should call the grand old champion."[8]

Important as these contributions are, House's life is even more significant for the historical issues it raises about the nineteenth and twentieth centuries. There are, of course, many such issues: the role of women in Japanese society, the quality of Western diplomacy in Asia, the relationship between diplomacy and a country's commercial interests, the role of music in Japan's national development, the influence of missionaries. For reasons of space, we will focus here on two matters: the role of image in shaping relations between nations, and the massive topic of imperialism, both its workings in Asia during House's time and its implications in the longer term.

Image. The threat to Japan's existence as an autonomous entity in the mid-1800s had little to do with image. The menacing black ships that sailed uninvited into its harbors were real, as were the treaties that deprived it of judicial and commercial sovereignty. Just as real, but more surprising, was the early leaders' understanding of the fact that success with foreigners depended almost as much on what the imperialist powers thought of Japan as on the country's actual policies. The American advisor Charles LeGendre may have constructed cogent arguments for government support of a friendly newspaper in the mid-1870s, but he was arguing points the Japanese already had made to each other. Restoration leader Shinagawa Yajirō had written to the powerful councilor Kido Takahashi in 1871 about the "indispensability of the newspaper" in governing a people. And almost from its inception, the Meiji government had issued laws intended to shape the images held by its various constituencies, to make sure, as an 1869 ordinance put it, that writers said only things that "are not harmful to society."[9] Nor did the officials stop with suppressing negative images. Equally concerned about disseminating positive pictures of the government, they purchased copies early on of the most prestigious newspapers for distribution in the provinces and subsidized those papers whose voices they wanted the public to hear. And to shape foreign understandings, they helped W. G. Howell to distribute his *Japan Mail* abroad and paid House so that he could publish the *Tokio Times* without financial worry. Lest anyone should doubt whether they were intentional in what they did, the 1889 letter extending House's annual allowance explained that he was being paid partly "in appreciation of your past services towards Japan" and partly in the expectation that he would "promote the interests of Japan whenever a suitable opportunity presents itself."[10]

Making this image consciousness pertinent to our discussion of historical issues is the fact that the Japanese continue into the twenty-first century to be among the world's most effective people at influencing policies by winning friends. Over the last several decades, the Japanese have engaged in a host of sophisticated programs designed in part to influence worldwide impressions of Japan. The Japan Foundation supports a plethora of Japan-related programs around the globe: scholarly exchange, research, the expansion of library holdings, traveling art exhibits. The JET program brings thousands of young people from English-speaking countries to Japan each year to assist in the teaching of English. People-to-people and sister-city relationships abound, as do private programs of all sorts. Japanese officials are little different from astute opinion makers elsewhere in recognizing what an important role image plays in international politics. Where they stand apart is in the quickness with which the Meiji leaders recognized this truth.

So how should one react to these image-making efforts—of which House was a pioneer? A frequent response is simply to decry them as shallow and dishonest. Unfortunately, whether they are that or not, such a response helps us little. Image is a part of reality; the effort to manage it is ubiquitous, even among the "purest" of analysts. And scholars have a problem much like the one House had: without funding from interested sources such as the Japan Foundation, much of the basic research on Japan never could be carried out.[11] Another common response is to engage in denial: either to ignore the question of whether funding has an impact on one's work or to claim to be so honest as to be beyond influence. The trouble with that approach is that, like denial of all forms, it is intellectually lazy. To deny one's susceptibility is to become a collaborator with the donor. What is needed among those who care about truth and scholarship is vigilance about the image-making, or narrative-creating, process. Those who write about Japan must ask certain questions repeatedly: Are there strings attached to grants that underwrite my research? Are there safeguards to ensure that I am not beholden to the benefactor? Do my conclusions bear rigorous scrutiny? And, of particular importance, do I openly disclose the sources of support that I receive? House's failure on several of these left him open to attacks by his rivals, even though his personal integrity provided a relatively firm safeguard against distortion. Like House, however, we are more effective when we insist on rigorous reflection than when we simply claim purity.

Imperialism. Nothing inspired a greater portion of House's work than the imperialist system. Imperialism impelled the Japanese government to send its first embassy abroad, and that embassy brought House into contact with the country that would give shape to his life. Imperialism provided the impetus for Japan's 1874 military mission to Taiwan, which clinched House's liaison with Ōkuma and the Japanese government. Imperialism also provided the grist of fully half of his writings about Japan. At the *Tokio Times,* he described imperialism as a "reprehensible course" and ran a piece saying the powers "maintain their conduct not by reason or moral principle, but depend on force."[12] Even the Christianity about which House wrote so bitterly came to Japan as part of the imperialist package. And Japan's own imperialist adventures onto the Asian mainland in 1894 became the source of his last fling at reporting. House may not have ever noticed the fact that the system he hated so much gave him a career. But it did, highlighting in the process many of the most important human issues with which any student of House's life, or of the nineteenth and twentieth centuries more generally, must grapple. We would be remiss to end a study of Edward House without looking briefly at a few of them.

1. *Inescapability.* We have seen, again and again, that it was impossible for House to escape the values of the male, Western-dominated system in which he grew to maturity. Similarly, his career suggests that it also was impossible for any nation to avoid the effects of the imperialist storms that swept Asia and Africa in the 1800s. A combination of happy circumstances, including geographical isolation, outstanding leadership, and a good deal of luck, kept Japan from being colonized, but the alternatives to colonization bore their own massive consequences. First, there was the forced entry. The Tokugawa officials used great cunning in dealing with the American, then Russian and British intruders in the 1850s, but in the end, the Western coming amounted to an invasion. And in its aftermath, no amount of vision and skill could have prevented Japan from being shaken to the core. Second came the loss of sovereignty. While House's view of the unequal treaties may have scandalized his contemporaries, it is hard to dispute today. Japan was deprived for decades of the right either to set its own tariff rates or to try foreigners accused of crime in its own courts. Third came the unnaturally rapid changes, propelled by the need to save the state and restore sovereignty. The wholesale destruction of old systems and creation of expensive new institutions, pushing large segments of the populations into economic misery, may have had salutary

results in the long term, but no fair accounting can dismiss the fact that they were monumentally disruptive—and inescapable. Fourth came Japan's own move toward imperialism, a move that resulted from both the need to defend itself against the West and the increasing conviction that no nation could be strong without colonies. To argue that each of these successive steps was inevitable is to argue the unprovable. To imagine scenarios, on the other hand, by which Japan could have avoided any of them, given the options presented by the imperialist system, is difficult indeed.

2. *Confronting the Challenge.* None of this should suggest that the Meiji experience with imperialism was wholly negative; far from it. Indeed, a second issue to be pondered is what lessons the Japanese response has to offer other nations in the midst of transformation. Many factors account for Meiji Japan's ability to modernize so rapidly. Even before the Restoration, the nation already was among the world's most highly developed countries in terms of literacy rates, urbanization, national integration, and political sophistication. In other words, the foundations for transformation were well laid. The nature of the Meiji leadership also played a crucial role. Few eras in Japanese history, or perhaps in the history of any country, have produced a more visionary or competent group of leaders than Japan did in the 1870s. These were the men whom House repeatedly declared to be at least the equals of their counterparts in the West. The leaders were not always unified; they fought over policies and power; some of them fomented rebellion. But taken as a whole, they provided the vision and the governing acumen that set this era apart from others. Then there were the policies that these men adopted. They unified the country administratively; they erased the old status system and eradicated the financially and spiritually burdensome samurai class; they created modern military and educational systems, along with an economic structure that has served as a model for contemporary times. And they threw great energy into creating a loyal people, by creating symbols and structures that would make even mountain villagers think of themselves as Japanese. The results of all of this were mixed, as we have seen, but compared to the experiences of other Asian and African countries subjected to imperialism, the picture looked grand at the time of House's death. If the total pattern was too complex to be replicated, it at least held options and ideas worthy of study by countries throughout the world.

3. *Unforeseen Consequences.* The last issue raised by House's engagement with imperialism, as it operated in Japan, has to do with seeds, with the unforeseen consequences that sprang from the system. One reason that the complex results of imperialism were not studied much until recent

decades is that the scribes of the imperialist nations have written the mainstream narratives. Another is that it has taken generations for many of the less direct results to become clear. Opacity has not, however, made those results less significant. Indeed, as the twenty-first century began, the havoc wreaked by imperialism continued to show itself around the globe, in more ways than most people dared imagine (or still want to believe). And Japan's own experience gave dramatic evidence to the ongoing impact of imperialist actions and ideas.

At home in Japan, we have seen how the concern about standing strong internationally served as justification for harsh treatment of Japanese citizens, how the interests of the state invariably took precedence over those of individuals or groups. That meant allowing girls to be mistreated in silk factories, so that Japan could compete with the industries of Europe. It entailed financial policies under Matsukata Masayoshi that pushed farmers into poverty, even into starvation in some cases. It meant suppressing freedoms and restricting suffrage in the name of national stability. Even a man like House, underdog champion that he considered himself to be, would overlook all of this, because he thought Japan had to win a place in the international system before it worried about justice at home; otherwise it would be devoured. As he wrote after the 1887 peace preservation law, "The occurrences . . . were in truth simple and necessary steps for the preservation of social order." That the measures had a draconian side, he tended to ignore, so convinced had he become that Japan must maintain tranquility in the face of the imperialist threat.[13] Few commentators at the time tied domestic statism directly to imperialism. But that is the point. The need to put national strength first in order to gain respect in an imperialist order gave Japan's rulers the justification they needed to ignore the interests of their own commoners.

Imperialism also justified Japan's development of a hierarchical view of the world. Certainly, the British and the Americans saw the world in hierarchical terms; indeed, they employed a whole vocabulary to justify that view: white man's burden, Oriental despotism, civilization, Christianizing the savages, exotic East. They also brought with them the ideology of social Darwinism, arguing that only those nations strong enough to devour weaker states would survive. The Japanese in response accepted both the social Darwinist view and the hierarchical standards that went with it. By the 1940s, this sense of hierarchy would lead to a desire "to establish permanent domination over all other races and peoples in Asia . . . as befitted their destiny as a superior race."[14] It was not quite that expansive, or arrogant, during the Meiji years, but it was then, in response to the threat and ideology of imperialism, that the hierarchical view took firm hold. It was then that the Japanese changed their appellation for

China from Chūgoku (Middle Country, which the Chinese called themselves) to Shina, a patronizing appropriation of the European word for China, and it was then that Fukuzawa Yukichi began calling for Japan to "cast off" Asia and become a European power. House had few misgivings about this typology. Indeed, he reaffirmed it when he said that "while China possesses the wealth of Asia, Japan has the brains."[15] He too (we repeat) had imbibed much of the ideology of his day. And he hardly could have conceived of how far that hierarchical sense would lead Japan in decades to come.

Perhaps the most unexpected result of imperialism, from the vantage point of Tokugawa Keiki or Matthew Perry, would have been the idea that Japan might become a colony *holder* and that its drive for power and respect would lead to prolonged war with the major colonial powers. It is simplistic to argue that Japan's march toward World War II was inevitable once it was forced by the United States to open its doors. In every era, different choices could have been made, with different consequences. But it is equally simplistic to deny a connection between Japan's experience as the victim of imperialism and its later role as a colonizer in its own right. It may not have been in the minds of Perry, or the British minister Harry Parkes, but the choice they gave Japan during the middle part of the century was to seek modernity or be devastated. The choice to survive necessitated becoming strong militarily as well as economically and politically, and the mainstream ideology of the day not only accepted but demanded aggressive military policies of the sort envisioned by Yamagata Aritomo and Katsura Tarō. When three of the powers pressured Japan in 1895 to return some of the territory that it had won in the Sino-Japanese War, opinion leaders and officials alike were convinced that the imperialist club was applying different rules to the new Asian member than to its charter members. So they vowed never again to be caught with a military that was not strong enough to fend off all challengers. As we have seen, the vast majority of Japanese had concluded by the time that House died in 1901 that colony-seeking was the only viable option in a world dominated by imperialism. And from that point, the march toward the tragic choices of the 1930s was inexorable, even if not inevitable.

The twenty-first-century world grapples still with the unforeseen consequences of imperialism, in the endless struggles over massive income inequities, in the instability of regions where colonial regimes nurtured sycophants and self-serving tyrants rather than enlightened leaders, in the post–September 11 struggle against terrorism, in angry struggles over globalization. Like Japan's own movement from seemingly glorious modernity in the nineteenth century to authoritarianism and chauvinism in the first half of the 1900s, those struggles highlight the fact that injustice creates troubles for its perpetrators as well as for its victims, even though the perpetrators' difficulties may come generations later, too late for most people to recognize the connection between early injustice and later conflicts. Put differently, repayment for historical, systemic injustice may take longer to occur than it does in individual situations, but for nations as well as for individuals, one's sins will find one out. The Nobel Prize–winning economist Amartya Sen argues that "virtually all the problems in the world come from inequality of one kind or another." When House worried in the 1870s about the problems imperialism was creating for Japan, he also should have been worrying about the difficulties Japan's *response* to imperialism would create for the imperialist nations themselves decades later.[16]

It was Saturday afternoon, February 20, 1999. Accompanied by my son James and my nephew Jeff, I was out to visit House's final resting place at Dairyūji in northern Tokyo. I had a sense of the location, but no address. Our first attempt landed us at the wrong train station, but with help from the police we found the spacious temple on our second try. The sign outside said the cemetery held the remains of the famed haiku poet Masaoka Shiki and the American journalist Edward H. House. Finding the marker itself took more searching still. It stood in a 440-square-foot, untended plot near the rear of the large cemetery, suggesting a life once revered but now forgotten. The stone was imposing: tall, beautifully inscribed with Koto's remembrances, overlooking the playground of an elementary school that House would have loved. But it was begrimed and lonely, having known more of pigeons than of people for many years now. We borrowed brooms and water from the temple to wash away the birds' droppings and sweep the earth around the marker. Then we went to a local shop and bought yellow chrysanthemums to put at the foot of the stone. And finally, after taking pictures and pausing for reflection, we walked a few blocks to a coffee shop, where we talked quietly about why a man of House's importance had been thus forgotten—and why the afternoon's activities had left each of us with such a sense that his spirit still spoke.

NOTES

1. *Japan Weekly Mail*, December 28, 1901.
2. *Osaka Mainichi Shimbun*, September 1, 1905.
3. For a discussion of "imperial democracy," see Andrew Gordon, *Labor and Imperial Democracy in Prewar Japan*, 1–10; "in the beginning," *Seitō* (*Blue Stockings*) (September 1911), in Shimura Akiko, "Meiji ki no josei jiyānarizumu," 667. I have discussed this growth of mass political consciousness more fully in Huffman, *Creating a Public*, 310–80.
4. Katsura's fears are in Kenneth Pyle, "The Emergence of Bureaucratic Conservatism in the Meiji Era," 26–27; and Ōkuma and Ukita are quoted in Carol Gluck, *Japan's Modern Myths*, 154.

5. "Public transcript," in James C. Scott, *Domination and the Arts of Resistance,* 2–3; and "European culture," Edward Said, *Orientalism,* 3.

6. *Tokio Times,* July 6, 1878.

7. The material on Koto is gleaned from my conversation with her daughter-in-law, Kuroda Hatsuko, May 5, 1999, and from Kuroda's books: *Aji to shizen no sanpodō* ("deep red," 107; "what's news,"109) and *Ikiiki kyūjūsai no seikatsu jutsu* ("delicious food," 101; "It is fine," 102). Kuroda died, at age 99, in 2002.

8. For "teachers," see Joseph M. Henning, *Outposts of Civlization,* 67; and for "groundwork," Ebihara Hachirō, *Nihon Ōji shimbun zasshi shi,* 128.

9. Shinagawa is quoted in Ryusaku Tsunoda et al., *Sources of Japanese Tradition,* vol. 2, 146. The 1869 law is in Midoro Masaichi, *Meiji Taishō shi: genron hen,* 373.

10. "Beikokujin 'Hausu' e nenkin oyobi teate kane kyūyo ikken," January 24, 1889, in Gaimushō gaikōshiryōkan, Tokyo.

11. One of my own previous research projects was supported in part by a grant from the government-funded Japan Foundation, and a paper that I presented on this study was given at the Midwest Japan Seminar, which also receives support from the Japan Foundation.

12. See *Tokio Times,* January 5, 1873 ("reprehensible"), and February 24, 1877 ("maintain their conduct").

13. February 16, 1888, letter by House to the *Evening Post,* in *Baba Tatsui zenshū,* 269.

14. John Dower, *War without Mercy,* 264.

15. House to John Hay, February 6, 1897, EHC, University of Virginia.

16. Quoted in David Barsamian, "The Progressive Interview: Amartya Sen," *The Progressive* (August 2001): 36.

Bibliography

Note: Japanese-language books are published in Tokyo unless otherwise indicated.

MANUSCRIPT AND DOCUMENT COLLECTIONS

British Library, London: Papers of Charles Dickens and William Ewart Gladstone

Brown University Library: John Hay Collection

University of California, The Bancroft Library: The Mark Twain Papers

Columbia University, Rare Books and Manuscript Library: Edmund Clarence Stedman Collection

Dokuritsu Gyōsei Hōjin Kokuritsu Kōbunshokan (Administratively Independent National Archives), Tokyo: Yakukō shūsei (Compilations of translated manuscripts), three series; Honyaku shūsei (Compilation of translations), nine volumes

Folger Shakespeare Library: Augustin Daly Papers

Gaimushō Gaikōshiryōkan (Diplomatic records of the Foreign Ministry), Tokyo: *"Beikokujin 'Hausu' e nenkin oyobi teate kane kyūyo ikken"* (An item on a pension and other monetary compensation to the American "House"); *Bunkyū sannen Shimonoseki ni okeru gaikoku gunkan hōgeki jiken ni kansuru shōkin Beikoku yori henkan kankei zassan* (Miscellaneous materials on the United States' return of the indemnity from Shimonoseki's bombardment of foreign warships in Shimonoseki in 1863); *Dainihon gaikō monjo* (Japan's diplomatic archives) 5 (1872); *Gaikokujin jokun zakken: Beikoku no bu* (Miscellaneous records of decorated foreigners: America); *Jōyaku misai Perokokufū hansen Mariya Rūtsugo Shinkoku kaimin rantai Yokohama e nyūkō ni tsuki shochi ikken* (A record of the handling of the Chinese coolies from the vessel *Maria Luz* of Peru, with which Japan had no treaty, when they entered Yokohama Harbor), 7 vols.; and *Kyōiku kankei zakken* (Miscellaneous records regarding education).

Harvard University, Houghton Library: Papers of Thomas Bailey Aldrich, William Warland Clapp, John Hay, Mark Antony DeWolfe Howe, and Henry Villard

Kunaicho Shoryōbu (Imperial Household Ministry Archives): *Ōshū ongaku kyōshi yatoinin roku ni,* Meiji 33–Taishō 14 (Records of Europeans employed to teach music, no. 2: 1900–1925)

Library of Congress, Manuscript Division: Papers of Thomas Bailey Aldrich, John Brown, James A. Garfield, Ulysses S. Grant, Horace Greeley, Townsend Harris, John Hay, Charles LeGendre, Charles Reade, Whitelaw Reid, Edmund Clarence Stedman, Benjamin Holt Ticknor, and John Russell Young, including "The Diaries of John Russell Young"

The London Library: Charles E. Reade Collection

Massachusetts Death Index, 1841–1895

National Diet Library, Tokyo: *Mutsu Munemitsu kankei monjo* (Archives related to Mutsu Munemitsu)

Oxford University, Bodleian Library: Benjamin Disraeli Papers, Earl of Kimberly (John Wodehouse) Papers, Manuscripts: English—Miscellaneous, Manuscripts: English Letters

Oxford University, Rhodes House Library: Papers of Sir John Pope-Hennessy

Peabody Essex Museum, Salem, Massachusetts, Phillips Library: Edward S. Morse Collection

Population Schedule of the Seventh Census of the United States, 1850: Massachusetts, Norfolk County, Washington D.C.: National Archives; Records Service, General Services Administration, 1963

Princeton University Library: Charles R. Reade Collection

Public Record Office, United Kingdom: Chancery Proceedings, Foreign Office Records

Rutgers University Library, Special Collections and University Archives: William Elliot Griffis Collection

The Theatre Museum, London: Dion Boucicault Papers, Princess's Theatre Collection, St. James's Theatre Collection

Tokyo-tō Kōbun Shokan (Public Archives of the City of Tokyo): *Fuka kyojū kakokujin meisaihyō* (Detailed register of city residents by nationality); *Gakuji nenpō* (Yearbook of educational matters), 1882, 1883; *Shiritsu kakushū gakkō shorui* (Documents on each type of private school), 1882; *Shiritsu shōgakkō kyōin shorui* (Documents on officials at private elementary schools), 1884; and *Shiritsu shōgakkō shorui* (Documents on private elementary schools), 1884, 1885

U.S. Department of State: Despatches from United States Ministers to Japan, 1869–1901: RG 59, National Archives, microfilm

University of Virginia, Clifton Waller Barrett Library: Collections of Samuel Langhorne Clemens (The Edward House Collection), James Russell Lowell, and Lafcadio Hearn

Waseda University: *Ōkuma monjo* (archives of Ōkuma Shigenobu)

Yale University Library: Charles A. Dana Family Collection, Knollenberg Collection, and Piatt Family Collection

UNPUBLISHED MANUSCRIPTS

Chang Lung-chih. "To Open up the Mountains and Pacify the Savages—The 1874 Mudanshe Incident and the Transformation of Qing Frontier Discourse in Taiwan." Cambridge, Mass.: Harvard University, 2000.

Clemens, Samuel Langhorne. "Concerning the Scoundrel Edward H. House." Berkeley: Bancroft Library, University of California, 1890.

Clemens, S. L., and E. H. House. "The Prince and the Pauper: A Romantic Drama of the Sixteenth Century." Washington, D.C.: Library of Congress, 1889.

Griffis, William Elliot. "Class Register Kaisei Gakkō." New Brunswick, N.J.: Griffis collection, Rutgers University, 1871.

———. "Four American Makers of Japan." New Brunswick, N.J.: Griffis Collection, Rutgers University, n.d.

———. "Japan's Foreign Helpers." New Brunswick, N.J.: Griffis Collection, Rutgers University, n.d.

———. "Student's Names, Kai Sei Gakko." New Brunswick, N.J.: Griffis Collection, Rutgers University, 1874.

House, Edward H. "The Japanese Soldier." Washington, D.C.: Benjamin Holt Ticknor Papers, Library of Congress.

———. "Nihon shi naka no ippen Kagoshima jiken" (An episode in Japanese history: The Kagoshima incident). Ōkuma monjo, Waseda University, April 1875.

———. "Shimonoseki shōkin ikken" (The Shimonoseki indemnity affair). Ōkuma monjo, Waseda University, November 1874.

House, Koto. "The Story of My Life." New Brunswick, N.J.: Griffis Collection, Rutgers University, n.d.

Spaulding, Robert. "Bibliography of Western-Language Dailies and Weeklies in Japan, 1861–1961." Ann Arbor: University of Michigan, n.d.

PUBLISHED SOURCES

Aldrich, Mrs. Thomas Bailey. *Crowding Memories.* Boston: Houghton Mifflin, 1920.

Allinson, Gary. *The Columbia Guide to Modern Japanese History.* New York: Columbia University Press, 1999.

Altman, Albert A. "Eugene Van Reed: A Reading Man in Japan, 1859–1872." *Historical Review of Berks County* 30, no. 1 (winter 1964–1965): 6–12, 27–31.

Anderson, Frederick, Lin Salamo, and Bernard L. Stein, eds. *Mark Twain's Notebooks & Journals,* vol. 2 (1877–1883). Berkeley: University of California Press, 1975.

Andrews, Kenneth R. *Nook Farm: Mark Twain's Hartford Circle.* Cambridge, Mass.: Harvard University Press, 1950.

Annual Catalogue of the Teachers and Pupils of Chauncy-Hall School, Boston. Boston: Dutton and Wentworth, 1849.

Aoyama Nao. *Jogaku zasshi shosakuin* (Indexes to *Jogaku zasshi*). Keiō Tsūshin, 1970.

Ariyama Teruo. *Kindai Nihon jiyānarizumu no kōzō* (Structure of modern Japanese journalism). Tokyo Shuppan, 1995.

——. *Tokutomi Sohō to Kokumin Shimbun* (Tokutomi Sohō and *Kokumin Shimbun*). Yoshikawa Kōbunkan, 1992.

Baba Tatsui. *Baba Tatsui zenshū* (Complete works of Baba Tatsui). Iwanami Shoten, 1988.

Baehr, Harry W., Jr. *The New York Tribune since the Civil War.* New York: Dodd, Mead and Company, 1936.

Baelz, Erwin. *Awakening Japan: The Diary of a German Doctor: Erwin Baelz.* Bloomington: Indiana University Press, 1974.

Baize. "Old Times in the Gazette Office." *Saturday Evening Gazette*, June 6, 1903, 4.

Barr, Pat. *The Coming of the Barbarians. A Story of the Western Settlements in Japan 1853–1870.* Tokyo: Charles E. Tuttle Company, 1967.

——. *The Deer Cry Pavilion: A Story of Westerners in Japan, 1868–1905.* London: Macmillan, 1968.

Battles and Leaders of the Civil War, vol. 1. New York: Thomas Yoseloff, 1956.

Beasley, W. G. *The Meiji Restoration.* Palo Alto, Calif.: Stanford University Press, 1972.

Beck, Clark, and Ardath Burks, eds. *Aspects of Meiji Modernization: The Japan Helpers and the Helped.* New Brunswick, N.J.: Rutgers University Libraries, 1983.

Beauchamp, Edward R., and Akira Iriye, eds. *Foreign Employees in Nineteenth-Century Japan.* Boulder, Colo.: Westview Press, 1990.

Berger, Meyer. *The Story of the New York Times.* New York: Simon and Schuster, 1941.

Bernstein, Gail Lee. *Recreating Japanese Women, 1600–1945.* Berkeley: University of California Press, 1991.

"Biography of the *Boston Courier*," *Historical Magazine* 10, no. 2 (February 1866): 45–47.

Bisland, Elizabeth, ed. *The Life and Letters of Lafcadio Hearn*. 2 vols. Boston: Houghton Mifflin, 1906.

Black, John R. *Young Japan*, vol. 2. Yokohama: Kelley and Company, 1881.

Boatner, Mark. *The Civil War Dictionary*, rev. ed. New York: David McKay Company, 1988.

Boston Advertiser.

Boston Daily Courier.

Boston Transcript.

Boucicault, Dion. *The Dolmen Boucicault.* Ed. David Krasue. Dublin: Dolmen Press, 1964.

Bowen, Roger. *Rebellion and Democracy in Meiji Japan: A Study of Commoners in the Popular Rights Movement.* Berkeley: University of California Press, 1980.

Braisted, William R., trans. *Meiroku Zasshi: Journal of the Japanese Enlightenment.* Tokyo: University of Tokyo Press, 1976.

Brinkley, Frank. "Why Japan Values American Good-Will." *Munsey's Magazine* 33, no. 1 (April 1905): 14–17.

Browning, Robert, Michael B. Frank, and Lin Salamo, eds. *Mark Twain's Notebooks & Journals*, vol. 3, 1883–1891. Berkeley: University of California Press, 1979.

Budd, Louis J., ed. *Mark Twain: The Contemporary Reviews.* New York: Cambridge University Press, 1999.

Burks, Ardath W. "Coercion in Japan: A Historical Footnote." *The Journal of Rutgers University Library* (June 1952): 33–52.

———. "William Elliot Griffis, Class of 1869." *The Journal of Rutgers University Library* (September 1966): 91–100.

Burks, Ardath W., ed. *The Modernizers: Overseas Students, Foreign Employees and Meiji Japan*. Boulder, Colo.: Westview Press, 1985.

Carrington, George Williams. *Foreigners in Formosa 1841–1874*. San Francisco: Chinese Materials Center, 1978.

"Case of the Peruvian Barque *Maria Luz*, with Appendix." Tokyo: Foreign Department, Japanese Government, 1872.

Chamberlain, Basil Hall. *Japanese Things: Being Notes on Various Subjects Connected with Japan*. London: John Murray, 1905.

"Chapel Hill–Chauncy Hall—An Historical Perspective." *The Chronicle* 4, no. 1 (fall 1987). Chaltham, Mass.: Chapel Hill–Chauncy Hall School.

"A Child of Japan; Or, the Story of Yone Santo." Review. *Athenaeum* (February 15, 1890): 206.

A Chronicle of the St. James's Theatre: From Its Origins in 1835. London: n.p., 1900.

Clemens, Clara. *My Father Mark Twain*. New York: Harper and Brothers, 1931.

Clemens, Samuel. *The Prince and The Pauper: A Tale for Young People of All Ages*. New York: Books, Inc., n.d.

Clemens, Susie. *Papa: An Intimate Biography of Mark Twain by Susy Clemens, His Daughter, 13*. Ed. Charles Neider. Garden City, N.Y.: Doubleday, 1985.

Cohen, Aaron M. "The Stage Is the World: Theatrical and Musical Entertainment in Three Japanese Treaty Ports." *Asian Cultural Studies: International Christian University Publications III-A* (March 1997): 137–59.

Cole, Edward H. *The Chauncy Hall Story*. Boston: Chauncy Hall School.

———. *A School—and a Man*. Newtonville, Mass.: The Oakwood Press, 1951.

Coleman, John. *Charles Reade As I Knew Him*. London: Anthony Treherne, 1904.

Conroy, Hilary. *The Japanese Seizure of Korea, 1868–1910*. Philadelphia: University of Pennsylvania Press, 1960.

Conroy, Hilary, Sandra T. W. Davis, and Wayne Patterson, eds. *Japan in Transition: Thought and Action in the Meiji Era, 1868–1912*. London: Associated University Presses, 1984.

Cortissoz, Royal. *The Life of Whitelaw Reid*. 2 vols. London: Thornton Butterworth Limited, 1921.

———. *The New York Tribune: Incidents and Personalities in its History*. New York: The New York Tribune, 1923.

Crozier, Emmet. *Yankee Reporters 1861–65*. New York: Oxford University Press, 1956.

Cushing, Thomas. *Historical Sketch of Chauncy-Hall School. 1828 to 1894*. Boston: Press of David Clapp & Sons, 1895.

"Daily Notes." *The Japan Gazette*, December 16, 1881.

Dainihon Bunmei Kyōkai. "Nihon bunka ni kiyoseru Ōeijin no ryakureki" (Brief biographies of Westerners who have contributed to Japanese culture). *Meiji Bunka Hasshō Kinengō* (December 7, 1924): 17–57.

Davidson, James W. *The Island of Formosa: Past and Present.* Taipei: SMC Publishing, 1988.

Davis, Elmer. *History of the New York Times: 1951–1921.* New York: The New York Times, 1921.

Davis, William C. *Battle at Bull Run: A History of the First Major Campaign of the Civil War.* Garden City, N.Y.: Doubleday, 1977.

Dictionary of American Biography. New York: Charles Scribner's Sons, 1932.

Dorwart, Jeffrey M. "James Creelman, the *New York World* and the Port Arthur Massacre." *Journalism Quarterly* 50, no. 4 (winter 1973): 697–701.

———. *The Pigtail War: An Involvement in the Sino-Japanese War of 1894–1895.* Amherst: University of Massachusetts Press, 1975.

Dower, John W., ed. *Origins of the Modern Japanese State: Selected Writings of E. H. Norman.* New York: Random House, 1975.

———. *War without Mercy.* New York: Pantheon Books, 1986.

Duncan, Barry. *The St James's Theatre: Its Strange & Complete History 1835–1957.* London: Barrie and Rockliff, 1964.

Duncan, Bingham. *Whitelaw Reed: Journalist, Politician, Diplomat.* Athens: University of Georgia Press, 1975.

Duus, Peter. *Modern Japan.* 2nd ed. New York: Houghton Mifflin, 1998.

———. *The Japanese Discovery of America.* New York: Bedford Books, 1997.

Ebihara Hachirō. "E. H. Hausu ni tsuite" (Concerning E. H. House), *Meiji Bunka Kenkyū* 1 (February 1934): 154–55.

———. *Nihon Ōji shimbun zasshi shi* (A history of Japan's Western language newspapers and magazines). Taiseidō, 1936.

Eble, Kenneth E. *Old Clemens and W. D. H.: The Story of a Remarkable Friendship.* Baton Rouge: Louisiana State University Press, 1985.

"Edward Howard House." *Saturday Review of Books, The New York Times,* January 25, 1901, 56.

"Eiji shimbun hatsuda no kyo" (Plans for the publication of an English-language newspaper). *Meiji Nippō,* March 16, 1882.

Eppstein, Ury. *The Beginnings of Western Music in Meiji Era Japan.* Lewiston, N.Y.: Edwin Mellen Press, 1994.

Eskildsen, Robert. "Of Civilization and Savages: The Mimetic Imperialism of Japan's 1874 Expedition to Taiwan." *The American Historical Review* 107, no. 2 (April 2002): 388–418.

Fält, Olavi K. *The Clash of Interests: The Transformation of Japan in 1861–1881 in the Eyes of the Local Anglo-Saxon Press.* Trans. Malcolm Hicks. Rovaniemi: Historical Association of Northern Finland, 1990.

Fatout, P. "Mark Twain, Litigant." *American Literature* 31 (March 1959): 30–45.

———. *Mark Twain on the Lecture Circuit.* Bloomington: Indiana University Press, 1960.

Fawkes, Richard. *Dion Boucicault: A Biography.* London: Quartet Books, 1979.

Fox, Grace. *Britain and Japan 1858–1883.* Oxford: Clarendon Press, 1969.

Fraser, Mrs. Hugh. *A Diplomatist's Wife in Japan: Letters from Home to Home.* 2 vols. London: Hutchinson and Co., 1899.

Frohman, Daniel. *Memories of a Manager.* London: William Heinemann, 1911.

Fujitani, Takashi. *Splendid Monarchy: Power and Pageantry in Modern Japan.* Berkeley: University of California Press, 1996.

Fukuchi Gen'ichirō, *Shimbun jitsureki* (My career in the newspaper). In Yanagida Izumi, ed., *Meiji bungaku zenshū* (Collected works of Meiji literature), vol. 11, *Fukuchi Ōchi shū* (Works of Fukuchi Ōchi). Chikuma Shobō, 1966.
Furendo Gakuen Hyakunenshi Hensan Iinkai, ed. *Furendo Gakuen hyakunen shi* (Centennial history of Friends School). Furendo Gakuen, 1987.
Gardiner, C. Harvey. *The Japanese and Peru, 1873–1873.* Albuquerque: University of New Mexico Press, 1975.
Garon, Sheldon. *The State and Labor in Modern Japan.* Berkeley: University of California Press, 1987.
Geismar, Maxwell. *Mark Twain: An American Prophet.* Boston: Houghton Mifflin, 1970.
"General Bibliography on the Impact of Western Culture in Japan." *Monumenta Nipponica* 19, nos. 3–4 (1964): 168–85.
Gluck, Carol. *Japan's Modern Myths: Ideology in the Late Meiji Period.* Princeton, N.J.: Princeton University Press, 1985.
Goldman, Merle, and Andrew Gordon, eds. *Historical Perspectives on Contemporary East Asia.* Cambridge, Mass.: Harvard University Press, 2000.
Gordon, Andrew. *Labor and Imperial Democracy in Prewar Japan.* Berkeley: University of California Press, 1991.
Gordon, Leonard. "Japan's Abortive Colonial Venture in Taiwan, 1874." *Journal of Modern History* 37, no. 2 (June 1965): 171–85.
Griffis, William Elliot. *The Mikado's Empire.* New York: Harper and Brothers, 1906.
———. *Verbeck of Japan.* New York: Fleming H. Revell Company, 1900.
Greenslet, Ferris. *The Life of Thomas Bailey Aldrich.* Boston: Houghton Mifflin Company, 1908.
Gribben, Alan. *Mark Twain's Library: A Reconstruction.* 2 vols. Boston: G. K. Hall and Company, 1980.
Groce, George C., and David H. Wallace. *The New York Historical Society's Dictionary of Artists in America 1564–1860.* New Haven, Conn.: Yale University Press, 1957.
Hackett, Roger. *Yamagata Aritomo in the Rise of Modern Japan, 1838–1922.* Cambridge, Mass.: Harvard University Press, 1971.
Hamilton, Sinclair. *Early American Book Illustrators and Wood Engravers 1670–1870.* Vol. 1. Princeton: Princeton University Press, 1968.
Hammersmith, Jack. *Spoilsmen in a "Flowery Fairyland": The Development of the U.S. Legation in Japan, 1859–1906.* Kent, Ohio: Kent State University Press, 1998.
Hane, Mikiso. *Modern Japan: A Historical Survey.* Boulder, Colo.: Westview Press, 1992.
———. *Peasants, Rebels, & Outcastes: The Underside of Modern Japan.* New York: Pantheon Books, 1982.
Hardin, Thomas L. "American Press and Public Opinion in the First Sino-Japanese War." *Journalism Quarterly* 50, no. 1 (spring 1973): 54–59.
Haruhara Akihiko. *Nihon shimbun tsū shi: 1861–1986* (History of the Japanese press, 1861–1986). Niizumisha, 1987.
"Hausu no seikyo" (House's death). *Kokumin Shimbun,* December 20, 1901.
"Hausu no omoide" (Memories of House). *Ōsaka Asahi Shimbun,* December 23, 1901.
"Hausu Nihon no kakusha ni yuku" (House dies at home in Japan). *Ōsaka Asahi Shimbun,* December 23, 1901.

Heibonsha. *Daijinmei jiten* (Dictionary of prominent people). Heibonsha, 1954.
Henning, Joseph M. *Outposts of Civilization: Race, Religion, and the Formative Years of American-Japanese Relations.* New York: New York University Press, 2000.
Henshū Iinkai, ed. *Za yatoi: oyatoi gaikokujin no sōgōteki kenkyū* (The yatoi: a synthesis of research on foreign employees). Shibunkaku Shuppan, 1987.
Hessler, Gene. *The Engraver's Line: An Encyclopedia of Paper Money & Postage Stamp Art.* Port Clinton, Ohio: BNR Press, 1993.
Hildreth, Richard. *Japan As It Was and Is.* Boston: Phillips, Sampson and Company, 1855.
Hill, Hamlin. *Mark Twain and Elisha Bliss.* Columbia: University of Missouri Press, 1964.
Hingston, Edward P. *The Genial Showman: Reminiscences of the Life of Artemus Ward.* London: Chatto and Windus, Piccadilly, 1881.
Historicus. "Japan's First Diplomatic Triumph: New Facts in the Maria Luz Affair." *Japan Times and Mail,* April 3, 1929.
Hoare, James E. "British Journalists in Meiji Japan." In Ian Nish, ed., *Britain and Japan: Biographical Portraits.* Kent, U.K.: Japan Library, 1994: 20–32.
———. *Japan's Treaty Ports and Foreign Settlements.* Kent, U.K.: Japan Library, 1994.
Hoffman, Andrew. *Inventing Mark Twain: The Lives of Samuel Langhorne Clemens.* New York: William Morrow and Company, 1997.
Hogan, Robert. *Dion Boucicault.* New York: Twayne Publishers, 1969.
Hohenberg, John. *Foreign Correspondence: The Great Reporters and their Times.* New York: Columbia University Press, 1964.
Hollingshead, John. *Gaiety Chronicles.* Westminster, U.K.: Archibald Constable and Comapny, 1898.
Holtham, E. G. *Eight Years in Japan 1873–1881: Work, Travel, and Recreation.* London: Kegan, Paul, Trench and Company, 1883.
House, Edward H. "Anecdotes of Charles Reade." *The Atlantic Monthly: A Magazine of Literature, Art, and Politics* 60, no. 360 (October 1887): 525–39.
———. "A Bit of Angling." *Harper's New Monthly Magazine* 20, no. 115 (December 1859): 110–15.
———. "Booth in London." *New York Herald,* November 7, 1880, 7.
———. "Bright Sides of History." *St. Nicholas for Young Folks* 26, nos. 1–7: (November 1898): 31–38; (December 1898): 140–47; (January 1899): 201–07; (February 1899): 332–39; (March 1899): 380–87; (April 1899): 485–93; and (May 1899): 602–06.
———. "Carnelian: A Romance of a Sleeping Car, In Two Parts." *Overland Monthly and Out West Magazine* 12, nos. 6–7 (June-July 1874): 9–17, 501–10.
———. "The Coolie Trade." *New York Tribune,* November 28, 1878.
———. "A Day in a Japanese Theatre." *The Atlantic Monthly: A Magazine of Literature, Art, and Politics* 30, no. 179 (September 1872): 257–71.
———. "Dejazet." *The Galaxy: An Illustrated Magazine of Entertaining Reading* 4 (April 1867): 179–90.
———. "Edwin Booth in London." *The Century Illustrated Monthly Magazine* 55, New Series 33 (November 1897–April 1898): 269–79.
———. "A First Interview with Lowell." *Harper's Weekly* 36, no. 1863 (September 3, 1892): 850.

———. "Foreign Jurisdiction in Japan." *New Princeton Review* (March 1888): 207–18.
———. "A Forgotten Literary Phenomenon." *The Atlantic Monthly: A Magazine of Literature, Art, and Politics* 60, no. 357 (July 1887): 134–36.
———. "How to Make a Boomerang." *Harper's Young People*, January 13, 1891.
———. "How the Snow Melted on Mount Washington." *Harper's New Monthly Magazine* 20, no. 116 (January 1860): 227–34.
———. "An Icy Flame." *Harper's New Monthly Magazine* 20, no. 119 (April 1860): 667–70.
———. "Japan." *The Atlantic Monthly: A Magazine of Literature, Art, and Politics* 5, no. 32 (June 1860): 721–33.
———. "A Japanese Doctor and His Works. Personal and Historical Memoranda." *The Atlantic Monthly* 28, no. 170 (December 1871): 678–89.
———. *Japanese Episodes.* Boston: James R. Osgood and Company, 1881.
———. "A Japanese Statesman at Home." *Harper's New Monthly Magazine* 44, no. 262 (March 1872): 589–600.
———. *The Japanese Expedition to Formosa.* Tokyo: n.p., 1875.
———. *The Kagoshima Affair: A Chapter of Japanese History.* Tokyo: n.p., 1875.
———. "A Leap in the Dark." *The Galaxy: An Illustrated Magazine of Entertaining Reading* 10 (July 1870–January 1871): 5–24.
———. "Love by Mishap." *Harper's New Monthly Magazine* 26, no. 155 (December 1862): 42–49.
———. "Martyrdom of an Empire." *The Atlantic Monthly: A Magazine of Literature, Art, and Politics* 47, no. 283 (May 1881): 610–23.
———. *Midnight Warning and Other Stories.* Boston: Harper and Brothers, 1892.
———. "Mien-Yaun." *The Atlantic Monthly, A Magazine of Literature, Art, and Politics* 3, no. 20 (June 1859): 671–85.
———. "Personal Characteristics of Charles Reade." *The Atlantic Monthly: A Magazine of Literature, Art, and Politics* 60, no. 358 (August 1887): 145–57.
———. "Political Tolerance in Japan." Letter. *New York Evening Post*, February 21, 1888.
———. "The Present and Future of Japan." *Harper's New Monthly Magazine* 46, no. 276 (May 1873): 858–64.
———. "The Sacred Flame of Torin Ji." *Scribner's Magazine* 2, nos. 3–4 (September-October 1887): 332–45, 420–35.
———. "The Silent Lover." *The Galaxy: An Illustrated Magazine of Entertaining Reading* 3 (January-April 1867): 426–31.
———. *The Simonoseki Affair: A Chapter of Japanese History.* Tokyo: n.p., 1875.
———. "The Sovereignty of the Inland Sea." *Japan Weekly Mail*, November 18, 1893.
———. "The Tariff in Japan." *New Princeton Review* (June 1888): 66–77.
———. "The Thraldom of Japan." *The Atlantic Monthly: A Magazine of Literature, Art, and Politics* 60, no. 362 (December 1887): 721–34.
———. "Transfer of the Temples of Ise." *Scribner's Magazine* 9 (May 1891): 569–75.
———. "Wagner and Tannhäuser in Paris, 1861." *The New England Magazine* 4, no. 4 (June 1891): 411–27.
———. "What *Was* the Grievance?" *Japan Weekly Mail*, February 24, 1883, 124–26.
———. *Yone Santo, A Child of Japan.* New York: Belford, Clarke, and Company, 1888. Also published in as "Child of Japan; Or, the Story of Yone Santo," *The Atlantic*

Monthly: A Magazine of Literature, Art, and Politics 61–62, nos. 363–70 (January-August 1888).

Howells, W. D. *Literary Friends and Acquaintances: A Personal Retrospect of American Authorship.* New York: Harper and Brothers Publishers, 1900.

Huffman, James L. *Creating a Public: People and Press in Meiji Japan.* Honolulu: University of Hawaii Press, 1997.

———. "Edward Howard House: In the Service of Meiji Japan." *Pacific Historical Review* 61, no. 2 (May 1987): 231–58.

———. "Edward H. House: Questions of Meaning and Influence." *Japan Forum* 13, no. 2 (2001): 15–25.

———. *Politics of the Meiji Press: The Life of Fukuchi Gen'ichirō.* Honolulu: University of Hawaii Press, 1980.

———. "That 'Naughty Yankee Boy': Edward H. House and Meiji Japan's Struggle for Equality." *Nanzan Review of American Studies* 22 (2000): 39–54.

Iddittie, Junesay. *Marquis Okuma.* Tokyo: Hokuseido Press, 1956.

Inwood, Stephen. *A History of London.* New York: Carroll & Graf Publishers, 1998.

Irokawa, Daikichi. *The Culture of the Meiji Period.* Princeton, N.J.: Princeton University Press, 1985.

Isono Naohide. *Misaki rinkai jikkenjo o kyoraishita hitotachi* (People connected with the Misaki marine laboratory). Gakkai Shuppan Sentā, 1988.

———. *Mōsuso no hi sono hi: aru oyatoi kyōshi to kindai Nihon* (Morse's Japan day by day: modern Japan and a foreign servant). Yūrindō, 1987.

Iwai Hajime. *Shimbun to shimbunjin* (Newspapers and journalists). Gendai Jiyānarizumu Shuppankai, 1974.

Jansen, Marius B., ed. *The Cambridge History of Japan,* vol. 5: *The Nineteenth Century.* Cambridge: Cambridge University Press, 1989.

———. *The Making of Modern Japan.* Cambridge, Mass.: Harvard University Press, 2000.

Jansen, Marius B., and Gilbert Rozman, eds. *Japan in Transition: From Tokugawa to Meiji.* Princeton, N.J.: Princeton University Press, 1986.

The Japan Advertiser.

The Japan Daily Herald.

The Japan Directory. The Japan Gazette Company, 1883, 1894, 1895, and 1902.

The Japan Gazette.

The Japan Punch, 1877–1880. Facsimile edition published by Tokyo: Yūshōdō Shoten, 1975.

The Japan Weekly Mail.

"Japanese Episodes." Review of *Japanese Episodes. The Nation* (November 3, 1881): 360.

"Jogakkō no ron ni fusu" (In regard to discussion of women's schools). *Jogakkō Zasshi,* no. 79 (October 8, 1888): 163–67.

Jones, F. C. *Extraterritoriality in Japan.* New York: AMS Press, 1970.

Jones, Hazel J. *Live Machines: Hired Foreigners and Meiji Japan.* Vancouver: University of British Columbia Press, 1980.

———. "The Meiji Government and Foreign Employees, 1868–1900." Ph.D. diss., University of Michigan, 1967.

Kaneko Fumiko. *The Prison Memoirs of a Japanese Woman.* Armonk, N.Y.: M. E. Sharpe, 1991.

Kaplan, Justin. *Mr. Clemens and Mark Twain: A Biography.* New York: Simon and Schuster, 1966.

Kasza, Gregory J. *The State and the Mass Media in Japan, 1918–1945.* Berkeley: University of California Press, 1988.

Kasahara Hidehiko. "Rujiyandoru to seifukei Eiji shimbun" (LeGendre and government-related English language newspapers). *Shimbun Gaku Hyōron* 33 (1984): 204–14.

Kennedy, W. S. "Hovenden's 'Last Moments of John Brown' (Correspondence)." *The Index,* September 17, 1885.

Keene, Donald. *Emperor of Japan: Meiji and His World, 1852–1912.* New York: Columbia University Press, 2002.

——. *The Japanese Discovery of Europe, 1720–1830.* Stanford, Calif.: Stanford University Press, 1952.

Keene, Donald, ed. *Modern Japanese Literature: An Anthology.* New York: Grove Press, 1956.

Kido Mataichi et al., *Kōza gendai jiyānarizumu* (Lectures: modern journalism), vol. 1, *Rekishi* (History). Jiji Tsūshinsha, 1974.

Kido Takayoshi. *The Diary of Kido Takayoshi,* vol. 2, 1871–1874. Trans. Sidney Devere Brown and Akiko Hirota. Tokyo: University of Tokyo Press, 1985.

"Kisha Hausu futatabi raichō" (Journalist House comes again). *Meiji Nippō Shimbun,* January 18, 1882.

Kobe Weekly Chronicle.

Kornicki, Peter, ed. *Meiji Japan: Political, Economic and Social History 1868–1912.* 4 vols. London: Routledge Library of Modern Japan, 1998.

Koseki Tsuneo and Kitamura Tomoaki, trans. *Kunippingu no Meiji Nihon kaisōki* (Knipping's recollections of Meiji Japan). Yūgen Kaisha, 1991.

Kunaichō, ed. *Meiji tenno ki* (Records of Emperor Meiji), vol. 9. Yoshikawa Hirobumi Kan, 1973.

"Kun nitō Hausu shi no sōgi" (Funeral of House, holder of merit order, rank two). *Tokyo Nichi Nichi Shimbun,* December 22, 1901.

Kuroda Hatsuko. *Aji to shizen no sanpodō* (Along the paths of flavor and nature). Hyōronsha, 1978.

——. *Ikiiki kyūjūsai no seikatsu jutsu* (How to live energetically at ninety). Sōshisha, 1993.

——. *Oryōri no ressun nanajūnen* (Seventy years of cooking lessons). Sōshisha, 1996.

Lane-Poole, Stanley. *The Life of Sir Harry Parkes.* 2 vols. Wilmington, Del.: Scholarly Resources, 1973.

"The Late Mr. E. H. House." *Japan Weekly Mail,* January 4, 1902.

Lawton, Mary. *A Lifetime with Mark Twain.* New York: Harcourt, Brace and Company, 1925.

Lehmann, Jean-Pierre. *The Image of Japan: From Feudal Isolation to World Power 1850–1905.* London: George Allen and Unwin, 1978.

"Literary Notes." Review of *Midnight Warning and Other Stories. Harper's New Monthly Magazine* (February 1893): 489.

Lockwood, William W. *The Economic Development of Japan: Growth and Structural Change 1868–1938.* Princeton, N.J.: Princeton University Press, 1954.

Lone, Stewart. *Army, Empire and Politics in Meiji Japan: The Three Careers of General Katsura Tarō.* New York: St. Martin's Press, 2000.

———. *Japan's First Modern War: Army and Society in the Conflict with China, 1894–95.* New York: St. Martin's Press, 1994.

Macqueen-Pope, W. *St. James's: Theatre of Distinction.* London: W. H. Allen, 1958.

McLaren, Walter W. "Japanese Government Documents." *Transactions of the Asiatic Society of Japan* 42, no. 1 (1914): 1–681.

McCormick, John. *Dion Boucicault (1820–1890).* Cambridge: Chadwyck-Healey, 1987.

McWilliams, Wayne C. "Soejima Taneomi: Statesman of Early Meiji Japan, 1868–1874." Ph.D. diss., University of Kansas, 1973.

"Mark Twain's Lawsuit." *Hartford Courant,* January 18, 1890, 1.

Maruyama, Masao. *Studies in the Intellectual History of Tokugawa Japan.* Princeton, N.J.: Princeton University Press, 1974.

Mason, W. B. "The Foreign Colony: Early Meiji Days III—Edward H. House, Editor of the First English Journal in Tokyo." *The New East* 3, no. 3 (March 1918): 243–44.

Matsumoto Tokutarō, ed. *Meiji hōkan* (Handbook of the Meiji era). Hara Shobō, 1940.

Meiji Nippō.

Midoro Masaichi. *Meiji Taishō shi: genron hen* (History of the Meiji and Taishō eras: the press). Asahi Shimbunsha, 1930.

"Missionary Terrorizing." *The Truth Seeker* 16, no. 6 (February 9, 1889): 86–87.

Mitchell, Richard. *Censorship in Imperial Japan.* Princeton, N.J.: Princeton University Press, 1983.

Miura Toshisaburō. *Honpō yōgaku hensenshi* (History of the evolution of Western music in Japan). Nittō Shoin, 1931.

Miyake Setsurei. *Dōjidai shi* (An account of my times), vol. 1. Iwanami Shoten, 1954.

"Mr. E. H. House." *Japan Weekly Mail,* December 21, 1901.

Monbushō. *Gakusei hyakunen shi* (Centennial history of the educational system). Teikoku Chihō Gakkai, 1972.

Mōri Toshihiko. *Taiwan shuppei* (Military expedition to Taiwan). Chūō kōron, 1996.

Morse, Edward S. *Japan Day by Day.* 2 vols. Boston: Houghton Mifflin Company, 1917.

Mutsu Munemitsu. *Kenkenroku: A Diplomatic Record of the Sino-Japanese War, 1894–95.* Trans. Gordon Berger. Tokyo: University of Tokyo Press, 1982.

Nagai Michio and Miguel Urrutia, eds. *Meiji Ishin: Restoration and Revolution.* Tokyo: United Nations University, 1985.

Nagatsuka Takashi. *Soil.* Trans. Ann Waswo. Berkeley: University of California Press, 1993.

Nakae Chōmin. *A Discourse by Three Drunkards on Government.* New York: Weatherhill, 1984.

Nakamura Shōmi, "Beikoku no Shimonoseki shōkin hensen ron ni tsuite" (Discussion on the return of America's Shimonoseki indemnity). *Ōkuma Kenkyū* 1 (1955): 68–79.

Nakayama Yasuaki, ed. *Shimbun shūsei Meiji hennen shi* (Chronological compilation of Meiji-era press articles). 15 vols. Honpō Shoseki, 1982.

Neider, Charles, ed. *The Autobiography of Mark Twain.* New York: Harper and Row, 1959.

"Newspaper Change." *The Pilot,* March 7, 1856, 4.

"Newspaper Sketches and Reminiscences." *Roxbury Gazette and South End Advertiser,* November 17, 1881.

Newton, James King. "Japanese Treaty Revision: Its Necessity and Our Responsibility Therefor." *Bibliotheca Sacra* 44, no. 173 (January 1887): 46–70.

New York Daily Tribune.

The New York Times.

New York World.

Nihon Fūzoku Gakkai. *Shiryō ga kataru Meiji no Tokyo hyaku wa* (One hundred tales of Meiji Japan, as seen through the records). Chirekisha, 1996.

Nihon Shimbun Renmei, ed. *Nihon shimbun hyakunen shi* (One-hundred-year history of the Japanese press). Nihon Shimbun Renmei, 1961.

Nish, Ian. *Japanese Foreign Policy 1869–1942.* London: Routledge and Kegan Paul, 1977.

Nish, Ian, ed. *Britain and Japan: Biographical Portraits.* Kent, U.K.: Japan Library, 1994.

———. *Contemporary European Writings on Japan.* Kent, U.K.: Paul Norbury Publications, 1988.

Nishida Taketoshi. *Meiji jidai no shimbun to zasshi* (Newspapers and magazines of the Meiji period). Shibundō, 1966.

Norman, E. H. *Japan's Emergence As a Modern State.* New York: Institute of Pacific Relations, 1940.

Notehelfer, F. G., ed. *Japan Through American Eyes: The Journal of Francis Hall 1859–1866.* Princeton, N.J.: Princeton University Press, 1992.

Ochanomizu Joshi Daigaku Hyakunen shi Kankō Iinkai, ed. *Ochanomizu Joshi Daigaku hyakunen shi* (Centennial history of Ochanomizu Joshi Daigaku). Ochanomizu Daigaku, 1984.

O'Connor, Peter. "The Captain, the Scribbler and the Professor: Foreign Failure and Imposture in Prewar Japan." *Tokyo Rikai Daigaku Kiyo,* no. 30, supplement (March 10, 1998): 137–51.

O'Connor, Peter, ed. "Special Issue: Informal Diplomacy and the Modern Idea of Japan." *Japan Forum* 13, no. 1 (2001).

Oka Yoshitake. *Five Political Leaders of Modern Japan: Itō Hirobumi, Ōkuma Shigenobu, Hara Takashi, Inukai Tsuyoshi, and Saionji Kimmochi.* Tokyo: University of Tokyo Press, 1986.

Okada Akio, Toyoda Takeshi, and Waka Moritarō, eds. *Nihon no rekishi: Meiji ishin* (Japanese history: Meiji Restoration), vol. 10. Yomiuri Shimbunsha, 1965.

Okano Takeo. *Meiji genron shi* (History of the Meiji press). Hō Shuppan, 1974.

Ōkuma Shigenobu, ed. *Fifty Years of New Japan.* 2 vols. London: Smith, Elders, 1910.

Ono Hideo. *Nihon shimbun hattatsu shi* (History of the development of the Japanese press). Gogatsu Shobō, 1982.

Ōtani Tadashi. "Edowādo Hawādo Hausu senkō" (Research on Edward Howard House). *Senō Hōgaku Ronshō* (Legal treatises of Senshū University) 48 (September 24, 1988): 235–60.

"A Pagan Saint." Review of *Yone Santo, A Child of Japan. The Critic* (February 2, 1889): 50–51.

Paine, Albert Bigelow. *Mark Twain: A Biography.* 3 vols. New York: Harper and Brothers, 1912.

Pope-Hennessy, James. *Verandah: Some Episodes in the Crown Colonies 1867–1889.* London: George Allen and Unwin, 1964.

Pullen, John J. *Comic Relief: The Life and Laughter of Artemus Ward, 1834–1867.* Hamden, Conn.: Archon Books, 1983.

Pyle, Kenneth B. "The Emergence of Bureaucratic Conservatism in the Meiji Period." *Undercurrent* 1 (March 1983): 13–29.

———. *The Making of Modern Japan.* 2nd ed. Lexington, Mass.: D. C. Heath, 1996.

———. *The New Generation in Meiji Japan: Problems of Cultural Identity, 1885–1895.* Stanford, Calif.: Stanford University Press, 1965.

Rasmussen, R. Kent. *Mark Twain A-Z: The Essential Reference to His Life and Writings.* New York: Oxford University Press, 1995.

Reade, Charles, and Compton Reade. *Charles Reade: A Memoir.* New York: Harper and Brothers, 1887.

Rosenstone, Robert A. *Mirror in the Shrine: American Encounters with Meiji Japan.* Cambridge, Mass.: Harvard University Press, 1988.

Rubin, Jay. *Injurious to Public Morals: Writers and the Meiji State.* Seattle: University of Washington Press, 1984.

Salsbury, Edith Colgate, ed. *Susy and Mark Twain: Family Dialogues.* New York: Harper and Row, Publishers, 1965.

Sanborn, Margaret. *Mark Twain: The Bachelor Years.* New York: Doubleday, 1990.

Sansom, George. *The Western World and Japan.* New York: Alfred A. Knopf, 1968.

Satow, Ernest. *A Diplomat in Japan.* London: Seeley, Service and Company, 1921.

Scheiner, Irwin, ed. *Modern Japan: An Interpretive Anthology.* New York: Macmillan Publishing, 1974.

Schnell, Scott. *The Rousing Drum: Ritual Practice in a Japanese Community.* Honolulu: University of Hawai'i Press, 1999.

Seitz, Don C. *Artemus Ward (Charles Farrar Browne): A Biography and Bibliography.* New York: Harper and Brothers, 1919.

———. *The James Gordon Bennetts, Father and Son.* Indianapolis, Ind.: Bobbs-Merrill, 1928.

Seiyō jinmei jiten (Biographical dictionary of Westerners). Iwanami Shōten, 1956.

Shiga Tadashi. *Nihon joshi kyōiku shi* (History of Japanese women's education). Biwa Shobō, 1977.

Shigehisa Tokutarō. *Oyatoi gaikokujin* (Foreign employees), vol. 5, *Kyōiku, shūkyō* (Education, religion). Tokyo: Kagoshima Kenkyūjo Shuppankai, 1968.

Shimura Akiko, "Meiji ki no josei jiyānarisuto" (Women journalists in the Meiji era). In Tanaka Hiroshi, ed., *Kindai Nihon no jiyārisuto* (Journalists of modern Japan). Ochanomizu Shobō, 1987: 645–72.

Shōwa Joshi Daigaku, ed. "E. H. Hausu (E. H. House)." *Kindai bungaku kenkyūshitsu: kindai bungaku kenkyū sōsho* (Modern literature studies department: Modern literature studies series), vol. 5. Shōwa Joshi Daigaku, 1957: 379–418.

Sievers, Sharon L. *Flowers in Salt: The Beginnings of Feminist Consciousness in Modern Japan.* Stanford, Calif.: Stanford University Press, 1983.

Snyder, Louis L. and Richard B. Morris, eds. *A Treasury of Great Reporting.* 2nd rev. ed. New York: Simon and Schuster, 1962.

Stedman, Edmund Clarence, and Ellen Mackay Hutchinson, eds. *A Library of American Literature, From the Earliest Settlement to the Present Time.* 11 vols. New York: C. L. Webster and Company, 1888–1890.

Stedman, Laura, and George M. Gould. *Life and Letters of Edmund Clarence Stedman.* 2 vols. New York: Moffat, Yard and Company, 1910.

Suzuki Yūga. "Aru Eijin hakkōsha o otte: A.W. Hansādo no kiseki" (Pursuing an English publisher: the legacy of A. W. Hansard). *Komiyunikēshiyon Kenkyū* 21 (1991): 45–50.

Takase Sōtarō, ed. *Kyōritsu joshi gakuen nanajūnen shi* (Seventy-year history of Kyōritsu Girls School). Kyōritsu Joshi Gakuen, 1956.

Takeuchi Hiroshi, ed. *Rainichi seiyō jinmei jiten* (Biographical dictionary of Westerners who lived in Japan). Tokyo: Tokyo Daigaku Shiryō Hensanjo, 1995.

Tanabe Hisao. *Japanese Music.* Trans. Sakabe Shigeyoshi. Kokusai Bunka Shinkokai, 1936.

———. *Japanese Music: Western Influences in Modern Japan.* New York: Institute of Pacific Relations, 1929.

Tezuka Tatsumaro. "Edward Howard House." In *Twenty-five Tales in Memory of Tokyo's Foreigners*: Supplement to Tokyo Municipal Library, vol. 23. Tokyo Metropolitan Government, 1989: 16–17.

———. "Japanophile Englishman: Francis Brinkley and His Son. The Introduction of Western Culture into Japan in the Age of Her Modernization." *Tokyo Municipal News*, supplement (1967): 2–4.

The Times (London).

The Tokio Times.

Tiedemann, Arthur. *Modern Japan: A Brief History.* New York: D. Van Nostrand, 1955.

"Tokio Taimusu" (*Tokio Times*). *Yūbin Hōchi Shimbun,* December 12, 1879.

"Tokio Taimusu kyūkan" (*Tokio Times* Discontinued). *Meiji Nippō Shimbun,* January 18, 1882.

"Tokio Taimusu saikō ka" (Will the *Tokio Times* be revived?). *Meiji Nippō Shimbun,* March 18, 1882.

Tokutomi Sohō. "Hausu sensei no omoide" (Recollections of Mr. House). *Shimbun kisha to shimbun* (Journalists and newspapers). Min'yūsha, 1929: 105–26.

———. *Shōrai no Nihon,* in Sumiya Mikio, ed. *Tokutomi Sohō, Yamaji Aizan.* Chūō Kōronsha, 1971.

Toyotaka, Komiya, ed. *Japanese Music and Drama in the Meiji Era.* Tokyo: Ōbunsha, 1956.

Treat, Payson, Jr. *Diplomatic Relations Between the United States and Japan.* 2 vols. Stanford, Calif.: Stanford University Press, 1932.

———. *Japan and the United States, 1853–1921.* Boston: Houghton Mifflin Company, 1921.

Tsuchida Mieko. "Edward H. House." *Gakugei* 9 (September 1942): 39–52.

Tsuge, Gen'ichi. *Japanese Music: An Annotated Bibliography.* New York: Garland, 1986.

Tsunoda, Ryusaku, Wm. Theodore De Bary, and Donald Keene, eds. *Sources of Japanese Tradition,* vol. 2. New York: Columbia University Press, 1958.

Tsurumi, Patricia. *Factory Girls: Women in the Thread Mills of Meiji Japan*. Princeton, N.J.: Princeton University Press, 1990.

Twain, Mark. *A Connecticut Yankee in King Arthur's Court*. Garden City, N.Y.: International Collectors Library, n.d.

Ubukata Toshirō. "Kenpō happu to Nisshin Sensō" (Promulgation of the constitution and the Sino-Japanese War), in Tsurumi Shunsuke, ed., *Jiyānarizumu no shisō* (Philosophy of the press), vol. 12, *Gendai Nihon shisō taikei* (Comprehensive outline of modern Japanese thought), ed. Matsumoto Sannosuke. Chikuma Shobō, 1965.

Uchikawa Yoshimi. "Shimbunshi hō no seitei katei to sono tokushitsu" (Characteristics of the process of developing newspaper laws). *Tokyo Daigaku Shimbun Kenkyūjo Kiyō* 13 (1967): 1–31.

——. *Shimbun shi wa* (Historical anecdotes from the press). Shakai Shisōsha, 1967.

Uchikawa Yoshimi and Matsushima Eiichi, eds. *Meiji niyūsu jiten* (Encyclopedia of Meiji news). 9 vols. Mainichi Komiyunikēshiyon Shuppanbu, 1983–86.

Uchikawa Yoshimi and Miyaji Masato, eds. *Gaikoku shimbun ni miru Nihon* (Japan as seen in foreign newspapers). 4 vols. Mainichi Komiyunikēshiyon, 1990.

UNESCO Higashi Ajia Bunka Kenkyū Sentā. *Shiryō oyatoi gaikokujin* (Sources on foreign employees). Shōgakukan, 1975.

Usui Chizuko. *Joshi kyōiku no kindai to gendai: Nichibei no hikaku kyōiku gakuteki shiron* (Women's education in early modern and modern times: A comparative sketch of education in Japan and America). Kindai Bungei, 1994.

Villard, Henry. *Memoirs of Henry Villard, Journalist and Financier 1835–1900*. 2 vols. Boston: Houghton, Mifflin and Company, 1904.

Walsh, Townsend. *The Career of Dion Boucicault*. New York: Benjamin Bloom, 1915.

Walthall, Anne, ed. *The Human Tradition in Modern Japan*. Wilmington, Del.: Scholarly Resources, 2002.

Waswo, Ann. *Modern Japanese Society, 1868–1994*. Oxford, U.K.: Oxford University Press, 1996.

Webster, Samuel Charles, ed. *Mark Twain, Businessman*. Boston: Little, Brown and Company, 1941.

Wecter, Dixon, ed. *Mark Twain to Mrs. Fairbanks*. San Marino, Calif.: Huntington Library, 1949.

Westney, D. Eleanor. *Imitation and Innovation: The Transfer of Western Organizational Patterns to Meiji Japan*. Cambridge, Mass.: Harvard University Press, 1987.

Wildes, Harry E. *Aliens in the East: A New History of Japan's Foreign Intercourse*. Reprint ed. Wilmington, Del.: Scholarly Resources, 1973.

——. *The Press and Social Currents in Japan*. Chicago: University of Chicago Press, 1927.

Williams, Harold S. *Foreigners in Mikadoland*. Rutland, Vt.: Charles E. Tuttle Company, 1963.

——. *Tales of the Foreign Settlements in Japan*. Rutland, Vt.: Charles E. Tuttle Company, 1958.

——. "Two Remarkable Australians of Old Yokohama." *The Transactions of the Asiatic Society of Japan, Third Series* 12 (1975): 51–69.

Wordell, Charles B. *Japan's Image in America: Popular Writing About Japan, 1800–1941*. Kyoto, Japan: Yamaguchi Publishing House, 1998.

Yamamoto Fumio. *Nihon shimbun hattatsu shi* (History of the development of the Japanese press). Itō Shoten, 1944.

Yokoyama Gennosuke, *Nihon no kasō shakai* (The lower strata of Japanese society). Chūō Rōdō Gakuen, 1949.

"Yone Santo, A Child of Japan." Review of *Yone Santo, A Child of Japan*. *The Nation* (January 10, 1889): 40.

Young, John Russell. *Around the World with General Grant*. 2 vols. New York: The American News Company, 1879.

———. *Men and Memories: Personal Reminiscences*. New York: F. Tennyson Neely, 1901.

Yūbin hōchi Shimbun (known as *Hōchi Shimbun*, after 1894).

Yumoto Kōichi. *Meiji jibutsu eigen jiten* (Dictionary of the origins of Meiji affairs). Kashiwa Shobō, 1996.

Yutani, Eiji, trans. "*Nihon no Kaso Shakai* of Gennosuke Yokoyama." Ph.D. diss., University of California at Berkeley, 1985.

Zen Nihon Shimbun Renmei, ed. *Kindai Nihon shimbun taikan* (Overview of the modern Japanese press). 3 vols. Zen Nihon Shimbun Renmei, 1980–1982. (The word *Kindai* is omitted from vol. 3.)

Zinn, Howard. *A People's History of the United States*. New York: Harper Perennial, 1980.

Index

About the Author

James L. Huffman is H. Orth Hirt Professor of History at Wittenberg University in Springfield, Ohio. A former newspaper reporter at the *Minneapolis Tribune,* he has spent a career studying the history of the Japanese press. He is the author or editor of numerous works, including *Creating a Public: People and Press in Meiji Japan* and *Modern Japan: An Encyclopedia of History, Culture, and Nationalism.*